MACROMEDIA®

Studio MX 2004

STEP-BY-STEP

Projects for Macromedia Flash™ MX 2004,
Dreamweaver® MX 2004, Fireworks® MX 2004, and FreeHand® MX

Official Macromedia
Education Curriculum

THOMSON
COURSE TECHNOLOGY™

Australia • Canada • Mexico • Singapore • Spain • United Kingdom • United States

THOMSON

COURSE TECHNOLOGY

Macromedia® Studio MX 2004 Step-by-Step
Projects for Macromedia Flash™ MX 2004, Dreamweaver® MX 2004,
Fireworks® MX 2004, and FreeHand® MX

Senior Vice President, School SMG
Chris Elkhill

Managing Editor
Chris Katsaropoulos

Product Manager
Robert Gaggin

Associate Product Manager
Meagan Putney

Sr. Marketing Manager
Kim Ryttel

Editor
Kirsti Aho

Development
Custom Editorial Productions Inc.

Director of Production
Patty Stephan

Production Management
Custom Editorial Productions Inc.

Print Buyer
Trevor Kallop

Cover Design
Abby Scholz

Illustrator
Paul Vismara

Compositor
GEX Publishing Services

Get Back to the Basics...
With these *exciting new products!*

Our exciting new series of Macromedia books will provide everything needed to learn about multimedia and Web site design.

NEW! Macromedia Studio MX 2004 Step-by-Step
Projects for Macromedia Flash MX 2004, Dreamweaver MX 2004, Fireworks MX 2004, and FreeHand MX
40+ hours of instruction

0-619-18390-X	Student Textbook, Soft-Perfect Cover
0-619-18391-8	Instructor Resources (PC)
0-619-18392-6	Instructor Resources (Mac)
0-619-18393-4	Review Pack (Data CD)

NEW! Multimedia Projects for Macromedia Flash MX 2004 and Dreamweaver MX 2004
20+ hours of instruction

0-619-18394-2	3-ring binder (extra projects)

NEW! Digital Design Curriculum Guide
150+ hours of instruction

0-619-18396-9	3-ring binder (for instructors)
0-619-18399-3	Instructor Resources
0-619-18400-0	Review Pack (Data CD)

HOW TO ORDER

To Order by Phone
Call toll free:
1-800-824-5179
8:00 AM – 8:00 PM EST (Mon.-Fri.)

To Order by Fax
Fax toll free 24 hours
1-800-487-8488

To Order by Mail
Write to:
Thomson Learning
Distribution Center
ATTN: Order Fulfillment
P.O. Box 6904
Florence, KY 41042-6904

To Order by Web
Go to:
www.course.com

Customer Support
Call toll free:
1-800-824-5179

Each Order Must Include

- Your complete name, shipping and billing address, ZIP Code, and daytime phone number with area code
- Your account number
- Complete title ISBN and quantity for each title ordered
- Purchase order number (for orders not accompanied by payment)
- Any special instructions or information clearly noted
- Credit card orders must be accompanied by the cardholder's complete name, address, phone number, card number, card expiration date, and shipping instructions (e.g., UPS, Federal Express, RPS). The school name, college name, or company name is essential. All written orders must contain the signature of the cardholder.

Join Us On the Internet **www.course.com**

How to Use This Book

What makes a good text about Web authoring applications? Sound instruction and hands-on skill-building and reinforcement. That is what you will find in *Macromedia Studio MX 2004 Step-by-Step*. Not only will you find a colorful and inviting layout, but also many features to enhance learning.

Objectives— Objectives are listed at the beginning of each lesson. This allows you to look ahead to what you will be learning.

Step-by-Step Exercises— Preceded by a short topic discussion, these exercises are the "hands-on practice" part of the lesson. Simply follow the steps, either using a data file or creating a file from scratch. Each lesson is a series of these step-by-step exercises.

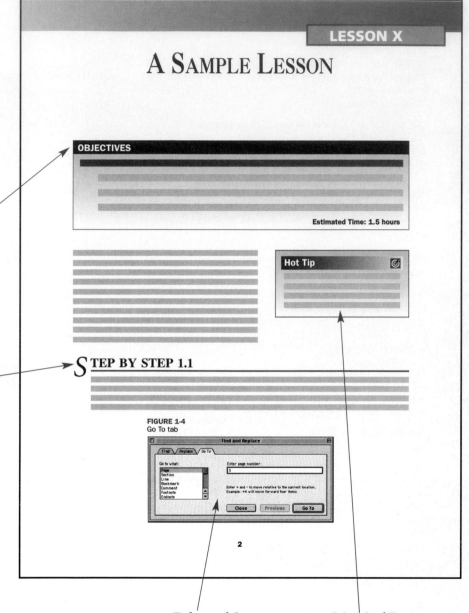

LESSON X

A SAMPLE LESSON

OBJECTIVES

Estimated Time: 1.5 hours

Hot Tip

STEP BY STEP 1.1

FIGURE 1-4
Go To tab

2

Enhanced Screen Shots— Screen shots now come to life on each page with color and depth.

Marginal Boxes— These boxes provide additional information about the topic of the lesson.

How to Use This Book

Special Feature Boxes— These boxes provide interesting additional information about the Internet.

Summary— At the end of each lesson, you will find a summary to prepare you to complete the end-of-lesson activities.

Web Design Skills

SUMMARY

PREFACE

Welcome to *Macromedia Studio MX 2004 Step-by-Step*. This course is designed to introduce you to Macromedia's suite of Web-authoring applications, and show you how to use them to create appealing and cutting-edge multimedia.

This course covers the applications for Microsoft Windows® or Macintosh® as described below.

Macromedia Flash™ MX 2004

Macromedia Flash MX 2004 is the professional-standard authoring tool for producing high-impact Web experiences. Whether you are creating animated logos, Web site navigation controls, long-form animations, entire Macromedia Flash Web sites, or Web applications, you'll find the power and flexibility of Macromedia Flash ideal for your creativity.

In the Macromedia Flash MX 2004 project, you will learn the Web publishing skills you need to:

- Work with the Macromedia Flash interface and drawing tools.
- Import a variety of file formats.
- Overlay and align images.
- Manipulate video.
- Create button, graphic, and movie clip symbols.
- Create frame-by-frame animation.
- Add sound effects.
- Generate an e-mail form.
- Publish and export Macromedia Flash movies.

Dreamweaver® MX 2004

Macromedia Dreamweaver MX 2004 is a professional visual editor for creating and managing Web sites and Web pages. You can use Dreamweaver to visually design your Web page in the convenient Layout view, or you can use the robust text-editing features when you want to hand-code your page. Either way, you'll find creating and managing your site easy with Dreamweaver and its intuitive workspace.

In the Dreamweaver MX 2004 project, you will learn the Web publishing skills you need to:

- Add text, graphics, and links.
- Add Macromedia Flash text and buttons.
- Create complex tables in Layout view.
- Add enhancements, such as rollover buttons and images.
- Manage the site.

Fireworks® MX 2004

Macromedia Fireworks MX 2004 is a graphics program used to create and edit sophisticated images for the Web. With Fireworks, you can quickly create image maps, rollover buttons, animations, and entire Web pages. You can then use the optimization features to shrink the file size of your graphics without sacrificing quality. When you're ready, simply export the HTML code to your favorite editor, such as Macromedia Dreamweaver MX 2004. The professional design tools in Fireworks even let you import digital camera files and scanned images, as well as files from popular image-editing programs and other graphics applications.

In the Fireworks project, you will learn the Web publishing skills you need to:

- Create graphics with both vector and bitmap images.
- Import objects from other applications.
- Work with grouped objects and layers.
- Create formatted text.
- Apply special effects.
- Build buttons.
- Add rollovers.
- Create animated GIF images.
- Optimize images.
- Use Export Preview to compare formats and palette choices.

FreeHand® MX

Macromedia FreeHand MX has the versatility to perform many functions. It is a superb vector illustration tool, a flexible page layout solution, and, most importantly, a powerful, integral part of a Web development workflow. FreeHand can import TIF, JPEG, GIF, Illustrator, EPC, DCS, and other FreeHand files, including older versions. You can also add links and site navigation with ActionScripts, laying the groundwork for the final Web page.

In the FreeHand MX project, you will learn the Web publishing skills you need to:

- Create logos, graphics, and buttons.
- Customize the FreeHand interface to suit your working preferences.
- Convert placed images into vector images.
- Add special effects to vector images.
- Create a storyboard workflow.
- Import FreeHand files into Macromedia Flash and create basic animations.
- Integrate FreeHand with other applications, such as Macromedia Fireworks and Dreamweaver.

About Macromedia Studio MX 2004

People expect more from the Internet now—richer content and more dynamic applications. Whether you're a designer or developer, you need tools to work effortlessly and cost effectively while delivering the intuitive, effective experiences users demand. Macromedia Studio MX 2004 brings the power of Macromedia Flash™, Dreamweaver®, Fireworks®, and FreeHand® together into one highly integrated and approachable solution—with everything you need to create the full spectrum of Internet solutions, from Web sites to Web applications and Rich Internet Applications.

Acknowledgments

EDITOR:

Kirsti Aho

AUTHORS:

Dreamweaver MX 2004: Patti Schulze, Skip Pickle, and Abie Hadjitarkhani

Fireworks MX 2004: Patti Schulze, Scott Tapley, and Skip Pickle

Macromedia Flash MX 2004: Michael Epstein and Scott Tapley

FreeHand MX: Walter Linsley, Ralph DiMarco, and Skip Pickle

COPYEDITORS:

Malinda McCain and Judy Ziajka

MACROMEDIA TECHNICAL REVIEWERS:

Julie Hallstrom, Mark Haynes, Clint Critchlow, Peter Davy, Bentley Wolfe, and Joanne Watkins

MACROMEDIA PROJECT MANAGERS:

Alisse Berger and Denise Costello

Macromedia would like to thank Betsy Newberry, Rose Marie Kuebbing, Jean Findley, Jan Clavey, and the rest of the team at Custom Editorial Productions Inc. for managing the editing, development, and production of this book. Thanks also to the team at Course Technology, namely Chris Katsaropoulos, Robert Gaggin, Meagan Putney, cover designer Abby Scholz, and illustrator Paul Vismara, and to the production house, GEX Publishing Services.

START-UP CHECKLIST

Macromedia Flash™ MX 2004 (Authoring)

Microsoft Windows

✓ 600 MHz Intel Pentium III processor or equivalent

✓ Microsoft Windows 98 SE, 2000, or XP

✓ 128 MB of free available system RAM (256 MB recommended)

✓ 190 MB of available disk space

Apple Macintosh

✓ 500 MHz Power PC processor or better

✓ Apple Mac OS X 10.2.6

✓ 128 MB of free available system RAM (256 MB recommended)

✓ 130 MB of available disk space

Macromedia Flash™ MX 2004 (Playback)

Microsoft Windows

PLATFORM	BROWSER
Microsoft Windows 98	Internet Explorer 5.x, Netscape Navigator 4.7 or Netscape Navigator 7.x, Mozilla 1.x, AOL 8, and Opera 7.11
Windows Me	Internet Explorer 5.5, Netscape Navigator 4.7, Netscape Navigator 7.x, Mozilla 1.x, AOL 8, and Opera 7.11
Windows 2000	Internet Explorer 5.x, Netscape Navigator 4.7, Netscape Navigator 7.x, Mozilla 1.x, CompuServe 7, AOL 8, and Opera 7.11
Microsoft Windows XP	Internet Explorer 6.0, Netscape Navigator 7.x, Mozilla 1.x, CompuServe 7, AOL 8, and Opera 7.11

Apple Macintosh

PLATFORM	BROWSER
Mac OS 9.x	Internet Explorer 5.1, Netscape Navigator 4.8, Netscape Navigator 7.x, Mozilla 1.x, and Opera 6
Mac OS X 10.1.x or Mac OS X 10.2.x	Internet Explorer 5.2, Netscape Navigator 7.x, Mozilla 1.x, AOL 7, Opera 6, and Safari 1.0 (Mac OS X 10.2.x only)

Macromedia Dreamweaver® MX 2004

Microsoft Windows

- ✓ 600 MHz Intel Pentium III processor or equivalent
- ✓ Microsoft Windows 98 SE, 2000, XP, or .NET Server 2003
- ✓ 128 MB of available RAM (256 MB recommended)
- ✓ 275 MB of available disk space

Apple Macintosh

- ✓ 500 MHz Power PC G3 processor or better
- ✓ Apple Mac OS X 10.2.6
- ✓ 128 MB of available RAM (256 MB recommended)
- ✓ 275 MB of available disk space

Macromedia Fireworks® MX 2004

Microsoft Windows

- ✓ 600 MHz Intel Pentium III processor or equivalent
- ✓ Microsoft Windows 98 SE, 2000, or XP
- ✓ 128 MB of free available system RAM (256 MB recommended)
- ✓ 150 MB of available disk space

Apple Macintosh

- ✓ 500 MHz Power PC G3 processor or better
- ✓ Apple Mac OS X 10.2.6
- ✓ 128 MB of available RAM (256 MB recommended)
- ✓ 100 MB of available disk space

Macromedia FreeHand® MX

Microsoft Windows

✓ Intel Pentium II 300MHz+

✓ Microsoft Windows 98 SE, ME, NT 4 (Service Pack 6), 2000, or XP

✓ 64 MB of free available system RAM (128 MB recommended)

✓ 70 MB of available disk space

✓ 16-bit (thousands of colors) color monitor capable of 1024 × 768 or better

✓ CD-ROM drive

✓ Adobe Type Manager version 4 or later for use with Type 1 fonts (Windows 98, ME, NT 4)

✓ Postscript Level 2-Compatible printer or higher (recommended)

Apple Macintosh

✓ Apple Power Mac G3+

✓ Apple Mac OS 9.1 or higher, OS X 10.1 or higher

✓ 64 MB of free available system RAM (128 MB recommended)

✓ 70 MB of free hard disk space

✓ 16-bit (thousands of colors) color monitor capable of 1024 × 768 or better

✓ CD-ROM drive

✓ Adobe Type Manager version 4 or later for use with Type 1 fonts (OS 9.x)

✓ Postscript Level 2-Compatible printer or higher (recommended)

✓ QuickTime 6 (OS 9.x)

GUIDE FOR USING THIS BOOK

Please read this Guide before starting work. The time you spend now will save you much more time later and will make your learning faster, easier, and more pleasant.

Conventions

The different type styles used in this book have special meanings. They will save you time because you will soon automatically recognize from the type style the nature of the text you are reading and what you will do.

WHAT YOU WILL DO	TYPE STYLE	EXAMPLE
Text you will key	**Bold**	Key **Don't litter** rapidly.
Commands you will select	**Bold**	Click **File, Open**
Individual keys you will press	**Bold**	Press **Enter** to insert a blank line.
WHAT YOU WILL SEE	TYPE STYLE	EXAMPLE
Filenames in book	**Bold upper and lowercase**	Open **Diving.htm** from the data files.
Glossary terms in book	***Bold and italics***	The ***menu bar*** contains menu titles.
Words on screen	*Italics*	Highlight the word *pencil* on the screen.
Menus and commands	**Bold**	Choose **Open** from the **File** menu.
Options/features with long names	*Italics*	Select Normal from the *Style for following paragraph* text box.

Student Files

All data files necessary for this book are located on the *Review Pack* CD-ROM supplied with this text. These data files are also available on the Course Technology Web site; go to *www.course.com* and select Student Downloads.

Instructor Resources CD-ROM

The *Instructor Resources* CD-ROM contains a wealth of instructional material you can use to prepare for teaching this course. The CD-ROM stores the following information:

- Both the data and solution files for this course.

- ExamView® tests for each lesson. ExamView is a powerful testing software package that allows instructors to create and administer printed, computer (LAN-based), and Internet exams. ExamView includes hundreds of questions that correspond to the topics covered in this text, enabling learners to generate detailed study guides that include page references for further review. The computer-based and Internet testing components allow learners to take exams at their computers, and also save the instructor time by grading each exam automatically.

- Electronic *Instructor's Manual* that includes lecture notes for each lesson and references to the solutions for Step-by-Step exercises.

- Instructor lesson plans as well as learner study guides that can help to guide students through the lesson text and exercises.

- Copies of the figures that appear in the student text, which can be used to prepare transparencies.

- Suggested schedules for teaching the lessons in this course.

- Additional instructional information about individual learning strategies, portfolios, and career planning, and a sample Internet contract.

- PowerPoint presentations outlining features for each lesson in the text.

- 30-day trial software.

TABLE OF CONTENTS

MACROMEDIA DREAMWEAVER MX PROJECT

MACROMEDIA FIREWORKS MX PROJECT

MACROMEDIA FLASH MX PROJECT

Macromedia FreeHand MX PROJECT

MACROMEDIA DREAMWEAVER MX

Project

LEARNING THE BASICS

OBJECTIVES

Upon completion of this lesson, you should be able to:

- Use the Dreamweaver graphical user interface.
- Recognize how Flash text differs from HTML text.
- Define a new site.
- Name, title, and save your documents.
- Specify preview browsers.
- Specify background, text, and link colors.
- Put text on a page and format it.
- Use the Assets panel to select and apply color to text.

Organizing Your Site

Before you begin creating your Web pages, you should have some idea what to put on the pages. Developing Web pages is similar to designing print material: you develop the concept first. You need to ask yourself—or your client—some basic questions. Why is the Web site needed? What are you trying to communicate? Who are the potential viewers of the pages? What do you want your visitors to take away with them?

Consider also what browsers your users might have. Do they probably have the most up-to-date version with all the latest plug-ins? Or are they more likely to have older computers and older browsers? The answer to the browser question determines whether you can use Cascading Style Sheets or layers on your pages.

You also need to develop an outline of the site. The outline is similar to a storyboard for a multimedia project or a movie, giving you an idea of the scope of the project and a starting point for setting up the file structure you need. When you have gathered the text and graphics for your Web pages, you are ready to start using Macromedia Dreamweaver MX 2004 to put those ideas together.

Dreamweaver Basics

When you open Dreamweaver, you'll notice a workspace area (where you can work in a Document window), the Insert bar above the workspace, the Property inspector below the workspace, and a group of panels to the right of the workspace, as shown in Figure 1-1. Use the Insert bar for adding objects such as images, tables, layers, or Macromedia Flash animations to the page. In the Property inspector, you can change the attributes of selected text or an object on the page. The panels enable you to modify elements of your page or to manage your site. You access the panels and the Property inspector from the Window menu.

FIGURE 1-1
The workspace

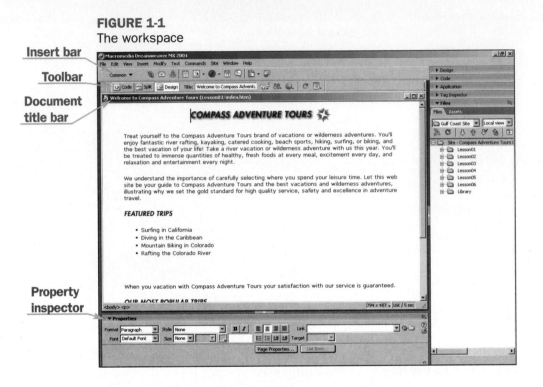

A check mark next to an item on the Window menu indicates that the panel is open, but it could be hidden beneath another panel or the Document window. To display a hidden panel, select it again from the Window menu.

If a panel is selected but still doesn't appear, click the Window menu and then click Arrange Panels to reset all open panels to their default positions. The Insert bar moves to the upper left of the screen, the Property inspector moves to the bottom of the screen, and all other open panels move to the right of the screen, with no overlap.

The Document Window

You'll do most of your work in the Document window. It gives you an approximate representation of your page as you add and delete elements. The title bar shows the document's title and filename. The Document toolbar lets you select the document view and enter the document title.

The Insert Bar

The Insert bar contains the objects or elements you want to add to your page, as shown in Figure 1-2. Among them are images, tables, special characters, forms, and frames. To insert an object, drag the object's icon from the Insert bar to its place in the Document window. Another method is to place the insertion point in your document where the object should appear and then click the object's icon on the bar. The object is inserted into the document at the insertion point.

FIGURE 1-2
The Insert bar showing the Common category

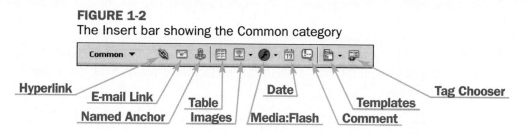

You can select from a number of categories on the Insert bar. To change categories, choose the category name from the pop-up menu on the left of the Insert bar. For example, you can access the objects you need to create a form by choosing the Forms category.

The Property Inspector

In the Property inspector, you can view and change the attributes of an object, as shown in Figure 1-3. The inspector is context sensitive—it relates to whatever you have selected in the Document window. Depending on the selected object, there might be additional properties that are not visible. To see all the properties, click the expander arrow in the lower-right corner of the inspector.

FIGURE 1-3
The Property inspector

Dockable Panels

By default, Dreamweaver panels are docked in collapsible groups in the docking area on the right side of the workspace. This maximizes your screen area while giving you quick access to the panels you need.

You'll also notice that the Document window and the panels snap to each other or to the sides of your screen. This helps you better manage your workspace.

To undock or move a panel group or panel, drag the gripper on the upper-left corner of the panel group away from the panel docking area on the right side of the screen.

To collapse or expand a panel group or panel, do one of the following:

■ Click the title of the panel group or panel. (The title bar is still visible when the panel group or panel is collapsed.)

■ Click the expander arrow in the upper-left corner of the panel group or panel.

S TEP-BY-STEP 1.1

Undocking and Docking a Panel Group or Panel

1. Start Dreamweaver.

2. Move the pointer over the gripper for the **Files** panel. You can tell you are over the gripper when the pointer changes to a four-headed arrow (Windows) or a hand (Macintosh).

3. Click on the panel gripper and drag the **Files** panel over the document area. Notice that the panel above the place where the **Files** panel had been located expands to fill in the space created by moving the **Files** panel.

4. Drag the **Files** panel back onto the panel docking area. As you drag a panel or panel group over the panel docking area, a placement preview line or rectangle shows where it will be placed among the groups.

5. Drop the **Files** panel back at the bottom of the docking area to return it to its original location. Remain in this screen for the next Step-by-Step.

Renaming a Panel Group

To change the name of a panel group, click the icon at the upper right of the panel group (this is known as the options menu) and choose Rename Panel Group. Enter the new name in the dialog box and then click OK. This is most useful if you decide to reorganize the panels or set up your own panel groups.

Hiding All Panels and the Property Inspector

If you find there are panels you do not use often or at all, you can hide them so there is less clutter on your screen and so you can more easily see and access the panels you do use. To hide entire panel groups, select Close Panel Group from the options menu. You can also choose to hide all the panels as well as the Property inspector by choosing Hide Panels from the View menu. This allows you a full screen view of your document.

To view hidden panels, select Show Panels from the View menu. Panels that are hidden when you choose Hide Panels remain hidden when you show the panels again.

Defining a Local Site

Before you begin to create individual Web pages, you need to create the site that contains those pages. This local site on your hard drive will mirror the actual pages on the Web server. The local site is where you do all your initial development and testing. To set up a local site, create a folder on your hard drive. The name of the folder can be the name of the site or any name

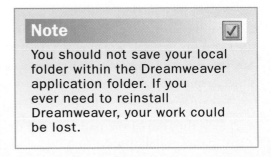

Note ☑

You should not save your local folder within the Dreamweaver application folder. If you ever need to reinstall Dreamweaver, your work could be lost.

you choose. For example, in this course you have a folder called compass_tours that contains all the files and folders you will use in this unit.

After you define the main folder, it becomes the root folder for your site. All your files and subfolders are contained within that root folder. Dreamweaver needs a properly defined site with a unique local root folder to maintain and update links between pages. When you upload a site, the relative links that worked within the local root will also work on the server. When you are ready to publish your site, all you have to do is copy that folder and all its files to the remote server. The images and links should all work (assuming they work locally).

If you connect a local site to a remote site, Dreamweaver maintains identical directory structures to ensure that links and references are not accidentally broken. If directories do not exist in the site where you are transferring files, Dreamweaver automatically creates them.

You must first save a document within a local site before site-root-relative or document-relative links will work. In all dialog boxes where you link a file to the current document, you can choose to define the path as site-root-relative, document-relative, or absolute.

Site-Root-Relative Paths

Site-root-relative paths provide the path from the site's root folder to a document. You might want to use these types of paths if you are working on a large Web site that uses several servers or on one server that hosts several different sites.

If you move a document or folder out of a local site, site-root-relative links stop working. If you move folders containing linked files to a different defined local site, site-root-relative links continue to work as long as the folder structure branching from the root is the same as the original site's structure.

Absolute Paths

Absolute paths provide the complete URL of the linked document, including the protocol to use (usually HTTP for Web pages). For example, an absolute path would be http://www.macromedia.com/support/dreamweaver/getting_started.html. You must use an absolute path to link to a document on another server. You can also use absolute paths for local links (to documents in the same site), but that approach is discouraged; if you move the site to another domain, all your local absolute links will break.

Document-Relative Paths

Document-relative paths are the best choice to use for local links in most Web sites. Document-relative paths define the path to take to find the linked file, starting from the document. For example, a path to a file in the same folder would be expressed as myfile.htm. To link to a file in a subfolder of the current document, the path would be expressed as content/myfile.htm. To link to a file in the parent folder of the current file, the path would be expressed as ../myfile.htm.

STEP-BY-STEP 1.2

Creating a New Local Site

1. Using the file management tools on your system, copy the entire **compass_tours** folder from the data files for this unit to the location where you will store your solution files (ask your instructor for specific directions).

2. Switch back to Dreamweaver. Click the **Site** menu, and then click **Manage Sites**.

STEP-BY-STEP 1.2 Continued

If you have already defined at least one site in Dreamweaver (or a previous version of Dreamweaver), the Manage Sites dialog box opens, as shown in Figure 1-4. This dialog box lists all the sites you have previously defined and lets you create new ones. If you haven't previously defined a site, the Site Definition dialog box opens, as shown in Figure 1-5.

FIGURE 1-4
The Manage Sites dialog box

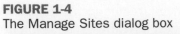

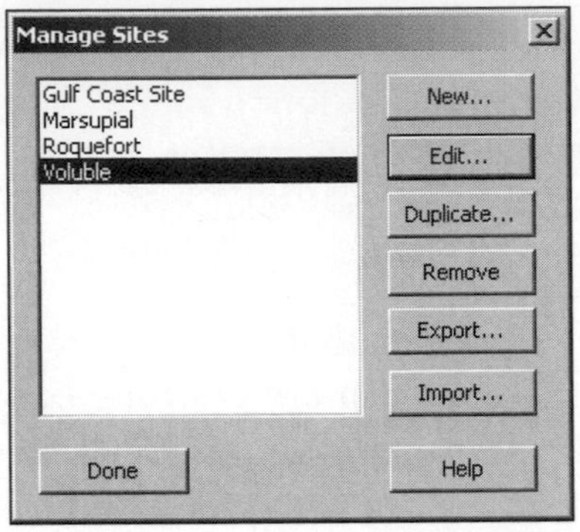

3. Click **New** and then click **Site** to create a new site. The Site Definition dialog box opens. If the dialog box opens in Advanced mode, click the **Basic** tab to start the Site Definition Wizard shown in Figure 1-5.

FIGURE 1-5
The Site Definition Wizard

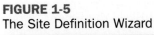

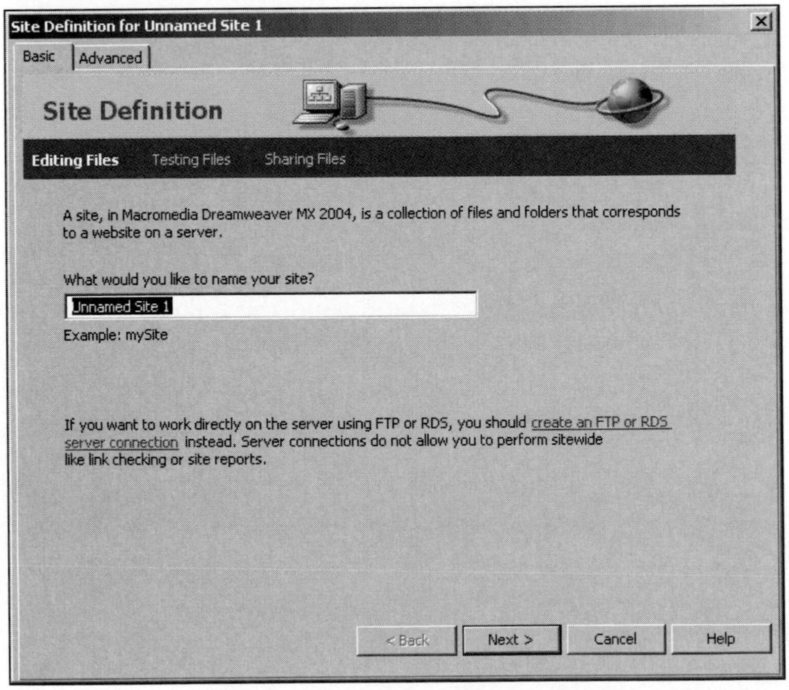

STEP-BY-STEP 1.2 Continued

4. The wizard starts with *What would you like to name your site?* The name you assign to the site can be anything that identifies the site—this is for your reference only. For this course, key your name as the site name.

5. Click **Next** to move to the next step in the wizard.

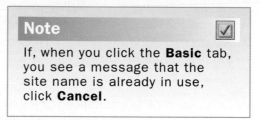

Note ☑

If, when you click the **Basic** tab, you see a message that the site name is already in use, click **Cancel**.

6. Under *Do you want to work with a server technology such as ColdFusion, ASP.NET, ASP, JSP, or PHP?* click **No, I do not want to use a server technology**. Then click **Next**.

7. Under *How do you want to work with your files during development?* click **Edit local copies on my machine, then upload to server when ready (recommended).** Later in this course you will learn how to move your files to a remote Web server.

8. Under *Where on your computer do you want to store your files?* click the folder icon next to the text box. The Local Root Folder text box specifies the folder on your hard drive where the files for this site are stored. It is the local equivalent of the site root folder at the remote site. Dreamweaver creates all site-root-relative links relative to the local root folder.

9. Locate your compass_tours folder (the one you copied in step 1).

   For Windows, select the **compass_tours** folder and click **Open**. Then click **Select** to use the compass_tours folder as your root folder.

   For the Macintosh, select the **compass_tours** folder and click **Choose**.

10. Click **Next** to move to the next step in the wizard.

11. "How do you connect to your remote server?" Click on the arrow to see the list of options and then select **None**.

12. Click **Next** to move to a summary of your site definition settings. Review your settings.

13. Click **Done** to finish defining your site. A message box might appear to notify you that the initial site cache will be created. Click **OK**.

14. Click **Done** to close the Manage Sites dialog box. Remain in this screen for the next Step-by-Step.

Did You Know? 💡

Once you have defined a site, whenever you open Dreamweaver, it will automatically load the site information from the last site used. If you have multiple sites in which you work, you can switch between them through the Files panel.

Specifying Preview Browsers

As you develop your Web pages, you will want to view your efforts in a browser—or in fact, in several browsers. In the Preferences dialog box (shown in Figure 1-6), you can specify which browsers you would like to use to preview your pages. Click the plus (+) button to add a browser to the list. When the dialog box opens, find the browser application.

FIGURE 1-6
The Preferences dialog box for Preview in Browser

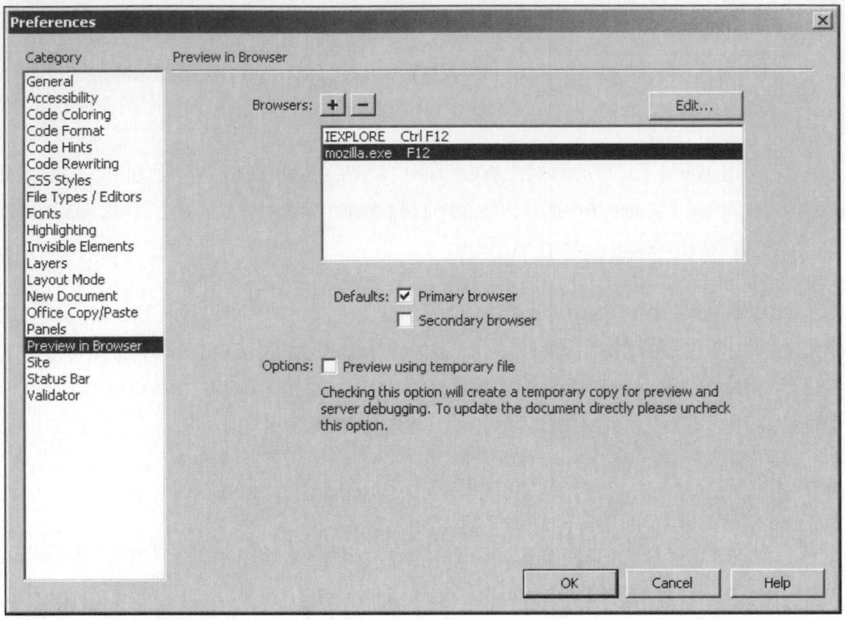

Select the primary browser by highlighting it in the list and then selecting the Primary Browser check box. Select the secondary browser in the same fashion. These selections allow you to utilize the keyboard shortcuts Dreamweaver has made available to simplify the preview process. To view a page in the primary browser, press the F12 key on the keyboard. To view a page in the secondary browser, press Ctrl + F12 (Windows) or Command + F12 (Macintosh). (You'll be using these shortcuts often, so memorize them quickly.) You can also access the preview through the Preview/Debug in Browser button on the toolbar and then selecting from the list the browser in which you want to view your work.

To remove a browser from the list, select the browser name in the list and then click the minus (–) button. To change a browser choice, select the browser name in the list. Then click Edit and locate a different browser.

*S*TEP-BY-STEP 1.3

Selecting Preview Browsers

1. Click the **Edit** menu, and then click **Preferences** (Windows), or click the **Dreamweaver** menu, and then click **Preferences** (Macintosh). Select **Preview in Browser** from the Category list on the left.

2. Click a browser name in the window on the right to identify whether it's a primary or secondary browser, or neither.

3. Follow the directions of your instructor or technical support personnel for adding any browsers and for setting the primary and secondary browsers.

> **Hot Tip** ◎
>
> You can also access the Browser Preferences dialog box from the File menu: point to **Preview in Browser** and then click **Edit Browser List**. Or you can click the **Preview/Debug in Browser** button on the toolbar and then click **Edit Browser List**.

4. Click **OK** when you finish adding or changing browsers. Remain in this screen for the next Step-by-Step.

Saving Your File

You should save your documents in Dreamweaver as soon as you open a new document. Don't wait until you have text or graphics on the page. If you save before you import graphics or other media, all references will be created properly.

Naming an HTML File

Naming your files for use on a Web server is a little different from naming your files for your hard drive. It helps to know what type of machine will be used: Windows, UNIX, or Macintosh. The naming structure might be different on each of these machines. UNIX systems are case sensitive, which means *myfile.htm* does not equal *MYFILE.HTM*. Here are some guidelines to follow:

■ Your best bet is to use lowercase names for your files and keep the filenames short. That way, your filenames work on all servers.

■ Don't use spaces within your filenames. Use the underscore or dash character to simulate a space to separate words.

■ Use letters and numbers, but no special characters, such as %, *, or /.

■ Avoid beginning your filenames with a number.

■ Make sure you don't leave a space at the end of the filename.

■ The same goes for folder names—don't use spaces. If you do, you'll notice that browsers substitute %20 for the spaces.

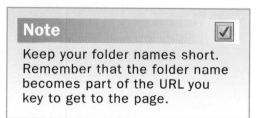

> **Note** ☑
>
> Keep your folder names short. Remember that the folder name becomes part of the URL you key to get to the page.

Setting Up a Page: Surf Hawaii Page

For the remainder of this lesson, you will create a simple Web page like that shown in Figure 1-7. In the process of creating this page, you will learn many different ways to format text and customize the look of your page.

FIGURE 1-7
The completed surf_hawaii.htm file

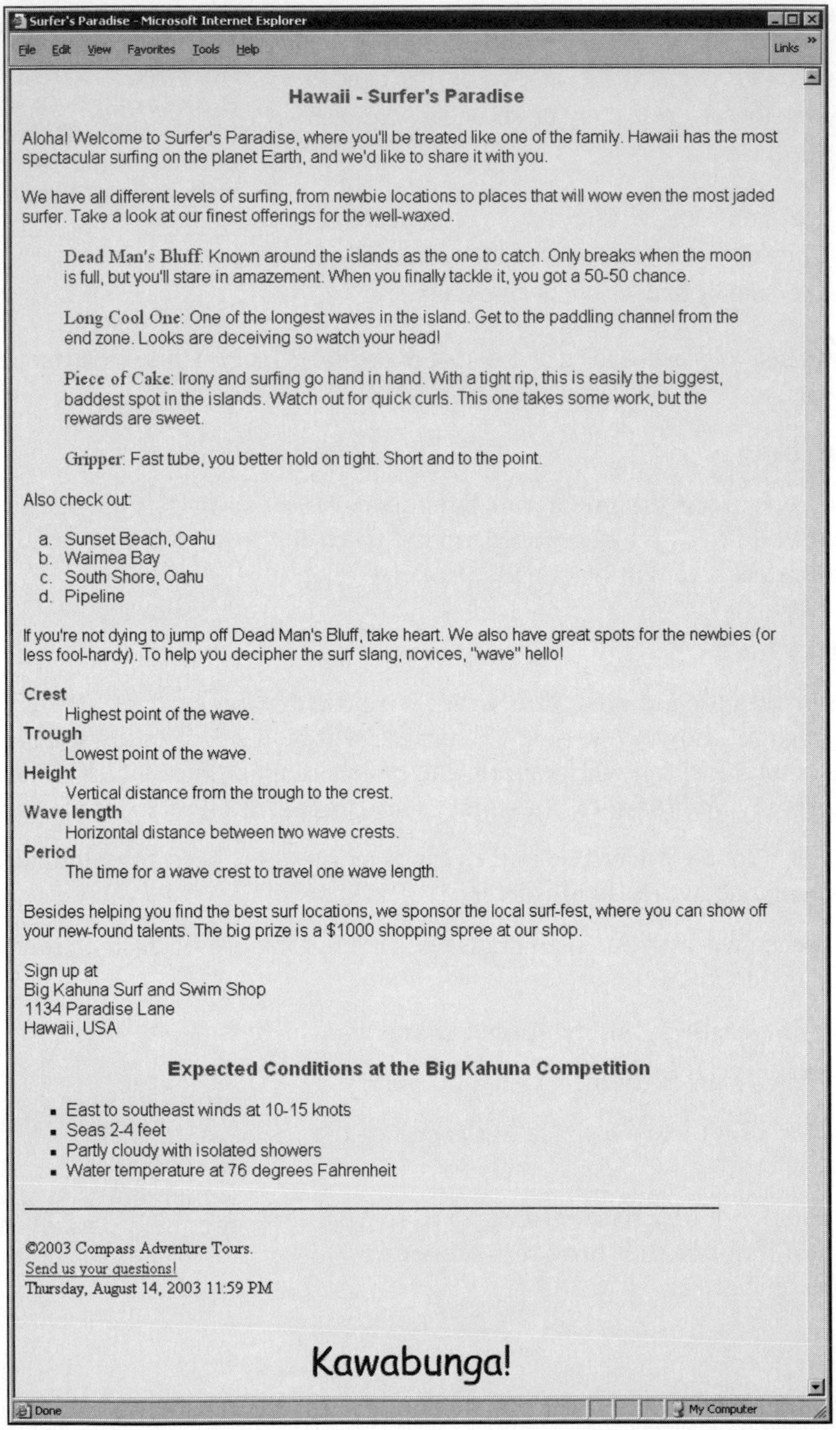

Giving Your Page a Title

Every HTML document should have a title. The title, used primarily for document identification, is displayed in a browser's title bar and as the bookmark name. Choose a short phrase that describes the document's purpose. The title can be of any length: you can crop it if it's too long to fit in the browser's title bar.

Get in the habit of adding the title to each page you create before you add text or graphics to the page. If you forget, Dreamweaver defaults to Untitled Document—you don't want to keep that for the page name.

S TEP-BY-STEP 1.4

Adding the Page Title

1. Click **Open** on the **File** menu. Because you have already set the compass_tours folder as the folder for this site, the Open dialog box will go to that folder automatically.

2. Open the **Lesson01** folder and then open the **surf_hawaii.htm** file.

3. If you don't see the Title text box at the top of the Document window (below the menu bar), click the **View** menu, point to **Toolbars**, and then click **Document**.

4. Key **Surfer's Paradise** in the Title text box and then press **Enter** (Windows) or **Return** (Macintosh) or click in the document.

> **Note** ☑
>
> Dreamweaver uses the Document window title bar to remind you to title your page. It contains the title and the filename of the current document. If you see "Untitled Document (filename.htm)" in the title bar, you haven't titled your document.

5. Use the scroll bar on the right side of the Document window to see all of the text. Note that most of the text for this page is present but that it does not yet look at all like the page in Figure 1-7.

6. Save your document (click the **File** menu and then click **Save**). Remain in this screen for the next Step-by-Step.

Specifying a Background Color

In Dreamweaver, you can easily change the background color of a page by using a preset palette of colors known as the Web-safe color palette. You access that palette in the Page Properties dialog box. For more colors, click the arrow located in the upper-right corner of the color picker and select a color palette from the menu.

STEP-BY-STEP 1.5

Selecting a Background Color

1. Click the **Modify** menu, and then click **Page Properties**. The Page Properties dialog box opens.

2. Make sure **Appearance** is selected in the Category list.

3. Click the **Background Color** box. A color picker opens.

4. Move the eyedropper over a color swatch. The swatch's hexadecimal equivalent is shown at the top of the color palette.

5. Click the pale blue color to select it, or key **CCFFFF** in the Background Color text box, as shown in Figure 1-8.

> **Hot Tip**
>
> You do not need to include the number sign (#) before the hexadecimal color code—it is added automatically when you close the Page Properties dialog box.

FIGURE 1-8
The 1Page Properties dialog box

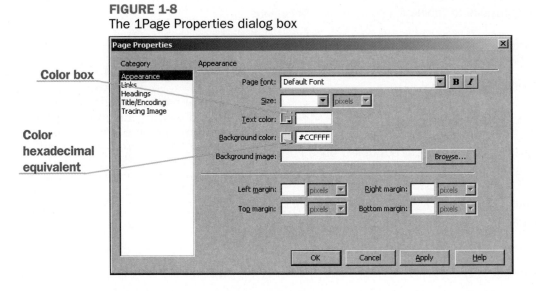

6. Click **Apply** to view the color change to your document without leaving the Page Properties dialog box. Remain in this screen for the next Step-by-Step.

Specifying the Default Font Color

When you change the background color, you might also need to change the color of the text that is displayed. Obviously, for example, black text won't be visible on a black background. But you also might find that certain color combinations are more visually appealing or are easier to read.

S TEP-BY-STEP 1.6

Changing the Default Font Color

1. In the Page Properties dialog box, click the **Text Color** box. A color palette opens.

2. Select a color for your text—dark blue would look good—and click **Apply** to view the color change in your document. Remain in this screen for the next Step-by-Step.

Specifying Link Colors

In addition to changing the default text color, you can change the color of text links on your page. There are three different link types that are described below.

- **Links:** The initial color of a link—the color a user sees before clicking the link. The normal default browser color for a link is blue.

- **Visited Links:** The color the link changes to when a user clicks the link. The normal default color for a visited link is purple.

- **Rollover Links:** The color the link changes to when a user positions the pointer over the link. If you do not select a color, then the link color doesn't change when the pointer is over the link.

- **Active Links:** The color the link turns to when a user holds down the mouse button after clicking the link. The normal default color for an active link is red.

S TEP-BY-STEP 1.7

Changing Link Colors

1. From the Page Properties dialog box, choose Links from the Category list.

2. Click the color box next to the link type you want to change, as shown in Figure 1-9.

FIGURE 1-9
Page Properties, showing link color selections

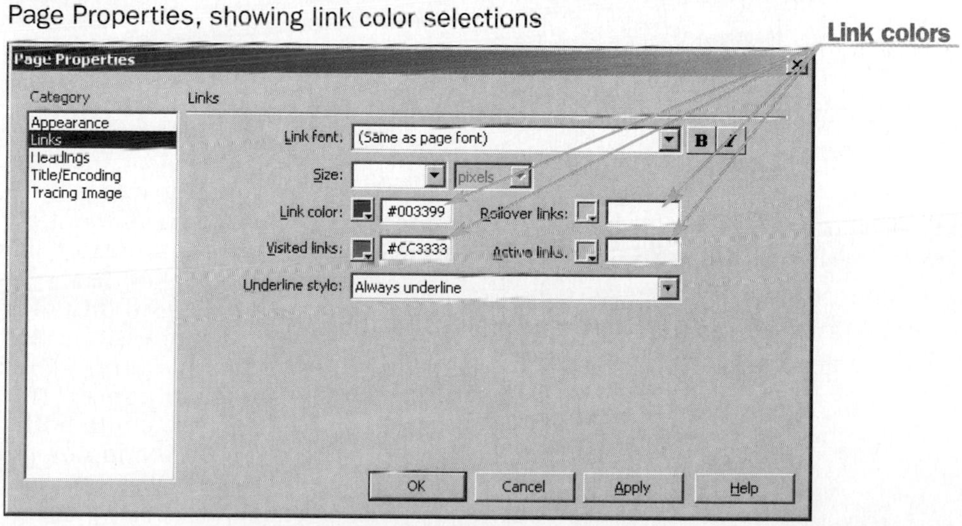

Link colors

STEP-BY-STEP 1.7 Continued

3. Using Figure 1-9 as a guide, select the colors for your links.

4. Click **OK** to close the Page Properties dialog box and return to your document.

5. Save the document and remain in this screen for the next Step-by-Step.

Working with Text on a Page

You can add text to a page by typing it or by copying and pasting from an existing text document. If the text is from an application that supports drag-and-drop copying (for example, Microsoft Word on the Macintosh), you can open both Dreamweaver and that application and either copy and paste or drag the text into Dreamweaver.

STEP-BY-STEP 1.8

Adding Text to a Page

1. Insert a new line at the top of the page by pressing **Enter** (Windows) or **Return** (Macintosh).

2. Key **Hawaii - Surfer's Paradise** in that new line.

3. From the Property inspector's **Format** menu, select **Heading 3**, as shown in Figure 1-10. You have now tagged the text as a Level 3 heading.

FIGURE 1-10
The Property inspector's Format menu

4. Save your document and remain in this screen for the next Step-by-Step.

HTML has six levels of headings—numbered 1 through 6—with Heading 1 having the largest font size. Headings are displayed in larger or bolder fonts than the normal body text. Tagging a paragraph as a heading automatically generates a space below the heading.

> **Note** ☑
>
> In many documents, the first heading is identical to the title. For multipart documents, the text of the first heading should be related information (such as a chapter title), and the title tag should identify the document in a wider context (for example, it could include both the book title and the chapter title).

Indenting Text

Often you'll want to indent the text on the page. You can use the Text Indent and Text Outdent icons in the Property inspector to do this, as shown in Figure 1-11. Using Text Indent indents text at the left and right margins of the page.

FIGURE 1-11
The Text Indent and Text Outdent icons

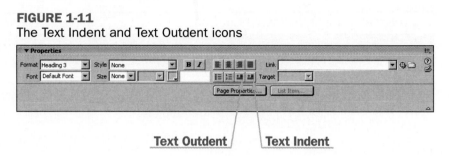

Text Outdent   Text Indent

S TEP-BY-STEP 1.9

Indenting Paragraphs and Removing Indentation

1. Select the first six body paragraphs of your surf_hawaii.htm document, starting with the word **Aloha**.

2. Click **Text Indent** in the Property inspector or click the **Text** menu and then click **Indent**.

3. Select the first two body paragraphs of the document.

4. Click **Text Outdent** in the Property inspector or click the **Text** menu and then click **Outdent**.

5. Save the file and preview it in the browser by pressing **F12**.

6. Close the browser and remain in this screen for the next Step-by-Step.

Making Lists

Dreamweaver gives you three kinds of lists: ordered (numbered), unordered (bulleted), and definition lists (a term and its definition).

ORDERED LISTS

An ordered list consists of list items that are ordered numerically or alphabetically. You have the option of using Arabic or Roman numerals or using uppercase or lowercase letters.

S TEP-BY-STEP 1.10

Creating an Ordered (Numbered) List

1. Select the four lines of text: **Sunset Beach**, **Oahu**, **Waimea Bay**, **South Shore**, **Oahu**, and **Pipeline**.

STEP-BY-STEP 1.10 Continued

2. Click the **Ordered List** button in the Property inspector shown in Figure 1-12, or click the **Text** menu, point to **List**, and then click **Ordered List**. The selected text is indented and numbered.

FIGURE 1-12
The Ordered List and Unordered List icons

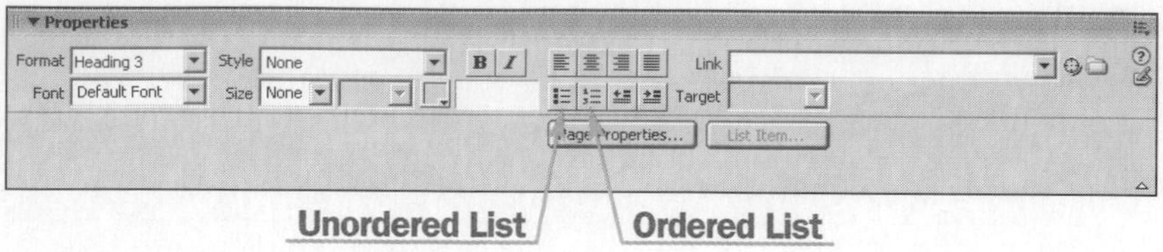

Unordered List   **Ordered List**

3. Save the document and remain in this screen for the next Step-by-Step.

You can change the numbering scheme of ordered lists by modifying the list's properties, which are accessed through the List Item button in the Property inspector. To use the List Item button, click in only one line from the list. If you select multiple lines, the List Item button is dimmed and not available for you to use. If the List Item button is not visible, click the expander arrow in the lower-right corner of the Property inspector.

STEP-BY-STEP 1.11

Changing Ordered List Properties

1. Click in the line with the text **Sunset Beach** or in any line in the list.

2. Click **List Item** in the Property inspector, or click the **Text** menu, point to **List**, and then click **Properties**. The List Properties dialog box opens, as shown in Figure 1-13.

FIGURE 1-13
The List Properties dialog box

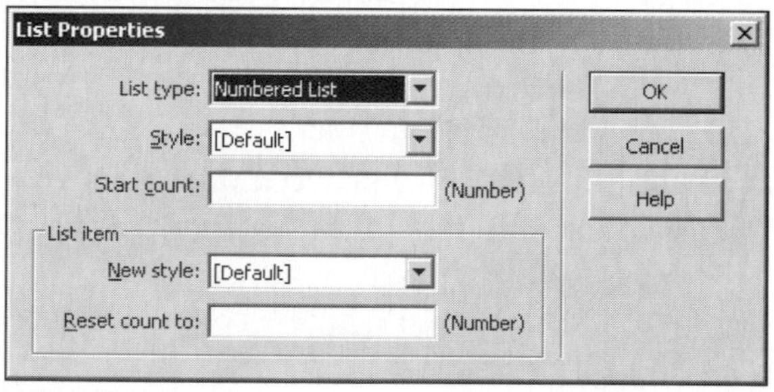

3. From the **Style** menu, select **Alphabet Small (a, b, c)** and then click **OK**. All items in the list are alphabetized.

4. Save the file and preview it in the browser.

5. Close the browser and remain in this screen for the next Step-by-Step.

UNORDERED LISTS

Unordered lists are often called bulleted lists because each list item has a bullet in front of it. The bullet symbol Dreamweaver displays by default can be changed to a circle or a square.

STEP-BY-STEP 1.12

Creating an Unordered (Bulleted) List

1. Select the text starting with **East to southeast winds** and ending with **Water temperature at 76 degrees Fahrenheit** (at the bottom of the document).

2. Click **Unordered List** in the Property inspector, or click the **Text** menu, point to **List**, and then click **Unordered List**. The selected text is indented and bulleted.

3. Save the document and remain in this screen for the next Step-by-Step.

You can change the default bullet symbol of unordered lists by modifying the list's properties.

STEP-BY-STEP 1.13

Changing Unordered List Properties

1. Click in any line in the list.

2. Click **List Item** in the Property inspector, or click the **Text** menu, point to **List**, and then click **Properties**. The List Properties dialog box opens, as shown in Figure 1-14.

FIGURE 1-14
The List Properties dialog box

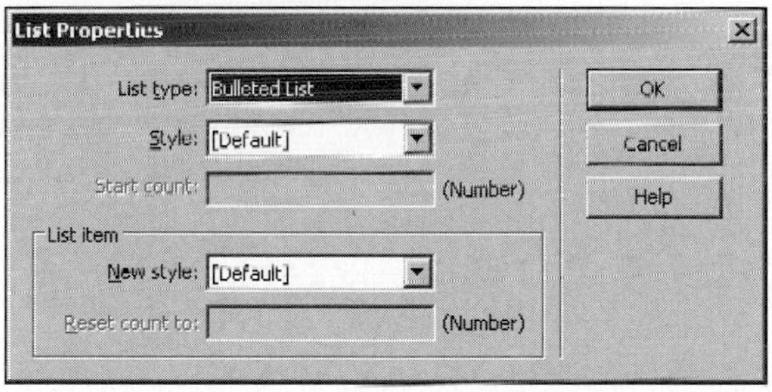

3. From the **Style** menu, select **Square** and click **OK**. All items in the list now use the square bullet symbol.

4. Save the document and remain in this screen for the next Step-by-Step.

DEFINITION LISTS

A definition list consists of a series of terms and their definitions. The word or term to be defined is left-justified; the definition is indented and placed on the next line. For this formatting to work, a term and its definition must each be a separate paragraph.

S TEP-BY-STEP 1.14

Creating a Definition List

1. Select the text starting with **Crest** and ending with **The time for a wave crest to travel one wave length**.

2. Click the **Text** menu, point to **List**, and then click **Definition List**. The terms are now at the left margin, and their indented definitions are on succeeding lines.

3. Save the file and preview it in the browser.

4. Close the browser and remain in this screen for the next Step-by-Step.

LIST TIPS

When you're creating lists, keep these tips in mind:

- To change a bulleted list to a numbered list or a numbered list to a bulleted list, select the entire list and then apply the other list format.

- To convert a list to plain text, select the list and apply the list type again. This procedure works like a toggle to turn off the list formatting.

- If you had extra text selected when you applied the formatting for the list, select the extra text and apply the formatting again to remove the list formatting.

- If you are keying within an already formatted list and you want to end the list, press Enter (Windows) or Return (Macintosh) twice.

- List items are single-spaced by default. If you want extra spacing between the lines, select all the items in the list and then choose Paragraph from the Format list of the Property inspector.

Character Formatting

Occasionally you will need a word or phrase to look different from the surrounding text. For example, you might want a word to be bold or italicized to visually set it apart from other text.

Many times you will find yourself repeating the most recent formatting you applied on another paragraph or other selected text. The Redo command makes that task easier, with a simple keystroke. The first two items listed on the Edit menu are the Undo and Redo commands. You'll want to remember their keyboard shortcuts:

- **Undo:** Ctrl + Z (Windows) and Command + Z (Macintosh)
- **Redo:** Ctrl + Y (Windows) and Command + Y (Macintosh)

S TEP-BY-STEP 1.15

Making Text Bold

1. Select the word **Crest** in the definition list you just created.

STEP-BY-STEP 1.15 Continued

2. Click **Bold** (the dark capital B) in the Property inspector, or click the **Text** menu, point to **Style**, and then click **Bold**. The selected text now has bold formatting applied to it.

3. Select the word **Trough** in the definition list.

4. Press **Ctrl + Y** (Windows) or **Command + Y** (Macintosh). Because you used the Bold command most recently, it is applied to the selected text.

5. Repeat the bold formatting on the other terms in the definition list.

6. Save the document and remain in this screen for the next Step-by-Step.

Positioning Text

If you want to force a line break in the text without creating a new paragraph, you need to insert a line-break character. This would be useful for an address line, for example, where you want a new line for each line in the address, without the extra spacing of a paragraph. You can create a line break by holding down the Shift key and then pressing Enter (Windows) or Return (Macintosh) You also might find that you want to make other adjustments to text, such as centering a heading, to make it more prominent.

S TEP-BY-STEP 1.16

Creating a Line Break and Centering Text

1. In the paragraph that begins with *Besides helping you find*, position the insertion point before the text **Big Kahuna Surf and Swim Shop**.

2. Press **Shift + Enter** (Windows) or **Shift + Return** (Macintosh). The text after the insertion point moves to the next line. A new paragraph has not been created, so there is no additional spacing between the two lines.

3. Repeat steps 1 and 2 to move the text **1134 Paradise Lane** to the next line and **Hawaii, USA** to a new line.

4. Position the insertion point before the text *Sign up at* and then press **Enter** (Windows) or **Return** (Macintosh) to insert a new paragraph.

5. Position the insertion point in the heading **Hawaii - Surfer's Paradise**.

STEP-BY-STEP 1.16 Continued

6. Click **Align Center** in the Property inspector, as shown in Figure 1-15. The heading is now centered.

FIGURE 1-15
The Align Center button

Align Center

7. Save the file and preview it in the browser.

8. Close the browser. Remain in this screen for the next Step-by-Step.

Changing Font Properties

To make your page more interesting and easier to read, you might want to change the typeface used to display the text. Although a great deal of information is available concerning how type is used for print, not all of that knowledge translates to the Web. You have to consider the fact that users are free to change the screen size or to change the font size and color of the text. The way type flows on a page can easily change from user to user. There is also a dramatic difference between font sizes in Windows and on a Macintosh. The same text displays smaller on Macintosh computers than in Windows.

If you are accustomed to print work, you might be frustrated by the lack of typographic control in HTML, such as line and letter spacing. You also can't control widows (a single word on a line) in Web text, and you can't control line breaks in paragraphs. You should remember that text support on the Web is still primitive (although Cascading Style Sheets can help—more on that later). You need to work within the constraints of the medium.

Changing the Font Face

You can change the font for the entire page or for selected text on the page. However, for users to see your page as you designed it, the font you choose must be installed on the user's computer. Do not make the assumption that all fonts are loaded on everyone's computer. If your first choice is not available, the browser will attempt to use the second choice and then the third. If none of the fonts are available on the user's computer, the text will be displayed in the browser's default font. In the following Step-by-Step, you will make some simple font changes to the text on the page.

S TEP-BY-STEP 1.17

Changing the Font Face

1. Select the text **Hawaii - Surfer's Paradise**.

STEP-BY-STEP 1.17 Continued

2. From the Property inspector's Font list, choose **Arial**, **Helvetica**, **sans serif**, as shown in Figure 1-16. The selected text changes to another font, depending on the fonts installed on your computer.

FIGURE 1-16
The Property inspector's Font menu

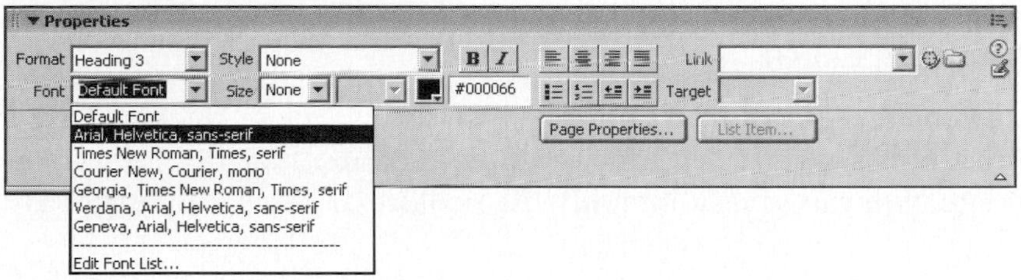

3. Select the remainder of the text on the page.

4. From the Property inspector's **Font** menu, choose **Arial**, **Helvetica**, **sans serif**. All the text now has the same font face.

5. Save the file and preview it in the browser. Remain in this screen for the next Step-by-Step.

Removing Font Face Settings

In some cases you might not want text to have a font setting but would rather have it displayed in the user's default font. To make this change in settings, select the text whose font you want to remove. Choose Default Font from the Font list in the Property inspector, as shown in Figure 1-17, or click the Text menu, point to Font, and then click Default Font.

FIGURE 1-17
The Property inspector, with Default Font selected

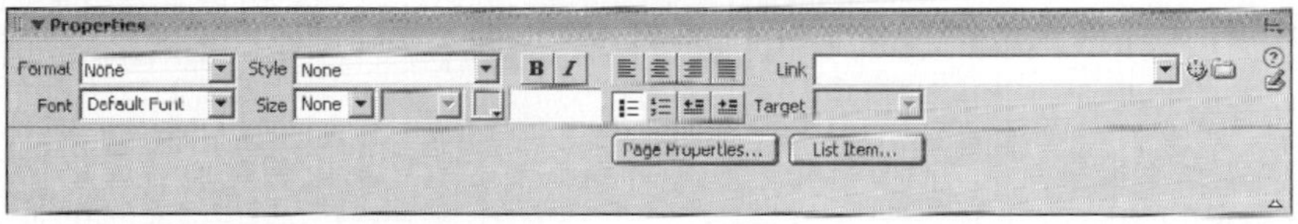

Modifying Font Combinations

You can also modify the choices that appear as font combinations and adjust the order in which the fonts will be used. From the Property inspector's Font list, choose Edit Font List, or click the Text menu, point to Font, and then click Edit Font List. The Edit Font List dialog box opens. Select a font combination (such as Arial, Helvetica, sans serif) from the Font list at the top of the dialog box. The fonts in the selected combination appear in the Chosen Fonts list at the lower left of the dialog box. To its right is a list of all fonts installed on your system.

You can choose from the following options:

- To add or remove fonts, select the font and then click the directional buttons between the Chosen Fonts list and the Available Fonts list.

- To add or remove a font combination, click the plus (+) or minus (−) button at the top left of the dialog box.

- To add a font not installed on your system, key the font name in the text box below the Available Fonts list and click the directional arrow to add it to the combination. Adding a font not installed on your system is useful; for example, you might want to specify a Windows-only font when you are authoring on a Macintosh.

- To move a font combination up or down in the list, click the directional arrow buttons at the top right of the dialog box.

Changing the Font Color

You can easily change the color of your text in Dreamweaver. All colors used at your site are listed on the Assets panel in the Files panel group. To ensure that the colors you use are consistent across your site, you can save commonly used colors on the Assets panel as Favorites.

S TEP-BY-STEP 1.18

Adding Colors to Assets Favorites

1. Click the **Window** menu, and then click **Assets** to display the Assets panel. If you have the Files panel group open, you can also click the Assets tab to open the panel.

2. Make sure the Colors icon is selected and then select **Site** at the top of the Assets panel, if necessary.

> **Note** ☑
>
> If your Site list has only black (#000000) and white (#FFFFFF), choose the **Options** menu and click on **Refresh Site List**.

STEP-BY-STEP 1.18 Continued

3. Select **#003366** to add to the Favorites list.

4. Select **Add to Favorites** from the **Options** menu, as shown in Figure 1-18.

> **Note** ☑️
>
> If you see a message that says the selected assets have been added to the Favorites list, click **OK**.

FIGURE 1-18
The Add to Favorites button

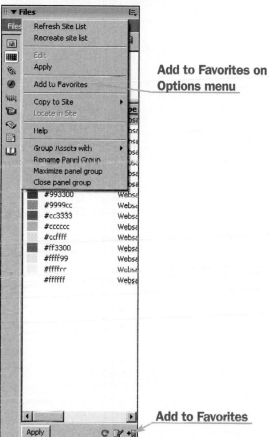

Add to Favorites on Options menu

Add to Favorites

> **Note** ☑️
>
> Some colors have already been set up for you in the Favorites panel. These are stored in a folder named _notes in the data files supplied with this course and are automatically available when you choose compass_tours as the folder for your site.

STEP-BY-STEP 1.18 Continued

5. At the top of the Assets panel, select **Favorites** as shown in Figure 1-19.

FIGURE 1-19
The Colors icon on the Assets panel

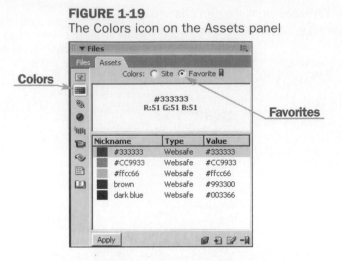

6. Select **#003366** and then select **Edit Nickname** from the **Options** menu.

7. Key **dark blue** as the nickname for this color and then press **Enter** (Windows) or **Return** (Macintosh).

STEP-BY-STEP 1.19

Changing the Font Color

1. Select the text **Hawaii - Surfer's Paradise**.

2. Select **turquoise (#006699)**. Then click **Apply**.

3. Save the file and preview it in the browser.

4. Close the browser and remain in this screen for the next Step-by-Step.

CSS Styles

As you design your Web pages, you will want to use font changes to make your pages more interesting. You can easily change the font face, including its size and color, but if you want the same color, the same font face, and the same size for all your pages, you would have to remember the settings from page to page.

Good news: Cascading Style Sheets (CSS) saves the text and paragraph formatting from selected text, making it easy for you to apply that style to other paragraphs in your document or to any document in your site. If you change a CSS style, text originally formatted with that style does not change.

Creating and Applying CSS Styles

The following exercises demonstrate the use of CSS styles on a page. You will format some text, define a CSS style, and then apply that formatting style to other portions of a document.

S TEP-BY-STEP 1.20

Creating a CSS Style Based on Existing Text

1. Select **Crest**, the first term in the definition list. You applied bold formatting to this word earlier.

2. Apply the color **turquoise (#006699)** from the Assets panel. This word now has the same color as the page's heading.

   The remaining definition terms on this page need the same formatting, as do any other lists you create for your site. You'll use a CSS style to accomplish this.

3. On the Property Inspector, click the **Style** pop-up menu and choose **Rename** from the list. The Rename Style dialog box opens, as shown in Figure 1-20.

FIGURE 1-20
The Rename Style dialog box

4. In the dialog box, name the style **Term** and click **OK**.

5. In the third paragraph, select the text **Dead Man's Bluff**. Change the font to **Times New Roman, Times, Serif**. Change the color to **#993300**. Use the Size menu to change the size to **Medium**.

6. Use the Rename Style dialog box to name the style **Place**.

7. Save the document and remain in this screen for the next Step-by-Step.

> **Note** ✓
>
> To apply a style to a selection, you have to highlight all of the appropriate text before applying the style. To apply a style to an entire paragraph, you just have to place the insertion point within the paragraph—you don't have to select each word in the paragraph.

S TEP-BY-STEP 1.21

Applying a CSS Style

1. Select the definition term **Trough**. The style is to be applied to a paragraph—so you can either select the whole word or just place your insertion point within the text.

2. Click **Term** on the Style menu on the Property inspector. The style is applied to the paragraph.

3. Repeat steps 2 and 3 for the remaining definition terms in the list.

4. Select the text **Long Cool One:**. This time you are applying a selection style, so make sure you highlight each word and the colon.

5. On the Style menu on the Property inspector click **Place**. The style is applied to the selected text.

6. Repeat steps 5 and 6 for **Piece of Cake**: and **Gripper:**.

7. Save the document and remain in this screen for the next Step-by-Step.

So far, you have created new CSS styles. But you can also use CSS to specify how existing HTML tags are displayed. In the next Step-by-Step, you'll redefine the Heading 3 tag.

S TEP-BY-STEP 1.22

Redefining an HTML Tag

1. t the top of the page, click anywhere in the heading **Hawaii - Surfer's Paradise**.

2. In the Property inspector, change the style to **None**. Even if the style is already set to None, set the selection to None again. This should remove the color you added earlier and set the font back to Default.

3. Click the **Align Left** button on the Property inspector.

4. Click the **Style** menu in the Property inspector, and then click **Manage Styles**.

5. In the Manage Styles dialog box, click **New**. The New CSS Style dialog box opens.

6. For Selector Type, choose **Tag**. For Define In, choose **This Document Only**. Then use the Tag pop-up menu to select **h3** (h3 is the HTML tag used to mark text as Heading 3). Then click **OK**. This will launch the CSS Style Definition dialog box for the new tag definition.

7. Start in the **Type** category. For Font, use the pop-up menu to select **Ariel**, **Helvetica**, **sans-serif**. For Size, key **medium** (or select it from the pop-up menu). For Color, key **#006699**.

8. Switch to the **Block** category. In the Text Align field, use the pop-up menu to select **center**.

9. Click **OK** to close the CSS Style Definition dialog box. Click **Done** to close the Manage Styles dialog box.

You should see that the heading is set to a style similar to what it was when we started. So why go through all that?

10. Here's why: Scroll down to the bottom of the page, and click anywhere in the line **Expected Conditions of the Big Kahuna Competition**. Then, in the Format menu on the Property inspector, select **Heading 3**.

Now every time you set some text to Heading 3, it will have all of the characteristics of your first Heading 3. And if you ever decide to change the characteristics of the heading 3 style, the change will be effective for the whole page.

11. Save the document and remain in this screen for the next Step-by-Step.

Deleting a CSS Style

If you want to delete a CSS style (one which you perhaps no longer need), click the Window menu and then click CSS Styles. On the CSS Styles panel, right-click the style you want to delete and choose Delete.

Clearing Text Formatting

If you want to clear some text formatting, first select the formatted text or, if you are clearing a paragraph style, you can place your insertion point anywhere in the paragraph. Then, from the Style menu on the Property Inspector, select None. All formatting is removed, regardless of how it was applied.

Adding Horizontal Rules

A horizontal rule is a line that goes across the page and provides a visual division between sections of your page.

STEP-BY-STEP 1.23

Adding a Horizontal Rule

1. Place your insertion point after the word *Fahrenheit* at the bottom of the document and press **Enter** (Windows) or **Return** (Macintosh).

2. In the Property inspector, deselect the **Ordered List** option.

3. From the HTML category on the Insert bar, click the **Horizontal Rule** button, or select the **Insert** menu, point to **HTML**, and then click **Horizontal Rule**.

4. With the horizontal rule selected, key **90** in the **W** (width) text box of the Property inspector, as shown in Figure 1-21.

FIGURE 1-21
The Property inspector for a horizontal rule

5. Select **%** from the list menu to the right of the W text box. The horizontal rule will now extend across 90 percent of the browser window regardless of the browser width. It is displayed as a shaded bar centered across the page.

> **Note** ☑
>
> You can select **pixels** from the menu to specify an absolute width. If you choose this option, the rule is not resized when users resize the browser window.

6. Deselect **Shading** to display a solid bar.

7. Key **3** in the H (height) text box. The horizontal rule is 3 pixels in height.

8. From the Align pop-up menu, select **Left**. The thick, unshaded bar moves to the left but still extends across 90 percent of the browser window.

9. Position the cursor to the right of the horizontal rule and press **Enter** (Windows) or **Return** (Macintosh).

10. Save the file and preview it in the browser.

11. Close the browser. Remain in this screen for the next Step-by-Step.

Adding Special Characters to Your Page

When working in Dreamweaver, you are generally typing at the keyboard. Sometimes you need characters and other information not directly accessible from the keyboard. With Dreamweaver, you can easily insert special characters, e-mail links, and dates.

The Characters pop-up menu on the Text category of the Insert bar contains the most commonly used special characters. To insert characters not found on this panel, click the arrow to the right of the Characters button from the Text category of the Insert bar, or click the Insert menu, point to HTML, point to Special Characters, and then click Other. The Insert Other Character dialog box opens, as shown in Figure 1-22. You can select any needed characters from this dialog box.

FIGURE 1-22
The Insert Other Character dialog box

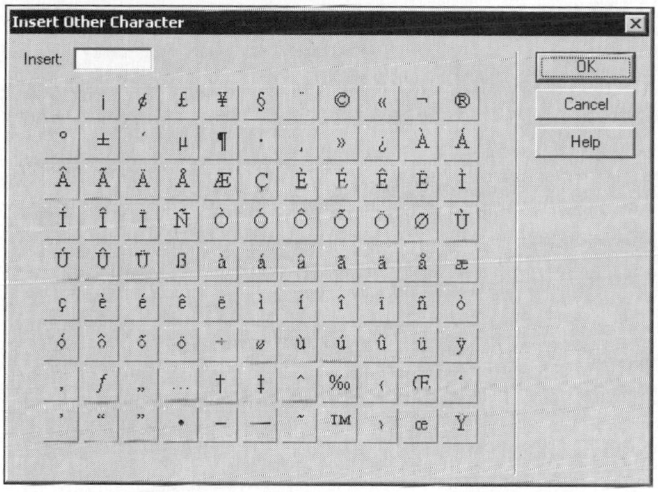

STEP-BY-STEP 1.24

Entering Special Characters

1. Make sure your cursor is positioned at the bottom of the page.

2. From the Text category on the Insert bar, click the Characters menu and choose the copyright character, as shown in Figure 1-23.

FIGURE 1-23
Choosing the copyright character

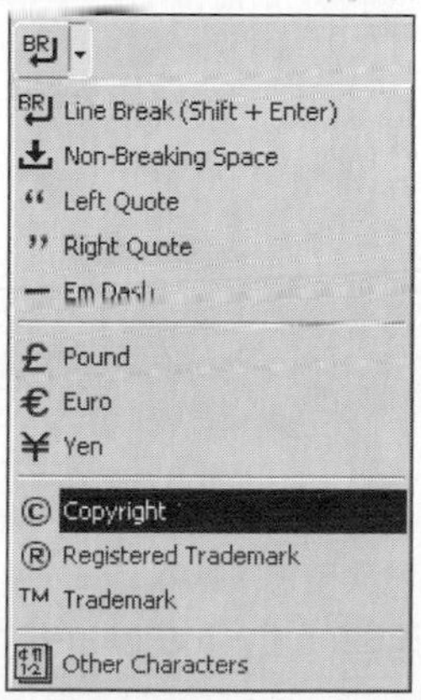

STEP-BY-STEP 1.24 Continued

3. To the right of the copyright symbol, key **2003, Compass Adventure Tours**.

4. Save the file and preview it in the browser.

5. Close the browser. Remain in this screen for the next Step-by-Step.

Adding E-mail Links

You can link to an e-mail address to give your visitors an easy way to contact you from a Web page. You should always include some method to allow visitors to correspond or interact with someone in your organization.

In addition to using the method described below to enter e-mail links, you can also manually enter an e-mail link. First you would select the text you want to make into an e-mail link. Then, in the Link text box of the Property inspector, key **mailto:** and then the e-mail address. Make sure you key the colon and no spaces (for example, *mailto:info@compassadventure.com*).

STEP-BY-STEP 1.25

Entering an E-mail Link

1. Place the insertion point at the end of the copyright line you created earlier. Press **Shift + Enter** (Windows) or **Shift + Return** (Macintosh) to create a new line just under the copyright notice.

2. Click the **Insert** menu, and then click **Email Link**. The Email Link dialog box opens, as shown in Figure 1-24.

FIGURE 1-24
The Email Link dialog box

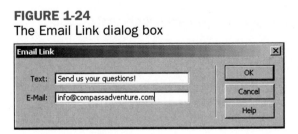

3. Make the following changes:

   a. For Text, key **Send us your questions!**

   b. For E-Mail, key your e-mail address.

4. Click **OK**. The text appears as a link. The Property inspector shows the e-mail address in the Link text box.

5. Save the file and preview it in the browser.

6. Close the browser. Remain in this screen for the next Step-by-Step.

Adding a Date Automatically

Sometimes you will need to keep track of the date when you last modified a page in your site. Dreamweaver lets you place the date and time on your pages to track this information. The date and time can be updated automatically so you don't have to do it.

Once you have an automatically updated date in your document, you can change its formatting by selecting it and then clicking Edit Date Format in the Property inspector. The Edit Date Format dialog box opens (just like the Insert Date dialog box shown in Figure 1-27 below). Make appropriate changes to the options and then click OK.

S TEP-BY-STEP 1.26

Inserting the Date

1. Make sure the insertion point is at the end of the line containing the e-mail link you created earlier. Press **Shift + Enter** (Windows) or **Shift + Return** (Macintosh) to create a new line just under the e-mail link.

2. Click **Date** from the Common category of the Insert bar or click the **Insert** menu and then click **Date**. The Insert Date dialog box opens, as shown in Figure 1-25.

FIGURE 1-25
The Insert Date dialog box

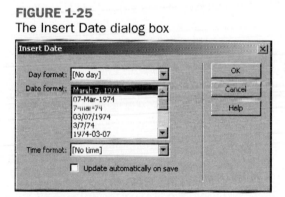

3. Make the following changes:
   a. Select **Thursday,** (with a comma) from the Day Format list menu.
   b. Select **March 7, 1974** from the Date Format list menu.
   c. Select **10:18 PM** from the Time Format list menu.
   d. Select **Update Automatically on Save** to update the date on your page each time you save your document.

4. Click **OK**. The current day, date, and time appear below the e-mail link. This information will change every time you save your document. Remain in this screen for the next Step-by-Step.

Adding Flash Text

When you add a heading to your page, your options are to use text and format it as a heading tag or to create a graphic and insert it on your page. Text formatted as a heading loads quickly because it is text, but your font choices are limited. Graphics as headings solve the font choice problem, but you might not have access to a graphics program, or you might not have enough time to create the graphic you need.

Flash text provides the best of both options. You can use any font you choose and create the text within Dreamweaver. The text you create is a small Flash file (a SWF file). Because it is Flash and not normal body text or a bitmap graphic, you can resize the text directly in the Document window.

> **Note** ☑️
>
> Resizing graphics (discussed in Lesson 2) within Dreamweaver is not recommended. But you can resize the Flash text image you create because it is a vector graphic. Vector graphics are scalable. Bitmap graphics (such as GIF and JPEG images) are not.

S TEP-BY-STEP 1.27

Adding Flash Text

1. Create a new line at the bottom of the document by pressing **Enter** (Windows) or **Return** (Macintosh). In the Property inspector, click **Align Center**.

2. Click the arrow to the right of the **Media** button on the Common category, and then click **Flash Text**, as shown in Figure 1-26. (Be sure you haven't selected Flash or Flash Button.) The Insert Flash Text dialog box opens.

FIGURE 1-26
The Common category on the Insert bar

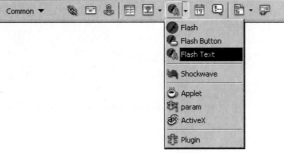

3. Make the following changes:
   a. From the Font pop-up menu, choose **Comic Sans MS**. (Choose another font if this is not available on your machine.)
   b. In the Size text box, replace the existing size with **22**.
   c. From the Color color picker, choose a maroon color (#660000).
   d. From the Rollover Color color picker, choose a blue color (#003366).
   e. In the Text text box, key **Kawabunga!**
   f. For Bg Color, key **CCFFFF**, or click on the color picker and use the eyedropper to click the background in the Document window.
   g. In the Save As text box, key **kawa_text.swf**.

STEP-BY-STEP 1.27 Continued

4. Your dialog box should look similar to Figure 1-27. Click **OK**.

FIGURE 1-27
The Insert Flash Text dialog box

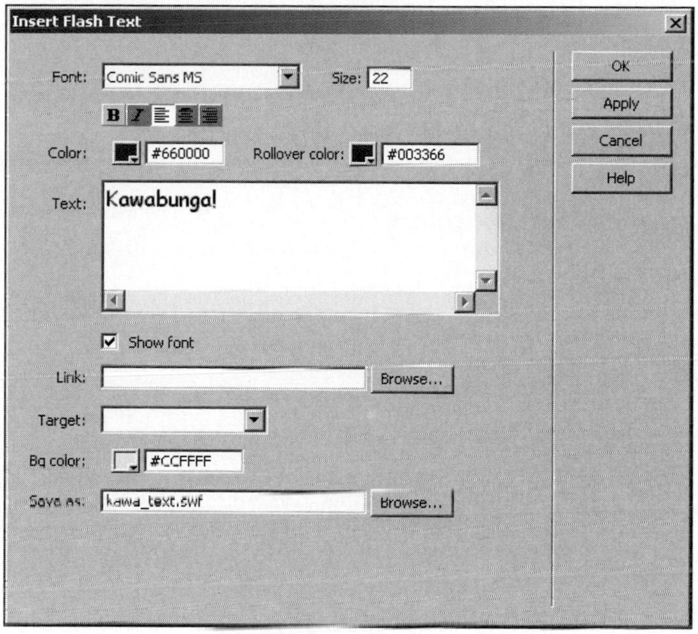

5. In the Property inspector, click **Play** to start the Flash animation.

6. In the Document window, place your pointer over the Flash text. The text changes to the rollover color you chose.

7. In the Property inspector, click **Stop**.

8. In the Document window, select the Flash text and increase its size by dragging one of the handles.

9. Save the file and preview it in the browser.

10. Close your browser and close Dreamweaver.

Modifying Flash Text

Once you have incorporated Flash text into your Dreamweaver document, you can make modifications to it. In the document window, double-click the Flash text. This opens the Insert Flash Text dialog box. Change the options to your liking. Click Apply to see the results of your changes. When you finish, click OK to close the Flash Text dialog box. The edited Flash text is placed on the page, and the SWF file is updated.

SUMMARY

In this lesson, you learned to:

- Use the Dreamweaver graphical user interface.
- Recognize how Flash text differs from HTML text.
- Define a new site.
- Name, title, and save your documents.
- Specify preview browsers.
- Specify background, text, and link colors.
- Put text on a page and format it.
- Use the Assets panel to select and apply color to text.

WORKING WITH GRAPHICS

OBJECTIVES

Upon completion of this lesson, you should be able to:

- Identify the graphics formats commonly used on Web pages.
- Insert graphics on a Web page.
- Use the Assets panel to manage graphics.
- Wrap text around graphics and work with alignment options.
- Insert buttons and animations from Flash.

Identifying Graphics Formats for the Web

All current Web browsers support both GIF and JPEG graphic formats. In general, use GIF if the artwork has large areas of solid color and no blending of colors, and use JPEG for photographic images or images with a large tonal range. For example, a picture of a blue sky with clouds looks "posterized" when saved as a GIF image. All the different shades of blue are mapped to only a few colors. GIF images are saved in 8-bit color mode, which means that only 256 colors can be represented. JPEG saves the image in 24-bit color mode, retaining all the colors.

If you're not sure whether to choose GIF or JPEG for your image format, check the file size. Whichever format gives you the smallest file size and still retains an acceptable level of quality for your image is the one you want to select. Helping you optimize your images is what Macromedia Fireworks MX 2004 is good for. When you use Macromedia Dreamweaver MX 2004, you'll want to make sure Fireworks is ready at hand.

You can use transparency options to mask the background of a graphic. Transparency properties don't always work as you might expect, however, so be sure to test your pages on as many machines and browsers as possible.

Interlacing is a method of defining the way the image is displayed in the browser. Interlacing displays every other pixel on every other line and then goes back and repeats the process, filling in areas not already displayed. Without interlacing, the graphic is "painted" on the screen line by line, starting at the top of the image. Interlacing increases the file size slightly, but its advantage is that it provides a visual clue to the user that something is happening.

Placing Graphics on the Page

Dreamweaver lets you choose how it references images: with document-relative or site-root-relative references. With document-relative referencing, Dreamweaver constructs the path to the image based on the relative location of your HTML document to the graphics file. Site-root-relative referencing constructs the path to the image based on the relative location of that image from your site root.

Generally, you should use document-relative links and paths. If you have an extremely large site, or if you plan to move pages frequently within the server, you might want to use site-root-relative referencing.

Until you save your file, Dreamweaver has no way to create the reference. You should always save your document before you insert graphics. If you don't, Dreamweaver displays an alert box and then fixes the filename path when you do save the Dreamweaver file.

S TEP-BY-STEP 2.1

Inserting a Graphic by Using the Insert Bar

1. Start Dreamweaver.

2. Click the **File** menu and click **New**. In the New Document dialog box, make sure **Basic Page** is selected in the Category list and **HTML** in the Basic Page list, and then click **Create**.

3. Save the document as **travel_log**, followed by your initials in the **Lesson02** folder of your **compass_tours** folder.

4. In the document Title box, key **Compass Extreme Adventures**.

> **Note** ☑
>
> Dreamweaver will automatically load the last site definition used on the system. It should load your information if you were the last user. If it does not, use the list menu in the upper-left corner of the Files panel to locate and select your site's name (and, hence, your site definition) as it was created in Lesson 1.

5. Click the **Modify** menu and then click **Page Properties**.

6. In the Page Properties dialog box, make sure **Appearance** is selected in the Category List. Change the Background color to **#006699** and the Text color to **#FFFFFF**. Then click **OK**.

7. Click in the document to make sure the insertion point is on the first line of the document.

STEP-BY-STEP 2.1 Continued

8. From the Common category on the Insert bar, click **Images** and then click **Image** (use your tooltips) or click the **Insert** menu and then click **Image** to insert a graphic on the page. The Select Image Source dialog box opens.

9. Locate and open your **compass_tours** folder, open the **Lesson02** folder, and locate the file **banner_head.gif** in the **Images** folder.

10. In the Relative To box, make sure **Document** is selected. The document filename *travel_log.htm* appears to the right of the menu.

11. Click **OK** (Windows) or **Choose** (Macintosh).

12. On the Property inspector, key **banner** in the image name text box (it's on the far left, under the word *Image*), as shown in Figure 2-1. Although naming your images is not essential, it is a good practice. Non-text objects in a Web page must have names if you want to include user interactivity enhancements (Lesson 5).

FIGURE 2-1
The Property inspector for the banner image

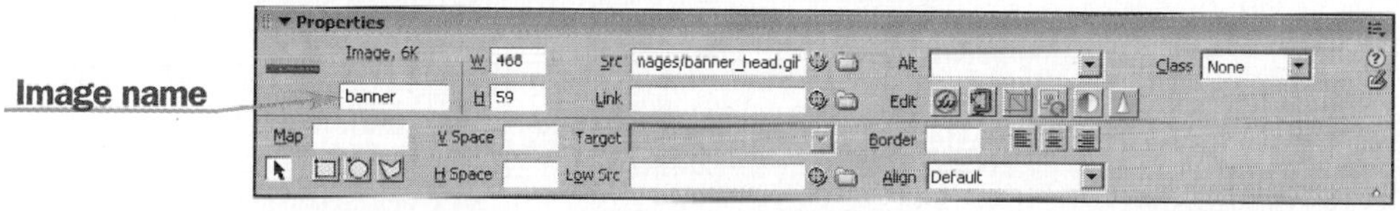

Image name

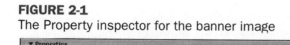

13. Save your work and remain in this screen for the next Step-by-Step.

When you import a graphic, the width and height of the graphic are automatically added on the Property inspector. This gives the browser the information it needs to define the layout of the page.

You can use the width and height attributes to create a special effect for a graphic without making the graphic larger or smaller in file size. For example, you can create a 1-pixel by 1-pixel graphic of a color—a solid dot. Use the width attribute to create a colored line across the page; use the height attribute to change its height.

> **Note** ☑
>
> Including the width and height of the image in the HTML code can make a difference in the time it takes for a browser to render your page. You can change these numbers in Dreamweaver, but don't! If you scale the image larger, the image quality diminishes. You could scale the image smaller and it would look OK, but you won't have changed the file size; thus, the graphic will take just as long to download. Always adjust the image size in Image-editing software (such as Fireworks) to ensure that you use the smallest file size possible.

The Alt attribute (Alt being a shortened form of *Alternate*) lets you specify text to be displayed on browsers when graphics can't be displayed. This is a significant feature to add to any graphic, particularly graphics that are critical for navigation. If users have disabled graphic display or are using a text-only browser, at least they can see some of the information they are missing. People with vision disabilities use a reader that speaks the Alt tags along with the text on a Web page. In some browsers, Alt text is displayed briefly when the user moves the pointer over the graphic.

STEP-BY-STEP 2.2

Working with Graphics and Adding Alt Text

1. Make sure the **banner_head.gif** image is selected.

2. On the Property inspector, key **Compass Extreme Adventure Tours** in the Alt text box.

3. On the Property inspector, click the **Align Center** button, shown in Figure 2-2. If you don't see the Align Center button, click the expander arrow at the bottom right of the Property inspector.

FIGURE 2-2
The Property inspector's Align buttons and expander arrow

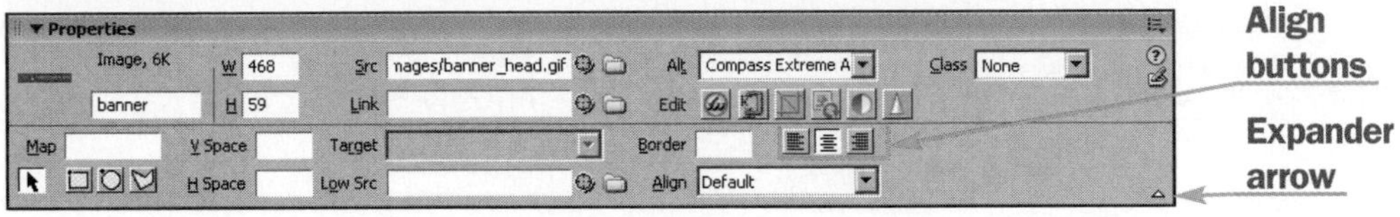

4. Click outside the banner graphic to deselect it. Press **Enter** (Windows) or **Return** (Macintosh) to move to the line below the banner graphic, and key **My Diving Travel Log**. Select the text, and click the **Italic** button, click the arrow on the Format box and select **Heading 2**, select the **Verdana, Arial, Helvetica** font, and click the **Align Left** button.

5. Create a new paragraph under the heading and make sure the line is set to **Paragraph** format and left alignment. Make sure that the **Italic** button is not selected.

   Next, you insert an image by using the Assets panel.

6. On the Assets panel, click the **Images** button. (If the Assets panel is not open, click the **Window** menu, and then click **Assets**.)

STEP-BY-STEP 2.2 Continued

7. Make sure **Favorites** is selected at the top of the Assets panel. Open the Lesson 2 folder by double-clicking it, as shown in Figure 2-3.

FIGURE 2-3
Assets panel with Favorites

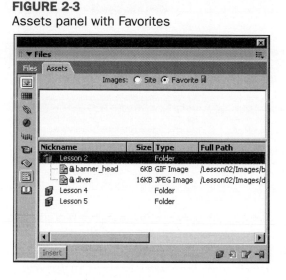

8. Drag the **diver** graphic from the Assets panel to the document and place it below the heading.

9. Key **Diver** in the Alt text box on the Property inspector. Key **diver** in the image name text box.

10. Save the document and remain in this screen for the next Step-by-Step.

Adding Images to Asset Favorites

All images used within a site are listed as site assets on the Assets panel. For images that are used repeatedly, placing them in Image Favorites can be a time-saver. You can organize your images into folders to make them easy to locate.

It might take a few seconds for the panel to create a listing of all the assets used by files in your site. If you haven't created a site cache for this site, the Assets panel prompts you to do so; the asset catalog can't be created without a site cache.

If you add a new asset to your site, it might not immediately appear on the Assets panel. To update the Assets panel to include all the images in your site, you need to refresh the site catalog. Click the Refresh Site List button at the bottom right of the Assets panel, as shown in Figure 2-4 (this button is only available when Site is selected in the Assets panel).

FIGURE 2-4
Assets panel for the site

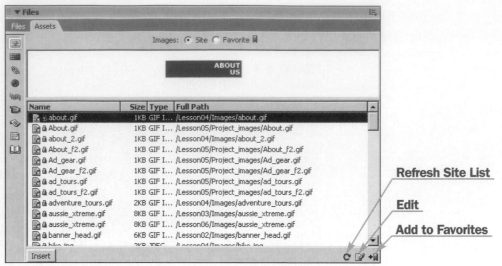

Refresh Site List

Edit

Add to Favorites

STEP-BY-STEP 2.3

Working with Asset Favorites

1. Click **Site** at the top of the Assets panel. Click the **Full Path** column heading to rearrange the images according to their folder structure (path), as shown in Figure 2-5 (you may need to resize the panel to see the column). This places all the images in the Lesson02 folder together.

FIGURE 2-5
Assets panel with figures organized by path

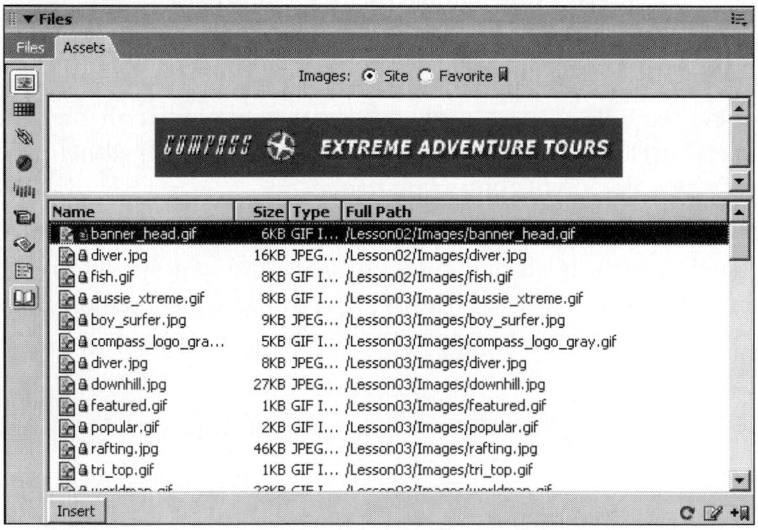

STEP-BY-STEP 2.3 Continued

2. Select the **fish.gif** graphic from the list of images.

3. Click **Add to Favorites** at the lower right of the panel. (And click **OK** if a message box appears.)

4. Click **Favorites** at the top of the Assets panel. The fish.gif image is listed in Favorites.

5. Drag the fish.gif image to the Lesson 2 folder. Remain in this screen for the next Step-by-Step.

To create a folder in Asset Favorites, click New Favorites Folder at the bottom of the panel. Once you have created a folder, you can collapse it or expand it by double-clicking it.

To remove an image from Asset Favorites, select the image from the list of images and then click Remove from Favorites. The image is no longer listed as a Favorite. You haven't deleted the image—it is still in its original location—you've simply removed it from the list of Favorites. To remove a folder from Asset Favorites, select the folder to delete, and then click Remove from Favorites at the bottom of the panel.

Note ✓

If a Favorites folder you want to remove contains any images you want to keep as Favorites, first move the images to another folder.

Wrapping Text Around Images

A common formatting preference is to have text wrap around a graphic on the page. You can achieve this easily by changing the Align attribute of the image. For text wrapping to work properly, make sure the image is inserted at the beginning of a paragraph. The text wraps to the bottom of the graphic and then returns to the left margin of the window.

Dreamweaver gives you several alignment options for images, including Top and Text Top. If you want your text to wrap or move to the top of the image, you might think that one of these options would work. Remember that multiline text can wrap only on either the left or the right side of an image, so the only options that will accomplish this are Left or Right. If you want to place the image on the left and wrap the text on the right, select the image and choose Left in the Align field. If you want to place the image on the right and wrap the text on the left, select the image and choose Right in the Align field.

The other alignment options on the pop-up menu are for the placement of a single line of text next to a graphic. You will work with these later.

S TEP-BY-STEP 2.4

Wrapping Text Around an Image

1. From the data files for this lesson, use the Files panel to open the file **diving.txt** from the **Text** folder. Double-click the file so that you can view it in Dreamweaver.

2. Select all the text, and click **Copy** on the **Edit** menu. Close the diving.txt file without saving.

3. In the **travel_log.htm** file, paste the copied text to the right of the diver graphic. Left-align all the text. You might need to insert paragraph breaks manually.

4. Select the diver graphic. On the Property inspector, choose **Left** from the Align pop-up menu, as shown in Figure 2-6. The text wraps around the diver graphic.

FIGURE 2-6
The Property inspector, showing Image properties

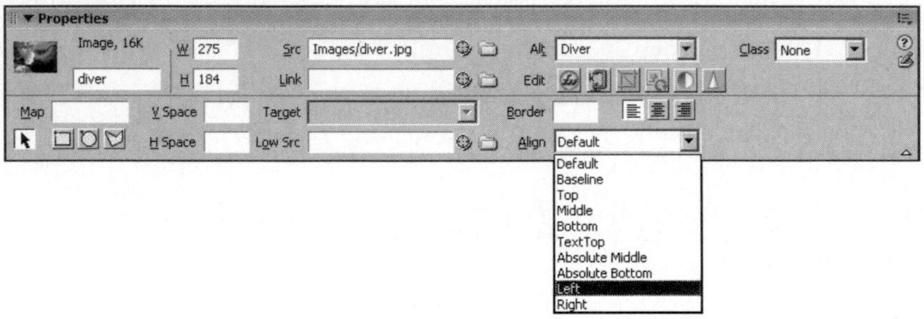

5. Save the file and preview it in your browser.

6. Close your browser and remain in this screen for the next Step-by-Step.

Modifying the Space and Adding a Border Around Images

When you use an Align option to wrap text around graphics, you'll probably want to adjust the space around the image as well. You can do this on the Property inspector.

S TEP-BY-STEP 2.5

Adding Space and a Border Around an Image

1. Make sure the Diver graphic is selected.

2. On the Property inspector, enter **15** in the H Space text box. This creates 15 pixels of space on both the left and right sides of the image. You cannot add space on only one side.

STEP-BY-STEP 2.5 Continued

3. Enter **2** in the V Space text box. This creates 2 pixels of space at both the top and bottom of the image.

4. In the Border text box of the Property inspector, enter **2**. Press **Enter** (Windows) or **Return** (Macintosh) to see the change. A 2-pixel border is added to the diver image.

5. Save your document and remain in this screen for the next Step-by-Step.

Aligning Images and Text

Often you'll want to control the placement of a graphic on the page in relation to a single line of text that appears near it. You can change the relative location of the graphic to the text by using options on the Property inspector.

STEP-BY-STEP 2.6

Aligning a Single Line of Text Near a Graphic

1. Press **Enter** (Windows) or **Return** (Macintosh) at the end of the document to add a new line.

2. On the Assets Favorites panel, drag the **fish.gif** image (from the Lesson 2 folder) to a new line after the body text. Key **Fish** in the Alt text box, and key **fish** in the image name text box.

3. On the Property inspector, click the **Align Center** button. Be sure to click the button; don't select Center on the Align menu.

4. Position the insertion point to the right of the Fish graphic and key **Check out some of the fish we saw.** The text is aligned with the bottom of the graphic and is too close to the graphic.

5. Select the **Fish** graphic and add a 2-pixel border to it.

6. On the Property inspector, enter **15** in the H Space text box. This will force the graphic and text to move apart.

7. From the Align pop-up menu, choose **Middle**. The baseline of the text is aligned with the middle of the graphic.

8. Save the file and preview it in your browser.

9. Close the browser and remain in this screen for the next Step-by-Step.

Image Alignment Options

You need to understand how the alignment options work. The following seven options work well for aligning a single line of text near a graphic. As you saw earlier, they don't work for wrapping multiple lines around a graphic (use Left or Right instead). Here's what happens when you use the Align pop-up menu:

- **Baseline:** Aligns the bottom of the image with the baseline of the text line.

- **Top:** Aligns the image with the top of the tallest item in the line.

- **Middle:** Aligns the baseline of the text line with the middle of the image.

- **Bottom:** Identical to Baseline.

- **Text Top:** Does what many people think Top should do, which is to align the image with the top of the tallest text in the line (this is usually, but not always, the same as Top).

- **Absolute Middle:** Aligns the middle of the text line with the middle of the image.

- **Absolute Bottom:** Aligns the bottom of the image with the bottom of the text line.

Adding Flash Objects

You can easily achieve special effects by using buttons and animations created in Flash. Because Flash graphics are vector-based, they have very small file sizes. This helps them load quickly in the user's browser.

Adding Flash Buttons

Flash buttons have several different states, depending on the position of the pointer and whether the mouse button has been clicked. The first state is the look of the button when the pointer is not on it. The second state appears when the pointer is on the button but the mouse has not been clicked. The third state appears when the pointer is on the button and the mouse has been clicked. You can create and maintain Flash buttons in Dreamweaver from a set of available button styles. Many of the button attributes are changeable. In the following Step-by-Step, you create a button and then modify it.

S TEP-BY-STEP 2.7

Creating and Modifying a Flash Button

1. Move to the end of the text and Press **Enter** (Windows) or **Return** (Macintosh) to position the insertion point below the Fish graphic and the text in the center of the Document window.

2. From the Common category of the Insert bar, click the small arrow to the right of the Media button, and then click **Flash Button**. The Insert Flash Button dialog box opens.

STEP-BY-STEP 2.7 Continued

3. Make the following changes:

  a. From the Style pop-up menu, choose **Blue Warper**.

  b. In the Button Text text box, key **Return Home**.

  c. From the Font pop-up menu, choose **Verdana** (or your font choice if Verdana is not available).

  d. In the Size text box, enter **12**.

4. For Bg Color, click the color picker. Then use the eyedropper to click anywhere on the background in the Document window. The background color code #006699 appears in the Bg Color text box.

5. In the Save As text box, key **home_button.swf** and then click **OK**. The Insert Flash Button dialog box closes and the button you created appears in the document.

6. With the Flash button still selected, click **Play** on the Property inspector. The button is in its original state.

7. In the Document window, move the pointer over the **Return Home** button. The button changes to its rollover state.

8. Click the button. It changes to its clicked state.

9. Click **Stop** on the Property inspector.

10. Save the file and preview it in your browser. The button changes states just as it did in Dreamweaver, depending on the pointer position and mouse click.

11. Close your browser.

  Next, you modify the Flash button.

12. In the Document window, double-click the button. The Insert Flash Button dialog box opens.

13. Make some changes to the options. For example, change the font to **Arial**.

14. Click **Apply** to see the changes.

15. Click **OK** when you finish.

16. Save your work and remain in this screen for the next Step-by-Step.

Adding Flash Animations

You can add Flash animations to your document as easily as adding an image, provided the animation has already been created. You can resize the animations to your specification by dragging the handles. Unlike Flash buttons, you cannot create these animations directly within Dreamweaver.

STEP-BY-STEP 2.8

Adding a Flash Animation

1. Press **Enter** (Windows) or **Return** (Macintosh) to position the insertion point below the Flash button on your page. If your insertion point is not centered, click **Align Center** on the Property inspector. The insertion point is now centered on the page. The next object you add to the page will be centered.

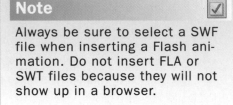

> **Note** ☑
>
> Always be sure to select a SWF file when inserting a Flash animation. Do not insert FLA or SWT files because they will not show up in a browser.

2. On the Assets panel, click **Flash**. You may have to adjust the column widths to see the Nicknames column.

3. From the Favorites list on the Flash Assets panel, select **surfAd** and click **Insert**. The Flash animation is placed on the page.

4. On the Property inspector, make sure Loop and Autoplay are selected. Autoplay causes the Flash animation to begin playing as soon as the page is loaded in the browser. The animation plays repeatedly because the Loop property is set in Dreamweaver. Click **Play** to view the animation in Dreamweaver.

5. Click **Stop** on the Property inspector.

6. Save the file and preview it in your browser.

7. When you are finished, close your browser, close the **travel_log.htm** file, and then close Dreamweaver.

SUMMARY

In this lesson, you learned to:

- Identify the graphics formats commonly used on Web pages.
- Insert graphics on a Web page.
- Use the Assets panel to manage graphics.
- Wrap text around graphics and work with alignment options.
- Insert buttons and animations from Flash.

CREATING LINKS

OBJECTIVES

Upon completion of this lesson, you should be able to:

- Define how linking works.

- Choose objects to use as links.

- Display linked content in a new browser window.

- Create text links, graphic links, and hotspots.

- Create named anchors to jump to a location within a Web page.

Working with Links

HTML's power comes from its capability to link regions of text and images to other documents. The browser highlights these regions (usually with color or underlines) to indicate that they are hypertext links. They are often called hyperlinks, or simply links. A link in HTML has two parts: the name of the file (or URL of the file) to which you want to link and the text or graphic that serves as the clickable link on the page. When the user clicks the link, the browser uses the path of the link to jump to the linked document. In some browsers, the path of the link is displayed in the status area of the browser window (the lower-left part of the window) when the pointer is positioned over the link.

In the next set of Step by Step exercises, you create text and graphics links on a Web page, add hotspots to an image to make it an image map, and link to named anchors within a page.

Creating Hypertext Links

Hypertext links can "jump" the user to another document within the current Web site or to a page at another Web site. The following Step-by-Step shows techniques for linking to a document within the site or for creating an external link.

STEP-BY-STEP 3.1

Creating Links to a Document and to an External Site

1. Start Macromedia Dreamweaver MX 2004. Click **Open** on the **File** menu. From your **compass_tours** folder, double-click the **Lesson03** folder to open it, and then open the **index.htm** file. This file contains all the text and graphics you will need to create links.

2. In the Document window, find the unordered list under *Featured Trips*. In the first item of the list, select the word **Surfing**.

> **Note** ☑
>
> Dreamweaver will automatically load the last site definition used on the system. It should load your information if you were the last user. If it does not, use the list menu in the upper-left corner of the Files panel to locate and select your site's name (and, hence, your site definition).

3. In the Property inspector, click the folder icon to the right of the Link text box. The Select File dialog box opens in the compass_tours/Lesson03 folder.

4. Select the **surfing.htm** file, and then click **OK** (Windows) or **Choose** (Macintosh). The filename *surfing.htm* appears in the Link text box.

5. Save the file and preview it in your browser. Close the browser.

6. Repeat steps 2 through 4 to link the word **Diving** to the **diving.htm** file, the words **Mountain Biking** to the **biking.htm** file, and the word **Rafting** to the **rafting.htm** file.

7. Save the file and preview it in your browser. Close the browser.

8. In the Document window, select the graphic at the bottom of the page.

9. In the Property inspector, key **http://www.australia.com** in the Link text box, as shown in Figure 3-1. You must key the complete URL, including *http://*.

FIGURE 3-1
The Property inspector, showing an URL link

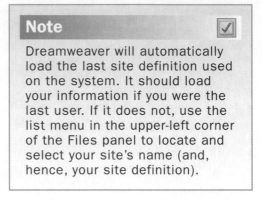

10. Save the file and preview it in your browser.

11. Close the browser and remain in this screen for the next Step-by-Step.

> **Hot Tip** ⊙
>
> If the URL is long or complex, you can go to that site in your browser, select the URL in the browser's address field, and copy and paste the URL into the text box.

Displaying Linked Content in a New Browser Window

When you link to a page, the linked page replaces the current browser page by default. Sometimes, however, you might want to display the browser page in a new location or window. For example, if you link to a site outside your site, you have just led your users out of your pages. If they haven't bookmarked your URL, users might not remember how to return to your pages. If your outside links open a new browser window, your page remains in the original window.

S TEP-BY-STEP 3.2

Targeting a Link

1. With the bottom graphic still selected, click the arrow on the Target box in the Property inspector and choose **_blank**, as shown in Figure 3-2.

FIGURE 3-2
The Property inspector's Target pop-up menu

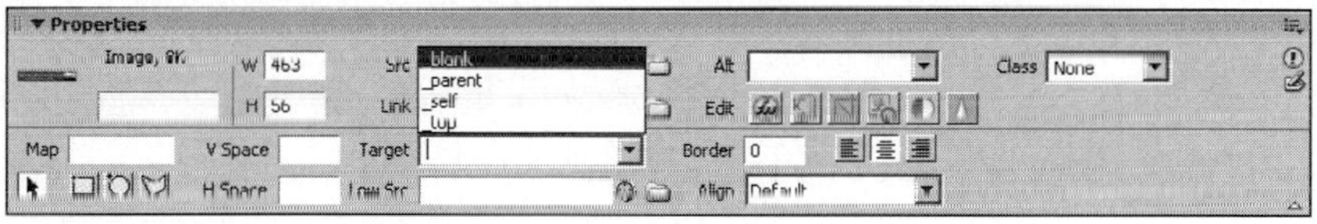

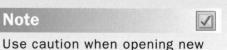

2. Save the file and preview it in your browser. When you click the bottom graphic, the resulting page opens in a new browser window.

3. Close the browser and the index.htm document. Leave Dreamweaver open for the next Step-by-Step.

In Dreamweaver, you can easily change the location where the linked page is displayed by using the following targets. (Targets other than _blank work only when you create frames for your page.)

- **_blank**: Loads the linked document in a new, unnamed browser window.

- **_parent**: Loads the linked document in the parent frameset or window of the frame that contains the link. If the frame containing the link is not nested, the linked document is loaded into the full browser window.

- **_self**: Loads the linked document in the same frame or window as the link. This target is implied, so you usually don't have to specify it.

- **_top**: Loads the linked document in the full browser window, thereby removing all frames.

> **Note** ☑
>
> Use caution when opening new browser windows. New windows impose extra RAM requirements on the user's computer as each window is opened.

Creating Image Maps

You've experienced how easy it is to link an image to a page. The user can click anywhere on the image to go to that linked page. You can also divide an image into several links by using an image map to place individual hotspots on the image.

S TEP-BY-STEP 3.3

Creating an Image Map

1. Make sure the Files panel is open (click Locate in Site on the site menu if necessary). Inside the **Lesson03** folder, double-click on the **map.htm** file to open it. This file has a large map graphic that needs to be divided into three hotspots.

2. Select the map graphic.

3. In the Property inspector, key **worldmap** in the Map text box, as shown in Figure 3-3. (If you don't see the Map text box, click the expander arrow at the bottom right of the inspector.) Don't use spaces or special characters in the name. You can have several image maps on a page, but each map name must be unique. Remain in this screen for the next Step-by-Step.

FIGURE 3-3
The Property inspector's Map text box

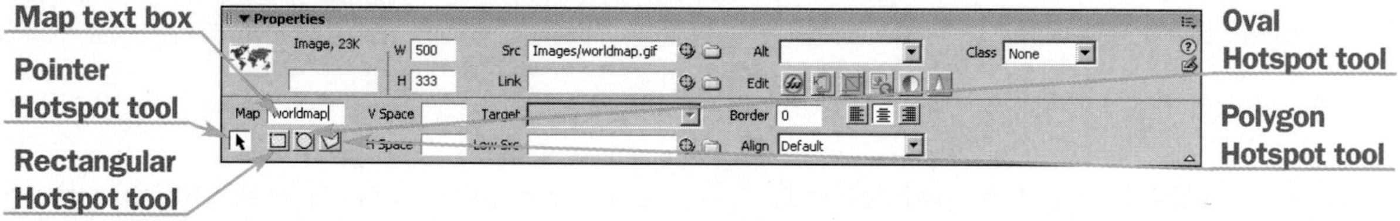

Map text box

Pointer
Hotspot tool

Rectangular
Hotspot tool

Oval
Hotspot tool

Polygon
Hotspot tool

Hotspots can be in a variety of shapes. In the following Step-by-Step, you add a rectangular hotspot, a circular hotspot, and a polygonal hotspot to an image.

S TEP-BY-STEP 3.4

Creating Hotspots

1. In the Property inspector, select the **Rectangular Hotspot** tool (refer to Figure 3-3).

2. Drag around the words *Hawaiian Islands*. A translucent blue-green area with handles appears around the text. The Property inspector changes to show hotspot properties, as shown in Figure 3-4.

FIGURE 3-4
The hotspot Property inspector

STEP-BY-STEP 3.4 Continued

3. In the hotspot Property inspector, select the **Pointer Hotspot** tool (refer to Figure 3-3). To resize the hotspot, drag a handle until the hotspot encompasses the small dot representing the Hawaiian Islands. To move the hotspot, position the pointer inside the hotspot and drag. (The hotspot must be contained within the boundaries of the image.)

4. Make sure the rectangular hotspot is selected. In the hotspot Property inspector, key **Hawaiian Islands** in the Alt text box. This text serves the same purposes as image Alt text.

5. Click the folder icon next to the Link text box and select **Lesson03/trips.htm**.

6. Save the file and preview it in your browser. Close the browser.

7. Select the large map graphic.

8. In the Property inspector, select the **Oval Hotspot** tool.

9. Drag a circle around Australia, including the words *Australia & South Pacific*. The hotspot area appears, and the Property inspector changes to show hotspot properties.

10. Make the following changes:
   a. In the Alt text box, key **Australia & South Pacific**.
   b. In the Link text box, key **http://www.australia.com**. Make sure you delete the number sign (#) from this text box.
   c. From the Target pop-up menu, choose **_blank** to open a new browser window.

11. Save your file and preview it in the browser. Close the browser.

12. Select the large map graphic.

13. In the Property inspector, select the **Polygon Hotspot** tool.

> **Note** ☑
>
> The more points that make up a hotspot shape, the more slowly the page will be processed. Simplify hotspot shapes as much as possible.

14. To draw a polygon, click around the North America graphic. Each click creates a point. Each subsequent point is connected by a line to the previous point. Continue clicking around North America until you have the shape you want. Adding points might make the hotspot seem to disappear at first. As you click, you'll see the translucent hotspot area begin to form.

15. Make sure the polygonal hotspot is selected. In the Alt text box of the hotspot Property inspector, key **North America**.

16. Use the folder icon next to the Link text box to locate and select **Lesson03/trips.htm**.

>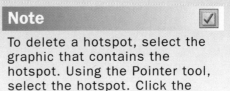
>
> **Note** ☑
>
> To delete a hotspot, select the graphic that contains the hotspot. Using the Pointer tool, select the hotspot. Click the **Edit** menu and then click **Clear**, or press **Delete**.

17. Save your file and preview it in the browser.

18. Close the browser and close the **map.htm** file. Leave Dreamweaver open for the next Step-by-Step.

Linking to Named Anchors

When a document is long or has many sections, you might want to create a link that jumps the user to a specific place in the document. This eliminates the tedium of scrolling through the document. To do this, you must create a jump-to point—a *named anchor*—that you can reference as the link.

The following Step-by-Step illustrates the use of named anchors and the links to jump to them.

S TEP-BY-STEP 3.5

Inserting and Linking to an Anchor

1. Open **Lesson03/trips.htm**. This file contains a large amount of text that requires scrolling to see the entire document.

2. Position the insertion point before the heading *Hawaii - Multisport* at the bottom of the document. Make sure you haven't positioned the insertion point in the top navigation area.

3. From the Common category of the Insert bar, click **Named Anchor**. Or you can click the **Insert** menu and then click **Named Anchor** to insert a named anchor. The Named Anchor dialog box opens, as shown in Figure 3-5.

FIGURE 3-5
The Named Anchor dialog box

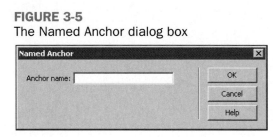

4. Key **hawaii** in the Anchor Name text box and then click **OK**. Don't use spaces or special characters in the name. A yellow anchor icon appears on the page to represent the anchor. (If you can't see the icon, make sure Invisible Elements is turned on by clicking the **View** menu, pointing to **Visual Aids**, and then clicking **Invisible Elements**.)

5. Scroll to the top of the trips.htm document. Select the text **Hawaii – Multisport**.

6. In the Link text box of the Property inspector, key **#hawaii**. Then press **Enter** (Windows) or **Return** (Macintosh). You must key the number sign (**#**) before the anchor name in the Link text box. Make sure the name you key is exactly the same as the anchor name. Anchor names are case-sensitive.

7. Save the file and preview it in your browser.

8. Close the browser and remain in this screen for the next Step-by-Step.

One of many areas where HTML is case-sensitive is in the naming of your anchors. If you name your anchor *top*, for example, and then enter *#Top* in the Link text box, your link might not work consistently in all browsers. To avoid keyboarding errors, you can use the Point to File icon in the Property inspector, as shown in Figure 3-6.

FIGURE 3-6
The Point to File icon in the Property inspector

Point to File icon

STEP-BY-STEP 3.6

Linking by Using the Point to File Icon

1. Add another named anchor before the *Alaska Vacations* heading and name the anchor **alaska**.

2. Select the words **Alaska Vacations** at the top of the document.

3. Drag the **Point to File** icon and point to the Alaska anchor you just created. Release the mouse button when you are directly over the anchor. The link is made.

4. Using the Point to File icon or the Link field in the Property inspector, insert anchors and links for the remaining headings.

5. Save your file and preview it in the browser.

6. When you finish, close the browser, close the document, and close Dreamweaver.

Extra Challenge

In this Step-by-Step, you linked the Hawaiian Island hotspot area to the trips.htm file. The link opens to the top of the page. You just created a named anchor to the Hawaii section in the trips.htm file. You can make the image map point directly to the Hawaii section instead of linking to the top of the page. Return to the **map.htm** page and drag the **Point to File** icon to the **Hawaii** anchor on the trips.htm page (make sure you can see both documents). When you release the mouse button, you'll see *trips.htm#hawaii* in the Link field.

In addition, you can try your hand at the following to practice what you've learned so far:

In the last paragraph of index.htm, link the phrase **popular trips** to **trips.htm**.

At the end of the last paragraph of index.htm, add the sentence **Our interactive map lets you traverse the globe.** Use the Property inspector to make sure the formatting of the new text matches the formatting of the old text. Link the word **map** to **map.htm**.

Insert the following sentence below the Flash movie at the bottom of index.htm: **E-mail us for more information.** Link the word **E-mail** to the address **info@compasstours.com**.

SUMMARY

In this lesson, you learned to:

- Define how linking works.
- Choose objects to use as links.
- Display linked content in a new browser window.
- Create text links, graphic links, and hotspots.
- Create named anchors to jump to a location within a Web page.

WORKING WITH TABLES FOR PAGE DESIGN

OBJECTIVES

Upon completion of this lesson, you should be able to:

- ■ Import images to use as tracing images.
- ■ Use tables to lay out your pages.
- ■ Work with tables in Layout, Standard, and Expanded mode.
- ■ Import tabular data.
- ■ Select elements of a table and modify their properties.
- ■ Sort tables.
- ■ Export a table.

Using Tracing Images

Sometimes you will be given a page design that someone else has designed in a graphics program such as Macromedia FreeHand MX, Adobe Photoshop, or QuarkXPress. If you can convert the page to a JPEG, GIF, or PNG graphic, you can import that image into Macromedia Dreamweaver MX 2004 and use it as a guide—or a tracing image—to re-create the HTML page.

The tracing image is visible only inside Dreamweaver. It is referenced in the HTML code but will not be downloaded or displayed by the browser. While you're using a tracing image, the background color or background image of your page will be hidden, but it appears in the browser.

S TEP-BY-STEP 4.1

Placing a Tracing Image

1. Start Dreamweaver. Create a new document and save it as **destinations**, followed by your initials, in your **compass_tours/Lesson04** folder. In the document Title box, enter **Featured Destinations**.

> **Note** ☑
>
> Dreamweaver will automatically load the last site definition used on the system. It should load your information if you were the last user. If it does not, use the list menu in the upper-left corner of the Files panel to locate and select your site's name (and, hence, your site definition).

2. Click the **View** menu, point to **Tracing Image**, and then click **Load**. The Select Image Source dialog box opens.

3. In the Lesson04 folder where you saved the page, double-click the **Images** folder and choose the file **table_trace.jpg**. Then click **OK** (Windows) or **Choose** (Macintosh). The Page Properties dialog box opens. Make sure Tracing Image is selected in the Category list.

4. Drag the **Image Transparency** slider to the left to about 30%. This will lighten the image considerably. You want to be able to see the image but not be distracted by it. Click **OK**.

5. Save the document and remain in this screen for the next Step-by-Step.

Altering a Tracing Image

You can change the position of a tracing image, align it to a selected object, or hide the image by using options on the View menu's Tracing Image submenu.

To show or hide the tracing image, click the View menu, point to Tracing Image, and then click Show.

To align the tracing image to a selected element, select an element in the Document window. Click the View menu, point to Tracing Image, and then click Align with Selection. The upper-left corner of the tracing image is aligned with the upper-left corner of the selected element.

To reset the position of the tracing image, click the View menu, point to Tracing Image, and then click Reset Position to return the tracing image to the upper-left corner of the Document window (0,0).

STEP-BY-STEP 4.2

Changing the Position of a Tracing Image

1. Click the **View** menu, point to **Tracing Image**, and then click **Adjust Position**.

2. Press the arrow keys to move the image 1 pixel at a time. Press **Shift** and an arrow key to move the image 5 pixels at a time. Enter coordinate values of your choice in the X and Y text boxes to precisely specify the position of the tracing image. Click **OK** when you finish.

3. To reset the position of the tracing image, click the **View** menu, point to **Tracing Image**, and then click **Reset Position** to return the tracing image to the upper-left corner of the Document window. Remain in this screen for the next Step-by-Step.

Using Tables for Page Design

Up to this point, you've had little control over the design of your pages. You've wrapped text around a graphic and indented the text on the page, but these options are limited and don't always provide the desired effect. Tables can give you more control.

Tables in HTML are very similar to tables in a spreadsheet. Tables in HTML were meant to be a means of presenting information in a very organized manner; they contain rows and columns where you can place data. But in HTML, tables also provide a way to design your pages with some control over placement of text and graphics. You can use the cells of a table to put graphics in a location other than just the next place vertically on the page, or you can use a cell to create a sidebar for your text.

If you've ever had to hand-code an HTML table, you know how tedious the task can be. To simplify the building of a table, Dreamweaver provides a Layout mode in which you can easily place the elements you want on the page. Dreamweaver then creates the table for you. Layout mode works much like page layout programs in which you draw boxes on the page and then fill the boxes with text or graphics. You can resize the boxes, and you can place the boxes anywhere on the page.

In Dreamweaver, you can view tables on the page in either Layout, Standard, or Expanded mode. In Standard mode, you see all the rows and columns of the table. In Expanded mode you see the rows and columns just as in Standard mode except that Dreamweaver adds cell padding and spacing and widens the borders to make editing easier. In Layout mode, you see just the cells (boxes) you draw.

You can switch to Layout mode by clicking the View menu, pointing to Table Mode, and then clicking Layout Mode, or by clicking Layout Mode on the Layout category of the Insert bar, as shown in Figure 4-1. When you are in Layout mode, you can add layout cells or a layout table to the page. If you add just a layout cell, Dreamweaver automatically draws a layout table as a container for the cell. The layout table is drawn as wide as the Document window and starts at the upper-left corner. You can resize the table to any size you need.

FIGURE 4-1
The Layout category on the Insert bar

Layout tables appear with a tab at the top, which helps you identify the table. The tab contains column numbers and a column menu and visually moves the table down from the top of the page. The tab will not be displayed in the browser.

Designing Tables in Layout Mode

In the next Step-by-Step, you build a Web page based on the tracing image you just imported. The graphics you need for this exercise are in the Lesson 4 folder of the Favorites section of the Assets panel (open the Assets panel, select the Images category, and select Favorites to see images). The text is in the student_table_project.txt file located in the Lesson04/Text folder, accessible via the Files panel. You do not have to exactly match the tracing image—just use it as a guide to help you place the text and images.

STEP-BY-STEP 4.3

Inserting a Layout Cell

1. In the Insert bar, use the category pop-up menu to switch to the **Layout** category. Then click the **Layout Mode** button.

2. Click the **Draw Layout Cell** button shown in Figure 4-2. The pointer changes to a crosshair.

> **Note** ☑
>
> You might see a message explaining the use of the Draw Layout Cell button and the Layout Table button. If you do, click **OK**.

FIGURE 4-2
The Draw Layout Cell button in the Layout category of the Insert bar

Layout Table

Draw Layout Cell

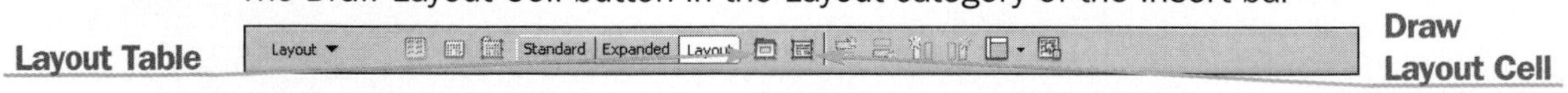

3. Place the pointer on the page and then drag to draw the cell. A table is automatically drawn to contain the cell. The cell is outlined in blue to distinguish it from the table, which appears in green. When you move the pointer over a cell border, the border turns red to indicate which cell you are over.

STEP-BY-STEP 4.3 Continued

4. Click the red border to select the cell. The cell border turns blue and handles appear, which you can drag to resize the cell. You can also hold down **Ctrl** (Windows) or **Command** (Macintosh) and click within a cell to display the resize handles.

5. Drag the border of the cell to move the cell to a new location. Move this cell to cover the plane on the left side of the page. Use the handles to resize the cell, if necessary.

6. Make sure the Assets panel is open and then select **Favorites**. Open the **Lesson 4** folder, and then open the **Student Project** folder. Insert the plane graphic by dragging it from the Student Project folder into the cell.

7. Draw six more cells to cover the Adventure Tours title, the Compass logo, and each of the four buttons across the top. To draw multiple cells without clicking the Draw Layout Cell button each time, hold down **Ctrl** (Windows) or **Command** (Macintosh) as you draw the first cell. You can then continue to draw new cells until you release the modifier key. If necessary, you can resize the cells later as you insert the graphics.

When you draw a cell on the page, white guides appear to help you place other cells you want to align with the first cell. Use the horizontal guides to align the top of each cell.

8. Insert the graphics **adventure_tours**, **compass_logo**, **feature_button**, **gear**, **about**, and **trip_button** in each of the other cells.

9. Draw cells to cover the Mountain Biking, Kayaking, and Surfing images and insert **biking_icon**, **kayaking_icon**, and **surfing_icon** in these cells. If there is space available around the cell, you can use the arrow keys to nudge the cells to the correct locations.

10. Draw four cells for the text areas.

11. Draw three more cells. Each cell will hold both the price and the More Details graphic for that trip.

12. In the Files panel group, click the **Files** tab. Select the **student_table_project.txt** file in the **compass_tours/Lesson04/Text** folder. This is a text (ASCII) file and opens in a text-editing window (Dreamweaver's Code view).

STEP-BY-STEP 4.3 Continued

13. To make the text wrap within the window, click **View Options** on the Document toolbar and select **Word Wrap** from the **View Options** menu, as shown in Figure 4-3. A check next to the menu item indicates that it is selected.

FIGURE 4-3
View Options menu on the toolbar

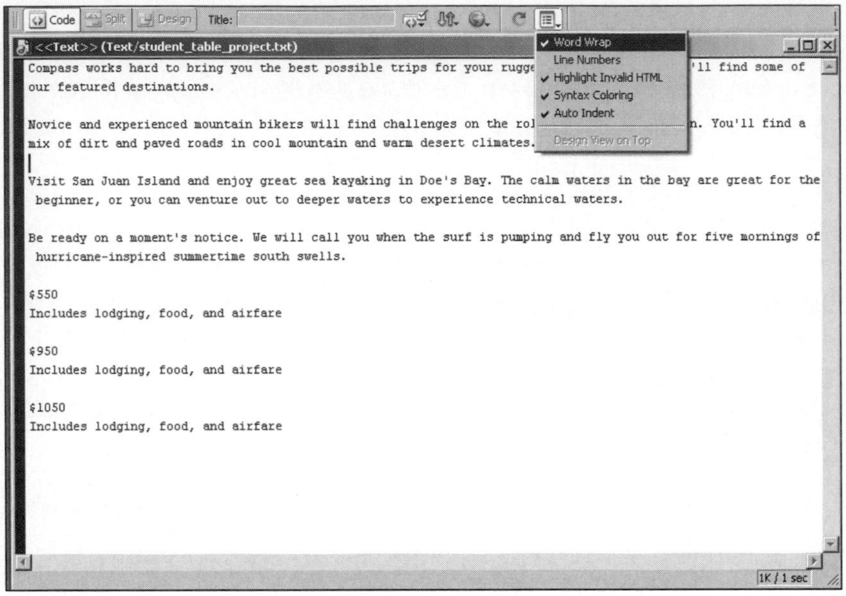

14. Select and copy the first paragraph. Return to your **destinations.htm** page (using the tab at the top of the Document window), place the insertion point in the top text cell, and click **Paste** on the **Edit** menu.

The text is copied to this cell. Adjust the cell size to accommodate the text by clicking and dragging the cell border. You might also need to change the font and font size. The tracing image uses Verdana for the font and 10 pixels for the font size. (Macintosh users might want to try –1 for the font size.)

15. Return to the text document and copy the remaining text into the other text cells you've drawn on the page. Use the Assets panel to insert the details image in each of the price cells.

16. When you have copied and pasted all of the text from student_table_project, close the text file.

STEP-BY-STEP 4.3 Continued

17. Resize and move the cells to make your page look like Figure 4-4.

FIGURE 4-4
Fine-tuning the table layout

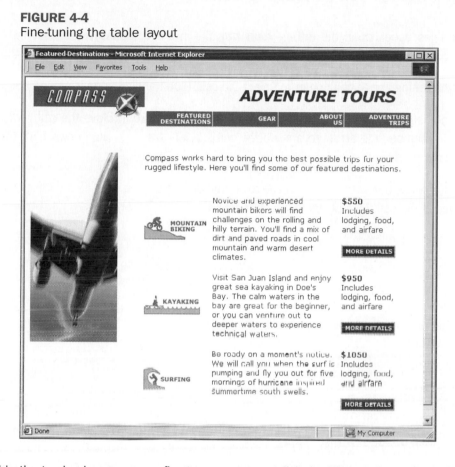

18. To hide the tracing image as you fine-tune your page, click the **View** menu, point to **Tracing Image**, and then click **Show**. This is a toggle to show or hide the tracing image.

19. Save your page and then preview it in your browser.

20. Close the browser and close the destinations.htm document. Leave Dreamweaver open for the next Step-by-Step.

As you design your pages in Layout mode, you will want to move or resize cells or add new cells to add more content. You can also add a background color to each cell or to the table. A layout cell cannot overlap other cells and cannot be moved outside the layout table.

STEP-BY-STEP 4.4

Moving a Layout Cell and Adding Color

1. In the Files panel, open the **rafting_tours.htm** file in the **compass_tours/Lesson04** folder. Make sure you are in Layout mode. This page has a table with some text and graphics in the cells.

2. Click the rafting image cell border to select the cell. Blue handles appear around the cell.

3. Drag the cell to a new location or use the arrow keys to move it. Move the cell vertically within the table. Remember, the arrow keys move the cell 1 pixel at a time. Hold down **Shift** to move the cell 5 pixels at a time.

4. Draw a new cell below the rafting image for a caption. Make it as wide as the image. Key **Rafting the Rockies** in the cell. Format the text as **Heading 4**.

5. Select the cell in which you added the caption.

6. Click the **Bg** color picker on the Property inspector and use the eyedropper to select the yellow color in the raft.

7. Save the document and remain in this screen for the next Step-by-Step.

> **Hot Tip**
>
> To add color to a table, select the table, click the **Bg** color box, and choose a color for the table.

Cell Formatting

You can change several options for each cell. You can control the alignment of objects in each cell in a table horizontally and vertically. The default HTML setting for horizontal alignment in a cell is along the left. The default HTML setting for vertical alignment in a cell is the middle of the cell. When you draw a cell in Layout mode, Dreamweaver changes the vertical alignment to Top, but you can easily change that setting.

STEP-BY-STEP 4.5

Changing the Cell Alignment

1. Select the caption cell and then choose **Center** from the Horz list menu on the Property inspector. This centers the text horizontally in the cell.

2. Change the Vert setting to **Middle**. This centers the text vertically in the cell.

3. Save the document and remain in this screen for the next Step-by-Step.

You can also control the width and height of the cell. The cell can be set to a fixed width or set to change width depending on the width of the browser. If you change a cell to Autostretch, Dreamweaver changes the entire column to Autostretch.

S TEP-BY-STEP 4.6

Setting a Column to Autostretch

1. Select the main text cell.

2. Click **Autostretch** on the Property inspector or click the number **235** at the bottom of the column to open the column header menu and choose **Make Column Autostretch**, as shown in Figure 4-5.

FIGURE 4-5
The column header menu

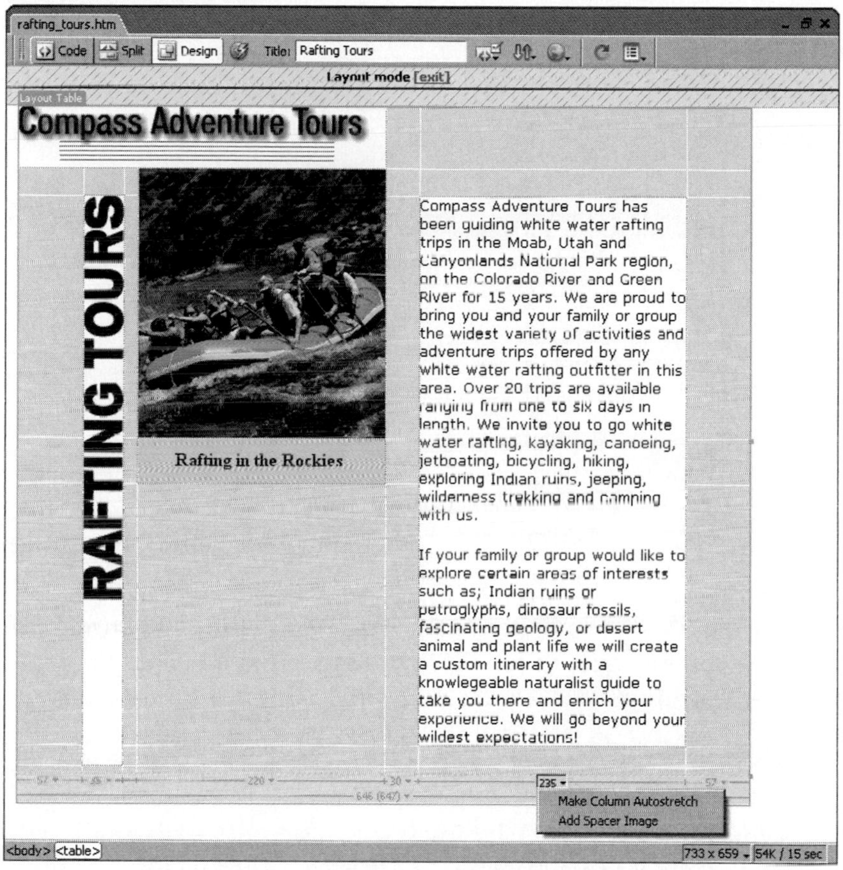

3. Save the document, and then preview the page in your browser and change the width of the browser. Notice that the column stretches as you change the width.

4. Close the browser and then close rafting_tours.htm. Leave Dreamweaver open for the next Step-by-Step.

When you select a column to Autostretch, you cause all cells in that column to Autostretch. Use the white guides on the page to determine if another cell is within the column you've selected. When you use Autostretch, Dreamweaver inserts spacer images to control the layout and sets the width of the table to 100%. A *spacer image* controls the spacing in the layout but is not visible in the browser window.

If you choose not to use spacer images, columns will change size or even visually disappear if they do not contain content. You can insert and remove spacer images in each column yourself or let Dreamweaver add them automatically when creating an Autostretch column. The spacer GIFs are added to a cell at the bottom of each column of the table.

To add a spacer image, select Add Spacer Image from the column header menu. If you have never created a spacer image for the site, the Choose Spacer Image dialog box opens, as shown in Figure 4-6.

Note ✓

The Choose Spacer Image dialog box (described in the next Step-by-Step) appears if a spacer image is not associated with your site. If the dialog box appears, click **Use an Existing Spacer Image File** and locate **spacer.gif** in the **Lesson04/Images** folder. The spacer file location is saved in your preferences. Click the **Edit** menu, point to **Preferences**, and then click **Layout Mode** to change or remove the spacer image.

FIGURE 4-6
The Choose Spacer Image dialog box

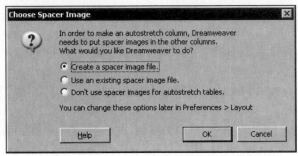

Choose from the following options:

- **Create a spacer image file:** If you choose this option and click OK, another dialog box opens in which you can navigate to the directory in your site where you want to store the spacer image file (for example, an images folder).

- **Use an existing spacer image file:** If you already have a spacer image created for your site, choose this option and then navigate to your spacer image in the next dialog box that opens.

- **Don't use spacer images for autostretch tables:** If you select this option, fixed-width columns in your layout might collapse to a small width, or even to zero width. Use this option only if you've already placed enough content in your fixed width columns to prevent them from collapsing, or if you have already added spacer images manually.

You can insert spacer images into specific columns, remove them from specific columns, or remove all spacer images on the page.

To insert a spacer image into a column, click Add Spacer Image from the column header menu to insert the spacer image into the column. You will not see the spacer image, but the column might shift slightly.

To remove a spacer image from a column, click Remove Spacer Image from the column header menu. The spacer image is removed and the column might shift.

To remove all spacer images from your page, click Remove All Spacer Images from the Table Header menu, or click Remove All Spacers on the layout table Property inspector, as shown in Figure 4-7. Your whole layout might shift slightly—or dramatically—depending on your content. If you do not have content in some columns, these columns might visually disappear completely.

FIGURE 4-7
Property inspector showing Remove All Spacers

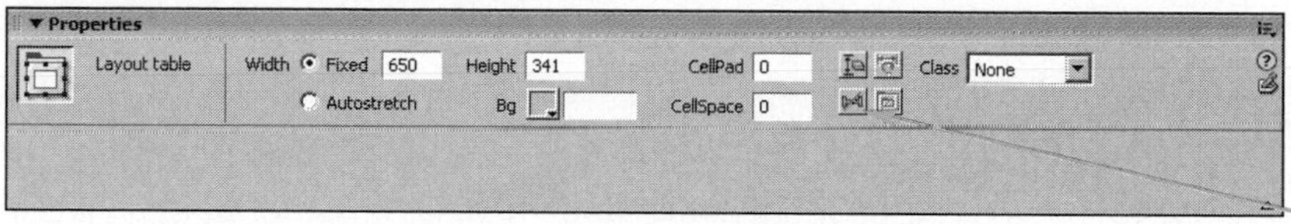

Creating Tables in Standard Mode

Although the Layout mode provides the easiest way to design your pages, you will often need to view your page in the Standard mode, which shows you the HTML table structure. You can create tables yourself in this mode or view the table Dreamweaver created when you drew a table in Layout mode. If the information you want to present is structured into rows and columns, using a standard table is easier than drawing the rows and columns yourself.

To switch to Standard mode, click Standard Mode on the Insert bar. If a table exists on the page, you'll see the table borders and all the cells of the table.

STEP-BY-STEP 4.7

Inserting a Standard Table

1. Open a new document and save it as **biking_table** (followed by your initials) in your compass_tours/Lesson04 folder. Title the page **Montana Mountain Biking**.

2. On the Insert bar, make sure the **Layout** category is selected. Click the **Standard Mode** button.

3. Open the **mt_biking.txt** file from the **compass_tours/Lesson04/Text** folder. Make sure the Word Wrap feature is turned on.

4. Copy the **Montana Mountain Biking** header and paste it at the top of your page. Change the header to **Heading 3** style.

5. Copy the paragraph from **mt_biking.txt** and close the text file. In your page, press **Enter** (Windows) or **Return** (Macintosh) after the header. Then paste the paragraph into your page.

6. Place the insertion point after the body text. Press **Enter** (Windows) or **Return** (Macintosh) to create a new paragraph.

7. Click the **Insert** menu and then click **Table**, or click **Table** in the Layout category of the Insert bar. The Table dialog box opens.

STEP-BY-STEP 4.7 Continued

8. Make the following changes in the Insert Table dialog box, as shown in Figure 4-8:

  a. Enter **2** in the Rows box and **4** in the Columns box.

  b. Change the Width to **500 Pixels**. You also have the option of setting the width as a percentage of the browser window. Tables specified in pixels are better for precise layout of text and images. Tables specified in percentages are a good choice when the proportions of the columns are more important than their actual widths.

  c. Set the Border thickness to **1**. This represents the width of the table border.

  d. Leave Cell Padding and Cell Spacing blank. Cell Padding refers to the amount of spacing between the cell content and the cell walls. Browsers use a default value of 1 pixel if you don't specify a value for the cell padding. Cell Spacing refers to the amount of spacing between table cells, not including the border. Browsers use a default value of 2 pixels if you don't specify a value for the cell spacing.

  e. Click **OK** to close the dialog box.

FIGURE 4-8
The Table dialog box

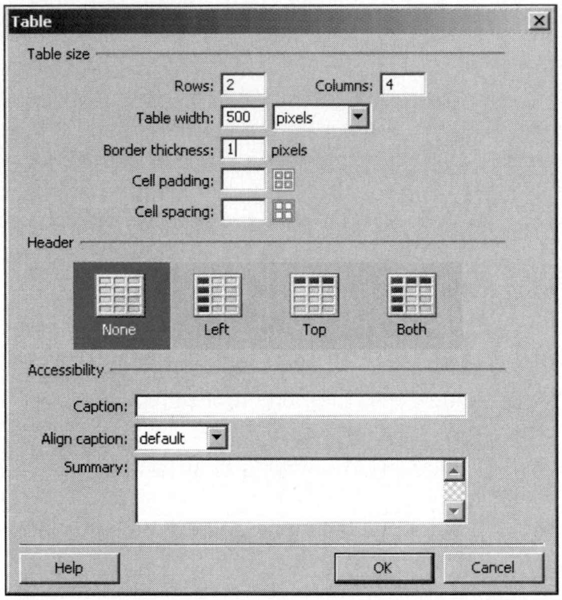

9. Key **Ride Name** in the first cell of the first row; then press **Tab** to move to the next cell. Key **Type**, press **Tab** again, key **Location**, press **Tab**, and key **Rating**.

10. Click to the right of the table and then press **Enter** (Windows) or **Return** (Macintosh). The insertion point is in a new paragraph. Remain in this screen for the next Step-by-Step.

You could continue to enter the remaining text for the table. In the next Step-by-Step exercise, however, you use another method to fill the table.

Importing Data from Spreadsheets

If you have text in a spreadsheet or even in a table in Microsoft Word, you can insert it very easily into Dreamweaver. You need to save or export the text as a tab- or comma-delimited file.

S TEP-BY-STEP 4.8

Inserting Data into a Table

1. Click the **Insert** menu, point to **Table Objects**, and then click **Import Tabular Data**, or click the **Tabular Data** button in the Layout category of the Insert bar. The Import Tabular Data dialog box opens, as shown in Figure 4-9.

FIGURE 4-9
The Import Tabular Data dialog box

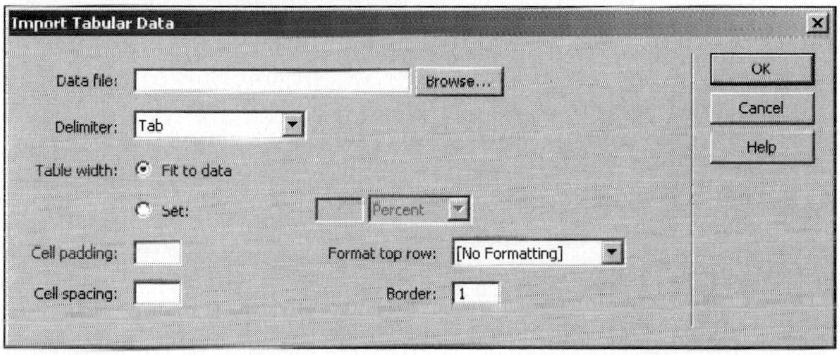

2. Click **Browse**, navigate to the **blkingtable.txt** file in the **Lesson04/Text** folder, and then double-click it.

3. In the Import Tabular Data dialog box, set the Delimiter to **Tab**, click the **Set** option under Table Width, enter **500** in the text box, click the arrow on the Percent box, select **Pixels**, make sure **(No Formatting)** is selected in the Format Top Row box, and that **1** is in the Border box.

4. Click **OK**. The data is imported, and a table is built for you with the settings you chose. Remain in this screen for the next Step-by-Step.

You have two tables: the first you created with the row headers and a second one with the data. You now want to combine the two tables.

Copying and Pasting Table Cells

You can copy and paste multiple table cells at one time, preserving the cell's formatting, or you can copy and paste only the contents of the cells.

Cells can be pasted at an insertion point or in place of a selection in an existing table. To paste multiple table cells, the contents of the Clipboard must be compatible with the structure of the table or the selection in the table in which the cells will be pasted.

S TEP-BY-STEP 4.9

Working with Cells and Cell Content

1. Select all the cells in the second table by dragging across the cells. Start in the upper-left cell and drag to the lower-right cell. The selected cells are displayed with a black border. To be cut or copied, the selected cells must form a rectangle.

2. Click the **Edit** menu and then click **Copy**, or use the keyboard shortcut **Ctrl + C** (Windows) or **Command + C** (Macintosh).

3. Click in the first cell of the second row in the top table. This is where the copied cells will be pasted.

4. Click the **Edit** menu and then click **Paste**, or use the keyboard shortcut **Ctrl + V** (Windows) or **Command + V** (Macintosh). All the cells from the second table should now be inserted in the first table.

5. Save the document and remain in this screen for the next Step-by-Step.

If you are pasting entire rows or columns, the rows or columns are added to the table. If you are pasting an individual cell, the contents of the selected cell are replaced if the Clipboard contents are compatible with the selected cell. If you are pasting outside a table, the rows, columns, or cells are used to define a new table.

Selecting Table Elements

To change or delete a table, you need to select the table. Dreamweaver provides several methods for selecting a table. You will find that some methods are easier than others, depending on the complexity of the table structure. You can easily select a row, a column, or all the cells in a table. You can also select noncontiguous cells in a table and modify the properties of those cells. (You cannot copy or paste noncontiguous cell selections.) You can use Expanded Tables mode to make it easier to select and edit cells. Expanded Tables mode temporarily adds space inside cells, between cells, and to the table border. That space disappears when you revert to Standard mode.

Following are options for selecting and working with parts of a table:

■ **Selecting rows or columns:** Position the pointer at the left margin of a row or at the top of a column and click when the selection arrow appears. Or click in a cell and drag across or down to select multiple rows or columns.

■ **Selecting one or more cells:** Click in a cell and drag down or across to another cell. Or click in one cell and then hold down Shift and click another cell to select all cells within the rectangular region defined by the two cells.

■ **Selecting noncontiguous cells:** Press Ctrl (Windows) or Command (Macintosh) and click to add cells, rows, or columns to the selection. Or select multiple cells in the table, and then press Ctrl (Windows) or Command (Macintosh) and click cells, rows, or columns to deselect individual cells.

- **Resizing a column:** Move the pointer over one of the column borders. When the pointer changes to a two-headed arrow, drag the column border.

- **Adding a new row:** Click in the last cell of a row and press Tab, or click the Modify menu, point to Table, and then click Insert Row. You can also right-click (Windows) or Ctrl-click (Macintosh) in the table, select the Table menu, and then click Insert Row from the submenu.

- **Deleting a row:** Click in the row, click the Modify menu, point to Table, and then click Delete Row. You can also use right-click (Windows) or Ctrl-click (Macintosh) while in the table row, select the Table menu, and then click Delete Row from the submenu.

- **Adding a row in the middle of the table:** Click in the row below where you want the new one, click the Modify menu, point to Table, and then click Insert Row. You can also right-click (Windows) or Ctrl-click (Macintosh) in the row below, select the Table menu, and then click Insert Row from the submenu.

- **Inserting a row and controlling placement before or after the current row:** Click the Modify menu, point to Table, and then click Insert Rows or Columns. A dialog box opens in which you can specify whether to insert before or after the current row.

- **Spanning columns or rows:** Drag to select multiple cells and then click Merge Cells on the Property inspector. You can also click the Modify menu, point to Table, and then click Merge Cells.

- **Splitting a cell:** Select the cell and then click Split Cell on the Property inspector, or click the Modify menu, point to Table, and then click Split Cell to return the number of cells to the original number (if you previously merged them) or to split a cell into any number of rows or columns.

S TEP-BY-STEP 4.10

Selecting Table Elements

1. Select one or more cells in the second table, but not an entire row or column.

2. Click the **Edit** menu, and then click **Clear** or press **Delete**. This removes cell content but leaves the cells intact.

3. Drag across all the cells in a row of the second table to select the row.

4. Press **Delete**. The row and all its contents are deleted. Remain in this screen for the next Step-by-Step.

5. Practice selecting an entire table by doing the following:
   a. Position the pointer on the upper-left corner of the second table or anywhere on the bottom edge. The pointer turns to a white arrow with a small table icon when you are close to the edge. Click when you see the pointer. Click outside the table to deselect it.
   b. Click once in the second table. Click the **Modify** menu, point to **Table**, and then click **Select Table**. Click outside the table to deselect it.
   c. Position the pointer anywhere inside the second table and select the **<table>** tag in the tag selector at the lower-left corner of the Document window.

   Selection handles appear around the table when it is selected. When the table is selected, you cannot see the black border around any of the cells.

STEP-BY-STEP 4.10 Continued

6. With the second table selected, press **Delete** to remove the second table.

7. Save the document and remain in this screen for the next Step-by-Step.

Changing Cell Attributes

You can change the attributes, or characteristics, of a cell, row, or column by using options in the Property inspector. Following are definitions of the options in the cell, column, or row Property inspector:

■ **Horz:** Sets the horizontal alignment of the cell's contents to the browser's default (usually Left for regular cells and Center for header cells), left, right, or center.

■ **Vert:** Sets the vertical alignment of the cell's contents to the browser's default (usually Middle), top, middle, bottom, or baseline.

■ **W** and **H:** Sets the width and height of selected cells in pixels. To use percentages, follow the value with a percent sign (%).

■ **Bg (top):** Sets the background image for the cells.

■ **Bg (bottom):** Sets the background color for the cells. Background color appears inside the cells only—that is, it does not flow over cell spacing or table borders. This means that if your cell spacing and cell padding are not set to zero, gaps will appear between the colored areas even if the border is set to zero.

■ **Brdr:** Sets the border color for the cells. Borders must be set for the entire table for this attribute to be recognized.

■ **No Wrap:** Prevents word wrapping, so cells expand in width to accommodate all data. Normally, cells expand horizontally to accommodate the longest word and then expand vertically.

■ **Header:** Formats the selected cell as a table header. The contents of table header cells are bold and centered by default.

S TEP-BY-STEP 4.11

Changing the Attributes of a Row, Column, or Cell

1. Select the **Location** column in the table.

STEP-BY-STEP 4.11 Continued

2. Click the arrow in the Horz box in the Property inspector and set the horizontal alignment to **Center**, as shown in Figure 4-10. Leave the vertical alignment set to **Default**.

> **FIGURE 4-10**
> The Property inspector with a column centered

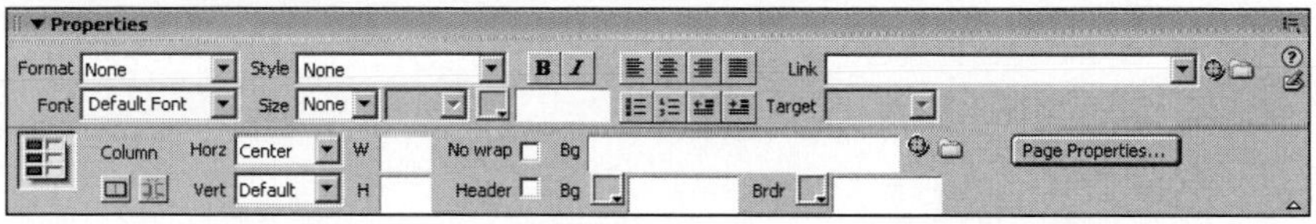

3. Select the **Rating** column and change the horizontal alignment to **Right**.

4. Select the top row of cells by positioning the pointer at the left margin of the row and clicking when the pointer changes to a selection arrow.

5. On the Property inspector, click the **Bg** color box to open the color picker.

6. Select a light gray color. The background color of the first row of cells changes accordingly.

7. Save the document and remain in this screen for the next Step-by-Step.

Sorting Tables

You can perform a simple table sort by sorting on the contents of a single column. You can also perform a more complicated sort by sorting on the contents of two columns. You cannot sort tables that contain merged cells.

The Sort Table dialog box offers a number of options:

- **Sort By:** This is the first column you will sort by.

- **Order:** Choose whether you want to sort the column alphabetically or numerically. This option is important when the contents of a column are numerical. An alphabetical sort applied to a list of one- and two-digit numbers results in an alphanumeric sort (such as 1, 10, 2, 20, 3, 30) rather than a straight numeric sort (such as 1, 2, 3, 10, 20, 30). Then choose Ascending (A to Z or low to high) or Descending for the sort order.

- **Then By:** Specify sort options here to perform a secondary sort on a different column.

- **Sort includes the first row:** Select this option to include the first row in the sort. If the first row is a heading that shouldn't be moved, leave this option unchecked.

- **Sort header rows:** Select this option if you have marked header rows for your table with the THEAD tag. The rows with THEAD tags will be sorted but will remain at the top of the table. If you expect your table to be printed (and for it to be printed across multiple pages), you can use the THEAD tag to have a consistent set of headings at the top of each page on which the table appears.

■ **Sort footer rows:** Select this option if you have marked footer rows for your table with the TFOOT tag. The rows with TFOOT tags will be sorted but will remain at the bottom of the table. TFOOT is similar to THEAD but applies to rows used as footers.

■ **Keep all row colors the same after the sort has been completed:** If you changed any attributes for a row, you can retain that attribute in the row by selecting this option. For example, suppose you sort a table with a color in the first row. After sorting, the data in the first row moves to the second row. If this option is selected, the color moves with the data to the second row. If this option is not selected, the color remains in the first row.

S TEP-BY-STEP 4.12

Sorting a Table

1. Click **View**, point to **Table Mode**, and make sure **Standard Mode** is selected. Select the table, click the **Commands** menu, and then click **Sort Table**. The Sort Table dialog box opens, as shown in Figure 4-11.

FIGURE 4-11
The Sort Table dialog box

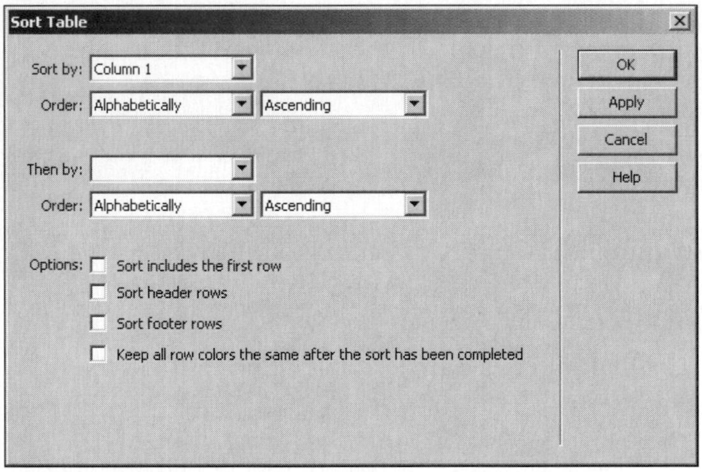

2. Make sure the following options are set in the Sort Table dialog box:
   a. Sort By: Select **Column 1**.
   b. Order: Select **Alphabetically**. Choose **Ascending**.
   c. Then By: Leave blank.
   d. Sort Includes First Row: Leave unchecked.
   e. Sort Header Rows: Leave unchecked.
   f. Sort Footer Rows: Leave unchecked.
   g. Keep All Row Colors the Same After the Sort Has Been Completed: Leave unchecked.

3. Click **OK**. Your table is sorted alphabetically by the first column, but the row headers remain in the first row.

4. Save the document and remain in this screen for the next Step-by-Step.

Exporting a Table

A table you create in HTML has all the tags needed to display the table in a browser. If you need to extract the table information to place it in a database, a spreadsheet, or a word-processing or page layout application, you can't just copy and paste the text. All you'll get is the text with no row and column formatting. However, you can easily export the table and save the file as a tab-delimited file that can be read by most applications.

S TEP-BY-STEP 4.13

Exporting a Table

1. With the table still selected, click the **File** menu, point to **Export**, and then click **Table**. The Export Table dialog box opens, as shown in Figure 4-12.

FIGURE 4-12
The Export Table dialog box

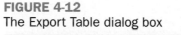

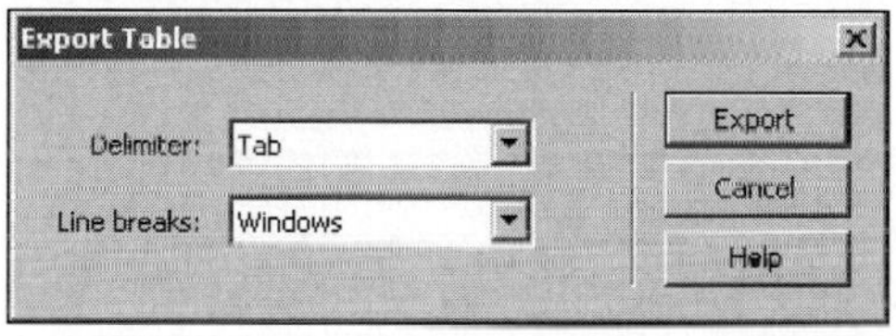

2. For the Delimiter (the character that separates cell data), Tab is the default selection. The other options are Space, Comma, Semicolon, or Colon. Make sure **Tab** is selected.

3. For the Line Breaks, choose line breaks for the operating system to which you are exporting the file. The options are Windows, Mac (Macintosh), or UNIX. Select the option that's running on your local machine.

4. Click **Export** to open the Export Table As dialog box.

5. Enter **new_biking_table** as the name of your file, followed by your initials and then the **.txt** extension. (The file you are creating is an ASCII text file. You should add the .txt extension to the filename.) Click **Save**.

6. Save and close the document, and then close Dreamweaver.

> ### Extra Challenge
>
> Use the Page Properties dialog box to change the background color of the **biking_table.htm** file to purple (**#9999CC**). Change the font of the text in biking_table.htm to **Verdana**. Change the font size of the text to 9. Format the names of the rides in the first column to be bold. Don't include the column label. Starting with the third row of the table in biking_table.htm, change the background color of every other line in the table to yellow.

SUMMARY

In this lesson, you learned to:

- Import images to use as tracing images.
- Use tables to lay out your pages.
- Work with tables in Layout, Standard, and Expanded modes.
- Import tabular data.
- Select elements of a table and modify their properties.
- Sort tables.
- Export a table.

ADDING USER INTERACTIVITY

OBJECTIVES

Upon completion of this lesson, you should be able to:

■ Add user interactivity to your pages by using behaviors.

■ Create and work with rollovers.

■ Attach behaviors to objects.

■ Modify behaviors.

■ Understand events.

■ Add multiple behaviors to one user action.

Defining a Behavior

Behaviors are used to add interactivity to your pages, enabling your users to change or control the information they see. A behavior combines a user event (for example, moving the pointer over a graphic button) with an action or series of actions that take place as a result of that event. Behaviors are prewritten JavaScript programs you can easily incorporate in your page when using Dreamweaver.

You can specify more than one event to trigger a behavior and more than one action for each event. Macromedia Dreamweaver MX 2004 includes several predefined behavior actions. If you are proficient with JavaScript, you can add your own behaviors. You can also download new behaviors from the Macromedia Exchange for Dreamweaver Web site by clicking the Dreamweaver Exchange link on Dreamweaver's start page. If you have an Internet connection, your primary browser will open and you will be taken directly to the Web site.

Creating Rollover Buttons

One common use of JavaScript on Web pages is for creating a rollover—an image that changes when the user moves the pointer over the image. You can create button rollovers in Dreamweaver without ever looking at the HTML or JavaScript code.

Here are a few things to remember when designing rollover buttons for your page:

■ Create each image the same width and height. If you don't, Dreamweaver resizes the second rollover image to the size of the first image. Resizing distorts the second image.

■ Make the buttons as small as possible. Remember, with rollovers you are displaying not one, but two images for the same button. The file size of the button is effectively doubled, because you have two images to download.

Using Insert Rollover Magic

Dreamweaver makes it easy to insert rollovers in your page. JavaScript behaviors rely on naming of objects (such as images). Using the Rollover Image command provides you with a field for naming the image, so you won't forget. If you haven't already placed your initial images on the page, you might find this method preferable because it steps you through inserting and naming the images.

STEP-BY-STEP 5.1

Inserting a Rollover Image

1. Start Dreamweaver and open the **latest.htm** file from your **compass_tours/Lesson05** folder.

2. This page contains a table with some graphics. Switch to **Layout** mode to view the table structure.

3. Place the insertion point in the blank cell to the left of *Welcome to Compass*. Then click the **Insert** menu, point to **Image Objects,** and then click **Rollover Image** to open the Insert Rollover Image dialog box shown in Figure 5-1.

> **Note** ✓
>
> Dreamweaver will automatically load the last site definition used on the system. It should load your information if you were the last user. If it does not, use the list menu in the upper-left corner of the Files panel to locate and select your site's name (and, hence, your site definition).

FIGURE 5-1
The Insert Rollover Image dialog box

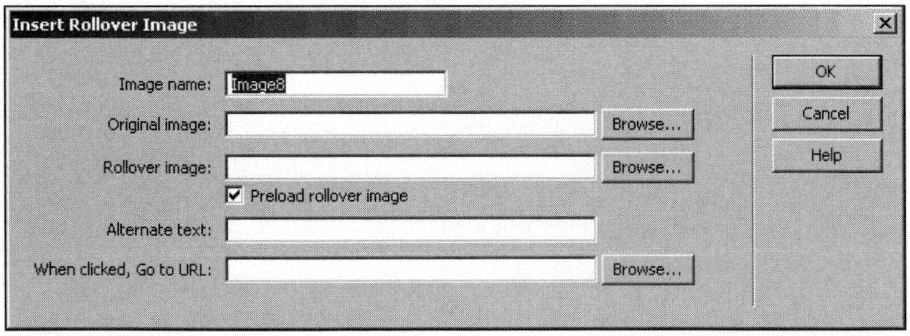

> **Note** ✓
>
> If you see the Getting Started in Layout mode message, click **OK**.

STEP-BY-STEP 5.1 Continued

4. Key **biking** in the Image Name text box. The name you enter here must be unique. No other object on this page can have the same name. Use lowercase for the name, and don't use any special characters or spaces in the name. Don't begin the name with a number.

5. Click **Browse** next to the Original Image text box and select **biking_button.gif** in the **Project_images** folder. (You're already in the Lesson05 folder of your compass_tours folder.) All the images you need for this exercise are located in that folder. Then click **OK** (Windows) or **Choose** (Macintosh).

6. Click **Browse** next to the Rollover Image text box and select **biking_button_f2.gif**. Click **OK** (Windows) or **Choose** (Macintosh).

7. Make sure the **Preload Rollover Image** option is selected.

8. Key **Biking** in the Alternate Text text box.

9. Click **Browse** next to When Clicked, Go To URL and link the biking button to **biking.htm** from the Lesson05 folder. Click **OK** (Windows) or **Choose** (Macintosh), and then click **OK** to close the Insert Rollover Image dialog box.

10. Save and test your file in your browser.

11. Place the insertion point after the image and press **Shift + Enter** (Windows) or **Shift + Return** (Macintosh).

> **Note** ☑
>
> If you want the graphic to link to another file, you need to click **Browse** next to When Clicked, Go To URL and find the file to link. If you're not linking, you leave this text box blank.

STEP-BY-STEP 5.1 Continued

12. Use the **Insert Rollover Image** command, repeating steps 3–11 to add the remaining buttons: **climbing_button.gif**, **diving_button.gif**, and **kayaking_button.gif**. For the rollover images, use the corresponding image files: **climbing_button_f2.gif**, **diving_button_f2.gif**, and **kayaking_button_f2.gif**. Don't forget to give each a unique name as well as Alternative Text. You don't need to link these buttons. The final page should look like that shown in Figure 5-2.

> **Note** ☑
>
> The number sign (#) in a Link text box on the Property inspector causes the browser to change the pointer to a pointing hand when the user rolls over the button.

FIGURE 5-2
The completed Adventure Travel page

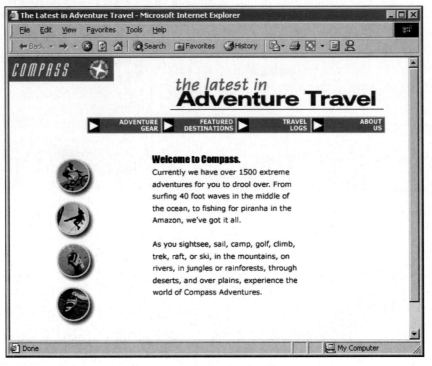

13. Save the document and remain in this screen for the next Step-by-Step.

Adding Rollovers to Existing Images

Using the Insert Rollover Image command makes it very easy to insert rollovers on your page. Sometimes graphics are already placed on the page and you want to add rollovers. You could delete the graphics and use the Insert Rollover Image command to put them back on the page, but there is a possibility of changing the page design, especially if the graphics are in a table. In the next Step-by-Step, you will add rollovers to the buttons across the top of the page.

STEP-BY-STEP 5.2

Adding Rollovers to an Image

1. Select the **Adventure Gear** image and key **gear** in the image name text box on the Property inspector (illustrated in Figure 5-3). The image name text box is under the word *Image* in the upper-left corner of the Property inspector.

FIGURE 5-3
The image name text box in the Property inspector

Name text box

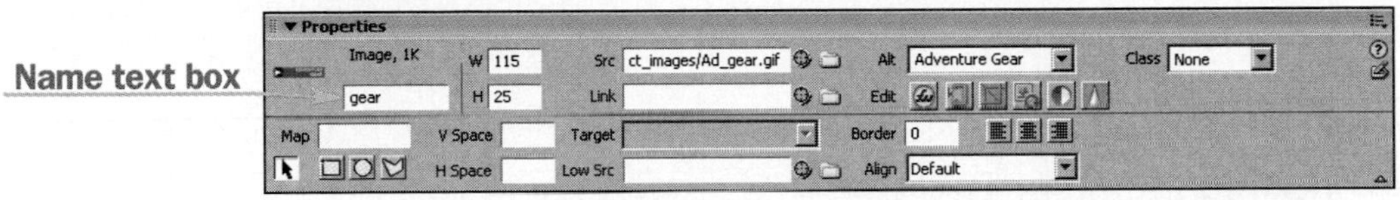

2. Click the **Window** menu, and then click **Behaviors** to open the Behaviors panel.

3. With the image still selected, click the Add Behavior (+) button at the top of the Behaviors panel and click **Swap Image** from the pop-up menu, as shown in Figure 5-4. The Swap Image dialog box appears, with the gear image selected.

FIGURE 5-4
The Behaviors panel with the Actions menu displayed

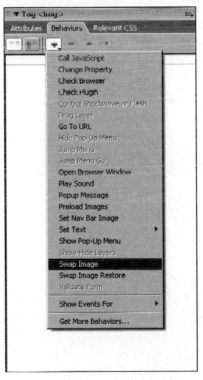

STEP-BY-STEP 5.2 Continued

4. In the Swap Image dialog box, click **Browse** and select the **Ad_gear_f2.gif** image from the **Project_images** folder. Click **OK** (Windows) or **Choose** (Macintosh). The Swap Image dialog box should look like Figure 5-5. Click **OK** to close the Swap Image dialog box.

FIGURE 5-5
The Swap Image dialog box

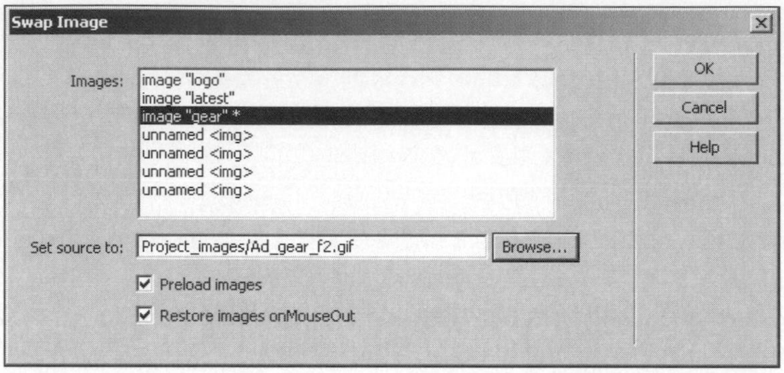

5. Save your file and preview it in your browser.

6. Repeat steps 1–5 to add rollovers to the remaining buttons, using the corresponding image files **featured_f2.gif**, **Travel_logs_f2.gif,** and **About_f2.gif**. Don't forget to name each image before you add the Swap Image behavior.

7. Save the document and remain in this screen for the next Step-by-Step.

> **Note** ☑
>
> In the Swap Image dialog box, Dreamweaver selects the Preload Images and Restore Images onMouseOut options by default. Leave these options on. Preload Images ensures that the rollover image loads when the page loads, so users do not have to wait the first time they roll over the image. Restore Images onMouseOut returns the button to the first image when users roll off the image.

Understanding Events

After you select an action, Dreamweaver adds that action to the list in the Behaviors panel. Dreamweaver also adds an appropriate event for that action. The event is what causes the action to occur; for example, an event could be the user clicking a button. The action is the result of the user interaction. You can see the list of events and actions for an object (such as a graphic) by selecting the object on the page. If you want to change the event, select the event in the left column of the Behaviors panel and then pick a new one from the pop-up menu (the arrow) to the right of the event, as shown in Figure 5-6. The events in the pop-up menu might change depending on the action and the browser type you choose. The Events pop-up menu appears only after you add an action and select the event. The Show Set Events button shows only those events that have been attached to the current document. The Show All Events button shows all available events.

FIGURE 5-6
The Events pop-up menu in the Behaviors panel

The Events pop-up menu displays events using two methods. In the top portion of the list, Dreamweaver displays events that need an anchor placed around the selected object. These events are listed with <A> preceding the event name. The bottom section shows events that can be directly attached to the selected object. Sometimes, the same event is listed in both sections. The difference is that if you choose from the bottom section, the behavior call is added to the object's tag. If you choose from the top section, the same behavior call is added to a hyperlink containing the selected object.

Adding Several Actions to an Object

After you define a user event, you can attach several actions to that event. To add another event, select the object with the first event and use the Behaviors panel to add another action. To change the order in which the actions are executed, use the Move Event Value Up arrow or Move Event Value Down arrow on the Behaviors panel, as shown in Figure 5-7.

FIGURE 5-7
The Behaviors panel with several actions assigned to one event

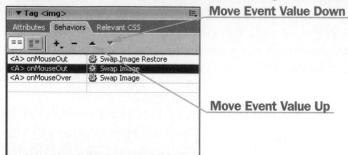

You can also have several images swap out with a single event. For example, you might want two images to swap out when the user rolls over one button. You might think you should create two separate Swap Image actions, but this behavior only works if you use the same Swap Image action for both images. The Swap Image Restore action restores only the last swapped image, so if you have two swap images, only the last one is restored. In the Swap Image dialog box, pick the first graphic and choose the image to swap. Then, before leaving this dialog box, pick the other image and choose its swapped image.

In the next Step-by-Step, you want two images to swap when the user rolls over the buttons on the left. You already have one of the rollovers done. Two actions need to occur on the same onMouseOver event. Instead of adding a new action, you edit the existing Swap Image action and add a new swap image.

STEP-BY-STEP 5.3

Swapping Out Two Images on a Rollover

1. In the latest.htm file, select the **Welcome to Compass** graphic. This is the graphic you want to change when the user rolls over each of the buttons.

2. Name the image **text**.

3. Select the round biking image to the left. This image has a Swap Image behavior assigned.

STEP-BY-STEP 5.3 Continued

4. Double-click the **Swap Image** action in the Behaviors panel. The Swap Image dialog box opens. Images that have an asterisk at the end of the name have been assigned a swap image. This is a quick way to verify which images will swap to other images.

5. Select **image "text"** in the list.

6. Click **Browse** and select **biking_text.gif** from the **Project_images** folder. Then click **OK** (Windows) or **Choose** (Macintosh). Your dialog box should look like the Swap Image dialog box in Figure 5-8. Click **OK** to exit the dialog box.

FIGURE 5-8
The Swap Image dialog box with two swap images assigned

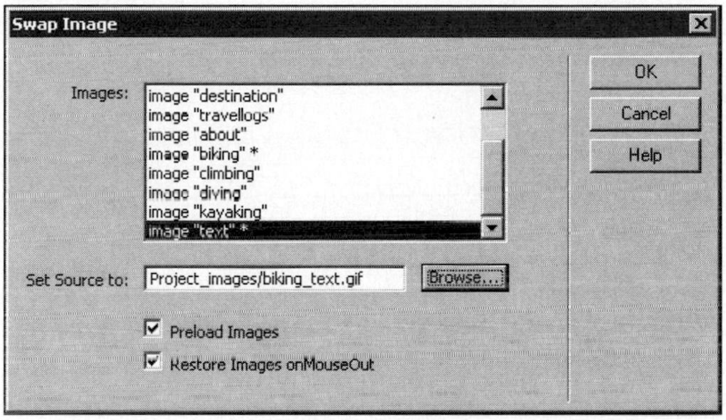

7. Repeat steps 3–6 for all the round buttons, using **climbing_text.gif**, **diving_text.gif**, and **kayaking_text.gif** from the **Project_images** folder.

8. Save your file again and test it in your browser. When you roll over each button, the button should swap and an image should swap in the Welcome area. When you roll off the button, both the button and the Welcome text graphic should restore to their original images.

9. Close the browser, close your file, and close Dreamweaver.

SUMMARY

In this lesson, you learned to:

■ Add user interactivity to your pages by using behaviors.

■ Create and work with rollovers.

■ Attach behaviors to objects.

■ Modify behaviors.

■ Understand events.

■ Add multiple behaviors to one user action.

MANAGING YOUR SITE

OBJECTIVES

Upon completion of this lesson, you should be able to:

- ■ Understand the purpose and uses of the Files panel.
- ■ Use the Files panel to perform site management functions.
- ■ Customize the Files panel.
- ■ Set up a connection to a remote site.
- ■ Copy files to and from a remote site.

Using the Files Panel

The Files panel displays the file and folder structure of your site. You can add and delete files or folders, rename files and folders, and move files and folders. By using the Files panel to maintain your files, you are assured that your link information stays correct. Conversely, if you make file or folder changes in Windows Explorer (Windows) or Finder (Macintosh), Macromedia Dreamweaver MX 2004 doesn't recognize the changes and can't keep your links updated.

To access the Files panel, click the Window menu, and then click Files. The Files panel opens in collapsed view, displaying only your local files, as shown in Figure 6-1.

FIGURE 6-1
The Files panel

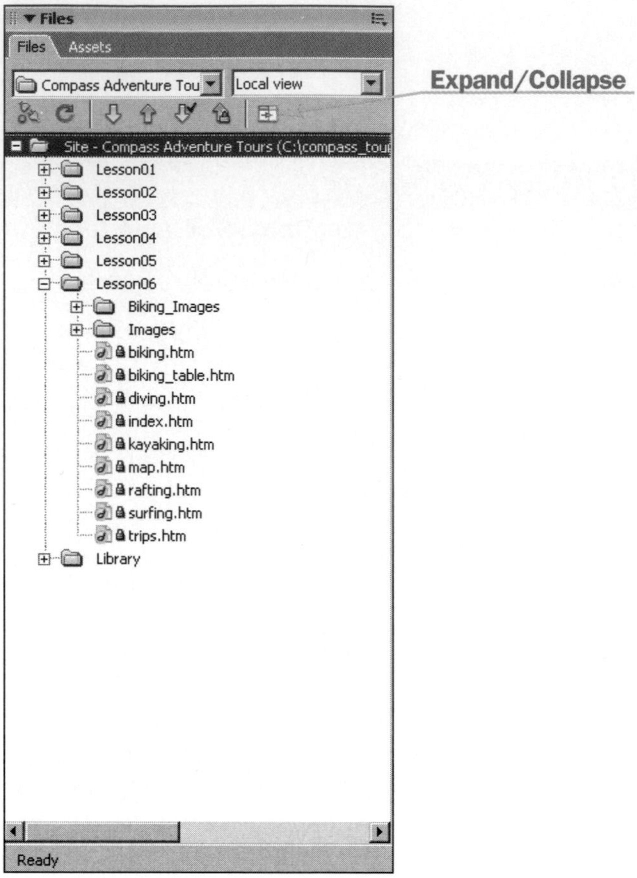

Expand/Collapse

S TEP-BY-STEP 6.1

Expanding the Files Panel

1. Start Dreamweaver and make sure the Files panel is open by clicking the **Window** menu, and then clicking **Files**.

2. With the Files panel open, drag the **Files** panel group away from the docking area. If you leave the Files panel docked before going on to the next step, you'll be able to view the expanded Files panel, but you won't be able to work on documents while the panel is expanded.

> **Note** ☑
>
> Dreamweaver will automatically load the last site definition used on the system. It should load your information if you were the last user. If it does not, use the list menu in the upper-left corner of the Files panel to locate and select your site's name (and, hence, your site definition).

STEP-BY-STEP 6.1 Continued

3. Click the **Expand/Collapse** button (refer to Figure 6-1). The Files panel expands to display two panes, as shown in Figure 6-2. By default, the pane on the right shows your local files. The pane on the left shows the files on the remote version of your site. If you haven't set up a remote site, the pane on the left is blank.

FIGURE 6-2
The Files panel expanded

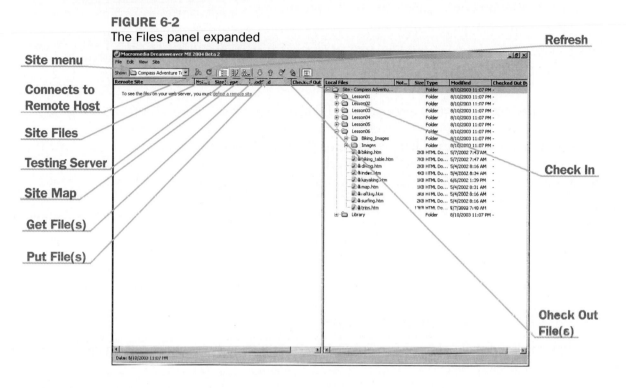

4. Review the tools and options available on the Files panel. Remain in this screen for the next Step-by-Step.

For the remainder of this lesson, you'll work with the Files panel expanded. Following are the options on the Files panel:

- **Site Files view:** Displays the file structure of the remote and local sites in the panes of the Files panel. This is the default view for the Files panel.

- **Testing Server view:** Displays the directory structure of the testing server (if you have defined one) and the local site.

- **Site Map view:** Displays a graphical map of your site, based on how the documents are linked to one another. Click and hold this button down to choose Map Only or Map and Files from the pop-up menu.

- **Site menu:** Indicates the name of the currently selected site. If you have defined more than one site on the local machine, you can use the pop-up menu to switch to one of your other sites.

- **Connects to Remote Host:** Connects to or disconnects from the remote site.

- **Refresh:** Refreshes the local and remote directory lists.

- **View Site FTP Log:** Shows you a record of the communication that goes back and forth between your machine and the remote server, including files that have been sent to or retrieved from the remote site. (This button is visible only when you have established a remote version of your site.)

- **Get File(s):** Copies the selected files from the remote site to your local site, overwriting any existing local copies. The files remain available on the remote site for other team members to check out.

- **Put File(s):** Copies the selected files from the local site to the remote site without changing the file's checked-in or checked-out status.

> **Note** ☑
>
> If Enable File Check In and Check Out is turned off in the Site Definition dialog box, getting a file transfers a copy of the file with both Read and Write privileges.

- **Check Out File(s):** Transfers a copy of the file from the remote server to your local site, overwriting any existing copies. The file is marked as "checked out" on the server. The Check Out feature makes collaborating on a Web site easier. When you check out a file on the remote server, others can tell that you're working on the file and know not to edit that file at the same time. This option is not available if file check-in and check-out is turned off for this site.

- **Check In:** Transfers a copy of the local file to the remote server and makes the file available for editing by others. The local file becomes read-only. This option is not available if file check-in and check-out is turned off for this site.

- **Expand/Collapse:** Toggles the Files panel between single-pane and dual-pane mode.

Adding New Files or Folders to a Site

You can easily add new pages and folders to your site directly from the Files panel.

S TEP-BY-STEP 6.2

Adding a New File or Folder to a Site

1. In the Local Files pane of the Files panel, **right-click** (Windows) or **Control-click** (Macintosh) the Lesson06 folder. A context menu opens, as shown in Figure 6-3.

FIGURE 6-3
The Files panel's context menu

2. Choose **New File**. A new, unnamed document is added to the Lesson06 folder. The name field is highlighted, indicating that you need to enter a name for this document.

3. Key **kayaking.htm** and press **Enter** (Windows) or **Return** (Macintosh) to name the new file. Don't forget the .htm extension for the filename. When you save a file in Dreamweaver from the Document window, the extension is added for you. When you add a file on the Files panel, you need to key the complete filename. Remain in this screen for the next Step-by-Step.

Note ☑
To add a new folder to a site, you would choose **New Folder** from the context menu and then name the folder.

Creating a Site Map

A *site map* is a visual representation of your site and all its linked pages. You can save the site map as a graphic to be used in documentation. To create a site map, you must first select your home page.

STEP-BY-STEP 6.3

Defining Your Home Page

1. In the Local Files pane of the Files panel, select **Lesson06/index.htm**.

2. On Windows, click the **Site** menu on the Files panel, and then click **Set as Home Page**. On Macintosh, click the **options** menu in the upper-right corner of the panel, point to **Site**, and then click **Set as Home Page**. Or, you can **right-click** (Windows) or **Control-click** (Macintosh) the file and choose **Set as Home Page** from the context menu.

   You will not see the result of this command until you create the site map. After you define the home page, you can create the site map.

3. To create the site map, click the **Site Map** button on the Files panel and make sure Map and Files is selected. Remain in this screen for the next Step-by-Step.

The site map is a graphical representation of your entire site, with the home page displayed at the top level, as shown in Figure 6-4. A link from one page to another is shown by a connecting line with an arrowhead. Pages containing links are displayed with a plus or minus sign. Clicking the plus sign displays the linked pages. If a link appears in red, the link is broken. Special links such as e-mail links or URLs are blue and display a small globe.

FIGURE 6-4
The site map

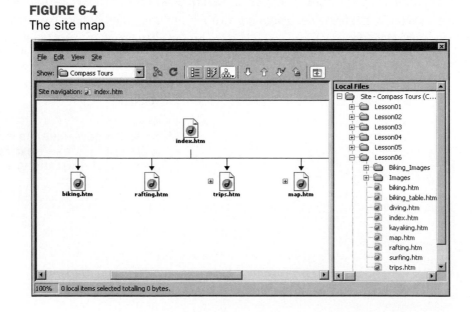

By default, Dreamweaver displays the site map horizontally. If the home page has many links, the site map might not have enough room to show all the pages. You can change the number of columns and the column width to make the site map fit a single page for printing. You can also switch the layout to a vertical format.

STEP-BY-STEP 6.4

Viewing the Site Map Vertically

1. In Windows, click the **View** menu on the Files panel, and then click **Layout**. In Macintosh, click the **options** menu, point to **View**, and then click **Layout**. The Site Definition dialog box opens, showing the Site Map Layout options.

2. In the Number of Columns text box, enter **1** and click **OK**. The site map is regenerated to show all the linked pages in a single column. Remain in this screen for the next Step-by-Step.

You can save the site map as a graphic. On Windows platforms, the site map graphic can be saved as a BMP or PNG file. On Macintosh computers, you save the graphic in PICT format.

STEP-BY-STEP 6.5

Saving the Site Map as a Graphic

1. In Windows, click the **File** menu on the Files panel, and then click **Save Site Map** to open the Save Site Map dialog box. In Macintosh, click the **options** menu, point to **File**, and then click **Save Site Map** to open the Save dialog box.

2. If you're using Windows, key **compass_site.bmp** in the File Name text box. If you're using Macintosh, key **compass_site.** in the Save As text box. Then click **Save**. The site map is saved as a graphic that can be printed or viewed in an image editor. Remain in this screen for the next Step-by-Step.

Viewing a Subset of the Entire Site

As your site becomes larger and more complex, the site map might become too big to see on the Files panel. You can refine the view to show just a selected page and its links.

S TEP-BY-STEP 6.6

Viewing the Site from a Branch

1. On the site map, select the **map.htm** page. You might need to scroll to see this page.

2. In Windows, click the **View** menu on the Files panel, and then click **View as Root**. In Macintosh, click the **options** menu, point to **View**, and then click **View as Root**. The site map changes to show the map.htm page as the root (the top level) and its links (the second level).

3. At the top of the site map is a gray bar displaying site navigation, as shown in Figure 6-5. You should see *index.htm → map.htm*. To remove the branch, click the Dreamweaver icon to the left of index.htm, the home page for this site. The site root is returned to your home page. Remain in this screen for the next Step-by-Step.

FIGURE 6-5
Site navigation on the Files panel

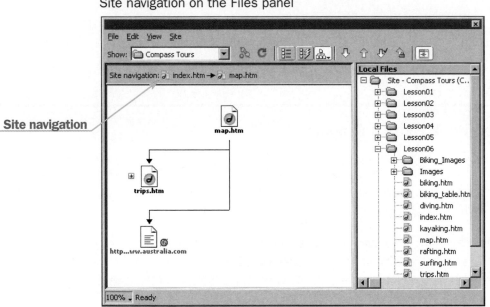

Modifying Pages from the Files Panel

As you view pages on the site map and move the pointer over the pages on the map, you'll see information about each page in the status area at the lower left of the Files panel. One of the pieces of information is the title of the page. If you have forgotten to title the page or want to change the title, you can do it on the Files panel.

S TEP-BY-STEP 6.7

Modifying the Title of a Page on the Site Map

1. On the site map, place the pointer over the **biking.htm** filename. The status area shows that the document is untitled. (Make sure you roll over the filename, not the icon of the file.)

2. In Windows, click the **View** menu on the Files panel, and then click **Show Page Titles**. In Macintosh, click the **options** menu, point to **View**, and then click **Show Page Titles**. The site map displays page titles instead of filenames.

3. Click the page title for the biking.htm page to select it. Then click the title again. A rectangle is placed around the title to indicate that it is editable.

4. Key **Mountain Biking** and press **Enter** (Windows) or **Return** (Macintosh). The site map shows the new title. Remain in this screen for the next Step-by-Step.

Opening Files on the Files Panel

You can open a page for editing from either the site map or the site files list.

S TEP-BY-STEP 6.8

Opening and Editing a File from the Files Panel

1. Do one of the following. On the site map, double-click **Compass North America Tours**, or in the Local Files pane, double-click **trips.htm**. The trips.htm document opens and is available for modification. You might need to move the Files panel aside to work on the document.

2. Select the text **cycling routes** in the first sentence under the heading *Montana Mountain Bike*.

3. Use the Property inspector to link the selected text to **biking_table.htm**.

STEP-BY-STEP 6.8 Continued

4. Close and save the document, but leave Dreamweaver open.

5. Verify that Montana Mountain Biking (biking_table.htm) has been added to the site map. You might need to expand the plus sign next to Compass Adventure Tours to see the linked document. Remain in this screen for the next Step-by-Step.

Renaming Files on the Files Panel

If you need to change the name of one of your files, change the name on the Files panel. This preserves the link information maintained by Dreamweaver. If you change the filename outside of Dreamweaver for either an HTML file or a graphics file that is linked, Dreamweaver has no way to track your changes. If you make the change on the Files panel, Dreamweaver updates all pages that link to the file or contain the graphic.

S TEP-BY-STEP 6.9

Changing a Filename on the Files Panel

1. In the Local Files pane of the Files panel, select **trips.htm**. The filename is highlighted.

2. Click the filename. A rectangle appears around the name, indicating it is editable.

3. Change the filename to **na_trips.htm** and then press **Enter** (Windows) or **Return** (Macintosh). The Update Files dialog box opens, listing all the files affected by this name change, as shown in Figure 6-6.

FIGURE 6-6
The Update Files dialog box

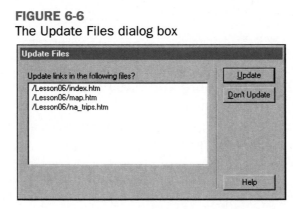

STEP-BY-STEP 6.9 Continued

4. Click **Update** to update the files with the new file-name. Dreamweaver opens each file in the list, makes the change, and then closes the file. If a file in the list is currently open, Dreamweaver makes the change but does not save or close the file. The site map and site files list now show the new name. Remain in this screen for the next Step-by-Step.

> **Note** ☑
>
> You might need to click the **View** menu, and then click **Show Page Titles** (Windows,) or click the **options** menu, point to **View**, and then click **Show Page Titles** (Macintosh) to see the altered filename.

Moving Files on the Files Panel

If a file or folder is not in its proper place, you can easily move the file or folder to its correct location. Doing this on the Files panel ensures that all the link information remains correct and intact.

STEP-BY-STEP 6.10

Moving a File on the Files Panel

1. In the Local Files pane of the Files panel, open the **Biking Images** folder in the **Lesson06** folder. Only one image, downhill.jpg, is in the folder.

2. Drag the image's icon to the **Images** folder located just below the Biking Images folder. The Update Files dialog box opens, asking if affected files should be updated.

3. Click **Update** to keep the link to this graphic correct. The graphic moves to the Images folder.

4. Select the **Biking_Images** folder and delete it. Remain in this screen for the next Step-by-Step.

Customizing the Files Panel

The information displayed on the Files panel might not be as useful to you as you might like. You can reorder existing information, show or hide columns, or even add your own columns.

S TEP-BY-STEP 6.11

Customizing the Columns of the Files Panel

1. Click the **site** pop-up menu in the upper-left corner of the Files panel, and then click **Manage Sites**. The Manage Sites dialog box opens.

2. Select your **site** from the list in the Manage Sites dialog box. Then click **Edit**. The Site Definition dialog box opens.

3. Make sure the **Advanced** tab is selected. Then click the **File View Columns** category to open it, as shown in Figure 6-7.

FIGURE 6-7
The File View Columns category of the Site Definition dialog box

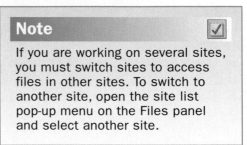

4. Select **Size** from the list and then click the down arrow located in the upper-right corner of the dialog box. "Size" moves down in the list.

5. Select **Modified** from the list and then deselect **Show**. *Hide* appears in the Show column.

6. Click the plus (+) button in the upper-left corner of the dialog box. In the Column Name text box, key **Priority**. Then click **OK** to close the Site Definition dialog box, and click **Done** to close the Manage Sites dialog box.

> **Note** ☑
>
> If you are working on several sites, you must switch sites to access files in other sites. To switch to another site, open the site list pop-up menu on the Files panel and select another site.

A Priority column is added to the end of the list, and the columns of the Files panel change to reflect your choices. Notice that the modification date no longer shows. (You can use the scroll bar at the bottom of the pane to see all the columns.) Remain in this screen for the next Step-by-Step.

Connecting to a Remote Site

In Lesson 1, you created a local site—that is, a folder on your hard drive to store all the folders and files needed for your site. You've been working in the local site, developing pages and testing links. For visitors to see your Web pages, however, you need to copy them to a remote site. Typically, the remote site is on a server specified by your Web administrator or client, but it could also be on a local network.

After creating your local site, you choose which remote site to connect to and the attributes of that remote site. To simulate a remote FTP site, you will create a "remote" site on your desktop. This will enable you to experiment with the Get and Put functions without the possibility of corrupting an actual remote site.

STEP-BY-STEP 6.12

Setting Up a Connection to a Remote Site

1. Click the **Site** menu, and then click **Manage Sites**. The Manage Sites dialog box opens, similar to that shown in Figure 6-8. (The actual names that appear will depend on what sites have been built on your system.)

FIGURE 6-8
The Manage Sites dialog box

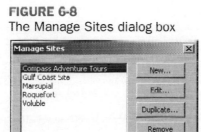

2. Select your site from the list and click **Edit**. The Site Definition dialog box opens.

STEP-BY-STEP 6.12 Continued

3. With the **Basic** tab selected, click **Next** until you come to the sharing files section of the Site Definition Wizard ("When you are done editing a file, do you copy it to another machine?"). On Macintosh, you may not see this screen; skip to step 5.

4. Click **Yes I want to use a remote server**. Then click Next to display the next question ("How do you connect to your Remote Server?") shown in Figure 6-9.

FIGURE 6-9
The Site Definition dialog box

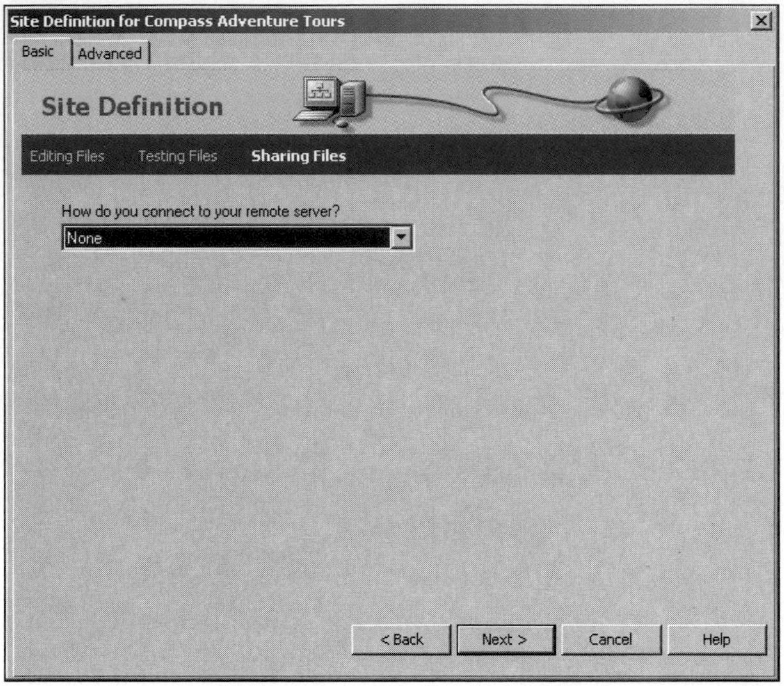

5. From the list menu, select **Local/Network**. A new field appears: What folder on your server do you want to store your files in?

6. Click the folder icon to specify the remote folder. The Choose Remote Root Folder dialog box opens.

7. Click **Desktop** from the **Select** (Windows) or **From** (Macintosh) pop-up menu, and then click **Create New Folder** (Windows) or **New Folder** (Macintosh).

8. Rename the new folder **MyRemote** and then select it. Click **Open** and then click **Select** (Windows) to make the MyRemote folder the remote folder for this site. Or click **Choose** (Macintosh) and the folder is selected as the remote folder.

9. Make sure the **Refresh Remote File List Automatically** check box is selected.

STEP-BY-STEP 6.12 Continued

10. Click **Next** until you reach the Summary section of the Site Definition Wizard.

11. Click **Done** to close the Site Definition Wizard and click **Done** to close the Manage Sites dialog box. Remain in this screen for the next Step-by-Step.

Uploading Files

If you've selected FTP or Local/Network access to connect to your remote site, you can use Dreamweaver to identify the newest files on your local site. This way, you can update only files that have changed.

STEP-BY-STEP 6.13

Selecting and Uploading New Files Only

1. Make sure that the **Site Files** view is selected in the Files panel, so that you see the remote site in the left pane and the local files in the right pane. In the Local Files pane, select the top-level folder.

2. Click the **Edit** menu, and then click **Select Newer Local** (Windows), or click the **options** menu, point to **Edit**, and then click **Select Newer Local** (Macintosh). Dreamweaver compares the modification dates of all local files to the corresponding file information at the remote site and selects only the newer local files. Since there are no files in the remote site, Dreamweaver selects all of the files.

> **Hot Tip**
>
> If your remote site were actually on a remote server, you would click **Connect** on the Files panel. This logs you on to the designated remote server. For this project, you've defined your remote site in a local folder; therefore, the Connect button is not active.

3. Click **Put File(s)** to upload only the selected files to the server. The Dependent Files dialog box opens, as shown in Figure 6-10. Note that there is a *Don't show me this message again* check box. If a previous user has checked this option, you will not see the Dependent Files dialog box.

FIGURE 6-10
The Dependent Files dialog box

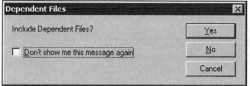

4. In the Dependent Files dialog box, your choices are Yes, No, or Cancel. Clicking Yes sends the images on the selected page, along with the HTML page, to the server. Clicking No sends only the HTML page. If you have made changes only to the HTML page and the images are already on the server, there is no reason to send the images again, so you would click No. If you have modified an image or added an image to the page, you would click Yes.

Click **Yes**. All the files in the Local Files pane are copied to the remote site on the Files panel. This option could take a long time, depending on the size of your site, so be prepared to wait. If you have only made changes to a few files, you might find it quicker to manually select the updated files and upload them.

5. Click the **Expand/Collapse** button to restore the Files panel to single-pane view. Close Dreamweaver.

Connecting to a Remote FTP Site

FTP access is commonly used to get files from or put files on a remote site. Consult your network administrator to set the options explained below correctly. Choose FTP from the pop-up menu in the Sharing Files section of the Site Definition Wizard as shown in Figure 6-11.

FIGURE 6-11
FTP settings in Site Definition dialog box

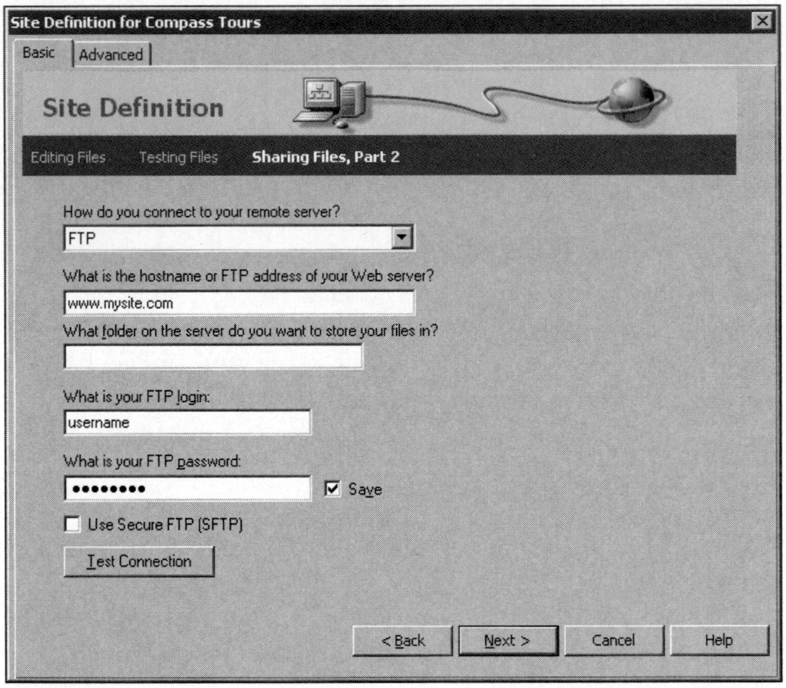

- **FTP hostname:** The host name of your Web server: for example, *ftp.everyone.com* or *www.mysite.com*.

- **Host folder:** The directory on the remote site where documents visible to the public are stored. Ask your FTP service provider what directory, if any, you should use.

- **Login and Password:** Your login name and password for the server. If you deselect the Save option, you'll be prompted for a password when you connect to the remote site.

SUMMARY

In this lesson, you learned to:

- Understand the purpose and uses of the Files panel.
- Use the Files panel to perform site management functions.
- Customize the Files panel.
- Set up a connection to a remote site.
- Copy files to and from a remote site.

MACROMEDIA FIREWORKS MX

Project

BITMAP EDITING

OBJECTIVES

Upon completion of this lesson, you should be able to:

- Define the difference between bitmap and vector graphics.
- Identify elements of the Fireworks interface.
- Create and set up a new Fireworks document.
- Make selections in Bitmap mode.
- Edit bitmap images.

Bitmap Versus Vector Graphics

Macromedia Fireworks MX 2004 functions as both a bitmap editor and a vector drawing program. Most images on the Web are bitmap graphics (GIF, JPEG, or PNG files). Bitmaps record information pixel by pixel and color by color. The size of a bitmap is determined by the number of pixels and colors used to define the image. Creating and editing bitmaps has its limitations. As with paint on a canvas, you need to completely remove a mistake. When editing bitmaps, you need to completely erase or "paint" over the mistake.

Vector graphics, on the other hand, use mathematical formulas to describe the image. They provide more precise control when creating the image and allow for more advanced editing and modification.

By combining these drawing methods in the same application, Fireworks gives you a very powerful and versatile set of tools. You get the features of photo editing and paint programs, along with the precision of a vector drawing program, and your finished graphics are optimized for use in Web pages.

Fireworks Editing Modes

Fireworks knows whether you want to create and edit vector objects, bitmap objects, or text, based on the current tool or selection. The Tools panel is divided into clearly labeled sections for easy tool selection.

Floating and Tabbed Panels

Panels provide easy access to controls that help you edit selected objects or elements of the document. Panels let you work on frames, layers, symbols, color swatches, and more. Each panel group is draggable, and you can group panels together in custom arrangements. By default, the panels are docked to the right side of the workspace. You can undock panel groups, add panels to a group, rearrange the order of docked panel groups, and collapse and close panel groups. To undock a panel group, drag the gripper in the upper-left corner of the panel group's title bar, as shown in Figure 1-1.

FIGURE 1-1
Fireworks 2004 panels

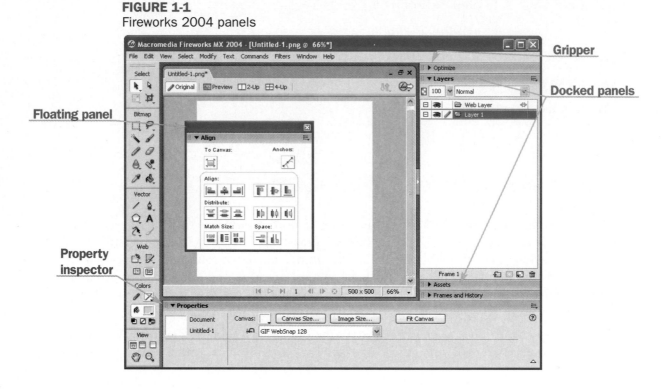

Many of the panels are divided into two or more tabs. You can create your own arrangement by selecting a panel or an individual tab, choosing Group [panel or tab name] With from the panel Options menu, and then selecting the new panel to group with. You can collapse and expand panel groups by clicking the panel group's title.

The Property Inspector

The Property inspector displays options that change according to the current object or tool selection. Open a document, and the Property inspector displays document properties. Choose a tool, and it displays tool options. Select a vector object, and it displays options such as stroke and fill. You can change these and other options right from the Property inspector. By default, the Property inspector is visible, but you can hide or show it by clicking the Window menu and then clicking Properties.

The Fireworks Tools Panel

The Fireworks Tools panel is divided into clearly labeled sections for easy tool selection, as shown in Figure 1-2. If the Tools panel is not visible, you can display it by clicking the Window menu and then clicking Tools. To select a tool, just click it. If a tool has a small black triangle in the lower-right corner, it is part of a group of tools; click and hold over the tool to access the pop-up tool group. Table 1-1 lists the tools and the tools in their tool group (if they have one), and a description of each.

FIGURE 1-2
Fireworks Tools panel

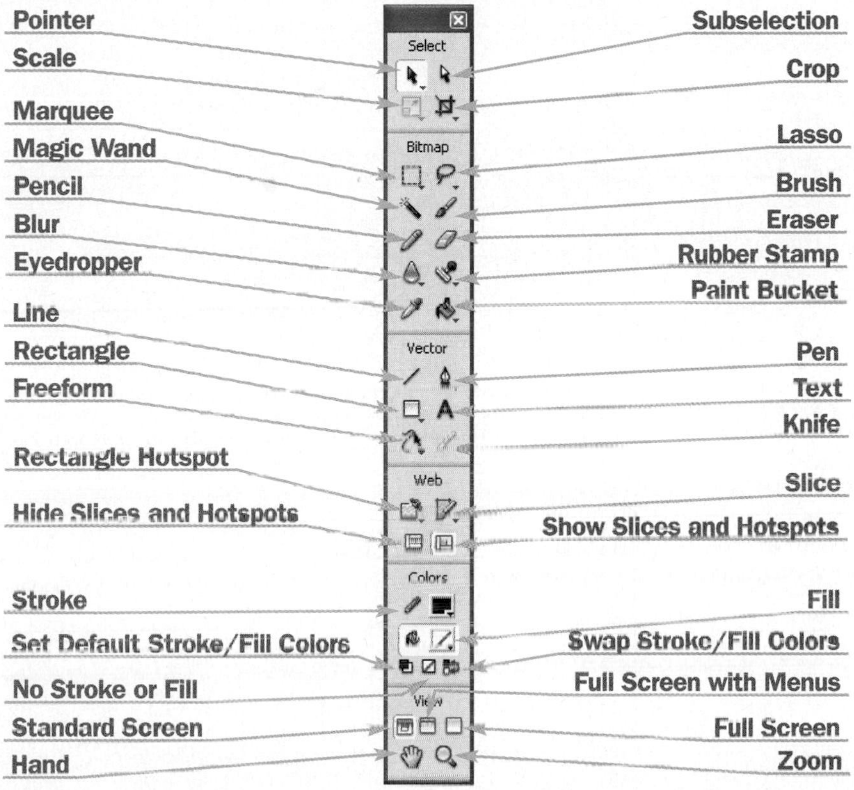

TABLE 1-1
Description of tools

SELECTION TOOLS	DESCRIPTION
Pointer	Selects and moves objects on the screen.
Select Behind	Selects an object behind the currently selected object.
Subselection	Selects and moves paths on the screen, selects an object within a group, displays points on a path, and selects points.
Scale	Resizes an object horizontally, vertically, or proportionally.
Skew	Transforms an object by slanting it along the horizontal or vertical axis or along both axes.
Distort	Changes the size and proportion of an object.

TABLE 1-1
Description of tools (continued)

SELECTION TOOLS	DESCRIPTION
Crop	Discards portions of a document.
Export Area	Exports a portion of a document.
BITMAP TOOLS	**DESCRIPTION**
Marquee	Selects a rectangular area of pixels.
Oval Marquee	Selects an elliptical area of pixels.
Lasso	
Polygon Lasso	Use these to select an irregularly shaped area of pixels.
Magic Wand	Selects an area of similarly colored pixels in an image.
Brush	Paints a brush stroke using the color and effects selected in the Brush tool Property inspector.
Pencil	Draws one-pixel freeform or constrained lines. If you zoom in, you can also use the Pencil tool to edit single pixels.
Eraser	Erases the pixels so they are transparent and so background objects and the canvas show through.
Blur	Decreases the focus of selected areas of the image.
Sharpen	Sharpens the focus of selected areas of the image.
Dodge	Lightens part of an image.
Burn	Darkens part of an image.
Smudge	Picks up color and pushes it in the direction you drag.
Rubber Stamp	Allows you to clone one area of an image to another.
Replace Color	Replaces one color with another, while keeping the tonal range of the original color.
Red Eye Removal	Changes the colors of pixels within a certain range of red to neutral grays and blacks.
Eyedropper	Picks up color from anywhere in a document to designate a new stroke or fill color.
Paint Bucket	Fills objects with solid colors.
Gradient	Fills objects with gradients or patterns.
VECTOR TOOLS	**DESCRIPTION**
Line	Draws straight lines with editable paths.
Pen	Draws vector objects by plotting points along a path.
Vector Path	Paints free-form lines with editable paths.
Redraw Path	Redraws or extends a segment of a selected path while retaining the path's stroke, fill, and effect characteristics.

TABLE 1-1
Description of tools (continued)

VECTOR TOOLS	DESCRIPTION
Rectangle Ellipse Polygon Smart Shapes	Use the Rectangle and other tools in this group to quickly draw basic shapes. Only rectangles are drawn as grouped objects, which allows you to adjust corner roundness after drawing. In all other instances, basic shapes draw paths. To move a rectangle corner point independently, you must ungroup the rectangle or use the Subselect tool. Smart Shapes are new in Fireworks 2004. They can also be found in this tool group. Smart Shapes are complex shapes you can modify by using special control points.
Text	Creates text blocks and selects and edits existing text.
Freeform	Pulls or pushes a selected path or part of a path to reshape it. Fireworks automatically adds, moves, or deletes points along a path as you edit it. With the Freeform tool selected, you can use the Property inspector to control the size of the push pointer. Use the arrow keys (left or right) to resize the push or pull pointer as you draw. You can also press 1 to make the pointer smaller or 2 to make the pointer larger.
Reshape Area	Modifies the shape of a vector object when you select the Reshape Area tool and drag across a selected path. The Reshape Area tool contains inner and outer circles. The outer circle controls the gravitational pull or size of the area that is reshaped. The inner circle controls the strength of the tool. A large inner circle produces a wide blunt shape. A narrow inner circle produces a narrower shape.
Path Scrubber—additive Path Scrubber—subtractive	Use these to change the appearance of a path. Using varying pressure or speed, you can change a path's stroke properties. These properties include stroke size, angle, ink amount, scatter, hue, lightness, and saturation.
Knife	Splits a path into two or more paths.
WEB TOOLS	DESCRIPTION
Rectangle Hotspot Circle Hotspot Polygon Hotspot	Use the Rectangle Hotspot and the other tools in the group to draw a hotspot on an image (hotspots are Web objects that specify interactive areas in a Web graphic). When exported as HTML and images, hotspots become image maps.
Slice Polygon Slice	Use these to create slices from an existing graphic. Slices cut an image into sections so you can apply rollover behaviors, animation, and Uniform Resource Locator (URL) links to parts of the overall image.
Hide Slices and Hotspots	Hides slices and hotspots while you work.
Show Slices and Hotspots	Displays slices and hotspots in the workspace.

TABLE 1-1
Description of tools (continued)

COLOR TOOLS	DESCRIPTION
Stroke Color	Shows the color currently set for the stroke.
Fill Color	Shows the color currently set for the fill.
Set Default Stroke/Fill Colors	Restores the color boxes to the default colors of black for the stroke and white for the fill.
No Stroke or Fill	Removes the stroke and fill of the selected object.
Swap Stroke/Fill Colors	Swaps the stroke and fill colors.
VIEW TOOLS	**DESCRIPTION**
Standard Screen mode	Sets the Standard Screen mode. Use the view mode buttons in the View area of the Tools panel to choose from any of three view modes to control the layout of your workspace. Standard is the default.
Full Screen with Menus mode	Sets a maximized Document window view against a gray background with menus, toolbars, scroll bars, and panels visible.
Full Screen mode	Sets a maximized Document window view against a black background with no menus, toolbars, or title bars visible.
Hand	Pans the document and views hidden areas when you are zoomed in and the document is not entirely visible.
Zoom	Moves in and out to view more or less of the workspace.

Setting Up a Document

When you begin a new document, you are presented with the New Document dialog box. This is where you set the size and color of your canvas and the image size for the new document. Each new document defaults to the settings you established in your most recently saved document, unless you have copied an image to the Clipboard. In that case, the Width and Height settings match the dimensions of the copied image.

S TEP-BY-STEP 1.1

Setting Up a New Document

1. Start Fireworks. Click the **File** menu, and then click **New** to create a new empty document. The New Document dialog box opens, as shown in Figure 1-3.

FIGURE 1-3
New Document dialog box

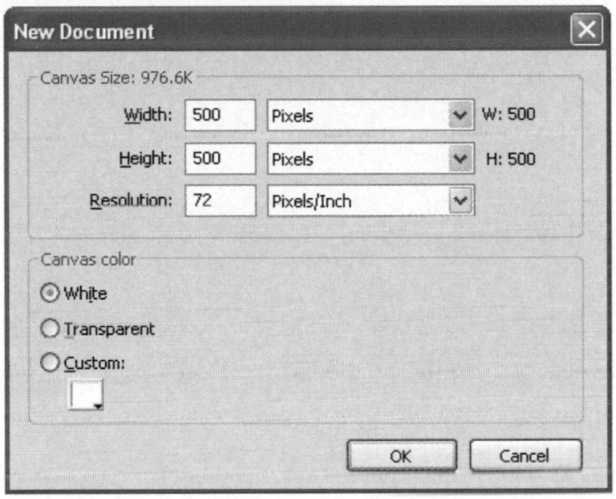

2. You can set the canvas size in the New Document dialog box, using pixels, inches, or centimeters. Set the canvas size to **554** pixels wide by **354** pixels high.

   In the New Document dialog box, the resolution is set to 72 pixels per inch. This is the default for Web graphics. (You can also change the resolution by selecting **Image Size** on the Property inspector or by clicking the **Modify** menu, pointing to **Canvas**, and then clicking **Image Size**. This opens the Image Size dialog box.)

3. The Canvas Color is the background color of your document. You can choose a white canvas, a transparent canvas, or a custom color canvas. To display the color palette, click the **Custom Color** box beneath the Custom button.

Hot Tip

You can also change the canvas size by selecting **Canvas Size** on the Property inspector, or by clicking the **Modify** menu, pointing to **Canvas**, and then clicking **Canvas Size**. You can also use the Crop tool to crop the document, or click the **Modify** menu, point to **Canvas**, and then click **Trim Canvas** to trim the empty edges of the canvas. Or you can click the **Modify** menu, point to **Canvas**, and then click **Fit Canvas** to expand the canvas to fit all objects in the document if any objects are in the gray area outside the canvas right of the Custom button. Finally, the Property inspector for the document has a handy Fit Canvas button in it.

STEP-BY-STEP 1.1 Continued

The pointer becomes an eyedropper you can use to select colors from anywhere on the screen, including the color pop-up window, as shown in Figure 1-4.

FIGURE 1-4
Custom Color box and palette in the New Document dialog box

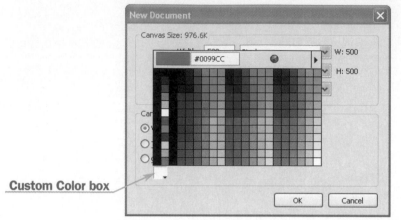

Custom Color box

4. Use the eyedropper to select a new color. Then click **OK**. The canvas color changes.

5. Make sure the **Pointer** tool is selected on the Tools panel. Then click the **Canvas** color box on the Property inspector, as shown in Figure 1-5. In the color pop-up window, select the color white. You can also change the canvas color by clicking the **Modify** menu, pointing to **Canvas**, and then clicking **Canvas Color**. This opens the Canvas Color dialog box.

> **Note** ☑
>
> The color you choose as the canvas color is also the color of the background page when you export to HTML. If your canvas color is set to Transparent, then the transparent background will export as a white background unless you select Index or Alpha Transparency on the Optimize panel or in Export Preview or unless you set the Matte color to some color other than white on the Optimize panel.

FIGURE 1-5
Document Property inspector

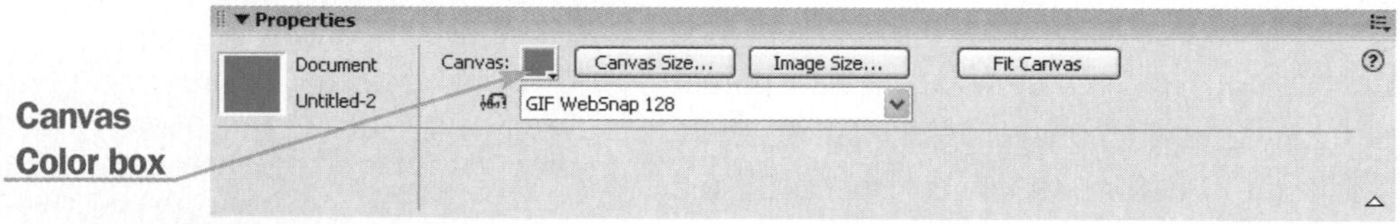

Canvas
Color box

6. Click the **File** menu and then click **Close**. If you are asked to save the file, click **No** (Windows) or **Don't Save** (Macintosh). Remain in this screen for the next Step-by-Step.

Editing Bitmap Objects

Fireworks provides a wealth of tools for creating new bitmap graphics and for editing existing ones. To edit an existing bitmap image, you must first open or import the file you want to edit. Fireworks recognizes the following bitmap file formats: Photoshop native files (PSD), TIFF, JPEG, GIF, BMP, PICT (Macintosh), PNG, and Targa.

STEP-BY-STEP 1.2

Editing a Bitmap Graphic

1. Click the **File** menu, click **Open**, and open the **girl_pumpkin1.png** file from the data files supplied with this course.

2. Click the **File** menu, click **Save As**, name the file **girl_pumpkin1**, followed by your initials, and click **Save**. Note that the .png file extension is added by default to the name of the file.

3. Select the **Pointer** tool from the Tools panel if necessary, and double-click the image. Double-clicking a bitmap image switches Fireworks to Bitmap mode.

4. To exit Bitmap mode, click the **Exit Bitmap Mode** button (the red circle with a white X) at the bottom of the Document window, as shown in Figure 1-6. You can also press **Escape** (Windows and Macintosh), **Ctrl + Shift + E** (Windows), **Command + Shift + E** (Macintosh), or **Command + period** (Macintosh). Remain in this screen for the next Step-by-Step.

FIGURE 1-6
Exit Bitmap Mode button

Exit Bitmap
Mode button |◁ ▷ ▷| 1   ◁| |▷ ⊗ | 366 x 555 | 100% ▾ |

Selecting Pixels

Bitmap graphics are made from a collection of colored picture elements called *pixels*. To make changes to a bitmap graphic, you can edit one pixel at a time, or you can select and edit several pixels. To work with bitmaps successfully, you must learn to select the exact part of the graphic you want to edit. Fireworks provides tools and commands for selecting groups of pixels. For example, you can use the Magic Wand tool to select a range of pixels with a similar color, such as the sky in a photograph. When you make a selection, a floating marquee indicates the area that is selected.

After you draw the selection marquee, you can manipulate it by moving it, adding to it, or basing another selection on it. You can edit the pixels inside the selection, apply filters to the pixels, or erase pixels without affecting the rest of your document.

Figure 1-7 shows the Bitmap section of the Tools panel. You might want to review the Bitmap Tools section of Table 1-1.

FIGURE 1-7
Bitmap portion of the Tools panel, showing selection tools for image editing

Using the Marquee Tools

The Bitmap section of the Tools panel contains the marquee selection tools. The Marquee and Oval Marquee tools are used for selecting specific shapes in the image. You can modify the style and edge of the marquee tools, using the settings on the Property inspector shown in Figure 1-8. For the Fixed Size style, type the exact width and height in pixels for the selection. For the Fixed Ratio style, type the proportion of width to height before making the selection. You can also change the appearance of the edges of the selection. You learn more about this in the section *Controlling the Edge of a Selection* later in this lesson.

FIGURE 1-8
Property inspector for the Marquee tool

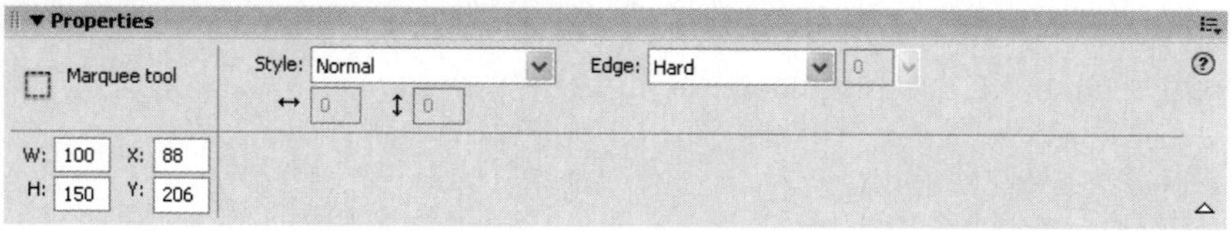

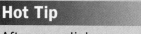

S TEP-BY-STEP 1.3

Working with the Marquee Tools

1. The **girl_pumpkin1.png** file should still be open. Select the **Marquee** tool from the Tools panel. Click the bitmap object at any spot where you want to begin your selection and then drag to the opposite corner to define the area. The area within the marquee is selected. You can now modify, move, or delete pixels.

2. To deselect, click outside the selection. You can also click the **Select** menu and then click **Deselect**.

> **Hot Tip**
>
> After you click, you can hold down **Shift** to constrain the shape of the selection. You can also hold down **Alt** (Windows) or **Option** (Macintosh) to draw the marquee shape from the center outward. Hold down **Shift-Alt** (Windows) or **Shift-Option** (Macintosh) to constrain the shape of the marquee as you select from the center outward.

3. Select the **Oval Marquee** tool from the Tools panel. To switch between the Marquee and Oval Marquee tools, click the **Marquee** tool to reveal the pop-up menu, and then click the tool you want to use. You can also press **M** to toggle between the marquee tools.

STEP-BY-STEP 1.3 Continued

4. Drag to draw a selection marquee around the girl's face.

5. Hold down **Shift**. A plus sign appears on the pointer.

6. Drag to draw a second marquee around the pumpkin. Be careful not to overlap the selections. Both areas are selected.

7. Make sure you still have selection marquees around the girl's face and the pumpkin.

8. Hold down **Shift**. A plus sign appears on the pointer.

9. Drag to draw a new marquee that overlaps the current selections. The original marquee expands to include the new selection, as shown in Figure 1-9. Click outside the image to deselect it.

FIGURE 1-9
Expanded selection

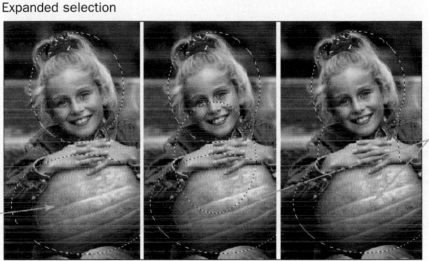

You can extend your selection by holding down the Shift key and overlapping selections

You can select multiple areas by using the Shift key

10. Use the rectangle Marquee tool to select the entire girl and the pumpkin.

11. Hold down **Alt** (Windows) or **Option** (Macintosh). A minus sign appears on the pointer.

STEP-BY-STEP 1.3 Continued

12. Drag to draw a new marquee that overlaps a portion of the current selection, as shown in Figure 1-10. The overlapped area is removed from the selection. Click outside the image to deselect it.

FIGURE 1-10
Modified selection

Using the Alt key (Windows) or Option key (Macintosh), you can subtract from a selection by overlapping selections

13. Use the rectangle Marquee tool to select the pumpkin.

14. Move the pointer within the selection. The pointer appears as a triangle with a small rectangle below it.

15. Drag the marquee until it surrounds the girl's face. This moves just the selection, not the pixels within the selection.

16. Press the right arrow key several times. (You can also use the up, down, and left arrow keys.) The selection moves a distance of one pixel each time you press an arrow key. Click outside the image to deselect it.

Hot Tip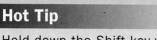

Hold down the Shift key while you use the arrow keys to move the selection 10 pixels at a time.

17. Use the rectangle Marquee tool to select the entire girl and the pumpkin.

18. Move the pointer within the selection and hold down **Ctrl + Alt** (Windows) or **Command + Option** (Macintosh). The pointer changes to a double-triangle pointer.

19. Drag the selection to the left while holding down the modifier keys. A copy of the image moves within the selection.

20. Click the **Edit** menu and then click **Undo Duplicate**. Click outside the image to deselect it.

STEP-BY-STEP 1.3 Continued

21. Switch to the Oval Marquee tool. Hold down **Alt** (Windows) or **Option** (Macintosh), click the girl's nose, and then drag to draw an ellipse around the girl's head and shoulders from the center of the ellipse, as shown in Figure 1-11.

FIGURE 1-11
Oval Marquee selection drawn from the center outward

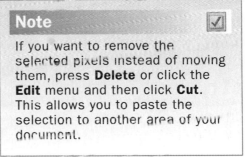

22. Move the pointer within the selection and hold down **Ctrl** (Windows) or **Command** (Macintosh). The pointer changes to a triangle and a pair of scissors.

23. Drag the selection while holding down the modifier key. The selected pixels of the bitmap object move from their original position. When you release, the moved pixels are pasted in the new location. This leaves a transparent hole in the position of the original pixels.

> **Note** ☑
>
> If you want to remove the selected pixels instead of moving them, press **Delete** or click the **Edit** menu and then click **Cut**. This allows you to paste the selection to another area of your document.

24. Click the **Edit** menu and then click **Undo Move**.

25. Save the file by clicking the **File** menu, and then clicking **Save**. Remain in this screen for the next Step-by-Step.

Fireworks provides many options and tools for enhancing and modifying the look of an image. In the next Step-by-Step, you use the Feather option to fade and soften the background of the image, and you use the Crop tool to remove portions of the image.

STEP-BY-STEP 1.4

Feathering and Cropping an Image

1. If necessary, use the Oval Marquee tool to draw an ellipse around the girl's head and shoulders, as shown in Figure 1-11.

STEP-BY-STEP 1.4 Continued

2. Click the **Select** menu, and then click **Feather**. In the Feather Selection dialog box, enter **25** in the Radius box, and click **OK**, as shown in Figure 1-12. (You won't be able to see the feathering until you delete the background.)

FIGURE 1-12
Feather Selection dialog box

3. Click the **Select** menu, and then click **Select Inverse** to select the background.

4. Press **Delete** to delete the background. This isolates the face with a soft edge.

5. Click the **Select** menu, and then click **Deselect** to deselect the image. Your results should look like Figure 1-13.

FIGURE 1-13
Final results of feathering

6. Select the **Crop** tool from the Tools panel. The Crop tool lets you crop unwanted parts of the canvas (review Figure 1-2 and Table 1-1).

7. Drag to select the feathered image. Handles appear along the borders of the crop marks. You can use these to fine-tune your selection.

8. Position the pointer within the image and the crop marks, and double-click to crop the image.

9. Save and close the file. Leave Fireworks open for the next Step-by-Step.

Using the Magic Wand

With the Magic Wand tool (review Figure 1-2 and Table 1-1), you can select neighboring pixels of the same or a similar color. The level of similarity depends on the tolerance level you set on the tool's Property inspector. The lowest level, zero, selects one color; you pick the exact color with the tip of the tool. The highest setting, 255, allows the greatest range of colors to be selected. The default tolerance level of 32 is generally a good starting point. Instead of increasing the tolerance level, try adding to the selection by holding down Shift and clicking another color.

S TEP-BY-STEP 1.5

Using the Magic Wand Tool

1. Open the **flower1.png** file from the data files supplied with this course. Save it as **flower1**, followed by your initials.

2. Select the **Magic Wand** tool on the Tools panel. The Property inspector now displays the settings for the Magic Wand tool, as shown in Figure 1-14.

FIGURE 1-14
Property inspector for the Magic Wand tool

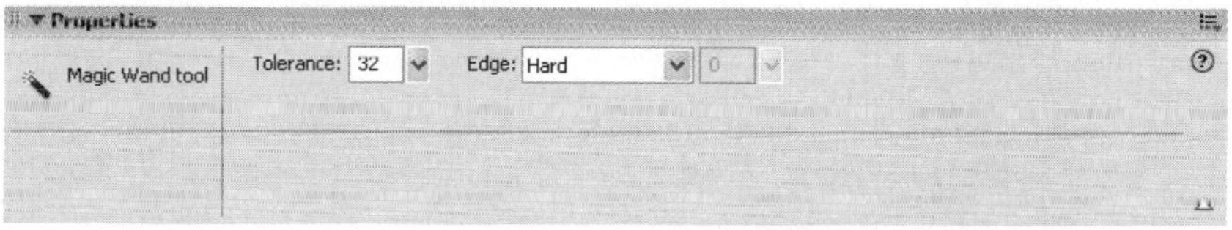

3. Highlight the value in the Tolerance box on the Property inspector and enter **255**.

4. Click anywhere in the blue sky area of the picture. A wide range of colors is selected.

5. Press **Delete**. Just about everything but the flowers is deleted.

6. Click the **Edit** menu, and then click **Undo Delete**. The picture returns to normal.

7. Click the **Select** menu, and then click **Deselect** to deselect the image. You will now try a different tolerance value.

8. Highlight the value in the Tolerance box and enter **32**.

9. Click anywhere in the blue sky area of the picture. A much narrower range of colors is selected.

10. Click the **Select** menu, and then click **Deselect** to undo this selection. Now you will make a selection based on similar colors.

11. Click one of the yellow petals on the large sunflower.

12. To add to your selection based on color similarity, click the **Select** menu, and then click **Select Similar**. Any similar colors in the image are added to the selection.

STEP-BY-STEP 1.5 Continued

13. Click the **Select** menu, and then click **Deselect** to undo the selection.

14. Save the file and remain in this screen for the next Step-by-Step.

Controlling the Edge of a Selection

You can change the appearance of the edge of a selection by selecting Hard, Anti-Alias, or Feather from the Edge menu on the Property inspector. A hard edge on any shape that is not a horizontal or vertical edge creates a stair-step effect, as shown in Figure 1-15. This is the result of trying to create a curve or a diagonal line from square pixels; it can't be done. Anti-aliasing makes the edges appear smooth by adding lighter-colored pixels on the edges. Feathering expands the border of the selection and applies a blur to the extra pixels in the border. If you select Feather, set the amount of the blur with the Feather slider control. You should make your edge choice before you make your selection. After the selection is made, you can't use the Property inspector to change the edge (although you can use commands on the Select menu to make certain changes).

FIGURE 1-15
Stair-step effect on a diagonal line

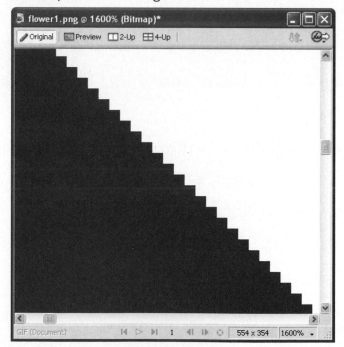

Using the Lasso Tools

The Lasso tool creates a free-form selection boundary around an area. Wherever you drag, you draw a selection outline. When you release, the selection area closes automatically. To close the selection area yourself, return to the first point of the selection. As you come close to the beginning, the pointer displays a small square, as shown in Figure 1-16. To close the selection, release when you see the square.

FIGURE 1-16
Lasso pointer in the document

Lasso

STEP-BY-STEP 1.6

Using the Lasso Tool

1. The **flower1** file should still be open. Select the **Lasso** tool on the Tools panel. The Property inspector displays the settings for the Lasso tool.

2. Locate the butterfly on the large sunflower. Drag to trace the edge of the butterfly. (Don't worry about the antennae.) When you have completely surrounded the butterfly, you will see a small square. Release to close the selection.

3. To fine-tune the selection, select the **Zoom** tool from the View section of the Tools panel.

4. Position the pointer within the selected butterfly. The pointer changes to a plus sign. Click on the butterfly until the image is at 400% magnification, as shown in the Set Magnification pop-up menu in Figure 1-17.

FIGURE 1-17
The Set Magnification pop-up menu

Set Magnification
pop-up menu

5. Hold down **Alt** (Windows) or **Option** (Macintosh) and the pointer changes to the Zoom Out tool with a minus sign on it. Click until the image is displayed at 300%.

6. Switch back to the **Lasso** tool.

7. You now want to add the antennae to your selection. Hold down **Shift**. A plus sign appears next to the pointer. Drag the Lasso tool around the area you want to add to your selection, and then release.

8. Now, you want to delete portions outside the butterfly image. Hold down **Alt** (Windows) or **Option** (Macintosh). A minus sign appears next to the pointer. Drag the Lasso tool around the area you want to delete from the selection, and then release.

9. Continue adding or subtracting pixels from the marquee until just the butterfly is selected.

STEP-BY-STEP 1.6 Continued

10. Click the **Set Magnification** pop-up menu on the status bar of the document and choose **100%**.

11. Switch to the **Pointer** tool, hold down **Alt** (Windows) or **Option** (Macintosh), and drag the selected butterfly to the right edge of the large sunflower. Then release to copy the butterfly.

    You can create fun effects by flipping a selection.

12. Make sure the copied butterfly is still selected.

13. Click the **Modify** menu, point to **Transform**, and then click **Flip Horizontal**. The butterfly is flipped.

14. Deselect the image and save the file. Remain in this screen for the next Step-by-Step.

> **Hot Tip** ⊚
>
> If you accidentally undo a complicated selection, just click the **Edit** menu, and use the Undo command to recover your selection.

> **Note** ☑
>
> The Polygon Lasso tool draws straight-line segments. Instead of dragging the tool to make the selection, click for your first point, release, move to a new location, and click again to define a line segment. As with the Lasso tool, you'll see a small square by the pointer when close to the beginning point. Click when you see the square to close the selection, or double-click to close the selection, even if you have not moved your pointer back to the beginning point.

As with the Magic Wand tool, you can control the edges of the selection you draw with the Lasso tool. You can read about this in the section *Controlling the Edge of a Selection* earlier in this lesson.

Using the Rubber Stamp Tool

The Rubber Stamp tool (review Figure 1-2 and Table 1-1) works well for retouching an image or copying a portion of an image.

When you use the Rubber Stamp tool, you are, in effect, painting a copy of some area of a bitmap object onto another area of the bitmap object. Here the process will be referred to as *cloning*. First, you have to designate the area that you plan to clone: your set point.

In the following exercise, you clone the small sunflower at the left of the image.

STEP-BY-STEP 1.7

Using the Rubber Stamp Tool

1. The **flower1** file should still be open. Select the **Rubber Stamp** tool on the Tools panel.

STEP-BY-STEP 1.7 Continued

2. On the Property inspector, make sure that **Source Aligned** is selected and that Use Entire Document is *not* selected, as shown in Figure 1-18.

FIGURE 1-18
Rubber Stamp tool Property inspector

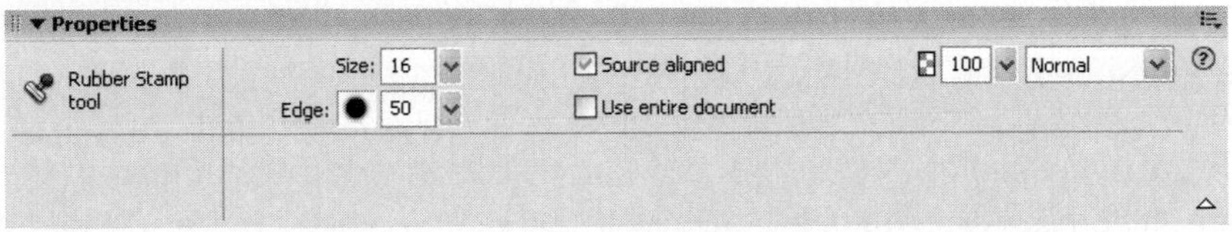

3. On the Property inspector, set Size to **10** and Edge to **90**. This creates a small stamp with a soft edge, allowing you to clone the small edges of the flower and blend the new image with the surrounding pixels.

4. Move the pointer over the center of the small sunflower at the lower left of the image. Hold down **Alt** (Windows) or **Option** (Macintosh) and click to mark the set point. A cross-hair marks the set point.

5. Position the pointer to the left of the small sunflower and drag to begin cloning. Try using small circular motions and work from the center outward as you clone. Since you have selected the Source Aligned option, the relationship (distance) between the original cloned area and the location of the new image remains constant. If you move the pointer to a new location, you can see this relationship. As you clone, a cross-hair appears above the set point and the cloned image appears where you drag.

6. Deselect **Source Aligned** on the Property inspector. The set point will remain the center of the small sunflower. You can now clone the sunflower to another area of the image.

7. Draw another sunflower just above the green leaves along the right edge of the picture. You may need to scroll to bring this area of the image into view.

8. Save the **flower1** file and remain in this screen for the next Step-by-Step.

Using the Brush Tool

You use the Brush tool in Bitmap mode to paint new pixels. You use the settings on the Property inspector to create the type of brush you want to paint with.

> **Hot Tip** ⊚
>
> If the document includes vector objects along with the bitmap, you can select **Use Entire Document** to clone the vector object as well as the bitmap image.

S TEP-BY-STEP 1.8

Using the Brush Tool

1. Select the **Brush** tool from the Tools panel and drag anywhere on the image. As you drag, pixels are replaced with the color indicated on the Property inspector.

2. Click the **Edit** menu, and then click **Undo Brush Tool**.

3. On the Property inspector (see Figure 1-19), click the arrow on the **Stroke category** box, point to **Basic**, and then click **Soft Rounded**. Highlight the value in the Tip size box and enter **5**. Click the **Color** box and select white. Highlight the value in the Edge softness box and enter **90**. Highlight the value in the Opacity box and enter **30%**.

FIGURE 1-19
Brush tool Property inspector

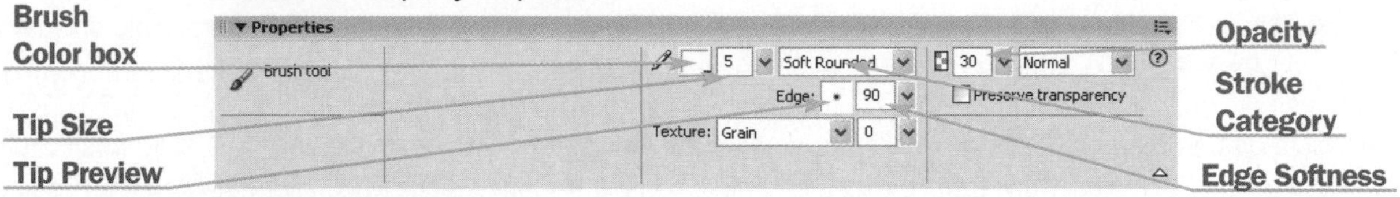

Brush
Color box
Tip Size
Tip Preview

Opacity
Stroke Category
Edge Softness

4. Click several times along the top of the image (you might need to scroll to bring this part of the image into view). This paints small round brush strokes on the image at 30% opacity, creating the visual effect of stars.

5. Save and close the **flower1** file.

Review of Selection Options

This lesson introduced you to several methods for selecting pixels in a bitmap graphic. Fireworks includes a Select menu with a comprehensive list of selection options, as shown in Figure 1-20. The following list provides an overview of the commands on the Select menu.

FIGURE 1-20
Select menu commands

- **Select All:** In Bitmap mode, selects all of the pixels in a bitmap object on a selected layer. In Vector mode, selects all visible objects on all layers.

- **Deselect:** Removes the selection marquee.

- **Superselect:** Selects an object's entire group or mask group when the object has already been selected by the Pointer tool.

- **Subselect:** Selects all of the objects individually within a group selected by the Pointer tool.

- **Select Similar:** Within a single bitmap object, creates an additional selection around colors bearing a similarity to colors in the existing selection. The Magic Wand tool (and, thereafter, Select Similar) can also select transparent pixels or the space outside of a bitmap object.

- **Select Inverse:** Selects all pixels not in the current selection and deselects the currently selected pixels.

- **Feather:** Feathers the edges of the selection.

- **Expand Marquee:** Expands the selection by a set number of pixels.

- **Contract Marquee:** Contracts the selection by a set number of pixels.

- **Border Marquee:** Creates an additional marquee to frame an existing marquee at a specified width.

- **Smooth Marquee:** Smoothes the selection by a set number of pixels.

- **Save Bitmap Selection:** Remembers the current selection within the document.

- **Restore Bitmap Selection:** Restores the last-saved selection.

Web Design Skills

VIEWING THE GAMMA SETTING

When creating graphics for the Web, how do you make the color look good on all machines? This is a nearly impossible task. Monitors are usually not calibrated accurately, nor are they calibrated the same from one machine to another. To make matters worse, on different computer platforms, shades of colors appear differently.

The *gamma setting* on your computer affects the apparent brightness and contrast of the monitor display. The gamma setting for the Macintosh is lower than that on Windows machines. This makes images created on the Macintosh appear darker when viewed on a Windows PC. Knowing this, you have to compensate as you create your images. If you are designing on a Macintosh, create your images a little lighter; on a PC, create them a little darker.

To make your job easier, Fireworks has a built-in function for viewing the gamma setting on the other platform. If you are using Windows, click the View menu, and then click Macintosh Gamma. This renders the image to simulate its display on a Macintosh. If you are using a Macintosh, click the View menu, and then click Windows Gamma. This renders the image to simulate its display on a PC.

SUMMARY

In this lesson, you learned to:

- Define the difference between bitmap and vector graphics.
- Identify elements of the Fireworks interface.
- Create and set up a new Fireworks document.
- Make selections in Bitmap mode.
- Edit bitmap images.

WORKING WITH VECTOR GRAPHICS

OBJECTIVES

Upon completion of this lesson, you should be able to:

- Combine simple shapes to create complex objects.
- Select points and paths in vector graphics.
- Use the ruler and guides for drawing.
- Draw with the basic drawing tools.
- Rotate objects.
- Use the History panel to save steps as commands.
- Use the Knife tool to cut paths.
- Scale objects.
- Apply stroke and fill settings.
- Use the Eyedropper tool to sample color.
- Trim the canvas and fit the canvas to your objects.

Making Selections in Vector Mode

In this lesson, you use the vector drawing tools to create a simple logo. Before you begin drawing from scratch, it's important that you have a few basic skills for selecting vector graphics. To gain these skills, you will work with a simple vector object.

Macromedia Fireworks MX 2004 provides a few tools for making selections in Vector mode: the Pointer tool, the Subselection tool, and the Select Behind tool, which are shown in Figure 2-1. A vector graphic is made up of two or more points that connect to form a path. You can use the Pointer tool to select the path, the Subselection tool to select the points on the path, and the Select Behind tool to select an object that is hidden behind another object.

FIGURE 2-1
Pointer and selection tools

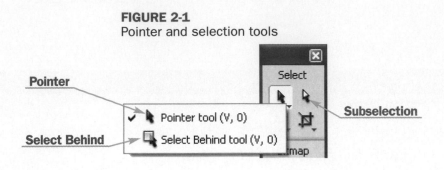

S TEP-BY-STEP 2.1

Selecting a Grouped Object

1. Open the **butterfly2.png** file from the data files provided with this course. This file contains a vector graphic of a butterfly. This graphic is stored on the layer named Butterfly. (*Hint:* To display the Layers panel, click the Window menu and click Layers.) The butterfly is a single graphic made from several smaller drawings that have been grouped. This file also contains colored rectangles on layers that are behind the butterfly. (You will learn more about grouping and layers in Lesson 3.)

2. Select the **Pointer** tool and position the pointer over the butterfly. When you point to this graphic, four red selection handles appear.

3. Click the butterfly. The red handles are replaced by blue handles, indicating that the graphic is selected. Remain in this screen for the next Step-by-Step.

Notice that when you click the butterfly, only the butterfly is selected and not the colored rectangles. This is because the colored rectangles are on layers "behind" the Butterfly layer. The butterfly is made up of multiple objects, but only one object is selected here, because the objects that make up the butterfly have been grouped. This is indicated for you on the Property inspector. The selected object is called Group (79), which tells you 79 different objects are grouped as one. If you view the Layers panel to the right of the graphic, you will see how each object or group is stacked.

S TEP-BY-STEP 2.2

Selecting Part of a Grouped Object

1. Choose the **Subselection** tool from the Tools panel.

STEP-BY-STEP 2.2 Continued

2. Move the pointer over different parts of the butterfly. As you roll over different parts of the graphic with the Subselect tool, the individual shapes that make up the butterfly are highlighted in red.

3. Click in the middle of the graphic and notice the blue line (the path) and the points on the path. Try clicking different parts of the butterfly.

4. Click the **Select** menu, and then click **Deselect**. Remain in this screen for the next Step-by-Step.

You can use the Subselection tool to select the parts that make up a grouped object.

STEP-BY-STEP 2.3

Selecting Objects Hidden Behind Other Objects

1. Choose the Select Behind tool from the Tools panel by clicking the arrow on the **Pointer** tool and then clicking **Select Behind**.

2. Click the butterfly graphic. Blue handles appear, indicating that the butterfly graphic is selected. The Butterfly layer is also highlighted on the Layers panel.

3. Click the butterfly graphic again. Now the orange rectangle is selected, and the Orange Frame layer is highlighted on the Layers panel.

4. Click the butterfly graphic again. Now the green rectangle is selected, and the Green Frame layer is highlighted on the Layers panel.

5. Click the butterfly graphic again. Now the black rectangle is selected, and the Black Frame layer is highlighted on the Layers panel.

6. Click the butterfly graphic again. You've clicked through every layer in the file. The butterfly is once again selected.

7. Close the **butterfly2.png** file. If you are asked if you want to save changes, click **No** (Windows) or **Don't Save** (Macintosh). Remain in this screen for the next Step-by-Step.

Displaying Rulers and Guides

You can use rulers and guides to lay out objects as precisely as possible and to help you draw. You can place guides in the document and snap objects to those guides or turn on the Fireworks grid and snap objects to the grid.

S TEP-BY-STEP 2.4

Setting Up the Canvas

1. Create a new document. Make the canvas size **400** × **400** pixels and the color white. You are going to draw a compass to be used in a logo like the one shown in Figure 2-2.

FIGURE 2-2
Finished compass

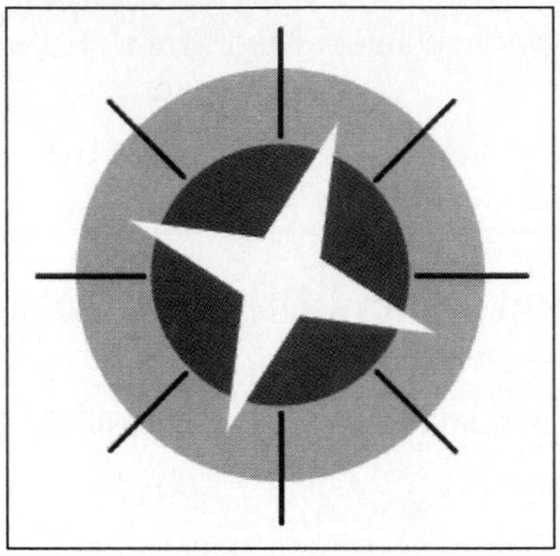

2. Save your file as **compass**, followed by your initials. Remain in this screen for the next Step-by-Step.

To make it easier to precisely draw the compass, you'll use grid lines and rulers. The grid lines will make it easier to size the circle, and the ruler guides will help you align the objects as you draw them.

S TEP-BY-STEP 2.5

Showing and Setting the Grid, Rulers, and Guides

1. Click the **View** menu, point to **Grid**, and then click **Edit Grid**. This displays the Edit Grid dialog box as shown in Figure 2-3 (Windows) or the Grids and Guides dialog box (Macintosh).

FIGURE 2-3
Edit Grid dialog box

STEP-BY-STEP 2.5 Continued

2. Make the grid size **24** × **24** pixels.

3. Make sure the **Show Grid** and **Snap to Grid** options are selected (a check will appear in each box).

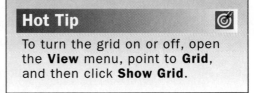

Hot Tip

To turn the grid on or off, open the **View** menu, point to **Grid**, and then click **Show Grid**.

4. Click the **Color** box and choose a pale blue color such as **#CCFFFF** for the grid.

5. Click **OK**. Pale blue gridlines now appear on the canvas.

6. Make sure the page rulers are visible, as shown in Figure 2-4. If they are not, click the **View** menu, and then click **Rulers**.

FIGURE 2-4
The rulers

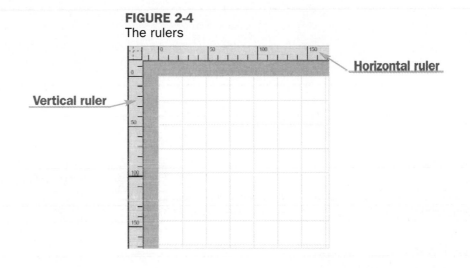

Horizontal ruler

Vertical ruler

7. Position the pointer over the vertical ruler (on the left). Drag from the ruler onto the canvas. Then release to add a vertical guide to the document.

8. Position the pointer over the horizontal ruler (on the top). Drag from the ruler onto the canvas. Then release to add a horizontal guide to the document. Remain in this screen for the next Step-by-Step.

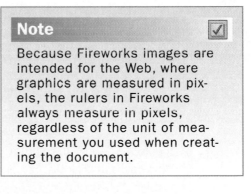

Note

Because Fireworks images are intended for the Web, where graphics are measured in pixels, the rulers in Fireworks always measure in pixels, regardless of the unit of measurement you used when creating the document.

You are going to use the intersection of the guides as the center of your logo.

S TEP-BY-STEP 2.6

Moving and Adjusting Guides

1. Make sure the Pointer tool is selected. Then position the pointer over the vertical guide. The pointer changes to indicate that you are positioned to drag the guide, as shown in Figure 2-5.

FIGURE 2-5
Dragging a guide

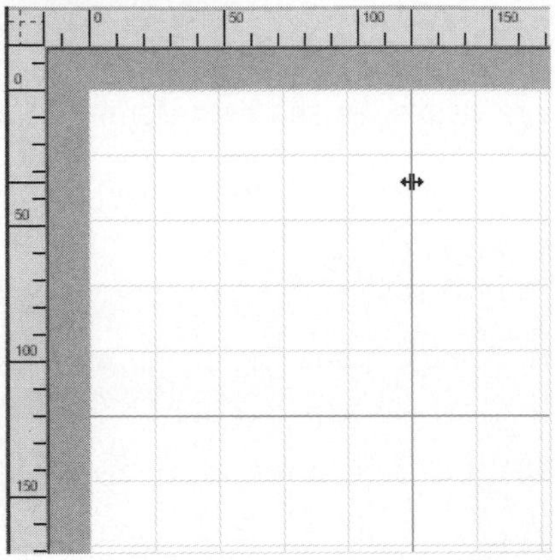

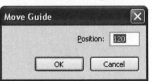

2. Drag the guide left or right.

3. Double-click the vertical guide. This opens the Move Guide dialog box, as shown in Figure 2-6. (*Note*: Don't worry if the value in your Position box differs from that shown.)

Hot Tip

To remove a guide, just drag it off the canvas.

FIGURE 2-6
Move Guide dialog box

4. In the Move Guide dialog box, enter **216** in the Position box, and click **OK**. You are placing the guides at position 216—not the exact center at 200—so the guides will align with the grid. This will help in drawing the final graphic.

Note

Double-clicking a ruler guide does not open the Move Guide dialog box if the guides are locked.

5. Repeat the same process for the horizontal guide: Double-click the guide, enter **216** in the Position box, and then click **OK**.

Once you set the position of a guide, you can lock it into place.

STEP-BY-STEP 2.6 Continued

6. Click the **View** menu, point to **Guides**, and then click **Lock Guides**. (You can also lock your guides from the Guides dialog box.) If your guides are locked, you cannot drag them.

7. To unlock guides, open the **View** menu, point to **Guides**, and then click **Lock Guides** again.

8. Click the **View** menu again, point to **Guides**, and then click **Edit Guides** to open the Guides dialog box, as shown in Figure 2-7 (Windows), or Grids and Guides dialog box (Macintosh).

   You can change the color of the guides, turn Snap to Guides on or off, lock the guides, and clear all guides from the page. With Snap to Guides selected, objects snap to align with guides as you position them in the document.

FIGURE 2-7
Guides dialog box

9. Make sure **Snap to Guides** is selected and click **OK**. Now you are ready to begin drawing the compass. Remain in this screen for the next Step-by-Step.

Drawing Basic Shapes

Most drawings, even complicated ones, are made from a variety of basic lines and shapes. Fireworks provides some basic shape tools for creating vector graphics: the Rectangle, Ellipse, and Polygon tools, which are shown in Figure 2-8.

> **Note** ☑
>
> Fireworks also includes a number of Smart Shapes. These are more complicated shapes, such as Bent Arrow, Rounded Rectangle, or Spiral, that can be controlled in a variety of ways.

FIGURE 2-8
Shape tools on the Tools panel

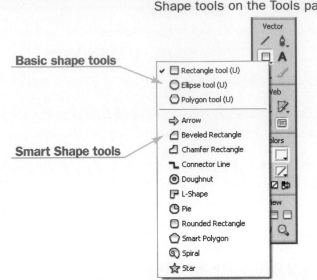

Basic shape tools

Smart Shape tools

S TEP-BY-STEP 2.7

Drawing an Ellipse

1. Choose the **Ellipse** tool from the Tools panel by clicking the arrow on the **Rectangle** tool and then clicking **Ellipse**.

   The ellipse you will draw needs to have a black stroke and no fill. You can use the Property inspector (shown in Figure 2-9) to set the options for the Ellipse tool.

FIGURE 2-9
Property inspector for the Ellipse tool

Fill Color box
Fill Category

Stroke
Color box

Stroke
Category

Tip Size

2. Make sure the **Stroke Color** box is set to black (**#000000**).

3. Make sure the **Tip Size** box is set to **1** (for 1 pixel).

4. Click the arrow on the **Stroke category** box, point to **Pencil**, and then click **1-Pixel Hard**.

5. Click the arrow on the **Fill category** box, and click **None**.

6. Position the pointer in the document where the guides cross. You will draw the circle from the center out.

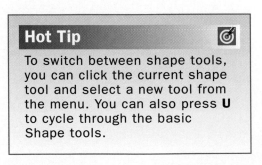

Hot Tip

To switch between shape tools, you can click the current shape tool and select a new tool from the menu. You can also press **U** to cycle through the basic Shape tools.

STEP-BY-STEP 2.7 Continued

7. Hold down **Alt** (Windows) or **Option** (Macintosh), press **Shift** to constrain the shape to a circle, and drag to create a circle that is three grid lines wide from the center point, as shown in Figure 2-10. Release the mouse before releasing the modifier keys.

FIGURE 2-10
Circle drawn from the center of the ruler guides

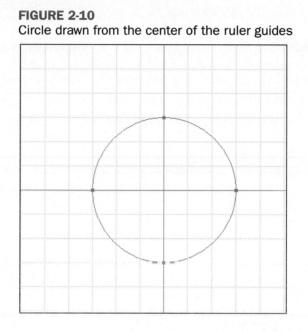

8. Click the **Select** menu, and then click **Deselect** to deselect the ellipse. Save your file and remain in this screen for the next Step-by-Step.

Using the Line Tool

Another important tool for drawing basic shapes is the Line tool. Using the Property inspector, you can experiment with the stroke and fill options to draw some interesting graphics using nothing but basic lines. In this task, you use the Line tool shown in Figure 2-11 to draw tick marks on the compass logo.

> **Hot Tip** ⊚
>
> The title bar of the Document window displays an asterisk when you make a change to the document. This is a great reminder that you should save your work.

FIGURE 2-11
Line tool on the Tools panel

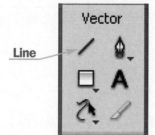

S TEP-BY-STEP 2.8

Drawing Lines

> **Note** ✓
>
> After you draw the vertical line, the ruler guide makes it difficult to select the line. You might find that you select the guide instead of the line. You can lock or hide the guides to make this task easier.

1. Select the **Line** tool from the Tools panel. On the Line tool's Property inspector, the line color should be set to black, the Tip size to **1** pixel, and the Stroke category to **1-Pixel Hard**.

2. Position the cross-hair on the vertical guide, about one-half a grid line above the top of the circle. Hold down **Shift** as you drag down to draw a straight line that extends one-half a grid line below the bottom of the circle.

3. Click the **Edit** menu, and then click **Clone** to make an exact copy of the line. The copy is placed directly on top of the line and is selected. Remain in this screen for the next Step-by-Step.

Rotating Objects

You can rotate objects in Fireworks by using the Scale tool or by pointing to Transform on the Modify menu and then choosing one of the preset rotation options. If you need to be more precise when rotating, you can use the Numeric Transform dialog box. From here, you can enter exact settings for scaling, sizing, and rotating objects. In this task, you use the Numeric Transform dialog box to rotate a line 45 degrees.

S TEP-BY-STEP 2.9

Rotating an Object

1. With the cloned line still selected, click the **Modify** menu, point to **Transform**, and then click **Numeric Transform**. The Numeric Transform dialog box appears, as shown in Figure 2-12.

FIGURE 2-12
Numeric Transform dialog box

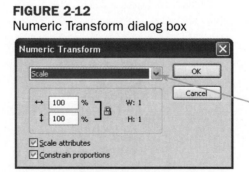

Click to choose Scale, Resize, or Rotate

2. Click the arrow on the drop-down text box and choose **Rotate**.

STEP-BY-STEP 2.9 Continued

3. Enter **45** in the Angle box and click **OK**. The line rotates from the center point of the circle. You need a total of four lines, each at a 45-degree angle from the last line. The lines cut the circle like a pie. You could repeat the process of cloning and then rotating the clone, but an easier way to repeat these steps is by using the History panel, which is discussed in the next section. Remain in this screen for the next Step-by-Step.

Using the History Panel

The History panel records each step you perform as you create objects on the canvas. Each time you use the Undo command on the Edit menu, you are stepping back a step on the History panel. The History panel makes it easy to see your steps and undo multiple actions. You can also use the History panel to repeat a set of actions. For example, you've just performed two actions: you cloned a line and then you rotated the line. You will now use the History panel to repeat those two actions.

STEP-BY-STEP 2.10

Viewing and Using the History Panel

1. Click the **Window** menu, and then click **History**. The History tab moves to the foreground of the Frames and History panel, as shown in Figure 2-13. (*Hint:* To display more of the History panel, you can collapse the other panels, such as Layers and Answers, by clicking the names of the open panel groups.)

FIGURE 2-13
History panel

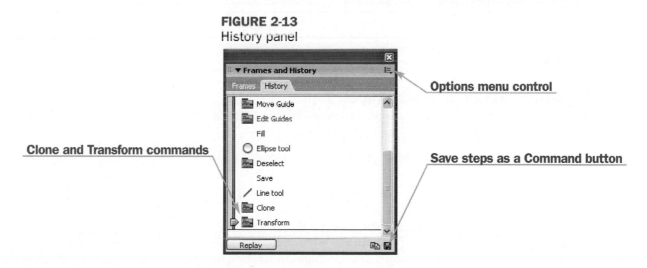

2. Make sure the line you are copying is still selected.

3. Scroll down to the bottom of the list in the History panel until you see the two actions Clone and Transform.

4. Hold down **Shift** and click **Clone** and then **Transform**.

5. Click **Replay** at the bottom left of the History panel. A new line is drawn at a 45-degree angle from the last line.

STEP-BY-STEP 2.10 Continued

6. Click **Replay** again to draw the last line. Your drawing should look like Figure 2-14. Remain in this screen for the next Step-by-Step.

FIGURE 2-14
Circle with four intersecting lines

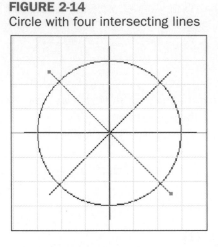

The History panel can replay steps, as you've just seen, and it can be used to step back through your actions, like a super Undo command. To undo your steps with the History panel, just drag the slider on the left side of the panel up; to redo the steps, drag the slider down. You can also save your steps for actions you will perform in the future. For example, in the preceding Step-by-Step exercise you cloned and rotated the line. You used the Replay button twice to create the other lines. If you know you will want to use that same action again, you can save the steps as a command that can be used over and over.

STEP-BY-STEP 2.11

Saving Steps as a Command

1. Hold down **Shift** and click the **Clone** and **Transform** actions on the History panel if they are not already selected.

2. Click the **Save Steps as a Command** button (see Figure 2-13) at the bottom of the History panel.

> **Note** ☑
>
> You can also open the Save Command dialog box by choosing **Save as Command** from the History panel **Options** menu (see Figure 2-13).

3. In the Save Command dialog box, enter **Clone and Rotate** and click **OK**. Those actions are now saved as a single command on the Commands menu for you to use again.

4. To experiment with the new Clone and Rotate command, draw another line off to the side of the compass you are drawing.

> **Hot Tip** ⊚
>
> To delete a saved command, click **Commands**, click **Manage Saved Commands**, choose the command you want to remove, click **Delete**, and then click **OK**.

STEP-BY-STEP 2.11 Continued

5. Click the **Commands** menu, and then click **Clone and Rotate**. The line is cloned and then rotated.

6. You don't need those extra lines, so delete them by clicking each with the **Pointer** tool and then pressing **Delete**. Remain in this screen for the next Step-by-Step.

Using the Knife Tool

When you draw basic shapes in Fireworks, your lines are called *paths*. You can dissect the paths into two or more paths by using the Knife tool shown in Figure 2-15.

FIGURE 2-15
Knife tool on the Tools panel

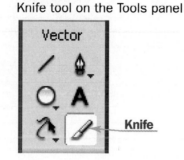

The finished compass logo has only tick marks (partial lines on the edges of the circle). The next step is to cut each line and remove the center portion. So you can more easily make the cuts, you will draw another circle, smaller than the first, and cut around the edges of the smaller circle.

S TEP-BY-STEP 2.12

Using the Knife Tool

1. Choose the **Ellipse** tool. Make sure the Fill category is set to **None** on the Property inspector, or the circle will cover your lines, making it difficult to complete this task.

STEP-BY-STEP 2.12 Continued

2. Hold down **Alt** (Windows) or **Option** (Macintosh) and **Shift** to draw a smaller circle from the center outward within the first circle. Use the grid lines to make this new circle two grid lines wide from the center point. The object should now look like Figure 2-16.

FIGURE 2-16
The inner circle acts as a guide as you work with the Knife tool

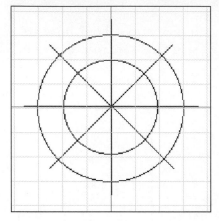

3. Select one of the lines with the Pointer tool.

4. Select the **Knife** tool from the Tools panel.

5. Drag the Knife pointer across the line where it intersects the smaller circle. You don't have to drag a huge amount—just enough to cut through the line. When you release, a point appears on the line. That is the cut you just made.

> **Note** ☑
>
> The guides could make it difficult to select your vertical and horizontal lines. You might need to turn off the guides while editing these lines. If you do, make sure to turn them back on when you are done. You will continue to use them in this lesson.

6. Repeat the process at the other end of the line.

7. Switch to the **Pointer** tool and click anywhere outside the circle to deselect the line.

8. Click the center portion of the line between the two cuts; then press **Delete** to remove the inner line.

STEP-BY-STEP 2.12 Continued

9. Repeat the process on the other lines. The objects should now look like Figure 2-17. Remain in this screen for the next Step-by-Step.

FIGURE 2-17
Circle with tick marks

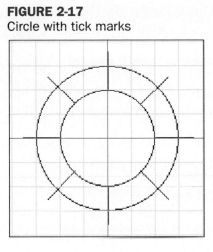

Scaling Objects

You can scale objects in Fireworks by using the Scale tool shown in Figure 2-18. Scale allows you to rotate the object freely. If you need to be more precise when scaling, you can use the Numeric Transform dialog box to enter exact settings for scaling, sizing, and rotating objects. In this task, you will reduce the size of the inner circle.

Hot Tip

If there appear to be breaks in your lines or circles, it might just be your view. Try zooming in by using the Zoom tool or the Magnification box.

FIGURE 2-18
Scale tool on the Tools panel

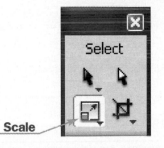

Scale

S TEP-BY-STEP 2.13

Scaling an Object

1. Select the inner circle by using the Pointer tool.

STEP-BY-STEP 2.13 Continued

2. Select the **Scale** tool on the Tools panel. Scale handles appear. You can use this tool to scale or rotate the selected object.

3. Drag the lower-right handle up and to the left. The circle is smaller, but it's no longer centered like you want.

4. Click the **Edit** menu, and then click **Undo Transform**.

5. Click the **Modify** menu, point to **Transform**, and then click **Numeric Transform**. The Numeric Transform dialog box appears.

> **Hot Tip** ⊙
>
> If you hold down the Alt key when scaling an object with the Scale tool, the transformation is performed from the center of the object.

6. Click the arrow on the drop-down list box and choose **Scale**.

7. Make sure **Constrain Proportions** is selected.

8. Enter **95** (for 95%) in either of the text boxes and click **OK**. The circle is scaled down.

9. Deselect the image. Save the file and remain in this screen for the next Step-by-Step.

Applying Strokes

Stroke refers to the width, color, and style of lines drawn in Fireworks, as well as the lines that border the shapes you create. When you select a drawing tool in Fireworks, you can adjust the stroke settings by using the Property inspector, as shown in Figure 2-19.

FIGURE 2-19
Property inspector showing Stroke and Fill settings

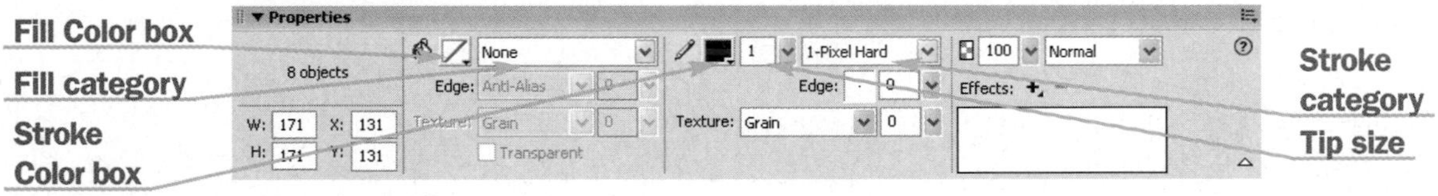

Fill Color box
Fill category
Stroke Color box

Stroke category
Tip size

STEP-BY-STEP 2.14

Changing the Stroke of a Line

1. Select all eight lines on the canvas by holding down **Shift** and clicking each line with the Pointer tool.

2. Click the arrow on the **Stroke category** box, point to **Basic**, and then click **Soft Line**.

3. Enter **2** (for 2 pixels) in the Tip size box.

4. Deselect the image.

STEP-BY-STEP 2.14 Continued

5. Select both circles, click the arrow on the **Stroke category** box, and click **None**.

6. Deselect the image. Save the file and remain in this screen for the next Step-by-Step.

Applying Fill Color

If you're working with Web tools such as Fireworks, you've probably heard the term *Web-safe colors*. You might have also heard them called browser-safe, the 216 palette, the Netscape cube, Explorer colors, and so on. These all refer to a set of 216 colors that can be viewed with computer systems that are set to display 8-bit colors. However, these days, most computers can display 64,000 colors or more. Many Web designers now use a WebSnap Adaptive palette or an Exact palette instead.

You might choose not to work at 16-bit color depth, because Web-safe colors might dither (making the image look grainy), and the eyedroppers in Fireworks often incorrectly sample colors at that depth.

When you select fill and stroke colors in Fireworks, you are presented with a palette of Web-safe colors, but you can also sample colors from another image by using the Eyedropper tool. Keep in mind that for you to get accurate color sampling, your monitor needs to be set to 24-bit or greater color depth.

In the following Step-by-Step, you will open another file, tile it side-by-side with the compass file, and sample a color to use as the fill color for the compass logo.

STEP-BY-STEP 2.15

Filling the Circles with Color

1. Open the **site_colors.png** file from the data files supplied with this course. This file contains the colors you will use for the circles.

2. Click the **Window** menu, and then click **Tile Vertical**. The two files now appear side by side. You might need to adjust the magnification of the compass file to 100% so you can see the entire graphic while the windows are tiled. You also might need to scroll to bring the entire image into view.

3. Click in the compass Document window to make sure it is the active document. Select the outer circle of the compass. The circle has no stroke or fill, so it might be hard to see. To select the circle, move the pointer over the image until the circle's selection handles appear in red; then click it.

4. Click the **Fill Color** box on the Property inspector and position the eyedropper over color 2 in the site_colors.png file. Click this color to change the color of the selected circle.

5. Deselect the outer circle and select the smaller, inner circle.

6. Click the **Fill Color** box on the Property inspector and position the eyedropper over color 3 in the site_colors.png file. Click this color to change the color of the selected circle.

7. Close the **site_colors.png** file. Click the **Maximize** button in the compass window and save the file. Remain in this screen for the next Step-by-Step.

Using the Polygon Tool

With the Polygon tool (see Figure 2-20), you can draw any equilateral polygon, from a triangle to a polygon with 360 sides. The last step to complete the compass logo is to draw a four-pointed star on top of the inner circle. Using the Polygon tool, drawing a simple star is a snap.

FIGURE 2-20
Polygon tool on the Tools panel

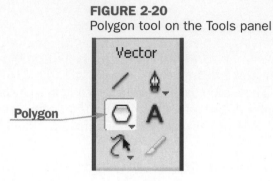

Polygon

S TEP-BY-STEP 2.16

Drawing a Star

1. Choose the **Polygon** tool on the Tools panel. (*Hint*: The Polygon tool is in the same tool group as the Rectangle and Ellipse tools.) The Property inspector shows the options for the Polygon tool.

2. On the Property inspector, click the arrow on the **Shape** box and choose **Star**.

3. Enter **4** in the Sides text box and **26** in the Angle text box.

4. Click the **Fill Color** box and select the color white (**#FFFFFF**).

5. If the guides are not visible, turn them back on by clicking the **View** menu, pointing to **Guides**, and then clicking **Show Guides**.

STEP-BY-STEP 2.16 Continued

6. Drag from the center point of the guides to draw the star. As you drag, rotate the star to position the points between the tick marks on the circle. The logo should now look like Figure 2-21. Remain in this screen for the next Step-by-Step.

FIGURE 2-21
The logo graphic with the star drawn by using the Polygon tool

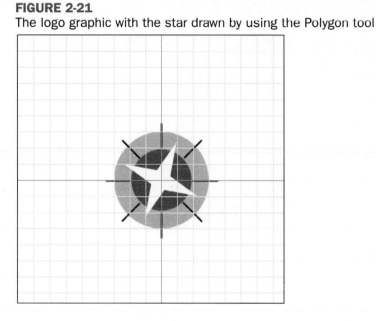

Trimming the Canvas

Your finished drawings aren't always evenly placed on the canvas. One way to correct this is to manually crop the unwanted areas of the canvas. Another method is to simply trim the canvas by using the Trim command.

STEP-BY-STEP 2.17

Trimming the Canvas

1. Click the **Modify** menu, point to **Canvas**, and then click **Trim Canvas**. Fireworks trims the canvas to an exact fit for the graphic.

2. Save and close the **compass** file.

SUMMARY

In this lesson, you learned to:

- Combine simple shapes to create complex objects.

- Select points and paths in vector graphics.

- Use the ruler and guides for drawing.

- Draw with the basic drawing tools.

- Rotate objects.

- Use the History panel to save steps as commands.

- Use the Knife tool to cut paths.

- Scale objects.

- Apply stroke and fill settings.

- Use the Eyedropper tool to sample color.

- Trim the canvas and fit the canvas to your objects.

IMPORTING, GROUPING, AND LAYERS

OBJECTIVES

Upon completion of this lesson, you should be able to:

- Import objects.
- Adjust import settings.
- Group and ungroup objects.
- Change the order of objects within a layer.
- Use the Info panel.
- Create and use layers.

Importing Objects

In this lesson, you learn to import graphic objects, group and ungroup objects, and use layers to manage your objects as you work. In the process, you create the final version of the compass logo you started in Lesson 2.

You begin by setting up a new document and then importing the objects you're going to work with. Macromedia Fireworks MX 2004 provides a wealth of tools for creating graphics, but you still might want to import graphics from other sources. For example, you might want to import a company logo created in Macromedia FreeHand or import a scanned image from Adobe Photoshop to combine with buttons you've created in Fireworks.

Fireworks can import these formats: PNG, GIF, JPEG, PICT, BMP, TIFF, ASCII, RTF, Adobe Photoshop PSD files, Adobe Illustrator 7, FreeHand 7 and later, and HTML.

To finish the compass logo, you need to add some text to the compass you created in the previous lesson. The text was created in FreeHand.

STEP-BY-STEP 3.1

Importing Objects to a Fireworks Document

1. Create a new document. Make sure the canvas size is **400 × 400** pixels and the canvas color is **white**. If the grid is visible when the document opens, turn it off by clicking the **View** menu, pointing to **Grid**, and clicking **Show Grid**.

2. Save your file as **compass_logo**, followed by your initials. Your finished logo will look similar to Figure 3-1.

FIGURE 3-1
Finished compass logo

3. Click the **File** menu, click **Import**, navigate to the **compass3.png** file supplied with the data files for this course, and double-click it. The pointer changes to an import pointer.

4. Position the pointer in the upper-left corner of the canvas and click to place the object in this location at its default size. This object is placed on the current layer, Layer 1. (If necessary, click the title of the Layers panel to display the panel.) You can see from the Layers panel that Layer 1 contains several objects.

Next you will import the FreeHand graphic.

5. Click the **File** menu, click **Import**, navigate to the **compass_text.fh11** file supplied with the data files for this course, and double-click it. The Vector File Options dialog box opens, as shown in Figure 3-2.

FIGURE 3-2
Vector File Options dialog box

Vector File Options	? X
Scale: 100	
Width: 210	Pixels
Height: 55	Pixels
Resolution: 72	Pixels/Inch
Anti-alias: ☑ Paths ☑ Text	Smooth

File conversion

Open a page   Page: 1

Remember layers

☐ Include invisible layers
☐ Include background layers

Render as images

☑ Groups over   30   objects
☑ Blends over   30   steps
☑ Tiled fills over   30   objects

OK   Cancel

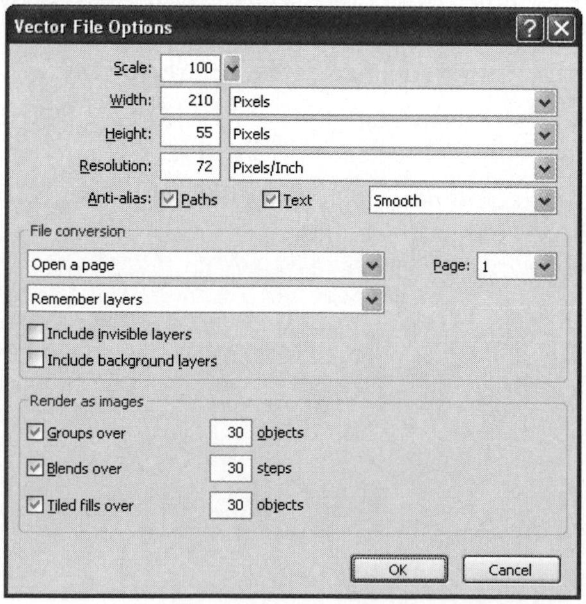

STEP-BY-STEP 3.1 Continued

6. Click **OK** to accept the default vector options. These options are discussed in the following section.

7. Position the pointer below the compass graphic and click to place the FreeHand object. The FreeHand text graphic is also placed on the current layer, Layer 1. Save the file and remain in this screen for the next Step-by-Step.

Understanding Vector File Options

In the Vector File Options dialog box, you can set the following options when you import vector files. The Vector File Options dialog box does not open when you paste or drag an image from another application.

- **Scale:** Specify the scale percentage for the imported file.

- **Width** and **Height:** Specify in pixels the width and height of the imported file.

- **Resolution:** Specify the resolution of the imported file.

- **Anti-Alias:** Anti-alias imported text and/or paths.

- **File Conversion:** These options specify how multiple-page documents are handled when imported. The options are:

    - **Open a Page:** Import only the specified page.

    - **Open Pages as Frames:** Import all of the pages from the document and place each on a separate frame in Fireworks.

    - **Remember Layers:** Maintain the layer structure of the imported file.

    - **Ignore Layers:** Delete the layer structure of the imported file. All objects are placed on the currently selected layer.

    - **Convert Layers to Frames:** Place each layer of the imported document in a separate frame in Fireworks. This can be useful if you are importing artwork for use in animations.

    - **Include Invisible Layers:** Import objects on layers that have been turned off. Otherwise, invisible layers are ignored.

    - **Include Background Layers:** Import objects from the document's Background layer. Otherwise, the Background layer is ignored.

- **Render as Images:** Rasterize (convert to bitmap) complex groups, blends, or tiled fills and place them as a single image object in a Fireworks document. Enter a number in the corresponding text box to determine how many objects a group or tiled fill can contain or how many steps a blend can use before it is rasterized during import.

Grouping and Ungrouping Objects

Most of the graphics you create in Fireworks will be made from several smaller objects. Once you complete a graphic or a portion of a graphic, you might want to group the individual objects to protect their relationship to one another. It's also a lot easier to work with one grouped object than to work with dozens of separate lines and shapes. When objects are grouped, they move together and can be manipulated as a single unit. You can scale and rotate all objects in the group at the same time. You can also combine two groups together. This is referred to as *nested grouping*.

The compass graphic you imported on Layer 1 is made from several smaller shapes, but they have not been grouped.

S TEP-BY-STEP 3.2

Grouping Selected Objects

1. Select the **Pointer** tool. Click in the upper-left corner of the canvas and drag to select the entire compass graphic. You can tell by the multiple sets of selection handles that you've selected several objects. Each of the selected objects is highlighted on the Layers panel.

2. Click the **Modify** menu, and then click **Group**. You can tell the objects are grouped because they now share one set of selection handles. They also appear as one group of 11 objects on Layer 1 of the Layers panel.

3. Select the **Subselection** tool from the Tools panel, as shown in Figure 3-3.

> **Hot Tip** ◎
>
> In Windows, you can also select the **Window** menu, point to **Toolbars**, click **Modify** to display the Modify toolbar, and use buttons on the toolbar to group and ungroup objects.

FIGURE 3-3
The Subselection tool on the Tools panel

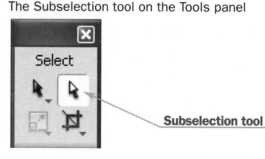

Subselection tool

4. Position the pointer over the grouped compass graphic. Point to several different parts of the graphic. As you roll over different parts of the graphic with the Subselection tool, you can see the individual objects that make up the compass.

5. Click in the middle of the graphic and notice the blue line (the path) and the points on the path. Try clicking different parts of the graphic.

    You can use the Subselection tool to select the parts that make up a grouped object. You can also subselect by using the Pointer tool and holding down **Alt** (Windows) or **Option** (Macintosh) as you click an object in the group.

6. Select any single element in the group, click the **Select** menu, and then click **Superselect** to select the group that contains the object. Remain in this screen for the next Step-by-Step.

Arranging the Stacking Order of Objects

Even if objects are sitting on the same layer, they can be stacked, one on top of the other. If you look on the Layers panel, you see that Layer 1 still contains two objects: the grouped compass and the imported text graphic. You can control the stacking order of these objects by dragging their positions up or down on the Layers panel or by using the Arrange commands on the Modify menu. The advantage of using the Arrange commands is that you can also control the stacking order of objects that have been grouped, such as the compass logo.

STEP-BY-STEP 3.3

Arranging the Order of Objects

1. Click the **Subselection** tool and select the star of the compass graphic.

2. Click the **Modify** menu, point to **Arrange**, and then click **Send to Back**. The star is still selected, but it's "hidden" behind the other objects.

3. Click the **Modify** menu, point to **Arrange**, and then click **Bring to Front**. The star returns to the front of the graphic.

4. Make sure the star object is still selected. Click the **Modify** menu, point to **Arrange**, and then click **Send Backward**. The star is sent back just one level. It's hidden behind the inner circle, but you can see the white tips of the star.

5. Click the **Modify** menu, point to **Arrange**, and then click **Bring Forward**. The star moves back up one level to the top of the stack. Save the file and remain in this screen for the next Step-by-Step.

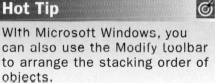

Hot Tip

With Microsoft Windows, you can also use the Modify toolbar to arrange the stacking order of objects.

Using the Info Panel

The Info panel provides information about the location and dimensions of selected objects and the exact coordinates of the pointer as you move it across the canvas. You can even use the Info panel to size an object by using exact height and width dimensions. You can also size an object by using the Property inspector.

In Step-by-Step 3.4, you use the Info panel to size the compass graphics.

S TEP-BY-STEP 3.4

Using the Info Panel

1. Click the **Window** menu, and then click **Info**. The Info panel opens, as shown in Figure 3-4. If the bottom half of the panel is not visible, click and drag the bottom border of the panel down to display it.

FIGURE 3-4
The Info panel

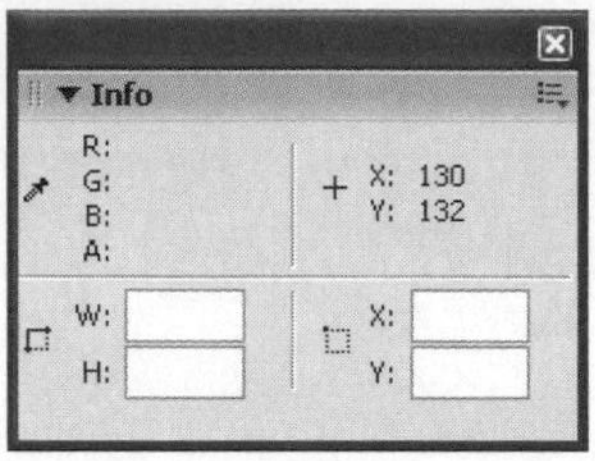

2. Click the **Pointer** tool and select the grouped compass graphic.

3. Enter **62** for both the width (W) and height (H), and then press **Enter** (Windows) or **Return** (Macintosh). The compass graphic is now 62 × 62 pixels. Save the file and remain in this screen for the next Step-by-Step.

Working with Layers

The Layers panel, as shown in Figure 3-5, is similar to the Layers panels in other graphics programs such as Macromedia FreeHand or Adobe Photoshop. Think of a layer as a transparent plane where you can create and place objects. Layers enable you to divide your artwork when building complex vector objects or composite images.

FIGURE 3-5
The Layers panel

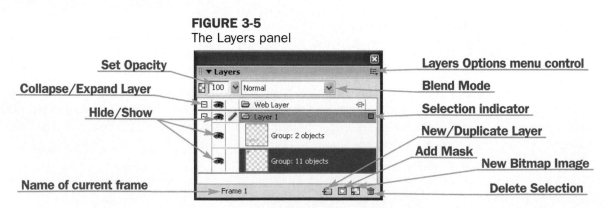

Different portions of an image can be stored on different layers and selectively turned off or on so you can isolate just the portion you are working with. Layers can contain either vector or bitmap objects, or a combination of both. On each layer, you can place one object or multiple objects. If you place multiple objects on the same layer, each object appears in a stack of objects contained within the layer. A thumbnail representation of the object is displayed to the left of the object name.

When you create a new document in Fireworks, you get two layers by default: Layer 1 and the Web Layer. All your objects and images are initially placed on Layer 1. The Web Layer is where slices and hotspots are stored. We discuss these in a later lesson.

Collapsing and Expanding Layers

If your document contains several layers, or several objects on a single layer, the Layers panel can become crowded. One way to help manage layers as you work is to collapse them. You can collapse and expand layers by clicking the plus and minus signs (Windows) or the down- and right-pointing arrows (Macintosh) beside each layer. Right now, Layer 1 contains two groups of objects.

S TEP-BY-STEP 3.5

Collapsing and Expanding Layers

1. Click the minus sign (Windows) or down arrow (Macintosh) beside Layer 1. Layer 1 collapses and the minus sign becomes a plus sign (Windows) or a right-pointing arrow (Macintosh).

2. Click the plus sign (Windows) or right-pointing arrow (Macintosh) beside Layer 1. Layer 1 expands. Remain in this screen for the next Step-by-Step.

Hiding and Showing Layers

As you create and build objects to form your final graphic, you might want to hide layers. Hiding layers allows you to isolate very specific parts of your work.

Right now, Layer 1 contains two groups of objects. In a moment, you'll create the rectangle that forms the border for the final compass logo. This might be easier to do with the compass and text hidden from view.

S TEP-BY-STEP 3.6

Hiding and Showing Layers

1. Click the eye icon beside the first object on Layer 1 (the compass text). The text graphic is hidden from view.

2. Click the spot where the eye icon used to be beside the first object in Layer 1. The text graphic reappears. You can also hide everything within a layer by using the eye icon beside the layer's name.

3. Click the eye icon beside Layer 1. Now every object on Layer 1 is hidden. You have a clean canvas for creating the last part of the logo. Remain in this screen for the next Step-by-Step.

Adding and Naming Layers

In this task, you add a new layer and name it Rectangle. You also change the name of Layer 1 to Imported Objects. Finally, you create the rectangle that will serve as the boundary for the final compass logo.

S TEP-BY-STEP 3.7

Adding and Naming a Layer

1. Click the **New/Duplicate Layer** button on the Layers panel (see Figure 3-5). Layer 2 is added above Layer 1.

2. Double-click the name **Layer 2** on the Layers panel.

3. In the Layer Name dialog box, key **Rectangle** and press **Enter** (Windows) or **Return** (Macintosh) to rename the layer.

4. Double-click the name **Layer 1** on the Layers panel.

5. Key **Imported Objects** and press **Enter** (Windows) or **Return** (Macintosh).

6. Click the **Rectangle** layer to select it.

7. Select the **Rectangle** tool and draw a rectangle on the canvas. Use the Info panel or the Property inspector to make the rectangle **288** pixels wide and **72** pixels high. In the Property inspector, make sure the rectangle's stroke is set to **None**.

8. Open the file named **site_colors.png** from the data files supplied with this course, click the **Window** menu, and then click **Tile Vertical**.

9. Make sure the rectangle in the compass_logo.png file is selected. You might need to scroll to bring the object into view. Click the **Fill Color** box on the Property inspector, and click the eyedropper on color 1 in the site_colors.png file.

10. Close the **site_colors.png** file, and then click the **Maximize** button in the compass_logo window. Save the file and remain in this screen for the next Step-by-Step.

Arranging Layers

You learned earlier how to change the stacking order of objects on the same layer. In the next Step-by-Step, you learn to arrange layers by using the Layers panel. Right now, the rectangle is on a layer above that of the imported graphics. You need to place the rectangle behind the graphics to complete the logo.

S TEP-BY-STEP 3.8

Arranging Layers and Objects on Layers

1. Select the compass with the Pointer tool and drag the compass to the right side of the rectangle. Notice that because of the way the layers are arranged, the compass is hidden behind the rectangle. That's not what you want.

2. On the Layers panel, drag the thumbnail of the rectangle graphic down. As you drag, you'll see a black line appear either above or below the other layers. The object you are moving is placed according to the position of the black line. Drag below the last layer and release. You have just moved the rectangle *out* of the Rectangle layer and *into* the Imported Objects layer. That's not what you want either.

3. Click the **Edit** menu, and then click **Undo Layer Change**.
   You'll move the whole layer instead to get the arrangement you want.

4. Drag the Rectangle layer's name or folder icon until it is below both objects on the Imported Objects layer. This places the entire Rectangle layer behind the Imported Objects layer, just as you want.

5. Select the text graphic and drag it to the left side of the rectangle, as shown in Figure 3-6. If necessary, you can select objects and fine-tune their positions by using the left, right, up, and down arrow keys. Remain in this screen for the next Step-by-Step.

> ### Hot Tip
> If a layer contains more than one object, you can move that object between layers by selecting the object and then dragging the selection indicator (blue square) beside the layer name to the desired new layer. Only the selected object moves.

FIGURE 3-6
The rectangle is now on a layer behind the compass and text

Locking Layers

To prevent your layers from being accidentally changed, you can lock them.

STEP-BY-STEP 3.9

Locking a Layer

1. Click the blank space between the Rectangle layer name and the eye icon. An icon of a padlock appears, indicating that this layer is now locked and cannot be edited.

2. Click the Layers panel **Options** menu, and then click **Lock All**, as shown in Figure 3-7. All three layers are locked.

Hot Tip

Single-layer editing, accessed from the Layers Options menu, makes only the currently selected layer accessible for editing. You can't select, edit, or change any objects on a locked layer. With single-layer editing, you can edit objects only on the selected layer; the other layers act as if they are locked.

FIGURE 3-7
Lock All command on the Layers panel Options menu

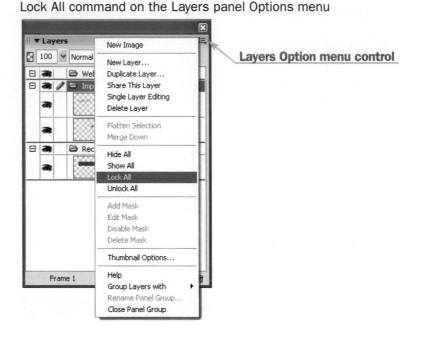

3. Click the **Modify** menu, point to **Canvas**, and then click **Trim Canvas**.

4. Save and close the **compass_logo.png** file.

SUMMARY

In this lesson, you learned to:

■ Import objects.

■ Adjust import settings.

■ Group and ungroup objects.

■ Change the order of objects within a layer.

■ Use the Info panel.

■ Create and use layers.

TEXT, MASKS, AND LIVE EFFECTS

OBJECTIVES

Upon completion of this lesson, you should be able to:

- Add text and special effects to your documents.
- Import text to your graphics and Web pages.
- Format text and position it in your documents.
- Add and edit Live Effects.
- Align and distribute objects.
- Create a mask by using Paste Inside.

Getting Started

In this lesson, you use Macromedia Fireworks MX 2004 to build a new Web page by using the compass graphic and compass logo you created in previous lessons. You add formatted text, apply filters called Live Effects, align objects, and use masking to isolate a part of an image to use as a button.

Your first step is to set up the new document and import some of the objects you'll work with. Your final Web page should look something like Figure 4-1. Refer to this figure often, because it will help you as you lay out your Web page.

FIGURE 4-1
Adventure Travel Web page

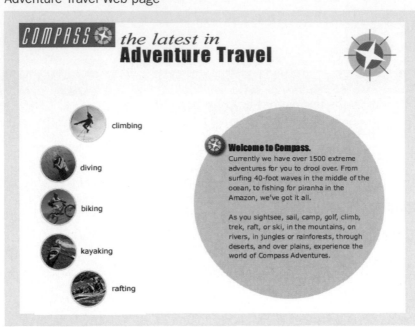

STEP-BY-STEP 4.1

Beginning the Web Page

1. Create a new document. Change the canvas size to **640** pixels wide by **480** pixels high and the color to **white**.

2. Click the **View** menu, point to **Grid**, and turn *off* the **Show Grid** and **Snap to Grid** features.

3. Save your file as **adventure**, followed by your initials.

4. Click the **File** menu, click **Import**, navigate to the **compass_logo4.png** file supplied with the data files for this course, and double-click it. Click to place the logo in the upper-left corner of the canvas.

5. Click the **File** menu, click **Import**, navigate to the **compass4.png** file supplied with the data files for this course, and double-click it. Position the pointer over the canvas and click to place the graphic in the document. Refer to Figure 4-1 as you do the next steps.

> **Hot Tip** ⊚
>
> If you select the logo, you can use the Info panel or the Property inspector to enter exact X and Y coordinates to position the logo. You can also use the rulers to help align objects.

STEP-BY-STEP 4.1 Continued

6. Scale the compass graphic to approximately 35% of its original size. Click the **Modify** menu, point to **Transform**, and then click **Numeric Transform**. Make sure **Scale** is selected, and enter **35%** in the scaling boxes.

7. Move the compass graphic to the upper-right corner of the canvas. Remain in this screen for the next Step-by-Step.

Adding Text

The Web has become an extremely visual medium, but no matter how well your images communicate, text will remain an important part of every Web page. In addition to large blocks of text, you'll want to use formatted text as headings and labels on your buttons and banners. In Fireworks, you can create text by using the Text tool, or you can import existing text.

The text you create in Fireworks is saved in the original PNG file where you can always edit it. However, after you export the image as a GIF or JPEG file, the text becomes part of the bitmap image and cannot be changed. You should keep the original Fireworks file (the PNG file) along with the exported images in case the text needs to be changed. To import text, the text must be saved as an ASCII (TXT) or rich text format (RTF) file.

STEP-BY-STEP 4.2

Using the Text Tool and Importing Text

1. Select the **Text** tool from the Tools panel, as shown in Figure 4-2.

FIGURE 4-2
Text tool on the Tools panel

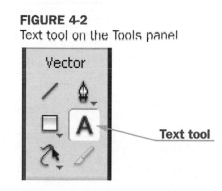

Text tool

2. Click on the canvas and key **Adventure Travel**.

3. Click the **File** menu, click **Import**, navigate to the **welcome.txt** file supplied with the data files for this course (Windows users should make sure Files of type is set to **All files**), and double-click it.

<u>STEP-BY-STEP 4.2 Continued</u>

4. Click on the canvas to place the imported text. Remain in this screen for the next Step-by-Step.

Formatting Text

Y̲ou can format both the text you create and the text you import by using the text options on the Property inspector. You can change the font, size (measured in points), kerning (letter spacing), leading (line spacing), horizontal scale, paragraph indents, alignment, color, transparency, and style (such as bold or italics).

Before you can format text, you must first select it. You can also select your formatting options before you begin typing.

S̲TEP-BY-STEP 4.3

Changing the Font, Size, Color, and Style

1. Click the **Pointer** tool and select the text **Adventure Travel**. The Property inspector shows the options for the Text tool, as shown in Figure 4-3.

FIGURE 4-3
Property inspector for the Text tool

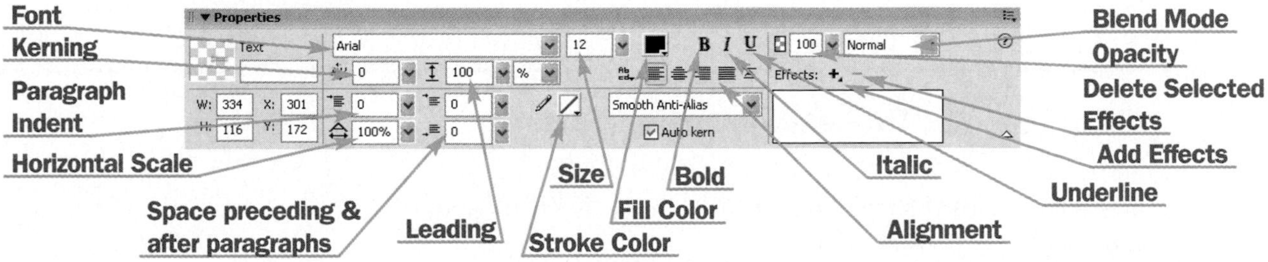

2. Click the arrow on the Font box and change the font to **Impact** (or **Arial Black** if Impact is not an available choice).

3. Highlight the value in the Size box and key **32**.

4. Click the **Fill Color** box and change the color of the selected text to black.

> **Note** ☑
>
> If you want to format just a portion of the text, you must use the Text tool to highlight the portion you want to format. To format the entire text object, just select it by using the Pointer tool.

5. Click the **Text** tool and drag to draw another text box about 1/2 inch high and 3 inches wide.

6. On the Property inspector, change the font to **Times** (or **Times New Roman**), the size to **27**, and the color to dark blue (**#000033**). Select the **Italic** style.

STEP-BY-STEP 4.3 Continued

7. Key **the latest in**. Your new text takes on the formatting you set on the Property inspector.

8. Click the **Text** tool, highlight the first line of the imported text, **Welcome to Compass**, and change it to a size of **15** and a font of **Impact** (or **Arial Black**). Highlight the rest of the imported text and change it to size **11 Verdana**. Remain in this screen for the next Step-by-Step.

Scaling, Kerning, and Leading

Changing the horizontal scale changes the width of the text without changing the height, as if you were stretching the text on a rubber band. Be careful not to overdo the stretching; you are electronically distorting the text without regard to its original design.

In the next Step-by-Step, you also work with kerning and leading formatting features. *Kerning* refers to the amount of space between letters, and *leading* controls the amount of space between lines of text.

STEP-BY-STEP 4.4

Changing Scale, Kerning, and Leading Formats

1. Click the **Text** tool and select the text **the latest in**.

2. Highlight the value in the Horizontal Scale box and key **130**. Then press **Enter** (Windows) or **Return** (Macintosh). The values are expressed as percentages. Values less than 100% condense the character width; values greater than 100% expand the character width, as shown in Figure 4-4.

FIGURE 4-4
Effects of horizontal scaling on text

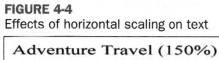
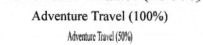

Adventure Travel (150%)
Adventure Travel (100%)
Adventure Travel (50%)

3. Select the text **Adventure Travel**.

4. Highlight the value in the Kerning box and key **6**. Then press **Enter** (Windows) or **Return** (Macintosh).

5. Select the entire imported text block, either by clicking it with the Pointer tool or by highlighting all the text with the Text tool.

6. Highlight the value in the Leading box and key **145**. Then press **Enter** (Windows) or **Return** (Macintosh). Remain in this screen for the next Step-by-Step.

Positioning Text

Now that you have your text formatted, you can place it where you want it to appear on the Web page. You can do that by selecting the text object with the Pointer tool and dragging the text to its new location, or you can use the Property inspector to position the text in an exact location on the canvas. Again, refer to Figure 4-1 as you position your text. After the text is where you want it, you will draw an ellipse as a stylish backdrop.

STEP-BY-STEP 4.5

Positioning the Text and Drawing the Backdrop

1. Move the text **Adventure Travel** to the top of the page. The final position of this text should be X:**165**, Y:**35**.

2. Move the text **the latest in** directly above *Adventure Travel*.

3. Move the imported text block to the right side of the page. The final position of this text should be approximately X: **343**, Y: **197**.

4. You can force the text to wrap by adjusting the width of the text box. Just select it and then drag the right side handle to the left or the right until the text wraps where you want. You can use Figure 4-1 as a reference.

5. Click the **Ellipse** tool and draw a circle that covers the imported text. To draw a perfect circle from the center of the text, hold down **Alt-Shift** (Windows) or **Option-Shift** (Macintosh) as you drag.

6. Use the Property inspector to change the stroke of the circle to **None** and the fill color to light gray, **#CCCCCC**.

7. With the circle still selected, click the **Modify** menu, point to **Arrange**, and then click **Send to Back** to move the circle behind the text. Remain in this screen for the next Step-by-Step.

Adding Live Effects

Live Effects are filters that apply to vector, bitmap, and text objects, as shown in Figure 4-5. Applying a Live Effect does not permanently change the original object. On the other hand, if you make a change to the original object, the Live Effect updates accordingly.

FIGURE 4-5
Effects section of the Property inspector

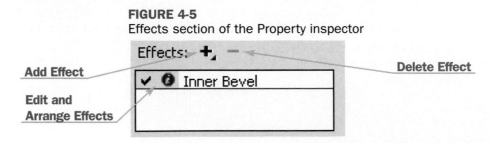

For example, if you create a button and then use Live Effects to apply a bevel and drop shadow, you can change the color and size of the original button, and the effects will be reapplied automatically to the new button. You apply or remove Live Effects by using the Effects pop-up menu on the Property inspector.

S TEP-BY-STEP 4.6

Applying and Editing an Effect

1. Click the **Ellipse** tool and draw a perfect circle that is **100** x **100** pixels. You can draw the circle anywhere on the page for now. You will complete the graphic and position it later. (You can use the Property inspector to enter exact height and width settings for the circle.)

2. Click the **Fill Color** box, and click the eyedropper on the blue color in the compass logo to change the circle's fill color to the same blue.

3. Click the **Add Effects** button on the Property Inspector, point to **Bevel and Emboss**, and then click **Inner Bevel**. A pop-up window opens, as shown in Figure 4-6.

FIGURE 4-6
Inner Bevel settings in the Effects pop-up window

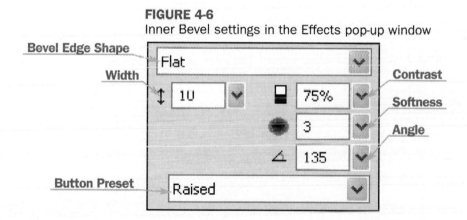

4. Click the arrow on the **Bevel Edge Shape** box and click **Smooth**. Make sure Contrast is set to **75**, Softness is set to **3**, and Angle is set to **135**. Enter **35** in the Width box. (*Hint:* If necessary, hover your mouse pointer on the options in the window to display their tooltips.) Click outside the pop-up window to close it.

5. Click the **Add Effects** button again, point to **Shadow and Glow**, and then click **Drop Shadow**. In the pop-up window, make sure the fill color is black (**#000000**). Enter **10** in the Distance box, **65%** in the Opacity box, **10** in the Softness box, and **315** in the Angle box. Click outside the pop-up window to close it.

STEP-BY-STEP 4.6 Continued

6. Make sure the circle with the Live Effects is selected. Notice that the Live Effects you applied to the object are represented by a list box in the right portion of the Property inspector, as shown in Figure 4-7. You can click the info button (the circle icon) next to an effect to open its pop-up window. Click the info button for each of the Live Effects and verify that you've entered the settings as described in steps 4 and 5. Click outside the pop-up window to close it.

FIGURE 4-7
Effects list with multiple effects

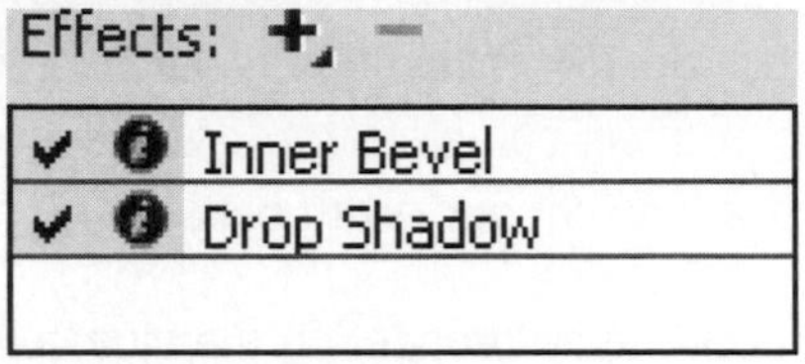

7. Save your file and remain in this screen for the next Step-by-Step.

When multiple effects are applied to an object, the order of the effects in the Effects list can change the look of the image.

S TEP-BY-STEP 4.7

Reordering Effects

1. Make sure the circle with the Live Effects is selected. Select the **Inner Bevel** effect name from the Effects list and then drag it down below the Drop Shadow effect. Changing the order of Inner Bevel and Drop Shadow changes the look of the circle.

2. Drag the **Drop Shadow** effect below the Inner Bevel. Deselect the circle. Remain in this screen for the next Step-by-Step.

Aligning Objects

T rying to align objects by using the rulers and guides can be a challenge. But by using the Align panel, you can quickly align several objects or evenly distribute them with the click of a button.

S TEP-BY-STEP 4.8

Aligning Objects

1. Click the **Window** menu, and then click **Align** to open the Align panel shown in Figure 4-8. (*Note*: If the Align panel doesn't look like that shown in Figure 4-8, click the **Anchors** button to deselect it.)

FIGURE 4-8
The Align panel

Click this button to align objects relative to the canvas

Click this button to apply alignment to selected points in a path

2. Shift-click to select the two text objects **the latest in** and **Adventure Travel** at the top of the Web page.

3. On the Align panel, click **Align Left Edge**. If necessary, hover your mouse pointer on the various buttons in the Align panel to display their tooltips.

4. Select the compass graphic in the upper right corner. Click the **Edit** menu, and then click **Duplicate**. A copy of the compass is offset from the original.

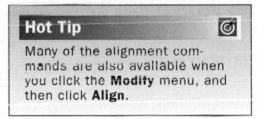

Hot Tip

Many of the alignment commands are also available when you click the **Modify** menu, and then click **Align**.

5. Drag the copy on top of the beveled circle. If the compass is behind the circle, bring it to the front.

6. Shift-click to select both the beveled circle and the compass graphic.

7. On the Align panel, click **Align Horizontal Center** and then click **Align Vertical Center**.

8. Click the **Modify** menu, and then click **Group** to group the beveled circle and the copy of the compass graphic. Then close the Align panel by clicking its **Close** button. The graphic should look like Figure 4-9.

FIGURE 4-9
The beveled circle and compass graphic grouped

STEP-BY-STEP 4.8 Continued

9. On the Property inspector, change the width and height of the grouped object to **32** x **32** pixels.

10. Move the grouped object to the left of the text *Welcome to Compass.* Remain in this screen for the next Step-by-Step.

Working with Masks

A *mask* is a window to something underneath. One way to create a mask in Fireworks is to use the Paste Inside command. You can think of the mask as a mat within a picture frame: only the area inside the mat is visible. Just as with a mat, you can use any shape for the mask. In fact, you can even use text or other objects to define the shape of the mask.

> **Hot Tip** 🎯
>
> Fireworks aligns objects on the left based on the leftmost object in the selected group and aligns objects on the right based on the rightmost object in the selected group. The topmost object controls Align Top, and the bottommost object controls Align Bottom. For Distribute Widths, Fireworks creates an equal amount of space between the objects, divided between the right edge of the leftmost objects and left edge of the rightmost objects. For Distribute Heights, Fireworks creates an equal amount of space between the objects, divided between the bottom edge of the highest and top edge of the lowest objects.

S TEP-BY-STEP 4.9

Creating a Mask by Using Paste Inside

1. Click the **File** menu, click **Import**, navigate to the **climber.gif** file in the **images** folder that's supplied with the data files for this course, and double-click it. Click to place it in the left section of the page.

2. Click the **Ellipse** tool and draw a circle that surrounds the climber in the picture (your finished circle should be about **60** x **60** pixels).

3. On the circle's Property inspector, click the arrow on the **Fill Category** box and select **None**. Click the arrow on the **Stroke Category** box, point to **Basic**, and then click **Soft Line**. Change the Tip Size to **2**. Change the stroke color to a dark yellow, **#FFFF00**.

4. Click the **Edit** menu, and then click **Duplicate** to make a copy of the circle. Use the Pointer tool to move the copy off to the side for now.

5. Click the **Pointer** tool and select the picture of the climber. Click the **Edit** menu, and then click **Cut** to copy the image to the Clipboard and delete it from the canvas.

> **Hot Tip** 🎯
>
> When you click the **Edit** menu and then click **Paste Inside**, the image is pasted in the same location on the canvas as when it was cut. If the image doesn't appear to be "inside" the selected circle, select the circle and then use the blue star-shaped move handle to reposition the image within the circle.

STEP-BY-STEP 4.9 Continued

6. Select the circle. Click the **Edit** menu, and then click **Paste Inside**. The image is pasted within the boundaries of the circle. Remain in this screen for the next Step-by-Step.

After you create the mask, you can change the position of the object within the mask, and you can split apart a mask and its object.

STEP-BY-STEP 4.10

Working with Objects in a Mask

1. Select the masked circle with the Pointer tool. Notice the small blue star within the selection. This is the move handle.

2. Drag the move handle to move the image within the mask.

3. Click the **Modify** menu, and then click **Ungroup**. The elements are now separated.

4. Click the **Edit** menu, and then click **Undo Ungroup**. Remain in this screen for the next Step-by-Step.

The only thing left to do on the Web page is to add the remaining masked images.

STEP-BY-STEP 4.11

Completing the Page

1. Select the copy of the circle you made in step 4 of Step-by-Step 4.9, and make three more copies by using the **Duplicate** command on the **Edit** menu.

2. Click the **File** menu, click **Import**, navigate to the **diver.gif** file in the **images** folder that's supplied with the data files for this course, and double-click it. Click to place it under the climber object.

3. With the diver image selected, click the **Modify** menu, point to **Arrange**, and click **Send to Back**.

STEP-BY-STEP 4.11 Continued

4. Drag one of the copies of the circle and position it on the diver, as shown in Figure 4-10.

FIGURE 4-10
The finished Compass Adventure page

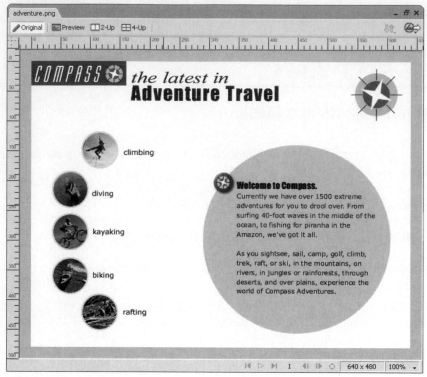

5. Select the picture of the diver. Click the **Edit** menu, and then click **Cut** to copy the image to the Clipboard and delete it from the canvas.

6. Select the circle. Click the **Edit** menu, and then click **Paste Inside**. The image is pasted within the boundaries of the circle.

7. Repeat steps 2 through 6 to place the **kayak.gif**, **biker.gif**, and **rafting.gif** images on the page. Refer to Figure 4-10.

8. Use the **Text** tool to create the one-word descriptions next to the masked images and position them as shown in Figure 4-10. Set the descriptions in size **12 Verdana**.

9. Save and close the **adventure** file.

SUMMARY

In this lesson, you learned to:

- Add text and special effects to your documents.

- Import text to your graphics and Web pages.

- Format text and position it in your documents.

- Add and edit Live Effects.

- Align and distribute objects.

- Create a mask by using Paste Inside.

CREATING BUTTONS

Understanding Rollover Buttons

A *button* is simply an object that performs some action when you click it. Most Web pages contain buttons that direct you to other information on the Web.

In Macromedia Fireworks MX 2004, a button is a symbol that has its own frames, slice, and code to enable the button behaviors. You can use the drawing tools and the Button Editor to create new buttons, or you can make a button from an existing graphic.

A rollover button changes appearance when the user moves the pointer over or clicks the button. There are four common rollover states: Up, Over, Down, and Over While Down. Each state reflects a particular type of user interaction with the button: when the user is not interacting with the button, when the user moves the pointer over the button, when the user clicks the button, and when the user holds the pointer over the button on a page where that button is already depressed. A button will always have the Up and Over states; the Down and Over While Down states are optional.

In this lesson you first change the look of the button for each state. Then Fireworks creates the HTML and JavaScript needed to make the rollover work in your browser.

Creating a Rollover Button

When you create a button in Fireworks, your button appears in the Button Editor. This window contains tabs for each state and makes creating new buttons a cinch.

When you create a new button, it is added to the library automatically. You can then use it over and over again by placing instances of the same button throughout your document.

A simple rollover requires only two graphics: for the Up and Over states. In Step-by-Step 5.1, you create a simple rollover button.

S TEP-BY-STEP 5.1

Creating the Up and Over States of a Button and Working in the Button Editor

1. Start Fireworks and open the **adventure5** file from the data files supplied with this course. Save it as **adventure5**, followed by your initials.

2. Click the **Window** menu and then click **Tile Vertical**. (This will allow you to switch between the Button Editor and the Document window.)

3. Click the **Edit** menu, point to **Insert**, and then click **New Button**. This opens the Button Editor window. You might need to drag the Button Editor window by its title bar so you can see the entire window. Figure 5-1 shows what the Up state will look like when you are finished drawing.

FIGURE 5-1
Button Editor showing the finished Up state of the new button

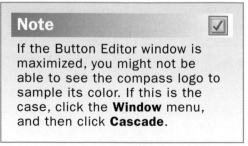

4. Click the **Rectangle** tool and draw a rectangle **115** pixels wide by **25** pixels high. (You can use the Property inspector to set or verify the size as you draw your rectangle.) Apply a fill color by sampling the color blue in the compass logo. (*Hint*: Click the **Fill Color** box, and then click the eyedropper on the blue color in the compass logo.)

5. Add a smaller rectangle **21** pixels wide by **25** pixels high. Color the small rectangle dark gray, **#333333**. Click the **Pointer** tool and drag the smaller rectangle on top of the first rectangle.

> **Note** ☑
>
> If the Button Editor window is maximized, you might not be able to see the compass logo to sample its color. If this is the case, click the **Window** menu, and then click **Cascade**.

6. Use Shift-click to select both rectangles. Click the **Modify** menu, point to **Align**, and then click **Left** to align the left edge of the second rectangle on top of the left edge of the first rectangle. Align their top edges as well.

STEP-BY-STEP 5.1 Continued

7. Select the **Polygon** tool (which is in the tool group with the Rectangle tool). On the Property inspector, click the arrow on the **Shape** box, and click **Polygon**. Highlight the value in the Sides box and enter **3**. Highlight the value in the Angle box and enter **38**. Set the fill color to white.

8. Move the pointer within the Button Editor, hold down **Shift** to constrain the shape of the triangle, and drag to draw a triangle small enough to fit within the gray rectangle. As you drag, move the pointer around to position the triangle with one of the angles pointing to the right, as shown in Figure 5-1.

9. Click the **Pointer** tool and drag the triangle on top of the gray rectangle.

10. Click the **Text** tool, click in the blue area of the rectangle, and key the name **ADVENTURE** (in all caps). Press **Enter** (Windows) or **Return** (Macintosh), and key **TRAVEL** (again, in all caps).

11. Highlight the text you just keyed. On the Property inspector, format the text to size **11**, **Arial**. Change the color to white, click the **Bold** button, and then click **Right Alignment** to align the text to the right. Make sure Horizontal scale is set to **100%** and Kerning is set to **0**.

12. Using Figure 5-1 as a reference, position the text within the rectangle.

13. Now, create the Over state of the button. Select the **Over** tab to create the rollover image. The rollover image is usually based on the original image, with perhaps just the color of the text or shade of the button changed.

14. Click the **Copy Up Graphic** button in the Button Editor window to make a copy of the button you just created.

15. Change the color of the triangle to red (**#FF0000**) and change the larger rectangle to dark blue (**#000066**).

16. Select the **Active Area** tab. The Active Area tab displays a green translucent area—a slice—over the button and red slice guides. The slice contains all of the link information about your button, and the slice guides display the exact size and position of the slice.

The size of the slice is set automatically based on the size of all states of the button. You can deselect the Set Active Area Automatically option to manually change the size of the slice for the button. The slice triggers the rollover in the browser when the user rolls over the object on the page. If your buttons are small, you might want to make the slice larger than the button to give the user a larger target for activating the button. For now, stick with the current settings.

17. Click the **Done** button at the bottom of the Button Editor window. Your button is visible, and you see the slice (a green translucent overlay) and the red slice guides. The slice guides are very helpful for placing other buttons on the page relative to this first one. The slice guides also determine the cells for the HTML table that is created if you export and save as an HTML file.

STEP-BY-STEP 5.1 Continued

If the guides are not visible, click the **View** menu and then click **Slice Guides** to display them. If the slice is not visible, click the **Show Slices and Hotspots** button on the Tools panel, as shown in Figure 5-2. Remain in this screen for the next Step-by-Step.

FIGURE 5-2
Web section of the Tools panel

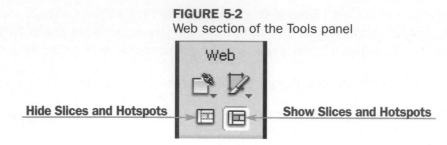

Hide Slices and Hotspots   **Show Slices and Hotspots**

You can modify a button by double-clicking it and making changes to it in the Button Editor. You can also preview how your button will look on the Web page by clicking the Preview button (Windows) or tab (Macintosh) in the Document window.

S TEP-BY-STEP 5.2

Modifying and Previewing a Button

1. Click the **Pointer** tool, and then double-click the **Adventure Travel** button to open the Button Editor. You can make changes to your button in the Button Editor. Remember that you have two images: the Up state and the Over state. Changing one does not automatically change the other—they are separate images. If you change the size of the first button, you might want to delete the rollover image and re-create the Over state of the button.

2. Click **Cancel** to close the Button Editor without making any changes.

3. Click the **Preview** button (Windows) or tab (Macintosh) in the Document window to view your button.

4. Move the pointer over the button to see the rollover image.

5. Click the **Original** button (Windows) or tab (Macintosh) to return to the Document window.

STEP-BY-STEP 5.2 Continued

6. Click the **Pointer** tool and move this button above the climbing button, as shown in Figure 5-3. Remain in this screen for the next Step-by-Step.

FIGURE 5-3
Final position of the Adventure Travel button

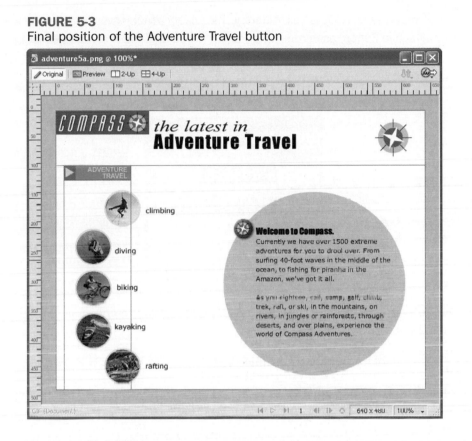

Using the Library Panel

The reusable objects stored on the Library panel are symbols. There are three types of symbols: graphic symbols, button symbols, and animation symbols. Once you add a symbol to the Library panel, you can place copies of the symbol—called instances—in your document. When you create a new button, Fireworks stores it in the library. You can then use the button over and over again by placing instances throughout your document. The library stores the master copy of your button, so if you make a change to the button, every instance of the button will be updated automatically. You can also use the Library panel to duplicate buttons and edit the copies to make new buttons based on an existing design.

In this task you use the Library panel to rename the button you just created. Then you make four new buttons based on the original.

STEP-BY-STEP 5.3

Working with Buttons

1. Click the **Window** menu, and then click **Library**. The Library panel moves to the foreground. The Library panel contains one button, as shown in Figure 5-4. (If you don't have a good view of the Library panel, you can undock it or collapse some of the other panels.)

FIGURE 5-4
Library panel

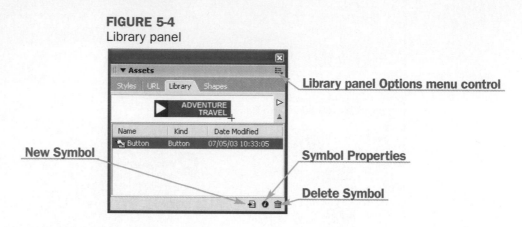

Library panel Options menu control

New Symbol

Symbol Properties

Delete Symbol

2. Double-click the button name, **Button** (one of the three types of symbols in Fireworks). The Symbol Properties dialog box opens.

3. Change the name of the button to **Adventure Travel** and click **OK**.

4. Click **Duplicate** on the Library **Options** menu, as shown in Figure 5-5. This creates a new button named *Adventure Travel 1*.

FIGURE 5-5
The Duplicate command on the Library Options menu

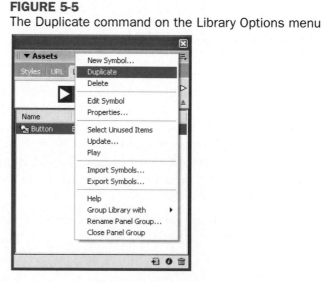

5. Double-click **Adventure Travel 1**, rename it **Featured Destinations**, and click **OK**.

   Now you need to edit the new button.

STEP-BY-STEP 5.3 Continued

6. With the **Featured Destinations** button still selected, double-click the preview of the button at the top of the Library panel. This opens the Featured Destinations Button Editor window.

7. Click the **Text** tool, highlight the label (**ADVENTURE TRAVEL**) on the button, and change the label to **FEATURED DESTINATIONS** (key the label in all caps, and remember to press **Enter** or **Return** after the word "FEATURED"). Click outside the text box. A message box opens, asking if you want to update the text in the other button states.

8. Click **Yes** and then click **Done**. You've just created a new button based on the original.

9. Follow steps 4 through 8 to add three more buttons. Name them **Adventure Gear**, **Travel Logs**, and **About Us**. Change the labels of the buttons to **ADVENTURE GEAR** (press **Enter** or **Return** after "ADVENTURE"), **TRAVEL LOGS** (press **Enter** or **Return** after "TRAVEL"), and **ABOUT US** (press **Enter** or **Return** after "ABOUT"). When editing the buttons, be sure to click outside the text box and click **Yes** to update the text in all button states. Then click **Done**.

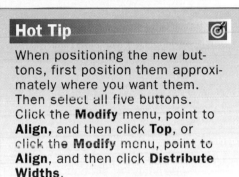

Hot Tip

When positioning the new buttons, first position them approximately where you want them. Then select all five buttons. Click the **Modify** menu, point to **Align,** and then click **Top**, or click the **Modify** menu, point to **Align**, and then click **Distribute Widths**.

10. To add the new buttons to the document, drag them from the Library panel to the canvas. Position them as shown in Figure 5-6. Save the document and remain in this screen for the next Step-by-Step.

FIGURE 5-6
Completed buttons

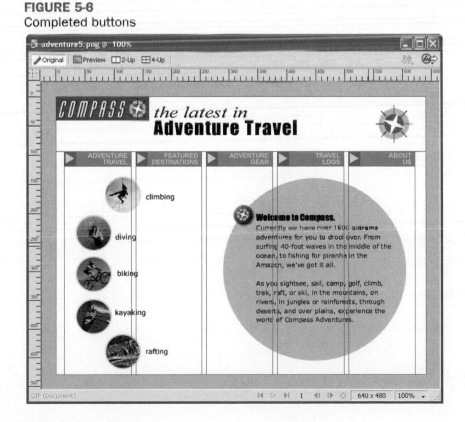

Establishing Links

The buttons you've created look great, but after you export the file, clicking your buttons doesn't do anything. You still need to set up your links. After all, the purpose of a button is to link to another HTML page. You could set up the links in another program such as Macromedia Dreamweaver MX 2004, but you can also take care of the links right in Fireworks.

S TEP-BY-STEP 5.4

Linking Buttons to HTML Pages

1. Select the **ADVENTURE TRAVEL** button. Make sure it's the only object selected.

2. Click in the **Link** box on the Property inspector and key the complete path name for the data file **travel.htm** (you may need to ask your instructor for the complete path name). Now when you export the file and click the **Adventure Travel** button, it will open the travel.htm Web page. You can also link to pages stored in other directories or to other URLs on the Web.

3. Click in the **Alt** box and then key **Adventure Travel**. The Alt box is used to create an alternative text description of the button for display in a browser.

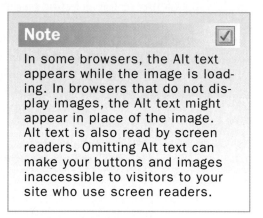

Note ✓

In some browsers, the Alt text appears while the image is loading. In browsers that do not display images, the Alt text might appear in place of the image. Alt text is also read by screen readers. Omitting Alt text can make your buttons and images inaccessible to visitors to your site who use screen readers.

4. Repeat steps 1 through 3 to establish links for the remaining four buttons. Use the following links: FEATURED DESTINATIONS button links to **featured.htm**, ADVENTURE GEAR button links to **gear.htm**, TRAVEL LOGS button links to **logs.htm**, and ABOUT US button links to **about.htm**. Use the button labels as the alternative text descriptions. Remain in this screen for the next Step-by-Step.

Creating a Button from a Graphic

So far, you've seen how easy it is to create a new button by using the Button Editor. But you can also turn your existing graphics into buttons. For example, the Adventure Travel Web page contains five graphics representing different types of adventures, such as rock climbing and diving.

Right now, these are bitmap graphics. If you click them, the Property inspector displays bitmap options. In other words, they're not buttons, and you can't use them currently to link to another HTML page. However, you can fix that if you convert the graphics to Fireworks buttons.

S TEP-BY-STEP 5.5

Converting Graphics to Buttons

1. Select the climbing graphic. You can tell by the selection border that the graphic is much larger than it appears. This means you will probably need to adjust the active area of the button.

2. Click the **Modify** menu, point to **Symbol**, and then click **Convert to Symbol**. The Symbol Properties dialog box opens.

3. Key **Climbing**, click the **Button** option, and click **OK**. The graphic is converted to a button, the Property inspector displays button options, and a copy of the new button is added to the Library panel.

    The large green area tells you that the slice for this button is much larger than it needs to be. You want the active area for this button to include the circle and the text to the right of the graphic. You also want the button to change when the user rolls over the image to show that it's a button.

4. Double-click the button to open the Button Editor.

5. Click the **Over** tab and click **Copy Up Graphic**.

6. Make sure the climbing graphic is selected. In the Layers panel, click the thumbnail next to the label "Bitmap." The Property inspector now shows the properties for a vector mask.

7. In the Property inspector, change the stroke color of the yellow circle to green, **#00FF00**.

8. Click the **Active Area** tab and deselect the **Set Active Area Automatically** option.

9. Drag the top slice guide to the top edge of the circle. Drag the bottom slide guide to the bottom edge of the circle. Drag the left slice guide to the left edge of the circle. Drag the right slice guide about one inch to the right edge of the circle. The width of the slice should be approximately 130 pixels. Then click **Done**. The slice should now look like Figure 5-7.

> **Note** ☑
>
> If your slice did not adjust, you probably did not deselect the **Set Active Area Automatically** option in step 8. It's an easy step to miss.

FIGURE 5-7
Edited slice

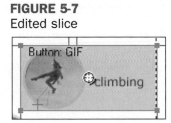

STEP-BY-STEP 5.5 Continued

10. On the Property inspector, link the climbing button to the **climbing.htm** file included in the data files supplied for this course. Be sure to key the complete path name for the file in the Link box, and key the button label **Climbing** in the Alt box.

11. Convert the four remaining circular graphics to buttons with green Over states and link them as follows: the diving button links to **diving.htm**, the biking button links to **biking.htm**, the kayaking button links to **kayaking.htm**, and the rafting button links to **rafting.htm**. Provide the alt text for each button. Your document should look like Figure 5-8.

FIGURE 5-8
The completed adventure5.png file

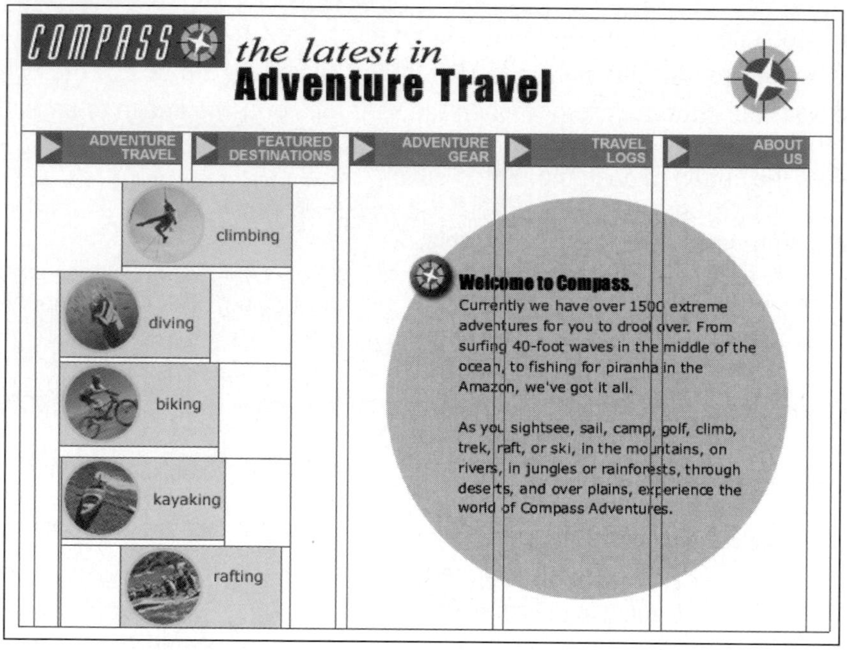

STEP-BY-STEP 5.5 Continued

12. Click the **File** menu, point to **Preview In Browser**, and select your default browser. You can now see what the file will look like when exported as HTML and viewed in your default browser. It should look similar to Figure 5-9.

FIGURE 5-9
The completed adventure5 file previewed in a browser

13. Close the browser window to return to the document.

14. Save and close the **adventure5** file.

SUMMARY

In this lesson, you learned to:

■ Create and edit rollover buttons.

■ Make new buttons from an existing one.

■ Use the library to add instances of a button.

■ Add links to your buttons.

■ Create a button from an existing graphic.

OPTIMIZING AND EXPORTING

Exporting Images

One of the most satisfying moments when working in Macromedia Fireworks MX 2004 is when you put the final touches on your artwork. But then what? Most likely you've created an image intended for a larger project, such as a Web site. That's why Fireworks gives you complete control when outputting your images to their final destination. With controls such as the Export Wizard and the Optimize panel, you can fine-tune the settings of your files before you export them for use in another program. Whether you're using your images on the Web or for multimedia, Fireworks provides several methods for creating the best-quality images with the smallest file size. Fireworks exports the following formats: GIF, JPEG, PNG, TIFF, PICT (Macintosh), WBMP, BMP, PSD, AI, SWF, and HTML.

The native file format of Fireworks is PNG. You should always keep a copy of your original PNG files in addition to the exported files you create. If you need to make changes to your images, simply change the PNG files and export them again.

There are several ways to export files from Fireworks. One is to follow the step-by-step advice of the Export Wizard. Another is to optimize the file manually by using the settings on the Optimize panel and then export the file by using the Export command or by using the Quick Export feature. Quick Export lets you select export options for Macromedia Flash, Dreamweaver, FreeHand, and Director; for Adobe Photoshop, GoLive, and Illustrator; for Microsoft FrontPage; and for previewing.

Using the Export Wizard

The Export Wizard walks you step-by-step through the process of exporting files. The wizard asks a series of questions and then suggests file types and optimization settings. You can also set a file size for the Export Wizard to use as a target for the optimization. At the end of the question dialog boxes, the Export Preview dialog box opens with optimization suggestions.

S TEP-BY-STEP 6.1

Exporting an Image to a Set Size

1. Open the **banner6.png** file from the data files supplied with this course.

2. Click the **File** menu, and then click **Export Wizard**. The Export Wizard dialog box opens, as shown in Figure 6-1.

FIGURE 6-1
First step of the Export Wizard

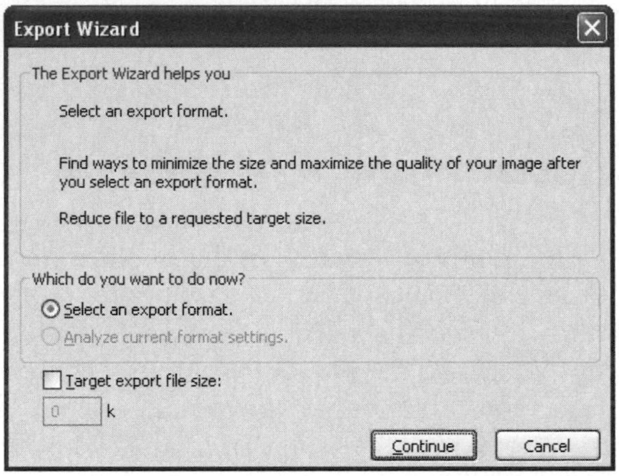

> **Note** ✓
>
> If you select the **Target Export File Size** option, Fireworks attempts to optimize the file at that size by adjusting the quality of JPEG files, modifying the smoothing for JPEG files, changing the number of colors for GIF files, and changing dithering settings for GIF files. This feature is especially important when you want to create images or animated GIF files that don't exceed maximum file size limits for banner ads on commercial sites.

STEP-BY-STEP 6.1 Continued

3. Click the **Target Export File Size** check box, enter **15**, and click **Continue** to go to the second step of the wizard, as shown in Figure 6-2.

FIGURE 6-2
Second step of the Export Wizard

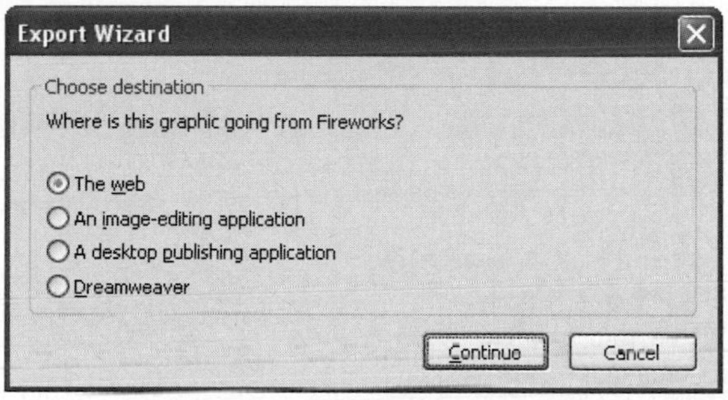

4. This is where you select a destination type for the image. Make sure **The Web** is selected. Then click **Continue** to go to the final step of the wizard. The wizard recommends optimization settings based on your feedback, as shown in Figure 6-3.

FIGURE 6-3
Analysis Results step of the Export Wizard

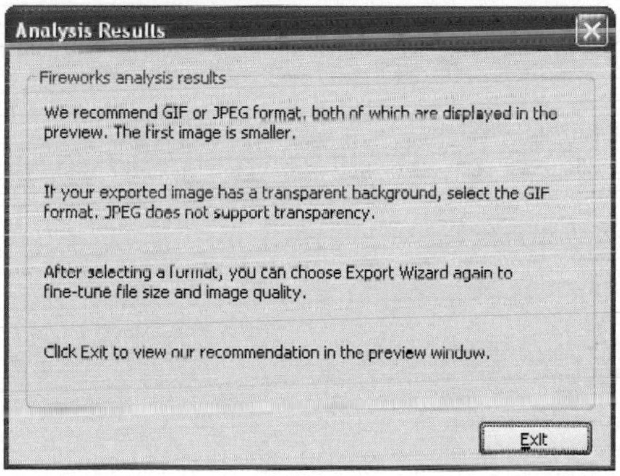

STEP-BY-STEP 6.1 Continued

5. Click **Exit** to go to the Export Preview window shown in Figure 6-4. The upper-right panel displays the image in GIF format; the lower-right panel displays the image in JPEG format. The left panel shows the recommended optimization settings for the currently selected panel—in this case, the GIF format. Exporting now would export the file as a GIF file.

FIGURE 6-4
Export Preview window

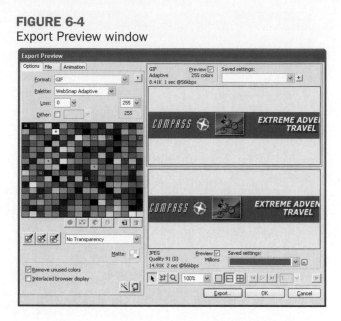

6. Click twice (Windows—*not* a double-click) or click once (Macintosh) on the JPEG image in the lower-right panel to display the recommended JPEG settings. Exporting now would export the file as a JPEG file.

7. Change back to the GIF settings by clicking twice (Windows) or clicking once (Macintosh) on the GIF image, and click **Export**. The Export dialog box opens.

8. Make sure the new filename is **banner.gif** and that **Images Only** is selected in the Save as Type (Windows) or Save As (Macintosh) box.

9. Display the folder to which you are saving course files, and click **Save** to export. A new file named banner.gif is placed in the folder.

10. Close the **banner6.png** file. Do not save changes if you are asked. Leave Fireworks open for the next Step-by-Step.

Optimizing the Image

When you use the Export Wizard, Fireworks recommends optimization settings based on how you answer the wizard's questions. You can also select your optimization settings by using the Optimize panel. The first step is to determine which type of file you plan to export, such as GIF or JPEG. You can then select the detailed settings.

Exporting GIF Images

GIF images are generally used for line art and images with solid colors. GIF images can contain transparent areas and can be used for animation files. If you choose GIF as your export file format, you need to pick the color palette for the export. The disadvantage of GIF images is that they are restricted to 256 colors.

When you export GIF images, you choose a color palette for the file. The color palette is a group of colors from which the image is created. Fireworks contains 10 preset palettes. The following list describes the default palettes:

- **Adaptive:** Creates a custom palette containing the majority of the colors in the image.

- **WebSnap Adaptive** (also called **Web Adaptive** on the Optimize panel): Creates a bridge between the Web 216 palette and the Adaptive palette. Colors within a tolerance of seven color steps are snapped to the closest Web-safe color.

- **Web 216:** A palette of the 216 colors that have a similar appearance on both Windows and Macintosh computers. This is sometimes called a Web-safe or browser-safe palette because it generates the most consistent results on different platforms and different browsers.

- **Exact:** Contains the exact colors in the image when the image contains 256 colors or fewer.

- **Macintosh, Windows:** Contains 256 colors as defined by either the Windows or Macintosh system colors.

- **Grayscale:** A palette of 256 (or fewer) shades of gray. Using this palette converts your image to grayscale.

- **Black & White:** A palette of only two colors: black and white.

- **Uniform:** A mathematical palette based on RGB pixel values.

- **Custom:** Gives the user the option of importing another color table (an *.act file). You can also import another GIF file that contains the colors you want to use.

STEP-BY-STEP 6.2

Selecting GIF Optimization Settings and Exporting a GIF File

1. Open the **compass_logo6.png** file from the data files supplied with this course.

   Click the **Window** menu, and then click **Optimize** to open the Optimize panel shown in Figure 6-5. You can change the format for the exported file by using the Export File Format pop-up menu.

FIGURE 6-5
Optimize panel

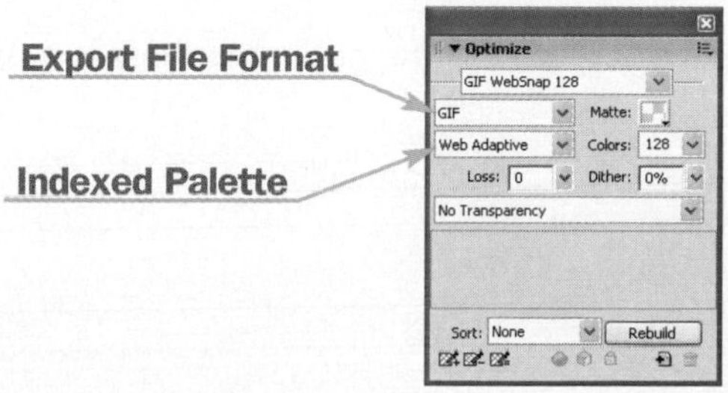

Export File Format

Indexed Palette

STEP-BY-STEP 6.2 Continued

2. Click the arrow on the **Export File Format** box. You see several formats, such as GIF, Animated GIF, JPEG, WBMP, PNG, and TIFF, from which you can select.

3. Make sure **GIF** is selected.

4. Click the arrow on the **Indexed Palette** pop-up menu. As shown in Figure 6-6, you see several color palettes from which you can choose.

FIGURE 6-6
Indexed palette pop-up menu

5. Make sure **Web Adaptive** is selected. You can set the number of colors for the palette by using the Maximum Number of Colors pop-up menu. If you want a smaller file size, use a smaller number. If you pick a number that is smaller than the actual number of colors in the image, some colors are lost. The pixels with the lost colors are converted to the closest remaining colors on the palette.

6. Make sure Maximum Number of Colors is set to **128**. You can enter a dither amount if you want that option.

7. Make sure Dither is set to **0%**. If your image was intended to include transparent areas, you could use Index Transparency to create the transparent areas based on color. You could also click the Matte box and use the eyedropper to pick a color that is used as the background color when exported.

> **Note** ☑
>
> Dithering is a process of approximating colors not on the current palette. A dithered image often looks "noisy" (grainy); however, dithering can help smooth the banding created by a gradient-like transition of colors.

8. Make sure **No Transparency** is selected.

9. Click **Rebuild** to update the palette based on your current selection and the colors in your image.

10. Click the **File** menu, and then click **Export** to open the Export dialog box.

11. Make sure the new filename is **compass_logo6.gif** and that **Images Only** is selected in the Save as Type (Windows) or Save As (Macintosh) box.

STEP-BY-STEP 6.2 Continued

12. Display the folder to which you are saving course files, and click **Save** to export. A new file named compass_logo6.gif is placed in the folder.

13. Close the **compass_logo6.png** file. Do not save changes if you are asked. Leave Fireworks open for the next Step-by-Step.

Exporting as JPEG

> ### Hot Tip
> For even more optimization settings, open the **Options** menu on the Optimize panel. For example, you can choose **Remove Unused Colors** to create the smallest file with the least number of colors. Or choose **Interlaced** if you want images to partially load in the browser at a low resolution and then transition to full resolution as they continue to download.

Use JPEG to export photographs or any artwork with gradations or millions of colors in the image. JPEG files cannot be transparent or animated. Unlike GIF images, JPEG images don't need a color palette. JPEG uses a lossy compression scheme, meaning it looks at your image and removes information as part of its compression algorithm. This causes a loss in quality. You set the level of quality for the compression on the Optimize panel.

STEP-BY-STEP 6.3

Selecting the JPEG Optimization Settings and Exporting a JPEG File

1. Open the **girl_pumpkin6.png** file from the data files supplied with this course.

2. On the Optimize panel, make sure the **Export File Format** pop-up menu is set to **JPEG**. The Optimize panel displays settings for JPEG files, as shown in Figure 6-7. JPEG images are always saved in 24-bit color, so you can't optimize a JPEG image by editing its color palette. The color table is empty when a JPEG image is selected.

FIGURE 6-7
Optimization settings for the JPEG format

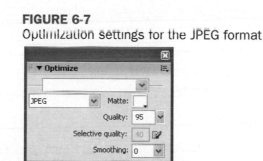

3. Highlight the value in the Quality box and enter **100**. Quality determines the amount of data loss when compressing the file. The lower the number, the greater the compression and the smaller the file, but the poorer the quality of the image.

STEP-BY-STEP 6.3 Continued

4. Make sure the value in the Smoothing box is **0**. Smoothing blurs the hard edges of the image, which do not compress well in JPEG format. The higher the number, the greater the blurring and the smaller the files.

5. Click the **File** menu, and then click **Export** to open the Export dialog box.

6. Make sure the new filename is **girl_pumpkin6.jpg** and that **Images Only** is selected in the Save as Type (Windows) or Save As (Macintosh) box.

7. Display the folder to which you are saving course files, and click **Save** to export. A new file named girl_pumpkin6.jpg is placed in the folder. Remain in this screen for the next Step-by-Step.

> **Hot Tip**
>
> Selective Quality compression lets you compress different areas of a JPEG image at different levels. If the area is of particular interest, it can be compressed at a high level. Areas of lesser significance, such as backgrounds, can be compressed at a low level, reducing the overall size of the image while retaining the quality of the more important areas.

Previewing in the Workspace

You can preview your images within the Document window before exporting them. The Preview button (Windows) or tab (Macintosh) displays the graphic as it would appear in a Web browser, based on your optimization settings. You can even preview rollover and navigation behaviors, as well as animation.

By splitting the window into two or four preview panes, you can compare multiple optimization settings side by side before exporting. Fireworks also displays the file size and the approximate download times within each preview window.

> **Hot Tip**
>
> For even more optimization settings, open the Optimize panel **Options** menu. You can choose **Progressive JPEG**, which is a JPEG format that supports a higher compression rate. Some browsers and image-editing programs might not support this format. Or you can choose **Sharpen JPEG Edges** to preserve edges between two colors. You can use this option to preserve the crispness of text against a solid color. This option increases the file size.

STEP-BY-STEP 6.4

Previewing an Image

1. Click the **Preview** button (Windows) or tab (Macintosh) at the top of the Document window. With Optimization set to JPEG, you see what the girl_pumpkin6.jpg file will look like in a browser. Because the Matte Color is set to white, the image will look best when placed over a white background.

> **Hot Tip**
>
> Because this image has a feathered edge and JPEGs cannot be transparent, you'll want to make sure the Matte Color you select is the same as the background where you plan to use the exported image.

STEP-BY-STEP 6.4 Continued

2. Click the **2-Up** button (Windows) or tab (Macintosh). This divides the document into two panes. Size the Document window so you can see both panes. Use the Preview pop-up menu at the bottom of each pane to make sure one pane is showing the Original image and the other pane is showing the Export Preview (JPEG).

3. Click the **4-Up** button (Windows) or tab (Macintosh). This shows one original and three JPEG preview options, as shown in Figure 6-8.

   You can compare various settings by selecting a pane and then changing settings for that image on the Optimize panel.

> **Note**
>
> The original image appears in the left pane when 2-Up is selected. It appears in the upper-left quadrant when 4-Up is selected.

FIGURE 6-8
Preview window showing 4-Up tab

4. Click the preview image in the lower-left corner, highlight the value in the Quality box on the Optimize panel, and enter **40**. At 40 the file size is much smaller, but the quality isn't very good. You can compare the results of different optimization settings by experimenting with the preview panes.

5. Click the preview image in the lower-right corner and change the JPEG quality to **95**. At 95, the file size and download times are much better than before, and the image quality still looks good.

6. Click the **Original** tab to accept the settings in the selected preview pane. The JPEG quality is now set to 95 for the original file.

7. Close the **girl_pumpkin6.png** file. Do not save changes if you are asked to. Leave Fireworks open for the next Step-by-Step.

Using Quick Export

The Quick Export button, located in the upper-right corner of the Document window, offers easy access to common options for exporting Fireworks files to other applications. By using the Quick Export button, you can export to a variety of formats, including Macromedia applications and other applications such as Microsoft FrontPage.

For example, you can export Dreamweaver HTML, or you can export a Macromedia Flash SWF file. You can even use the Quick Export button to launch other applications or to preview Fireworks documents in a preferred browser. By streamlining the export process, the Quick Export button saves time and improves the design workflow.

When you use the Quick Export button, Fireworks exports graphics and slices with the settings you specify on the Optimize panel, so be sure you've optimized your graphic before using Quick Export.

S TEP-BY-STEP 6.5

Using Quick Export

1. Open the **adventure_travel6.png** file from the data files supplied with this course. This file was designed to be an entire HTML page, so use the Quick Export button to export the file as Dreamweaver HTML.

2. Click the **Quick Export** button to open the Quick Export pop-up menu shown in Figure 6-9.

FIGURE 6-9
Quick Export button and pop-up menu

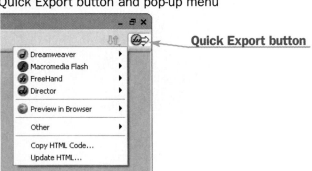

3. Point to **Dreamweaver**, and then click **Export HTML**.

4. Make sure the new filename is **adventure6.htm** and that **HTML and Images** is selected in the Save as Type (Windows) or Save As (Macintosh) box. **Export Slices** should be selected in the Slices box.

5. Make sure **Include Areas Without Slices** is selected.

6. Navigate to the Adventure Travel folder, and click **Save** to export. A new file named adventure6.htm is placed in the folder, along with several related images. You can open this file in a Web browser and try it out.

7. Close the **adventure_travel6.png** file. Do not save changes to the file if you are asked.

SUMMARY

In this lesson, you learned to:

- Export graphics by using the Export Wizard.
- Optimize your file before exporting it.
- Select a color palette when exporting.
- Export an image as a GIF or JPEG file.
- Preview a document in the workspace.
- Use the Quick Export menu to export graphics.

CREATING ANIMATIONS

Animating with Fireworks

There was a time when most Web sites were filled with page after page of text. But these days, Web surfers demand much more. At the very least, your site should contain colors and graphic images to help communicate and make your site more interesting. You can take that to the next level by adding animation to your pages. Animation is good for getting the reader's attention, and it's also a great way to illustrate concepts and model ideas.

The most common animations you'll find on the Web are simple animated GIF images. They're popular because they're typically fairly small files, and they don't require any special software to view them. They appear in your Web browser along with the rest of your images. The animations you create in Macromedia Fireworks MX 2004 are most commonly exported as GIF animations.

Animating in Fireworks is done by placing an object in a frame and then placing a slightly different copy of the object in the next frame—maybe with the object moved, made more transparent, or rotated. Once you have a series of frames, you can play them back quickly to get the appearance of motion.

In Fireworks, you can build your animations one frame at a time, or you can automate the process by using features such as tweening. With tweening, you set the first and last frames of an animation and then tell Fireworks to fill in the gap; Fireworks automatically creates the in-between frames.

If you want to use an animation over and over again, you can create an animation symbol. The symbol is added to the library, and you can add instances of the animation to different parts of your document. You can even export the symbol for use in other documents.

Creating Animation Symbols

The main advantage of symbols is that you can create the object once, store it in the library, and use it over and over again. You can place several copies, or instances, of the symbol in your document and then make changes to the instances without altering the original symbol. Fireworks uses three types of symbols: graphic symbols, animation symbols, and buttons.

S TEP-BY-STEP 7.1

Creating and Previewing an Animation Symbol

1. Create a new document. Make the canvas size **600** pixels wide by **150** pixels high and the color **white**.

2. Make sure the **Show Grid** and **Snap to Grid** options are turned off (click the **View** menu and point to **Grid** to deselect these options).

3. Save the file as **animated_logo**, followed by your initials.

4. Click the **Window** menu, and then click **Frames** to view the Frames panel. This document contains one frame, as shown in Figure 7-1. (You might want to collapse one or more of the other panels, such as Optimize, to get a better view of the Frames panel.)

FIGURE 7-1
Frames panel

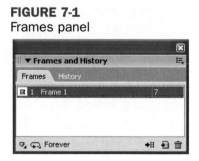

5. Import the **compass_logo7.png** file from the data files supplied with this course. Click to place it in the center of the canvas.

STEP-BY-STEP 7.1 Continued

6. With the logo still selected, click the **Modify** menu, point to **Symbol**, and then click **Convert to Symbol**. This opens the Symbol Properties dialog box, as shown in Figure 7-2, where you can give your symbol a name and choose whether it is to be a graphic, an animation, or a button.

FIGURE 7-2
Symbol Properties dialog box

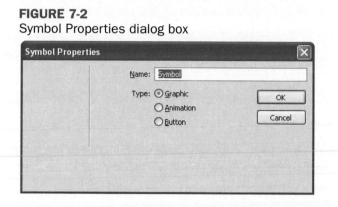

7. Key **Faded Logo** for the name of the symbol, click the **Animation** option, and click **OK** to open the Animate dialog box.

8. Enter **5** in the Frames text box. The more frames, the smoother the animation, but the bigger the file.

9. Make sure the Move and Direction text boxes are set to **0**. The Move option determines how far the object will move, and Direction tells it which direction to move. Because this will be a fade only, you don't want the object to move at all.

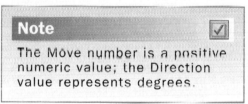

> **Note** ☑
> The Move number is a positive numeric value; the Direction value represents degrees.

10. Make sure the Scale To text box is set to **100**. These settings tell the object to start out smaller or larger and then scale during the animation.

11. Enter **0** (for 0 percent) in the first Opacity text box and **100** (for 100 percent) in the second Opacity text box. The object will seem to materialize right before the viewer's eyes.

12. Make sure the Rotate text box is set to **0** (for 0 degrees). Rotating creates the effect of a spinning object.

13. Click **OK**.

When you see a message that you need to add frames to accommodate the animation, click **OK** to accept the new frames. The document now contains five frames, as shown on the Frames panel.

STEP-BY-STEP 7.1 Continued

14. In the frame controls at the bottom of the Document window shown in Figure 7-3, click **Play**. The animation loops repeatedly.

FIGURE 7-3
Frame controls in the Document window

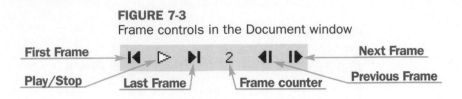

15. Click the **Stop** control. The animation stops. You can use the Previous Frame and Next Frame buttons in the frame controls to view the animation frame by frame.

16. Click **First Frame** to move to the beginning of the animation. Because this animation fades up from 0 opacity, the first frame is transparent. Remain in this screen for the next Step-by-Step.

The advantage of using animation symbols over frame-by-frame animation is that the initial image—the symbol—controls the overall look of all the other images. If you change something in the symbol (color, size, or rotation, for example), the instances are changed as well. They are, in a sense, linked together. If you had created the animation frame by frame, you would need to make your changes in each frame. That could take a long time.

STEP-BY-STEP 7.2

Editing an Instance of the Symbol

1. Click the **Faded Logo** symbol on the canvas to select it. Because you are in frame 1, the logo is transparent, but you can select it. Move the pointer over the logo until you see the red handles and then click. The red handles are replaced by blue handles, indicating that the logo is selected.

2. On the Property inspector, enter **12** in the Frames text box. Then press **Enter** (Windows) or **Return** (Macintosh), and click **OK** again to accept the added frames.

3. Click **Play** to preview the animation. This instance now plays for 12 frames, which creates a smoother animation than five frames. The document now contains 12 frames.

4. Click **Stop** to stop the animation.

5. Return to frame 1 and move the Faded Logo symbol to the bottom center of the canvas. Even though it's transparent, you can select and move it. Save your work and remain in this screen for the next Step-by-Step.

> **Note** ☑️
>
> You can move between frames by using the frame controls at the bottom of the Document window or by selecting the desired frame on the Frames panel.

Creating Frame Animations

The next Step-by-Step demonstrates basic frame-by-frame animation for creating an animated GIF image. You import a graphic object and animate the object moving across the screen.

Right now, this document contains 12 frames. The Frames panel is visible, and you are viewing frame 1.

S TEP-BY-STEP 7.3

Creating a Frame-by-Frame Animation

1. Import the **compass7.png** file from the data files supplied with this course. Click to place the object in the upper-left corner of the canvas.

2. Make a duplicate of the grouped compass. You can click the **Edit** menu and then click **Duplicate** or begin dragging and hold down **Alt** (Windows) or **Option** (Macintosh) to make the copy. Place the copy to the right of the original.

3. Continue to make new copies until you have nine copies placed on the canvas. Line up the compasses in a row from left to right, as shown in Figure 7-4.

>
> ### Note ☑️
> The Alt or Option key is the keyboard shortcut for the Subselection tool. If you hold down the **Alt** or **Option** key first, the Pointer tool changes to the Subselection tool. Dragging with the Subselection tool duplicates and drags only a portion of the grouped object. Drag the object first and then add the Alt or Option key to make a copy of the compass.

FIGURE 7-4
Copies on the canvas

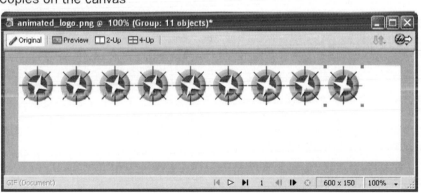

> ### Hot Tip 🎯
> After making and positioning your first duplicate, you can open the **History** panel, choose the **Duplicate** command, and click **Replay** to make additional duplicates.

STEP-BY-STEP 7.3 Continued

4. Select all nine objects. Make sure not to select the Faded Logo symbol by accident. (You can tell how many objects you have selected by looking on the title bar.)

5. Click the **Distribute to Frames** button on the Frames panel, as shown in Figure 7-5. This places each individual object in a separate frame. The first object you created is placed in the first frame. The remaining objects are placed in subsequent frames in the order they were created. Frames 1 through 9 now contain copies of the compass graphic. Frames 1 through 12 are used for the Faded Logo graphic.

FIGURE 7-5
Frames panel

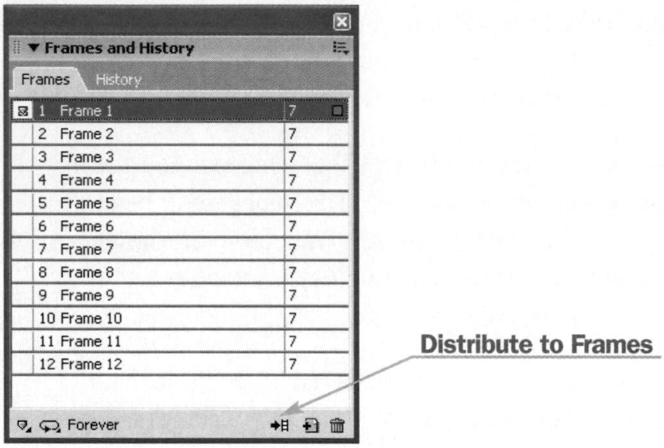

Distribute to Frames

6. Click each frame on the Frames panel to view successive frames of the animation.

STEP-BY-STEP 7.3 Continued

7. Click **Play** at the bottom of the Document window to pre-view the animation. The animation displays each com-pass object as the compass moves across the canvas.

8. Click **Stop** at the bottom of the Document window. Remain in this screen for the next Step-by-Step.

Using Onion Skinning

Onion skinning is a traditional animation technique that enables you to see and manipulate objects before and after the current frame. When you're creating frame-by-frame animation, this helps you position objects in each frame without flipping back and forth between frames. When onion skinning is turned on, objects in frames before and after the current frame are dimmed so you can distinguish them from objects in the current frame.

> **Hot Tip** ⊚
>
> When you create your anima-tions, Fireworks adds new frames for you automatically. You can also add and delete frames manually by using the **New/Duplicate Frame** (docu-ment icon with a plus sign) and **Delete Frame** (trashcan) buttons at the bottom of the Frames panel. Any frame selected when you click the trashcan will be deleted. You can Ctrl-click (Windows) or Command-click (Macintosh) to select more than one frame for deletion.

In the following Step-by-Step, you use onion skinning to reposition the Faded Logo symbol so it appears in line with the animated compass.

STEP-BY-STEP 7.4

Using Onion Skinning

1. Select frame **6** on the Frames panel.

2. Click the **Onion Skinning** button at the bottom of the Frames panel, as shown in Figure 7-6, and choose **Before and After** from the pop-up menu.

FIGURE 7-6
Onion Skinning button and pop-up menu

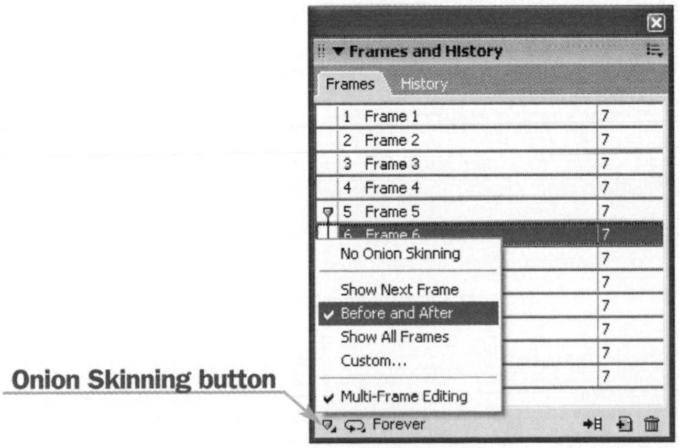

STEP-BY-STEP 7.4 Continued

A vertical bar appears on the Frames panel indicating all of the visible frames, as shown in Figure 7-7. You can add or remove frames from the view by clicking the frame numbers. Frame 6 is selected, so frames 5 and 7 are partially visible, making it easier to align the objects in the animation. When using onion skinning, only the current frame is 100% opaque; the others are partially visible to help you know which frame is selected.

FIGURE 7-7
Frames panel showing onion skinning

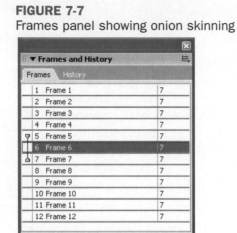

3. Click to the left of frame **9** on the Frames panel to view onion skinning for frames 5 to 9.

4. Drag the **Faded Logo** symbol so the compass in the logo lines up with the compass in frame 9, as shown in Figure 7-8.

FIGURE 7-8
Using onion skinning to align objects

STEP-BY-STEP 7.4 Continued

5. Click **Play** in the Document window to preview the animation.

6. Click **Stop** and turn off onion skinning (click **Onion Skinning** and choose **No Onion Skinning**). Remain in this screen for the next Step-by-Step.

> **Hot Tip** ◎
>
> You can choose **Custom** from the **Onion Skinning** pop-up menu to view more than three frames at once and to change the opacity of the frames before and after the current frame. You can also choose **Multi-Frame Editing** to enable other frames to be selected and edited (even though they are dimmed).

Controlling Playback

After you have the animation sequence working, you can change the playback speed by setting the frame delay. The frame delay determines the amount of time each frame is displayed. Frame delay is specified in hundredths of a second. For example, a setting of 100 displays the frame for a second, and a setting of 25 displays the frame for a quarter of a second.

STEP-BY-STEP 7.5

Setting the Frame Delay

1. Click frame **1** on the Frames panel to select the first frame. Hold down **Shift** and click the last frame to select all 12 frames in the animation.

2. Display the Frames panel **Options** menu. Then choose **Properties** to open the Frame Delay window, as shown in Figure 7-9.

FIGURE 7-9
Frames panel Options menu and Frame Delay window

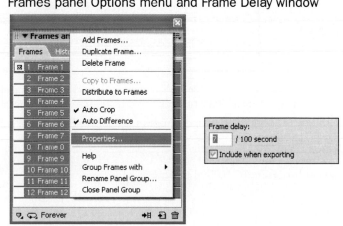

STEP-BY-STEP 7.5 Continued

3. Enter **5** in the Frame Delay box to speed up the animation.

4. Click outside the Frame Delay settings window to close it. Remain in this screen for the next Step-by-Step.

Setting Looping

Looping makes the animation play over and over. You can control the number of times your animation loops by using the GIF Animation Looping button on the Frames panel.

> **Hot Tip**   ◎
>
> You can also double-click the selected frame to display the properties. Double-click the **Frame Delay** column (the right column), not the frame name. You can rename each frame by double-clicking the name and entering a new name.

STEP-BY-STEP 7.6

1. Click the **GIF Animation Looping** button on the Frames panel. The GIF Animation Looping pop-up menu appears, as shown in Figure 7-10.

FIGURE 7-10
GIF Animation Looping pop-up menu

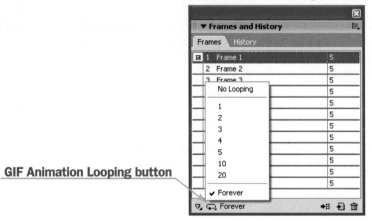

GIF Animation Looping button

2. Choose **No Looping** and then click **Play** to preview the animation with your new playback settings. Even though you selected no looping, your animation will loop when you play it back in the document. However, it will not loop when exported as an animated GIF image.

3. Click **Stop**. Remain in this screen for the next Step-by-Step.

Applying Tweening

Tweening is the process of defining beginning and end frames and then creating images in between to give the appearance that the first frame slowly changes to the end frame. You define an image as a symbol, place two instances of the symbol on the canvas, and then let Fireworks calculate (tween) the images in the middle. In this task, you use tweening to animate between two instances of a graphic symbol.

S TEP-BY-STEP 7.7

Using Tweening

1. Select frame **1**.

2. Click the **Text** tool and key the words **Adventure Travel** on the canvas. Make the text size **36**, **Impact**, and black. For now, position the text in the lower-left corner of the canvas.

3. With the text object selected, click the **Modify** menu, point to **Symbol**, and then click **Convert to Symbol** to open the Symbol Properties dialog box.

4. Key **Adventure Travel** as the name, make sure **Graphic** is selected, and click **OK** to convert the text to a graphic symbol. The text is converted to a graphic symbol and added to the library.

5. Drag another instance of **Adventure Travel** from the Library panel (if necessary, click the **Window** menu and click **Library** to display the Library panel), and position it below the Compass logo, as shown in Figure 7-11. Because the logo in the first frame is transparent, you may want to turn on onion skinning so you can see the Compass logo for better positioning.

FIGURE 7-11
Adventure Travel added below the Compass logo

STEP-BY-STEP 7.7 Continued

6. Select the first instance of Adventure Travel (the one that is *not* positioned below the logo). Use the Scale tool to stretch it both horizontally and vertically, making it much larger and distorted.

7. Highlight the value in the Opacity box on the Property inspector and change the opacity of the larger Adventure Travel instance to **0**.

8. Drag the large transparent **Adventure Travel** instance beyond the left edge of the canvas as far as you can. Even though it is transparent, you can position it by using its selection border.

9. Shift-click to select both instances of **Adventure Travel**. Click the **Modify** menu, point to **Symbol**, and then click **Tween Instances** to open the Tween Instances dialog box.

10. Make sure the Steps text box is set to **10**, click **Distribute to Frames**, and click **OK**.

11. Click **Play** to preview the animation and then click **Stop**. Remain in this screen for the next Step-by-Step.

Exporting a GIF Animation

When you have completed the animation, you can export the file as an animated GIF image and add it to your HTML pages.

You can use the Optimize panel to tell Fireworks you want the exported file to be an animated GIF image.

STEP-BY-STEP 7.8

Exporting a GIF Animation

1. Make sure the Optimize panel is open by clicking the **Window** menu and then clicking **Optimize**.

2. Click the arrow on the **Export File Format** box and select **Animated GIF**.

STEP-BY-STEP 7.8 Continued

3. Change the Indexed Palette to **Web Adaptive**. The Optimize panel should look like Figure 7-12.

FIGURE 7-12
Optimize panel with Animated GIF selected

4. Click the **File** menu, and then click **Export** to export the file. The Export dialog box opens. Make sure the new filename is **animated_logo.gif** and that **Images Only** is selected in the Save as Type (Windows) or Save As (Macintosh) box.

5. Display the folder to which you are saving course files, and click **Save** to export. A new file named animated_logo.gif is placed in the folder. You can now view this file in a Web browser.

6. Leave the **animated_logo.png** file open for the next Step-by-Step.

Using Export Preview

The default settings for animated GIF files will work for most of your animations, but if you'd like to experiment with the settings, use the Export Preview window. You can set any number of loops, change the disposal method, and even hide a frame from view.

The disposal method controls what happens to the previous frame after the current one is displayed. The types of methods are:

- **Unspecified:** No disposal method is specified. Fireworks automatically selects the disposal method for each frame. Select Unspecified to create the smallest possible animated GIF file and for full-frame animations.

■ **None:** The frame is not disposed of before the new frame is displayed. The next frame appears on top of the current frame. Select None to add a smaller object to the existing frame, for full-frame animations, and for frame optimization and transparency.

■ **Restore to Background:** This option erases the current frame's image and restores the area to the background color or pattern that appears in the Web browser. Select Restore to Background when moving an object in a transparent animated GIF file.

■ **Restore to Previous:** This option erases the current frame's image and restores that area to the previous frame's image. Select Restore to Previous to animate objects across a background image within the animation.

S TEP-BY-STEP 7.9

Controlling Settings with Export Preview

1. Click the **File** menu, and then click **Export Preview** to access the Export Preview window shown in Figure 7-13.

> **Note** ☑
>
> The Export Preview window lets you change your settings and see the results of your changes in a single window.

FIGURE 7-13
The Export Preview window

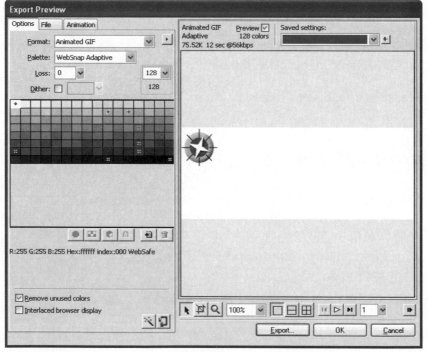

STEP-BY-STEP 7.9 Continued

2. Select the **Animation** tab of the Export Preview window.

3. Click the **Disposal Method** button to display the pop-up menu, as shown in Figure 7-14. Make sure the **Unspecified** option is selected.

FIGURE 7-14
Disposal Method pop-up menu

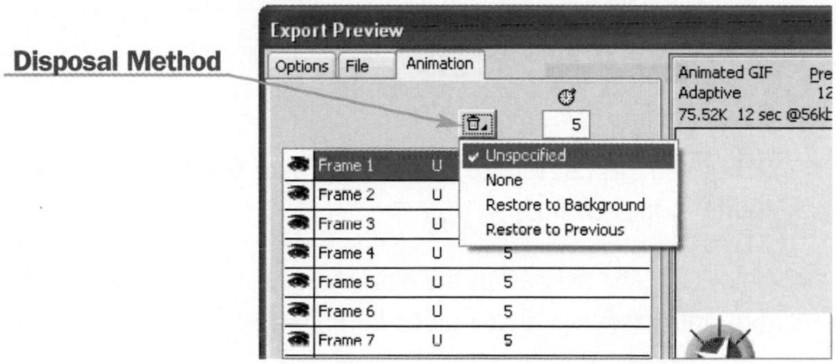

4. Select a frame on the Animation tab of the Export Preview window.

5. Click **Show/Hide Frame** (the eye) next to each frame to turn that frame on or off. If a frame is turned off, it is not visible when you preview the animation in Fireworks, and it will not be exported with the animation. Leave all the frames visible for now. Remain in this screen for the next Step-by-Step.

Animated GIF files used as banner ads typically need to be a set file size or smaller. By using the Export Preview window, you can let Fireworks determine the settings (color palette and number of colors) based on a set file size.

STEP-BY-STEP 7.10

Exporting to a Specific File Size

1. Click the **Options** tab of the Export Preview window.

STEP-BY-STEP 7.10 Continued

2. Click the **Optimize to Size Wizard** button to open the Optimize to Size dialog box shown in Figure 7-15.

FIGURE 7-15
Optimize to Size dialog box

Optimize to Size Wizard

3. Enter **75** (the file size in kilobytes) in the Target Size text box and click **OK**. Fireworks determines the optimization settings based on the target value.

4. When your settings are complete and the preview of the animation is to your liking, click **Export**. (You can also click **OK** to save your optimization and animation settings and return to the document without exporting.)

5. Enter a name, specify the location for the file, and click **Save**. If you are asked to replace a file of the same name, you can click **Yes** (Windows) or **Replace** (Macintosh) to overwrite the old file with your new settings. Remain in this screen for the next Step-by-Step.

Using the Library Panel

The Library panel is a repository for the symbols and buttons you create. When you create a symbol, it's automatically placed in the library for you. The library is document specific, which means the items within the library are only those created in that document. You can, however, export symbols from and import them into other documents.

In the following Step-by-Step, you learn how to export and import symbols.

STEP-BY-STEP 7.11

Exporting and Importing Library Symbols

1. The **animated_logo.png** file should still be open. Make sure the Library panel is open by clicking the **Window** menu and then clicking **Library**.

2. Open the Library panels **Options** menu, and click **Export Symbols** to open the Export Symbols dialog box.

3. Click **Select All** to select all the symbols to export, and then click **Export**.

4. Name the file **my_exported_symbols.png**, followed by your initials. Select the location to which you are saving course files, and click **Save**. Then close the file.

   Now, you will import symbols.

5. Create a new document, using the most recent settings in the New Document dialog box. Save the file as **my_imported_symbols.png**, followed by your initials.

6. Click the **Window** menu, and then click **Library** to view the Library panel, if necessary.

7. Open the Library panels **Options** menu, and click **Import Symbols**.

STEP-BY-STEP 7.11 Continued

8. Select the **custom_symbols.png** file from the data files supplied with this course and then click **Open** to open the Import Symbols dialog box shown in Figure 7-16. The custom_symbols.png file contains some symbols you can place on your page.

FIGURE 7-16
Import Symbols dialog box

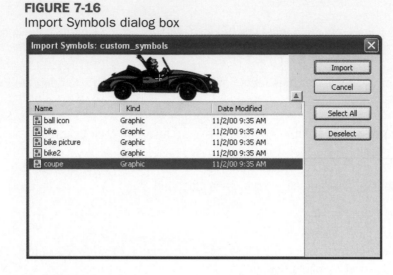

9. Click **Select All** to select all the symbols, and then click **Import**. The symbols are now placed in the library for the current document.

10. Save and close the file.

SUMMARY

In this lesson, you learned to:

- Add a reusable animation symbol to the library.
- Create animation by using frames.
- Preview and edit animations by using onion skinning.
- Control the playback of frame animations.
- Automate the animation process with tweening.
- Export an animation as an animated GIF file.
- Optimize your animation settings by using Export Preview.
- Import and export symbols for use in other files.

MACROMEDIA FLASH MX

Project

INTRODUCING
MACROMEDIA FLASH MX 2004

OBJECTIVES

Upon completion of this lesson, you should be able to:

■ Explain vector graphics and raster images and their role in streaming technology.

■ Use the Flash Player.

■ Recognize Flash file formats.

■ Recognize Flash in action on various Web sites.

What is Flash?

With Macromedia Flash MX 2004, you can produce rich, engaging Web content that doesn't require a fast computer or Internet connection. You might have seen Flash content on the Web before, marked by moving graphics or tied to interactive sound. Flash Web content consists primarily of vector graphics, but it can also contain imported video, bitmap graphics, and sounds. Flash movies can incorporate interactivity to permit input from viewers, even two-way messaging. Web designers use Flash to create navigation controls, animated logos, long form animations with synchronized sound, and complete, sensory-rich Web sites. Throughout the course of this unit, you will build an entire Flash Web site.

Streaming Animations

Flash movies use compact vector graphics that stream into a user's Web browser. The Macromedia Flash Player streams Flash movies as they download. This means the animation can begin before it's downloaded in its entirety. When you make your Flash movies correctly, users can start viewing your site within seconds without waiting for the whole movie to download. They have something to look at right away, keeping them from clicking the Back button.

Flash supports two types of image formats: vector and raster. *Vector graphics* are created with lines and curves and descriptions of their properties. Commands within the vector graphic tell your computer how to display the lines and shapes, what colors to use, how wide to make the lines, and so on. You might have already used a vector drawing program such as Macromedia FreeHand to create such images.

Raster images, also called bitmaps, are created with pixels. When you create a raster image, you map out the placement and color of each pixel, and the resulting bitmap is what you see on the screen.

Vector graphics have important benefits as well as limitations. They're small in file size and they scale wonderfully. However, complex vector graphics can have large file sizes, and vectors aren't the best choice for images with small gradations of color such as photographs.

Although Macromedia is a vector-based authoring tool, you can generate bitmap files by using the Export function. The biggest advantage of vector graphics is that they load quickly on the Internet and don't lose quality as their size increases, as illustrated in Figure 1-1.

Note

The term "bitmap" is commonly used to refer to raster graphics. It is also the name of a type of bitmap image, the Windows Bitmap (BMP) format. In this book, the term is used to refer to raster graphics—when we refer to the Windows Bitmap format, we call it BMP.

FIGURE 1-1
A scaled vector graphic maintains its smooth edges

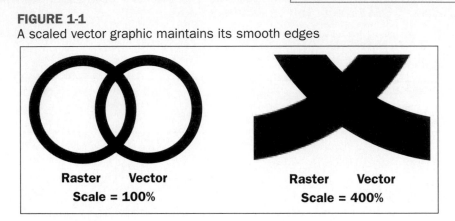

Simple bitmap images are often larger in file size than simple vector graphics, but complex bitmap images—for example, photographs—are often smaller than comparable vector graphics.

Image Formats Supported by Flash

Flash can use the following bitmap formats: Windows bitmap (BMP), GIF image, JPEG image, PNG image, Macintosh PICT image, MacPaint image (PNT), and TIFF image.

While you're developing your Flash animations for the Web or desktop, you'll create them inside the Flash authoring environment as FLA files, viewable only inside Flash. From these FLA files, you can create standalone movies, Web content (HTML and SWF files), and many different image formats. You will examine this further when you publish a Web site at the end of this project.

Macromedia Flash Player

You've probably watched and interacted with Macromedia Flash movies on many Web sites. A player is needed for viewing Flash on the Web. The Macromedia Flash Player is the most widely distributed software in the history of the Internet and is bundled with Internet Explorer, AOL, Netscape Navigator, Opera, and Windows XP. In Flash, you can create HTML pages that are preset to find the latest Flash Player so users can update their machines. The Flash Player is a very small file that can also be quickly and easily downloaded from Macromedia's Web site.

The Macromedia Flash Player resides on the local computer, where it plays back movies in browsers or as standalone applications. Viewing a Flash movie on the Flash Player is similar to viewing a DVD on a DVD player—the player displays the movies you create in the Flash authoring application.

You don't need the Flash Player installed to view files on your desktop. Just make sure the Flash movie has been turned into a *projector*, which is a standalone executable version of the movie, as shown in Figure 1-2. Flash also ships with the standalone Flash Player so developers can preview their movies without using a Web browser or creating projector movies.

FIGURE 1-2
A Flash movie can be turned into a projector

Flash file → home.fla   home.exe ← Stand-alone projector file

Seeing Flash in Action

Now that you know more about Flash, take some time to explore its use in the real world. The following Step-by-Step takes you through some excellent examples of Flash on the Web.

$\int$ TEP-BY-STEP 1.1

Seeing Flash in Action

1. Establish an Internet connection if necessary, and open your browser.

2. Visit the following sites. As you do, notice how quickly many of these sites load. Some sites might take longer to load, but they have engaging content to keep you occupied while the movie is loading.
   Axis Media Web Design Firm: **www.axis-media.com**
   Ryan Terry, Interactive Design student: **www.ry-guy.com**
   Artnomad Web Design: **www.artnomad.com**
   Sony Classical: **www.sonyclassical.com**
   Webvertising: **www.ihotelier.com/onescreen/onescreen.cfm**

3. Some of these sites have both bitmap and vector graphics—see if you can find the bitmaps in the sites.

4. As you move around a site, you should notice that some things are "clickable." Click these items and see what happens. Some sites even transport you automatically to another page or another part of the movie at a certain point.

5. When you finish browsing, close your Web browser.

SUMMARY

In this lesson, you learned:

- About streaming animations and the role vector graphics and raster images play in these.
- To use the Macromedia Flash Player.
- To recognize Flash file formats.
- What Flash products can look like when used in Web sites.

EXPLORING THE MACROMEDIA FLASH WORKSPACE

OBJECTIVES

Upon completion of this lesson, you should be able to:

■ Understand the purpose of the Stage, toolbar, panels, and Timeline.

■ Open, close, and configure the panels in your workspace.

■ Work with Flash and use layers.

■ Use drawing tools such as the Rectangle tool.

■ Use the Property inspector to modify an object's properties.

The Flash Workspace

The Macromedia Flash MX 2004 workspace is divided into five general areas. These are shown in Figure 2-1 and then described.

FIGURE 2-1
The Macromedia Flash workspace

Toolbar

Timeline

Stage

Panels

Property inspector

- *Stage*: The Stage is where you draw and import artwork, add text and sound, and add additional features such as navigation buttons or other user-interface components.

- *Toolbar*: The toolbar contains the tools for creating, placing, and modifying text and graphics.

- *Panels*: Panels in Flash help you view, organize, and modify the elements in the document.

- *Timeline*: The Timeline organizes and controls a document's content over time.

- *Property inspector*: The Property inspector enables you to specify the properties of a selected object.

Depending on whether you are a designer or a developer, you may choose to have a different collection of panels open while you work. There are several sets of panels available from the Window menu.

Design Panels

In this text, you will be using one of the Designer panel sets. This set contains the most commonly used panels and will provide you with all the tools and information you need to get started using Flash.

If you later find you need to change the panel set, you can do so through the Window menu. Point to Panel Sets on the Window menu and then select the desired panel set from the list that appears. Notice that Default Layout is also an option. This will set your screen to panel sizes that match your monitor resolution if the one you selected does not match.

S TEP-BY-STEP 2.1

Configuring the Flash Workspace

1. Start Flash. The Welcome dialog box appears. The Start page might appear. If so, click the Close button to close the Start page.

2. You can select a different panel set to meet your work needs. Click the **Window** menu, point to **Panel Sets**, and then click **Designer (1024 × 768)**. If Designer (1024 × 768) is not available on the menu, then click **Default Layout**. The panels are now configured for a designer. (When you select a panel set, the panels are sized to a standard screen resolution—1024 × 768 in this case. Notice that you can select higher resolutions if you have a higher resolution monitor.)

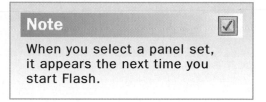

Note ✓

When you select a panel set, it appears the next time you start Flash.

3. Remain in this screen for the next Step-by-Step.

Opening and Closing Panels

You can close panels that you do not use frequently. For example, you might want to close the Info panel because the majority of this panel's information is also in the Property inspector. If you need to consistently open and use a panel that is not part of your workspace, you can add that panel to your workspace. For example, you might want to add the Actions panel to your workspace.

S TEP-BY-STEP 2.2

Closing and Opening a Panel

1. Click **Window**, point to **Design Panels**, and then click **Info** to open the Info panel. (You can click the title bar of any panel to expand or collapse it.)

STEP-BY-STEP 2.2 Continued

2. Click the **Options** menu in the upper-right corner of the Info panel and click **Close Panel**, as shown in Figure 2-2. The panel disappears. (You can display it again by clicking on the **Window** menu, pointing to **Design Panels**, and then clicking **Info**.)

FIGURE 2-2
Closing the Info panel

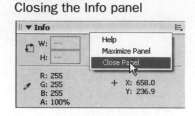

3. Add the Actions panel to the Stage by clicking the **Window** menu, pointing to **Development Panels**, and then clicking **Actions**. The Actions panel appears on the Stage, undocked.

4. Click the grip to the left of the panel title, as shown in Figure 2-3. Your pointer changes to a four-headed arrow. Drag the Actions panel between any two panels on the right. When you see a dark outline with a heavy line between the panels, drop the Actions panel. The panel docks with the panels to the right.

FIGURE 2-3
Moving the Actions panel

5. Click the Actions panel grip again and drag the panel above the Property inspector at the bottom of the Stage. When you see a dark outline over the Property inspector, drop the Actions panel. The Actions panel appears expanded above the Property inspector.

6. Click the Actions panel title bar. The Actions panel collapses.

STEP-BY-STEP 2.2 Continued

7. Click the Property inspector title bar. The Property inspector collapses, revealing more of the Stage, as shown in Figure 2-4.

FIGURE 2-4
Collapsed Actions panel and Property inspector

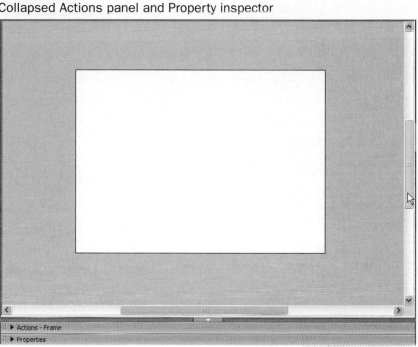

8. Click the Property inspector title bar again. The Property inspector opens. Remain in this screen for the next Step-by-Step.

Working in Flash

The Step-by-Steps in the following section and the rest of this lesson provide a short introduction to Flash through hands-on activities. Many of the steps are open-ended so you can explore the Flash interface and tool set prior to starting the project you will work on throughout the rest of this unit. If you are already familiar with Flash, you can move ahead to Lesson 3, *Creating a Logo*.

In your open Flash workspace, notice the title bar at the top of the window, displaying the document title. When you first open Flash, you have a new document named Untitled-1 until you save the file with a new name. Subsequent new documents are named *Untitled-2*, *Untitled-3*, and so on, until you exit Flash.

The menu bar at the top of the display contains access to all the tools, panels, and options within Flash and contains many of the design element and manipulation functions.

As you've learned, the Stage contains all the elements that make up a Flash document. It defines the border of the final file you create (the SWF file). The contents of the Stage reflect the frame currently on the Timeline.

The Timeline shown in Figure 2-5 is an example of an animation and illustrates many of the features you will see and use in this unit. The Timeline is a key organizational and navigational tool for your animations. Here graphics are animated over time. You coordinate the timing of the animation and assemble the artwork in separate layers on the Timeline.

FIGURE 2-5
Flash Timeline

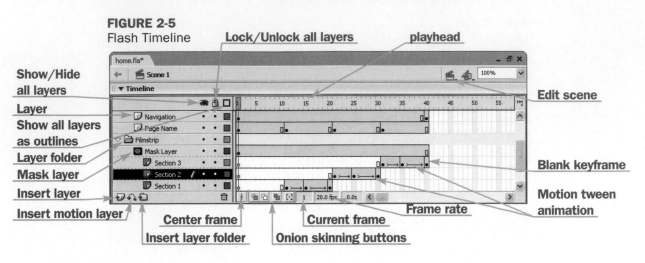

STEP-BY-STEP 2.3

Exploring the Flash Interface

1. The Flash workspace should still be open. Click **Edit** on the menu bar and review the options on this menu. You can click outside the menu to close it.

2. Click the **Insert** menu and review the options on this menu.

3. Click the **Modify** menu and review the options on this menu.

4. Click the **Control** menu and review the options on this menu.

5. Explore any of the other menus or submenus. This will familiarize you with the menu selections and locations and will aid you in accomplishing tasks in the future.

6. Position and hold the pointer over the icons on the Timeline to read the ToolTips. Remain in this screen for the next Step-by-Step.

Layers

Layers are a way of organizing the objects on the Stage, much like a stack of transparent sheets for an overhead projector. You must use separate layers to draw overlapping shapes. Each layer has controls for hiding or showing the layer, locking it (so you won't accidentally move its contents), and displaying its contents as outlines.

STEP-BY-STEP 2.4

Exploring Layers

1. Click the **File** menu, and then click **Open**.

2. Navigate to the data files provided for this lesson. In the **Sample_Movie** folder, double-click **Bouncing_Ball.fla**.

   The Bouncing Ball document opens. Notice that two layers are listed on the Timeline: Text and Ball, as shown in Figure 2-6.

   FIGURE 2-6
   Workspace for the Bouncing Ball document

   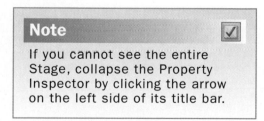

3. Click the **Control** menu, and then click **Play**. The short document plays.

4. Click the **Show/Hide Layer** column (the eye) next to the layer named Ball. The ball disappears from the Stage. A red X appears in that space, indicating that the layer is hidden from view.

5. Click **Control**, and then **Play**, or press **Enter** (Windows) or **Return** (Macintosh). The only visible object is the text.

> **Note** ☑
>
> If you cannot see the entire Stage, collapse the Property Inspector by clicking the arrow on the left side of its title bar.

STEP-BY-STEP 2.4 Continued

6. Click the **Show/Hide Layer** column next to the Ball layer to view the layer again.

7. Explore the Timeline.

> **Hot Tip**
>
> Pressing **Enter** (Windows) or **Return** (Macintosh) again pauses the playback. You can continue to use the **Enter/Return** key to play and pause the animation.

   a. Move the playhead to the first frame, and then using the Control menu, click **Step Forward One Frame** and **Step Backward One Frame** to advance and back up one frame at at time. (You can also use the period and comma keys on the keyboard to advance or back up one frame at a time.)

   b. Click the pointer in frames on the Timeline and on objects on the Stage. How does the icon change?

   c. Notice where the Pencil icon appears when you click different layers. Note what appears on each layer.

8. Close the Bouncing Ball document. Do not save any changes. Remain in this screen for the next Step-by-Step.

Working with the Drawing Tools

The toolbar, shown in Figure 2-7, contains tools you'll need for creating and manipulating graphics to make animations. The Tools section (at the top) contains drawing, painting, and selection tools. The View section contains tools for zooming and panning the application window. The Colors section contains modifiers for the selected tool that affect that tool's stroke and fill colors. The Options section contains particular settings you can add to tool functionality, such as straightening lines or curving edges of shapes.

> **Did You Know?**
>
> To create a perfect shape (i.e., a perfect square or a circle instead of an oval), hold down the **Shift** key as you drag to create the shape.

FIGURE 2-7
Flash toolbar

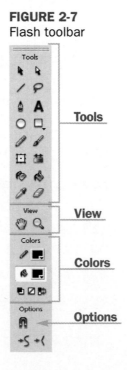

You can use the Rectangle tool to draw rectangular shapes, including squares. When you draw a rectangle, you draw both an outline of the shape and its fill.

S TEP-BY-STEP 2.5

Using the Rectangle Tool

1. If necessary, click the **File** menu, and then click **New** to create a blank document. The New Document dialog box opens with the General tab selected.

2. Click **Flash Document** to select it, and then click **OK**.

3. In the Colors section of the toolbar, click the **Stroke Color** (the pencil) pull-down menu and select a light blue color.

4. Click the **Fill Color** pull-down menu in the Colors section of the Tools toolbar and select a dark blue color.

5. Click the **Rectangle** tool. The pointer turns into crosshairs.

6. Drag the pointer across the middle of the Stage to draw a rectangle similar to the one shown in the middle of Figure 2-8.

> **Hot Tip** ⊚
>
> If a panel isn't expanded, click the triangle on the left side of the panel title bar to open the panel.

> **Note** ☑
>
> You can also select the colors for the Stroke and Fill from the Color Swatches panel.

> **Hot Tip** ⊚
>
> If you create an object you don't want, click the **Edit** menu, and then click **Undo**.

FIGURE 2-8
Creating and coloring rectangles

STEP-BY-STEP 2.5 Continued

7. Continue to use the Color tools, the Rectangle tool, and the Color Swatches panel to select colors and create rectangles using Figure 2-8 as a guide for your placement and colors. Remain in this screen for the next Step-by-Step.

Did You Know?

If the Color Swatches panel does not contain the exact color you want, you can use the Color Mixer panel to select the specific color you need.

Changing Object Properties

You can specify the properties of an object, such as its color, line width, or font size, with the Property inspector that appears below the Stage.

You use the Selection tool to select the stroke or fill of one of the rectangles. Four types of selections can occur on a shape:

■ Double-clicking the fill area selects the entire object (the fill and stroke); then the entire object can be edited (including its size, shape, and location).

■ Clicking the fill area selects just the fill.

■ Double-clicking the border selects the entire border (stroke).

■ Clicking the border selects one side of the border.

STEP-BY-STEP 2.6

Modifying the Properties of an Object

1. Click the **Selection** tool at the top left of the toolbar (the black arrow).

2. Double-click the rectangle in the middle of your Stage.

3. Make sure the Property inspector panel is open. The Property inspector should appear similar to that shown in Figure 2-9.

FIGURE 2-9
Property inspector for a rectangle object

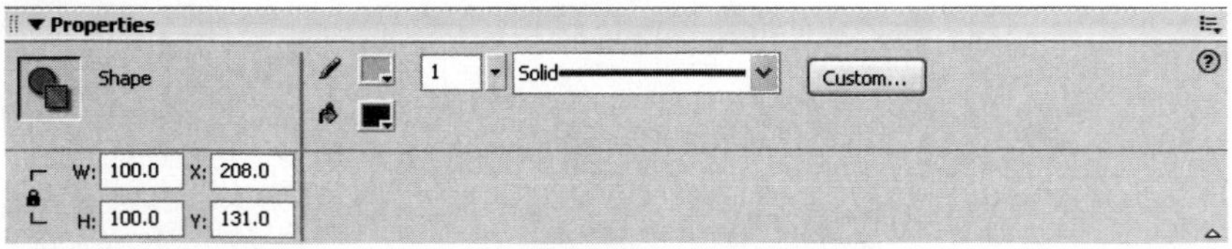

STEP-BY-STEP 2.6 Continued

4. Experiment with modifying the rectangle's properties. Using the Selection tool and the selection techniques described earlier, modify the following anyway you'd like:

Stroke color

Stroke height

Fill color

Rectangle width and height (using the W: and H: boxes)

Rectangle location on the Stage (using the X: and Y: boxes)

5. When you finish, close the document without saving it and exit Flash.

SUMMARY

In this lesson, you learned to:

■ Recognize the Stage, toolbar, panels, and Timeline.

■ Open, close, and configure the panels in your workspace.

■ Work with Flash, including how to use layers.

■ Use drawing tools such as the Rectangle tool.

■ Modify object properties by using the Property inspector.

CREATING A LOGO

OBJECTIVES

Upon completion of this lesson, you should be able to:

- Create ovals and circles with the Oval tool.

- Design gradient fills.

- Create and edit symbols.

- Import images into Flash.

- Export images from Flash.

The Gallery San Luis Project

You have been asked to create a logo for a local photo gallery, Gallery San Luis. The gallery said it might want to animate this logo, so you decide to build the logo in Macromedia Flash MX 2004.

> **Note** ✓
>
> You will work on the Gallery San Luis Web site throughout the rest of this project.

Creating a Folder Structure

Before you start building the logo, you need to create a folder structure for the project.

S TEP-BY-STEP 3.1

Creating Folders for a Web Site

1. Create a new folder on your hard drive and name it **build_GallerySanLuis**, as shown in Figure 3-1.

FIGURE 3-1
Creating the Gallery San Luis folder

build_GallerySanLuis

2. From the data files supplied for this project, copy all the subfolders from the **Macromedia Flash MX 2004** folder (images, photographs, Sample_Movie, scripts, and video) into the **build_GallerySanLuis** folder.

Now you're ready to start building the logo in Flash.

Creating a Flash Document

A Flash file is referred to as a "document" and carries the .fla extension. A FLA file can form a basis for several other types of media you can produce from a Flash document (bitmap images, SWF files, and HTML files, among others).

S TEP-BY-STEP 3.2

Saving a Flash Document

1. Start Flash.

2. With the blank document on the Stage, click the **File** menu, and then click **Save**. The Save As dialog box opens.

3. Name the file **logo** followed by your initials. From the Save in (Windows) or Where (Macintosh) list box, select the **images** folder inside the **build_GallerySanLuis** folder. Make sure Flash 2004 is selected as the document type.

4. Click **Save**. Remain in this screen for the next Step-by-Step.

Setting Document Properties

When you create any new document, you start by configuring its size, background color, and frame rate.

STEP-BY-STEP 3.3

Setting Document Properties

1. Click the **Modify** menu, and then click **Document**. The Document Properties dialog box opens.

2. Set the dimension to **100** × **100** pixels to create a space appropriate for the logo size.

3. Leave the Background color white and click **OK**. The Stage size shrinks to 100 × 100 with a white background.

4. Save your changes and remain in this screen for the next Step-by-Step.

Using Basic Drawing Tools

You need to consider two things in the design of the Gallery San Luis logo: The logo should look like a stylized lens, and it should include part of the Gateway Arch, the symbol of St. Louis from which the gallery took its name.

The Oval Tool

You will draw the lens part of the logo with the Oval tool and then add part of the arch on top of it, as shown in Figure 3-2.

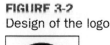
FIGURE 3-2
Design of the logo

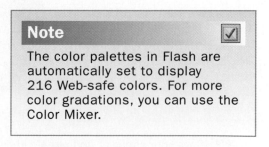

STEP-BY-STEP 3.4

Using the Oval Tool

1. The logo.fla document should be open. On the **View** menu, point to **Magnification**, and then click **Show Frame**. The Stage enlarges to full size for its view area.

2. Double-click the title of Layer 1 (on the Timeline panel) and rename it **Lens**. Press **Enter** (Windows) or **Return** (Macintosh).

3. On the Timeline, click frame **1** of the Lens layer.

4. Click the **Oval** tool in the toolbar.

> **Note** ☑
>
> The color palettes in Flash are automatically set to display 216 Web-safe colors. For more color gradations, you can use the Color Mixer.

STEP-BY-STEP 3.4 Continued

5. In the toolbar, change the **Stroke Color** and **Fill Color** both to black (**#000000**), as shown in Figure 3-3.

FIGURE 3-3
Stroke and Fill selections

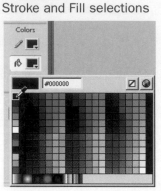

6. Hold down the **Shift** key and drag to draw a black circle in the center of the Stage. (Don't worry about exact size and placement; that will be set in the next steps.)

7. Select the **Selection** tool and double-click the circle.

8. In the Property inspector, set W: to **98** and H: to **98**.

9. Click the **Align** panel. The Align panel expands. Or click **Window**, point to **Design Panels**, and then click **Align**. If the Align panel opens undocked, you can dock it to the right.

10. Toggle the **To stage** button so it is on.

11. Click **Align horizontal center** and **Align vertical center** (position the pointer on the buttons to display their ToolTips if necessary). The circle aligns to the center of the Stage, as shown in Figure 3-4.

Hot Tip

Notice that there are two selection arrows in the toolbar. The black arrow is the Selection tool for selecting and moving an object. The white arrow is the Subselection tool for adjusting points on an object. In the following exercises you use the Selection tool. An easy mistake is to select only the fill of an object (the inside part). To avoid this, make sure you double-click to select an object.

FIGURE 3-4
Circle for the logo

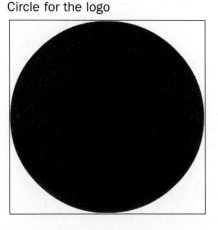

12. Save your changes and remain in this screen for the next Step-by-Step.

Gradient Fill

You now have the basis for the logo, but you can make it look more like a lens by adding a gradient fill. Gradient fills give depth and layered effects to a single object.

STEP-BY-STEP 3.5

Creating a Gradient Fill

1. Select the **Selection** tool and double-click the black circle to make sure both the fill and the stroke are selected.

2. Make sure the Color Mixer panel is expanded (click **Window**, point to **Design Panels**, and click **Color Mixer**), and change the fill style from Solid to **Radial**. The Gradient definition bar appears, with a color marker on each end.

3. Click the left color marker of the Gradient definition bar. Click the Color Proxy pull-down menu (above the Gradient definition bar) to change the marker's color to white.

4. Click the right color marker of the Gradient definition bar and change its color to black, as shown in Figure 3-5. The image displays a white gradient fill.

FIGURE 3-5
Changing gradient colors

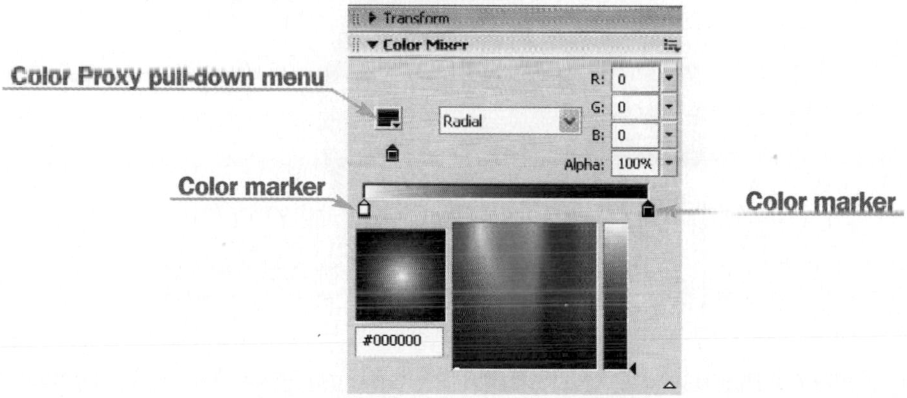

Color Proxy pull-down menu

Color marker

Color marker

5. Click the left (white) color marker and slide the Alpha of the left fill to **0%**. The image appears completely black again. The image now has a transparent fill. To create the actual lens look, you have to add more color markers to the gradient fill.

6. Click five times under the Gradient definition bar to create five new color markers, as shown in Figure 3-6. (Don't worry about the placement of the markers—these will be adjusted in later steps.)

FIGURE 3-6
Adding new color markers

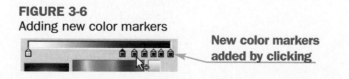

New color markers
added by clicking

STEP-BY-STEP 3.5 Continued

7. Change the color and alpha settings of the markers to the values shown in Table 3-1 (numbered from left to right).

TABLE 3-1
Changing marker settings

MARKER	1	2	3	4	5	6	7
Color	White	White	White	Black	Gray (#666666)	Black	Black
Alpha	0%	30%	100%	100%	100%	100%	100%

8. Adjust the locations of the markers to the approximate locations shown in Figure 3-7. With the markers set appropriately, the lens should look like Figure 3-8.

FIGURE 3-7
Gradient markers in position

FIGURE 3-8
Gradient fill effect on the lens (shown selected)

9. To save the gradient fill for use later (even in other documents), click Color Mixer **Options** button in the upper-right corner of the Color Mixer and choose **Add Swatch**, as shown in Figure 3-9. The gradient appears as a new color in the Color Swatches panel and in the document's color palette.

STEP-BY-STEP 3.5 Continued

10. Save your changes and remain in this screen for the next Step-by-Step.

FIGURE 3-9
Saving the gradient

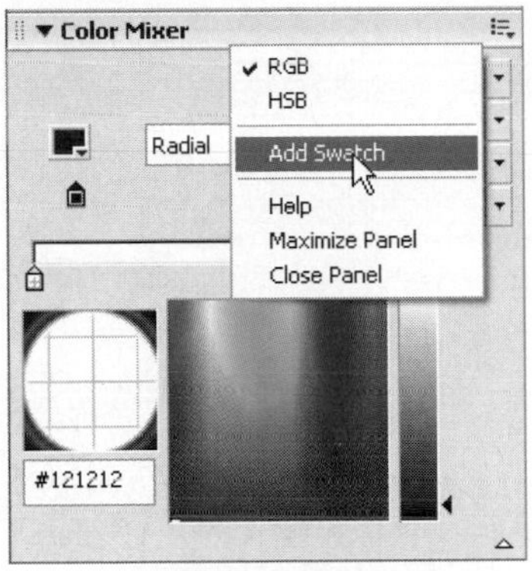

Creating Symbols

When you are working in Flash, you'll often find yourself reusing objects you have created on the Stage. Each object you create increases the size of your final document. In Flash, a *symbol* is a graphic, button, or movie clip that you create once and can reuse throughout a document. Symbols present several advantages in Web design:

- Converting a drawn object into a symbol creates a permanent object from which you can make many other copies.

- Symbols can overlap on the Stage and not affect each other. To keep a drawn object from being erased when another object moves on top if it, you can turn the drawn object into a symbol.

- Keeps file sizes small because symbols can be reused without significantly increasing file size.

- Symbols contain their own Timelines to create many rich, interactive areas on a Web page.

- Changing one symbol affects all copies of that symbol and thus makes updating easy.

Any symbol you create automatically becomes part of the library for the current document. The *library* in a Flash document stores symbols created in Flash and also imported files such as video clips, sound clips, bitmaps, and imported vector artwork. When you select a symbol in a library and drag it onto the Stage, you create an *instance* of that symbol, as shown in Figure 3-10.

FIGURE 3-10
Symbol and instance example

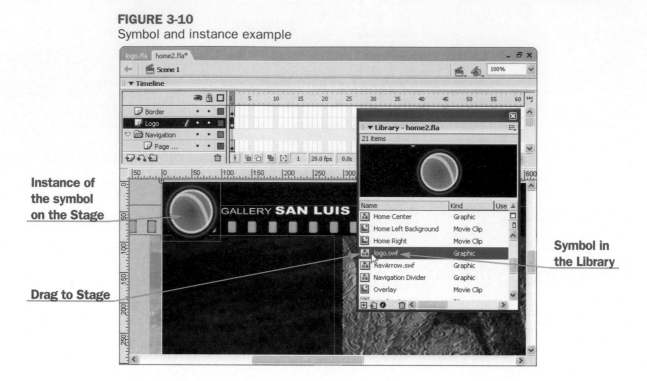

The great thing about symbols and instances is that you can change the size and color of instances without altering the original symbol, as shown in Figure 3-11. Flash also lets you change the behavior setting of an instance on the Stage or a symbol in the library at any time.

FIGURE 3-11
Variations of a single symbol as instances on the Stage

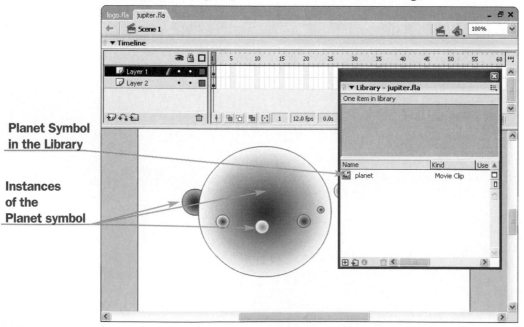

As mentioned previously, Flash has three different types of symbols: graphics, buttons, and movie clips. These types of symbols are discussed in more detail in the following sections. Understanding the differences in symbols is a key to working successfully in Flash.

Graphic Symbols

Graphic symbols are used for static images and simple animations. Graphic symbols operate in sync with the Timeline of the main movie. What does that mean? Each frame in a graphic symbol has to correspond to a frame on the main Timeline. If your main Timeline has 10 frames and your graphic clip has 15 frames, only the first 10 frames of the graphic clip will play. If your graphic clip has fewer frames than the main Timeline, the graphic clip will loop back to the beginning and play out as many frames as it can before the main Timeline runs out. Interactive controls and sounds won't work in a graphic symbol's animation sequence.

Movie Clips

Movie clips are more flexible than graphic symbols. They play independently of the main movie Timeline. In fact, a movie clip is like a movie within a movie. You can put actions, sounds, and buttons inside movie clips.

Button Symbols

Button symbols are used for creating buttons. The Timeline for a button is a little different from the regular Flash Timeline. A button has four states:

■ The *Up state* is how the button appears on the screen when it first appears.

■ The *Over state* becomes visible when you move your pointer over a button on the Stage.

■ The *Down state* is revealed when you click a button.

■ The *Hit state* is not visible in your document but defines the active area of a button. The active area can be larger or smaller than the visible button, and it can even have a different shape.

In creating the logo for Gallery San Luis, you will make a movie clip symbol containing graphic symbols.

S TEP-BY-STEP 3.6

Creating a Movie Clip Symbol

1. Select the **Selection** tool and double-click the gradient circle. The circle and its border are selected.

2. Click the **Modify** menu, and then click **Convert to Symbol**. The Convert to Symbol dialog box opens, as shown in Figure 3-12.

> **Note** ☑
>
> Figure 3-12 shows the Convert to Symbol dialog box with the Advanced options displayed. Your dialog box may open with only the Basic options displayed. To see the Advanced options, click the **Advanced** button. To close the Advanced options, click the **Basic** button.

STEP-BY-STEP 3.6 Continued

FIGURE 3-12
Convert to Symbol dialog box

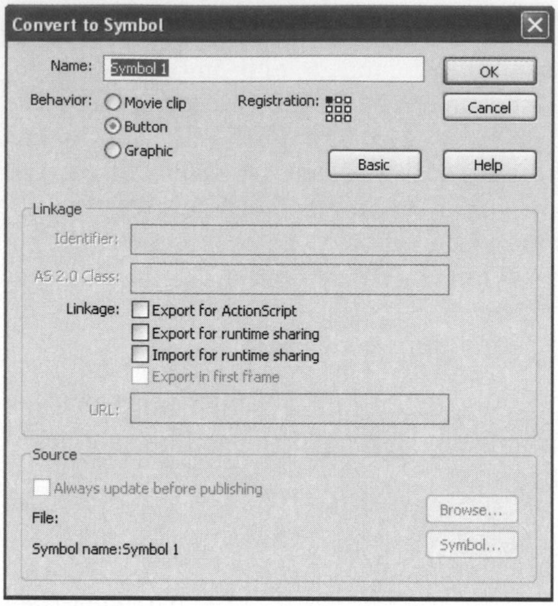

Convert to Symbol   [X]

Name:	Symbol 1		OK
Behavior:	○ Movie clip Registration:	▪□□	Cancel
	◉ Button	□□□	
	○ Graphic	□□□	Basic Help

Linkage
    Identifier: [   ]
    AS 2.0 Class: [   ]
    Linkage: □ Export for ActionScript
            □ Export for runtime sharing
            □ Import for runtime sharing
            □ Export in first frame
    URL: [   ]

Source
    □ Always update before publishing
    File: Browse...
    Symbol name:Symbol 1   Symbol...

3. Enter **Lens** in the Name box.

4. Select **Movie clip** as the Behavior. (You are making a movie clip symbol to allow for maximum functionality of the logo in animation and ActionScript. For example, it will be easy to make the logo a link to the home page.)

5. Click **OK**. The circle has a blue box around it, indicating that the instance of the symbol is selected.

6. Click the **Window** menu and then click **Library** to see the symbol description in the library.

7. Save your changes and remain in this screen for the next Step-by-Step.

Importing Images

Importing images into Flash is a flexible process. You can import bitmap images, vector graphics, or published movies. In the next Step-by-Step, you import a published Flash movie (a document with a .swf file extension). This document is the arch fill for the logo. When you import a Flash movie, the object is saved in the library, automatically creating a graphic symbol from the image.

STEP-BY-STEP 3.7

Importing a SWF Image into the Library

1. Create a new layer by clicking the **Insert Layer** button in the bottom-left corner of the Timeline panel, as shown in Figure 3-13.

FIGURE 3-13
Insert Layer button

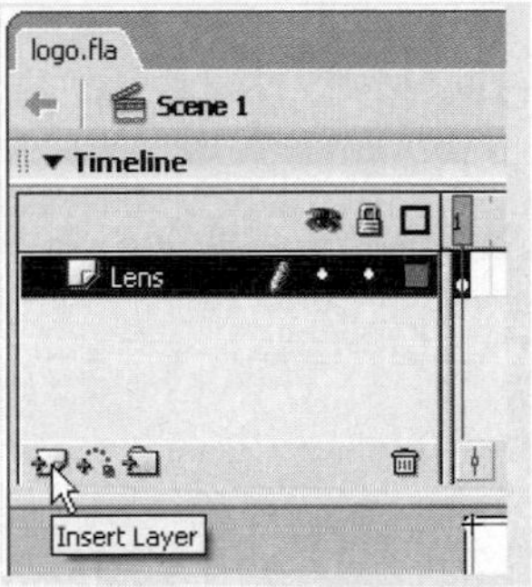

2. Double-click the **Layer 2** name and rename the layer **Lens Fill**. Press **Enter** (Windows) or **Return** (Macintosh).

3. Click the **File** menu, point to **Import**, and then click **Import to Library**. The Import to Library dialog box opens.

4. Navigate to the **images** folder in your **build_GallerySanLuis** folder, select **arch.swf**, and then click **Open** (Windows) or **Import to Library** (Macintosh). The file is imported to the library and the dialog box closes.

5. To see the file you just imported, locate the Library panel. The graphic symbol arch.swf appears in the library.

6. Make sure the **Lens Fill** layer is selected. Drag an instance of the **arch.swf** image from the library onto the Stage in the approximate center of the lens.

7. With the **arch.swf** image still selected in the Lens Fill layer, click the **Align** panel title bar to expand the panel, if it is not already expanded.

8. Make sure the **To stage** button is toggled to on.

9. Click the **Align horizontal center** and the **Align vertical center** buttons. Arch.swf is aligned to the center of the Stage.

10. Drag the **Lens Fill** layer below the Lens layer next to the Timeline. The image moves behind the gradient lens on the Stage.

STEP-BY-STEP 3.7 Continued

11. Click the **Control** menu, and then click **Test Movie**. A preview of the file appears and a SWF file is generated.

12. Close the Preview window.

13. Save your changes and remain in this screen for the next Step-by-Step.

Exporting Flash Files

You now have a FLA file and a SWF file. You will now create a JPEG version of this file to send to the client. The JPEG image would be appropriate for a static HTML version of the site.

STEP-BY-STEP 3.8

Creating Images to Export from Flash

1. On the **File** menu, point to **Export**, and then click **Export Image**. The Export Image dialog box opens.

2. Name the file **Logo** followed by your initials and set its type (or format) to **JPEG image (*.jpg)**.

3. Click **Save**. The Export JPEG dialog box opens.

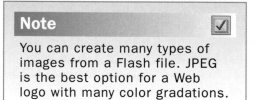

Note ☑

You can create many types of images from a Flash file. JPEG is the best option for a Web logo with many color gradations.

4. Set the Include text box to **Full Document Size**. The dimension boxes should show 100 × 100 pixels. (Edit them if they do not.)

5. Set the Quality to **90**.

6. The **Progressive display** option should be unchecked.

7. Click **OK**. A JPEG version of the logo is saved in the Images folder.

8. Close your logo file and exit Flash.

SUMMARY

In this lesson, you learned to:

■ Create ovals and circles with the Oval tool.

■ Design gradient fills.

■ Create and edit symbols.

■ Import images into Flash.

■ Export images from Flash.

DESIGNING A HOME PAGE

OBJECTIVES

Upon completion of this lesson, you should be able to:

- Understand the basics of site architecture and document sizing.
- Use a background (comp) image as a guide.
- Create and use graphic and movie clip symbols.
- Create and use layers and guides.
- Import and place JPEG files.
- Create a template movie clip.

The Gallery San Luis Home Page Requirements

Gallery San Luis is so happy with the logo you created that they would like you to design a Web site for them, all in Macromedia Flash MX 2004. They would like the site to contain the following:

- A Home page that is both appealing and speaks photography.
- A Featured Artist page with a slide show of photographs and featured photographer information (and perhaps video interviews with the featured artists).
- An Events page for requesting tickets to gallery events.
- An animated Map page to indicate where the gallery is located.
- Sound incorporated on buttons.
- Slick transitions between pages.
- An overall photography metaphor for the site.

Web Design Skills

FLASH AS A WEB DESIGN SOLUTION

Macromedia Showcase

SonyClassical.com

Developed by:
SonyClassical.com
http://www.sonyclassical.com

View Video Testimonial
QuickTime Player Required

SonyClassical.com
A division of Sony Music Entertainment, Sony Classical is a world leader in the field of recorded music.

Challenge
To create a rich multimedia experience —one that orchestrates video, audio and interactivity.

Solution
Macromedia Flash MX
Macromedia Flash

Benefit
Macromedia Flash enabled Sony Classical developers to re-make their static web pages into dynamic user experiences, all while realizing savings in development time and money. Now Sony Classical is choosing Macromedia Flash MX as the most powerful solution for integrating video -- generating a new level of interactive content.
More benefits.

Read More

This case study from the Macromedia Showcase[1] highlights how Flash solved particular design problems and video objectives for one company's Web site. Typically, Web designers look at several possible solutions or design options before deciding if they will use Flash. For your Gallery project, the photos could be displayed by using a JavaScript slide show or HTML links, but these can be complicated and increase download time. Furthermore, the Gallery is looking for a fresh, animated means of presenting itself on the Web. Most designers "think Flash" when clients want a rich, dynamic Web site.

[1]To see original case study, go to *www.macromedia.com* and click Visit the Showcase.

Site Architecture

As with any Web design lesson, so many site needs can seem overwhelming, so you must start with the most basic elements of the design. The site architecture diagram shown in Figure 4-1 gives a basic idea of what the Web site will include (arrows indicate links).

FIGURE 4-1
Gallery San Luis site architecture diagram

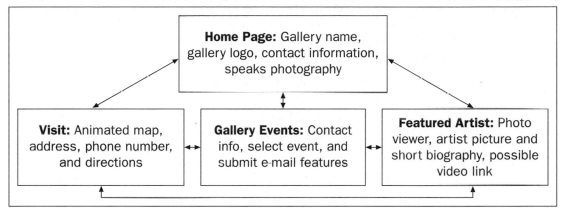

Sizing a Home Page

One of the major considerations for the design is size. The Gallery has indicated that they wish to target computers running Microsoft Internet Explorer set to at least an 800 × 600 display resolution. When designing for such resolutions, you must leave extra space for the browser's toolbar and title bar to display. For Internet Explorer windows, you have the actual display regions listed in Table 4-1.

TABLE 4-1
Internet Explorer display regions

SCREEN RESOLUTION[2]	ACTUAL DISPLAY AREA IN INTERNET EXPLORER
640 × 480	620 × 318
800 × 600	780 × 438
1024 × 768	1004 × 606
1280 × 1024	1260 × 862

[2]Canfield, Byron and Bentley Wolfe. "What is the Recommended Size (Height and Width) to Make a Flash Movie?" Available *http://www.macromedia.com/support/flash/ts/documents/movie_size01.htm.*

When it's time to publish the movie for the final site, we will discuss these size issues further (see Lesson 13, *Publishing a Macromedia Flash Movie*).

S TEP-BY-STEP 4.1

Setting Up a New Workspace

1. Launch Flash. A blank document opens.

2. Save the document as **home.fla** followed by your initials in the **Flash 2004 Document** format. Make sure you save the movie in the **build_GallerySanLuis** folder.

3. Click the **Modify** menu, and then click **Document**. The Document Properties window opens, where you can set the size, speed, frame rate, and background color of your document.

4. As shown in Figure 4-2, change the dimensions of the document to **780** × **438** pixels (the document is now set for the Internet Explorer browser in 800 × 600 pixels); change the background color to black (**#000000**); change the frame rate to **20**; and then click **OK**.

FIGURE 4-2
Document Properties window configured for 800 × 600 display

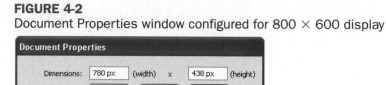

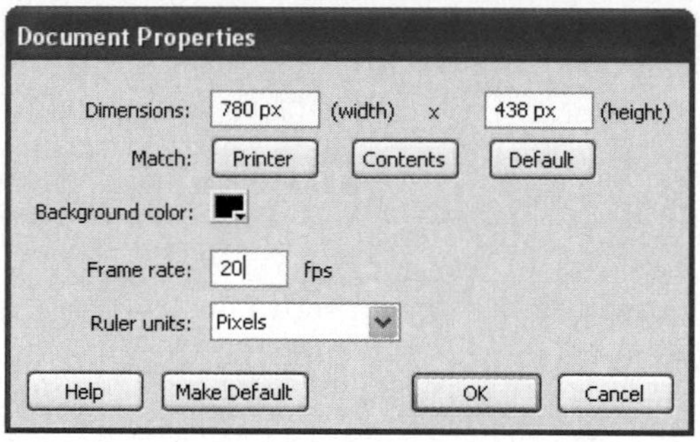

5. Save your changes and remain in this screen for the next Step-by-Step.

Drawing in Flash

Wh.hile focusing on construction of the home page, your guiding principles are the needs of the client. "A page that speaks photography" implies that the first page will have photographs and maybe even look like some sort of photographic device. You also know that you must include some basic functional and content components: the name of the gallery, a logo, contact information, and links to the other pages in the site. The first step in design is to draw on paper a rough design of what the site would look like.

You can use an image-processing program such as Macromedia Fireworks to construct a mock or rough design of the site like the one shown in Figure 4-3.

FIGURE 4-3
Mock image of the site

Like a professional designer, you will use this image as a guide when you build the site in Flash. Many designers put such an image in the background while building in Flash and then delete the image later. Before drawing, you need to configure the workspace for the size and type of media you are building.

From the design sketch, you have the dimensions for the home page. Sizing a document is the first step in creating a Flash file.

Creating the Filmstrip Movie

Your strategy for building the site is to work from the inside out. First you create the center filmstrip area. Then you design the navigation bar at the bottom and the title bar at the top.

> **Note** ☑
>
> It might seem a little weird to be drawing the same image twice. Traditionally, drawing was done outside the Web pages, and then the pages were built in another program. With the great variety of drawing tools in Flash, however, you can "comp" (create a composition—drawing) directly in Flash. But some designers still feel more comfortable creating comp images in an image-processing program such as Macromedia Fireworks or Adobe Photoshop, which provide a wider array of visual effects and layout features.

STEP-BY-STEP 4.2

Working with a Comp Image

1. Double-click **Layer 1** (on the **Timeline**) and rename it **Comp Image**. Then press **Enter** (Windows) or **Return** (Macintosh).

STEP-BY-STEP 4.2 Continued

2. Click the **File** menu, point to **Import**, click **Import to Stage**, and select the **comp.jpg** file from the **images** folder in the **build_GallerySanLuis** folder. (This image was created in Fireworks as the rough design for the Web site.) Click **Open** (Windows) or **Import** (Macintosh). A copy of the filmstrip appears on the Stage and is selected.

Note ✓

If you cannot see the image or you see only part of it, click **Zoom Out** on the **View** menu several times until the image appears. The image was created to scale in an image-editing program such as Fireworks.

3. Make sure the image is selected. Then use the arrow keys on the keyboard to slide the image up and to the left until the first two sprocket holes are outside the left edge of the Stage, as shown in Figure 4-4.

FIGURE 4-4
Aligning the comp image

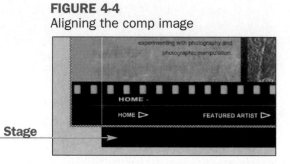

4. On the Align panel, toggle the **To stage** button on and click **Align vertical center** to center the filmstrip image vertically.

5. Click the **Comp Image** layer to select it.

6. Click the **Modify** menu, point to **Timeline**, and then click **Layer Properties**. The **Layer Properties** dialog box opens.

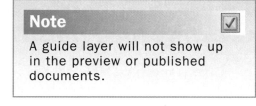

Note ✓

A guide layer will not show up in the preview or published documents.

7. Set the layer Type to **Guide**.

8. Lock the layer by clicking the **Lock** check box, as shown in Figure 4-5. Click **OK**.

FIGURE 4-5
The Layer Properties box with the layer locked

STEP-BY-STEP 4.2 Continued

9. Click the **Insert Layer** button to create a new layer. Rename the new layer **Background**.

10. Making sure this layer is still selected, select the **Rectangle** tool.

11. Set the stroke and fill colors to black (**#0000000**).

12. Draw a rectangle on top of the filmstrip. Make it approximately the same size (you'll adjust it more precisely in the next step). You might need to zoom out to see the entire filmstrip.

13. Use the Selection tool to select the rectangle. Make sure to double-click to select both the fill and stroke.

14. On the Property inspector, make sure the height and width boxes are unlocked. You can lock or unlock them by clicking the padlock icon. Locking them constrains the height and width proportions.

15. Set W: to **1090** and H: to **360**, and press **Enter** (Windows) or **Return** (Macintosh). The rectangle is sized to cover a large background area.

16. With the rectangle still selected, center it vertically on the Stage using the Align panel. Use the arrow keys to center the rectangle horizontally over the comp image, as shown in Figure 4-6.

FIGURE 4-6
Background rectangle centered over comp image

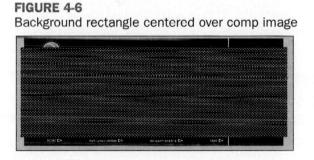

17. Convert the rectangle into a graphic symbol (from the Modify menu) and name it **Background**.

STEP-BY-STEP 4.2 Continued

18. Click the **Show As Outline** button (the square to the right of the padlock shown in Figure 4-7) for the Background layer. The black background appears as an outline only so it is no longer blocking the comp image.

FIGURE 4-7
Show the Background layer as an outline

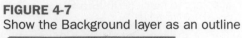

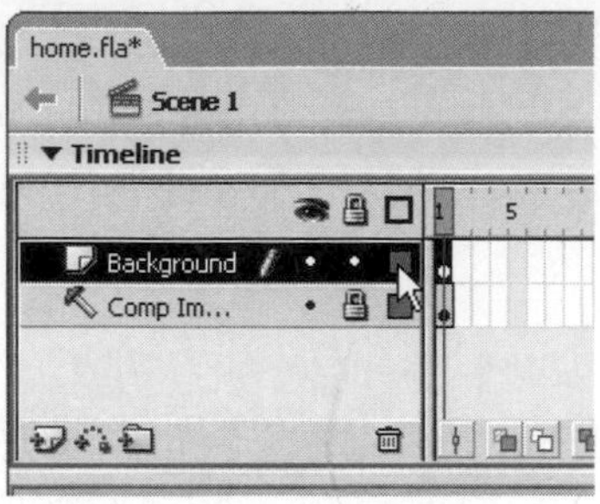

19. Save your changes and remain in this screen for the next Step-by-Step.

Creating the Filmstrip Sprocket Holes

The sprocket holes are important to your overall design. They make the words and the images seem like part of a filmstrip. If you were to draw so many sprocket holes individually, it would take a long time and unnecessarily increase the file size. You can use a single sprocket hole symbol to create the entire row.

*S*TEP-BY-STEP 4.3

Creating the Filmstrip Sprocket Holes

1. Insert a new layer and name it **Sprocket Holes**.

2. Make sure the layer is selected. On the **File** menu, point to **Import**, click **Import to Stage**, and import **sprocketHole.jpg** from the **Images** folder in the **build_GallerySanLuis** folder.

3. Double-click the sprocket hole image to make sure it is selected. A gray outline appears around the sprocket hole.

4. Convert the sprocket hole to a movie clip symbol and name it **Sprocket Hole**.

> **Hot Tip**
>
> You could have made the sprocket hole a graphic or even a button symbol, but a movie clip gives you the most flexibility for animation and interaction purposes. In any case, it is easy to change a symbol's behavior later on the Property inspector.

STEP-BY-STEP 4.3 Continued

5. Because there are 32 sprocket holes in each row, drag 31 instances of the Sprocket Hole movie clip from the Library to the Stage in the Sprocket Holes layer (anywhere will do). (You might need to open the Library panel from the Window menu.) Instances of the Sprocket Hole symbol accumulate on the Stage. Make sure all of them are on the Sprocket Holes layer.

6. Drag one of the sprocket holes to just below the right sprocket hole at the top of the filmstrip (visible from the Comp Image layer) and drag another sprocket hole to just below the far left sprocket hole at the top of the filmstrip. These are the two endpoints for the row of sprocket holes you are about to create, as shown in Figure 4-8.

FIGURE 4-8
Creating a row of sprocket holes

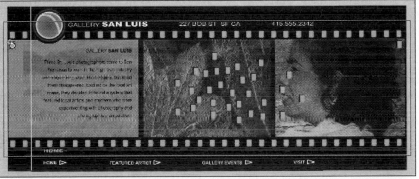

7. Select all the sprocket holes by clicking on the first frame of the Sprocket Holes layer.

8. On the Align panel, toggle the **To stage** button to off.

9. Click the **Space evenly horizontally** button and then click the **Align top edge** button. The sprocket holes align in a row, as shown in Figure 4-9.

FIGURE 4-9
Aligned sprocket holes

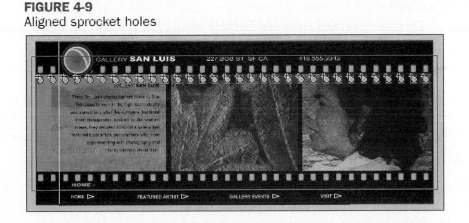

STEP-BY-STEP 4.3 Continued

10. Convert this row of sprocket hole instances into its own movie clip symbol and name it **Sprocket Hole Row**, as shown in Figure 4-10.

FIGURE 4-10
Sprocket Hole Row movie clip

You now have reached the third level of symbols: The main movie (home.fla) level within which there is a Sprocket Hole Row movie clip, within which there are 32 Sprocket Hole movie clips. Part of the power of movie clip symbols is that each sprocket hole symbol has an independent **Timeline**.

11. Align the **Sprocket Hole Row** movie clip over the top row of sprocket holes visible from the Comp Image layer. Align them as well as possible, using the arrow keys on the keyboard and zooming in if necessary.

12. Drag another instance of the **Sprocket Hole Row** movie clip onto the Stage from the library.

13. Cover the lower row of sprocket holes visible from the comp image as well as possible.

14. Save the movie and remain in this screen for the next Step-by-Step.

Inserting and Placing Images

Now you're ready to insert the images. When you are working in Flash and you are concerned about precise placement of elements on the Stage, you can use rulers and draggable guides.

S TEP-BY-STEP 4.4

Using Rulers and Guides and Inserting Images

1. Click the **View** menu and then click **Rulers**. Rulers appear above and to the left of the Stage.

2. On the **View** menu, point to **Snapping**, and make sure **Snap to Objects** and **Snap to Guides** are selected. Then, point to the **Guides** option on the **View** menu, and make sure **Show Guides** is selected. You will use these guides to align the inserted pictures on the three content areas of the filmstrip.

3. Drag a guide onto the Stage by clicking on the ruler at the top of the work area and dragging down toward the Stage without releasing your pointer. You might have to zoom in to align the guides correctly. A green line appears on the Stage. This is your guide line.

STEP-BY-STEP 4.4 Continued

4. Position the first guide so it is right on the top border of the three filmstrip "cels." Then drag another 11 guides to frame the three filmstrip cels and the Stage, as shown in Figure 4-11. You might have to hide the Comp Image layer to see the Stage. You might also want to zoom in so you can line up the guides precisely.

Did You Know?

The boxes in the filmstrip are referred to as "cels." This name comes from the fact that animated cartoons were originally drawn on celluloid.

FIGURE 4-11
Lining up the guides

5. On the **View** menu, point to **Guides**, and then click **Lock Guides**.

Now, you insert images along the guides.

6. Create a new layer and name it **Center**.

7. Import the image **floral.jpg** from the **images** folder into this layer.

8. Convert the image into a graphic symbol and name it **Home Center**.

9. On the Property inspector, set the width to **345** and the height to **260**.

Note

The width might automatically adjust to 344.9 and the height to 259.9 because it cannot cut off pixels.

STEP-BY-STEP 4.4 Continued

10. Drag **Home Center** up against the guides in the center cel. Use the Arrow keys to adjust the position of the images, as shown in Figure 4-12.

FIGURE 4-12
Aligning an image with the guides

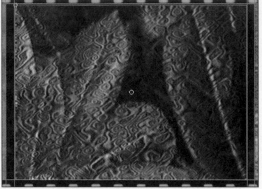

11. Insert a new layer above Center and name it **Right**.

12. Import the image **portrait.jpg** from the **images** folder into this layer.

13. On the Property Inspector, Set W: to **345** and H: to **260**.

14. Convert the image to a graphic symbol and name it **Home Right**.

15. Align the image to the guides in the cel on the right.

16. Insert a new layer above Right and name it **Left**.

17. Select the **Rectangle** tool. Change the Stroke to **None** and the Fill to purple **#9933FF**, as shown in Figure 4-13.

FIGURE 4-13
Choosing purple #9933FF from the Fill Color menu

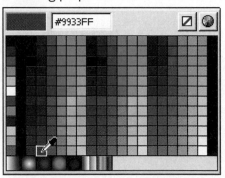

STEP-BY-STEP 4.4 Continued

18. Draw a rectangle approximately the same size as the left cel. The rectangle should "snap" to the guides. That is a major advantage of working with guides: creating precise drawing objects. If necessary, use the Property inspector to change the size of the rectangle to 345 × 260. Use the Arrow keys to adjust its position in the left cel if necessary.

19. Convert the rectangle to a movie clip symbol and name it **Home Left Background**.

20. On the Property inspector, select the **Color** drop-down box and set the Brightness to **50%**.

21. Save your work and remain in this screen for the next Step-by-Step.

Creating a Template Movie Clip

Because you will be creating many similar 345 x 260 cels for content later, it might be a good idea to create a template movie clip. Then you can just duplicate this movie clip in the library when you need to create new content.

S TEP-BY-STEP 4.5

Creating a Movie Clip for Future Content

1. Locate the Library panel (or, if necessary, open it) that contains all the symbols.

2. Click the **Home Left Background** symbol once to select it.

3. From the **Options** menu in the upper-right corner of the Library panel, choose **Duplicate**.

4. Name the new symbol **Cel Background** and click **OK**.

5. Double-click the icon beside the **Cel Background** movie clip in the library. This opens the Cel Background movie.

6. Rename Layer1 **Background**.

7. Use the Selection tool to double-click the rectangle.

8. On the Property inspector, change the Fill color to gray (**#CCCCCC**).

9. Click **Scene 1** on the information bar to return to the main **Timeline**.

10. Save the document, then close the file and exit Flash.

SUMMARY

In this lesson, you learned:

- The basics of site architecture and document sizing.
- To use a background (comp) image as a guide.
- To create and use graphic and movie clip symbols.
- To create and use layers and guides.
- To import JPG files.
- To create a template movie clip.

ADDING TEXT AND NAVIGATION TO THE HOME PAGE

OBJECTIVES

Upon completion of this lesson, you should be able to:

- Create and configure text.
- Line up objects with another layer.
- Create a transparent overlay image.
- Create navigation buttons.
- Create Layer folders.
- Insert Macromedia Flash movies (documents with .swf extensions).

Gallery San Luis Web Site Progress

When you started designing the Gallery San Luis Web site in Lesson 4, you outlined the list of items the client wanted incorporated into the site. Let's take a quick look at how the Gallery San Luis project has progressed:

- ❏ A Home page that is both appealing and speaks photography.
- ❏ A Featured Artist page with a Photo Viewer and featured photographer information.
- ❏ Video interviews with the featured artist (optional).
- ❏ An animated Map page to indicate where the gallery is located.
- ❏ An Events page for requesting tickets for gallery events.
- ❏ Sound incorporated on buttons.
- ❏ Slick transitions between pages.
- ☑ An overall photography metaphor for the site.

Working with Text

You start this lesson by adding text to the home page. The text description on the home page has two elements: a title and descriptive text. To give you the most flexibility in layout, you can create two separate text objects and align them separately to match the comp image on the Gallery Text layer.

You use the Text tool to create text in Macromedia Flash MX 2004. Here are some keys to working successfully with the Text tool:

- Click once on the Stage to create a text box.

- To size the text box, always drag the handle in the corner (don't use the width and height settings on the Property inspector or Transform panel).

- To increase the lettering size, use the Font Size box on the Property inspector.

- Click the Selection tool after you finish typing in a text box. If you don't, the Text tool is still active, and you will create a new text box if you click on the Stage again.

S TEP-BY-STEP 5.1

Creating Text

1. Launch Flash.

2. Open your **home.fla** movie, which should be in the **build_GallerySanLuis** folder you created in Lesson 4.

3. Click the **Insert Layer** button. Rename the new layer **Gallery Text**.

> **Note** ☑
>
> If you had problems with the previous lesson, ask your instructor for the **home1.fla** sample solution file. Once you open this file, save it as **home.fla** followed by your initials in the main **build_GallerySanLuis** folder (overwriting the file with which you had problems) and proceed with this lesson.

> **Note** ☑
>
> If the Missing Font warning box appears when you open home1.fla or any other file, click **Use Default** to close the box.

STEP-BY-STEP 5.1 Continued

4. Click the **Show Outline** button for the Left layer (the Background layer should already be in Outline view). The purple background disappears, revealing the comp image, as shown in Figure 5-1.

FIGURE 5-1
Showing a layer as an outline

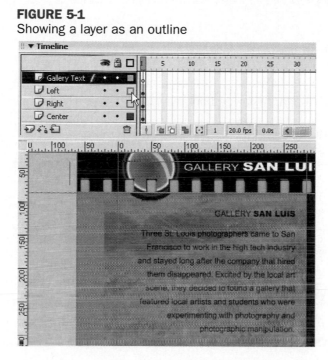

5. Select the **Text** tool.

6. Click and drag to create a text box on top of the title GALLERY SAN LUIS (this text is in the left cell over the purple background and is visible from the Comp Image layer).

7. On the Property inspector, set the text type to **Static**, the font to **Arial** or Helvetica, the size to 12 points, the color to black **(#000000)**, and the alignment to right-aligned.

8. Key **GALLERY** in all caps.

STEP-BY-STEP 5.1 Continued

9. On the Property inspector, change the font to **Arial Black**. If you don't have Arial Black, select Helvetica and select Bold.

10. Key **SAN LUIS** in all caps.

11. Select the **Selection** tool. The text is surrounded by a blue outline.

12. Use the Arrow keys to position the new text, GALLERYSANLUIS, over the same text in the Comp Image layer.

13. Click outside the text box to deselect it.

14. Select the **Text** tool, and click on the left edge of the top line of the paragraph text (visible from the Comp Image layer) to start a new text box, as shown in Figure 5-2.

FIGURE 5-2
Inserting a new text box

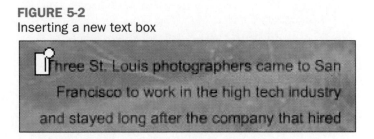

15. Drag the text box size handle and extend the text box to the right border of the background, as shown in Figure 5-3. (*Note*: You don't always have to size a text box, but it is helpful when creating a text box that will have more than one line, because it creates an automatic return when the border of the box is reached—similar to word-wrapping in a word-processing program.)

FIGURE 5-3
Resizing a text box

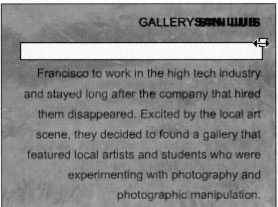
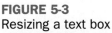

16. On the Property inspector, set the font and font size to **Arial** or **Helvetica**, **12**, and set the alignment to right-aligned.

STEP-BY-STEP 5.1 Continued

17. Key the following in the text box:

Three St. Louis photographers came to San Francisco to work in the high tech industry and stayed long after the company that hired them had disappeared. Excited by the local art scene, they decided to start a gallery that featured local artists and students who were experimenting with photography and photographic manipulation.

18. Use the Selection tool to select the text box and align it with the text in the Comp Image layer, as shown in Figure 5-4. If the body text is not lining up correctly, make sure the text box is wide enough that you can read "photographic manipulation" on the bottom line. You can also click the Format button on the Property inspector and change the line spacing. Try 7 pt. If you need to widen the text box, double-click the box and drag the resize handle in the upper-right corner. Do not stretch the box with the Transform tool or change its dimensions in the Property inspector (this just stretches the text)

> **Important**
>
> Sometimes text displays in different sizes in Windows and Macintosh browsers (text might display too large on Windows browsers to fit inside text boxes). If you develop on a Macintosh computer, check your text displays on a Windows computer before publishing to the Web. One way to avoid text size changes is to convert the text from a text object to a vector graphic object. You can do this by breaking apart the text into individual letters (use the Break Apart command on the Modify menu). However, once you break apart text, it is no longer selectable for edits with the Text tool.

> **Note**
>
> You might not be able to get your text to match up exactly. As long as the text comes close to filling the same area and is within the left box, it will be fine in the end.

FIGURE 5-4
Aligning the text to the comp image

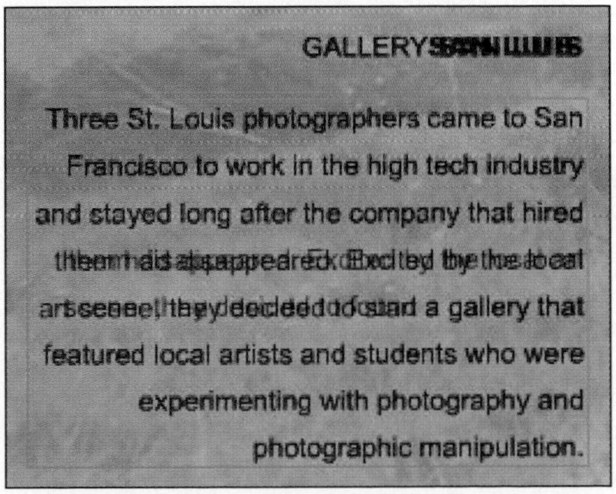

STEP-BY-STEP 5.1 Continued

19. Save the document and preview it by clicking the **Control** menu, and then **Test Movie**. The preview should look like that shown in Figure 5-5. The text should fill the left cel of the home filmstrip.

FIGURE 5-5
Previewing the aligned text

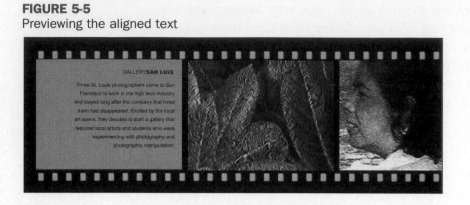

20. Click the **File** menu and then click **Close** to close the preview window. Remain in this screen for the next Step-by-Step.

Creating a Transparent Overlay Image

Although you have created the title, text, and purple background box, you have not yet created the texture. One way to create a texture is to use a semitransparent overlay image. This image is placed on top of the page like a clear, textured cover. Separating the texture from the text box background gives you more flexibility for designing and modifying it.

STEP-BY-STEP 5.2

Creating a Transparent Overlay Image

1. Click in the **Gallery Text** layer, and then click the **Insert Layer** button.

2. Rename the new layer **Overlay**.

3. Open the **File** menu, point to **Import**, and click **Import to Stage** to open the Import dialog box.

4. Navigate to the **images** folder in your **build_GallerySanLuis** folder, select **overlay.jpg**, and click **Open** (Windows) or **Import** (Macintosh). The Overlay image appears on the Stage in the Overlay layer. You might have to zoom out to see the entire image.

5. Click the **Modify** menu, and then click **Convert to Symbol**.

STEP-BY-STEP 5.2 Continued

6. In the Convert to Symbol dialog box, select **Movie clip**. Name it **Overlay** and click **OK**.

7. On the Property inspector, choose **Advanced** from the **Color** menu. Then click **Settings**. The Advanced Effect dialog box opens, as shown in Figure 5-6.

FIGURE 5-6
Advanced Effect dialog box

Advanced Effect	☒
Red = `100%` ▾ x R) `0` ▾	
Green = `100%` ▾ x G) `0` ▾	
Blue= (`100%` ▾ x B) + `0` ▾	
Alpha = `100%` ▾ x A) `0` ▾	
Help OK Cancel	

8. Set the left Alpha box to **25%** and set the right Blue box to **100**. Then click **OK**.

9. On the Property inspector, position the overlay on the Stage by entering **–20** in the X location coordinate, and **88** in the Y location coordinate.

10. Click the **Control** menu, and then **Test Movie**. The movie should play with the transparent overlay, as shown in Figure 5-7. (Although the images seem to run over the edge, they will automatically be cut by the Stage when you publish the final movie.)

> **Hot Tip** ◎
>
> The controls on the left side of the Advanced Effect dialog box let you reduce the color or transparency values by a specified percentage. The controls on the right let you reduce or increase the color or transparency values by a constant value.

FIGURE 5-7
Preview with overlay and text

11. Close the Preview window and save your document. Remain in this screen for the next Step-by-Step.

Building the Navigation Area

The filmstrip area of the site is now complete. You're ready to add the navigation layer at the bottom of the Stage with the page title and buttons for navigating to different areas of the site, including *Home*, *Featured Artist*, *Gallery Events*, and *Visit*. The text in the navigation area is designed to look like a filmstrip. If you've ever looked at a photographic negative, you might have noticed that the text and numbers on a filmstrip are long and flat. You can create similar-looking text by using the Transform panel.

S TEP-BY-STEP 5.3

Creating Elongated Text

1. Click in the **Overlay** layer, and click the **Insert Layer** button.

2. Rename the new layer **Page Name**.

3. Select the **Text** tool and click on top of the orange **HOME** (visible from the Comp Image layer).

4. Set the following attributes on the Property inspector: **Arial Black** or **Helvetica Bold**, **12**, and orange color **#FFCC00**.

5. Key **HOME** in all caps, as shown in Figure 5-8.

FIGURE 5-8
Creating page title text

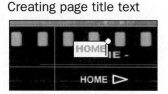

6. Select the Selection tool. The text is surrounded by a blue border showing that it is selected. If it is not, click the first frame of the Page Name layer.

7. Click the **Modify** menu, and click **Convert to Symbol** to open the Convert to Symbol dialog box.

8. Choose **Graphic**, name it **Title Home**, and then click **OK**.

9. Make sure the **Title Home** instance is still selected, open the **Window** menu, point to Design Panels, and then click **Transform**.

10. On the Transform panel, uncheck the **Constrain** check box. Double-click in the Horizontal Scale Width box (on the left), key **130**, and press **Enter** (Windows) or **Return** (Macintosh) as shown in Figure 5-9.

STEP-BY-STEP 5.3 Continued

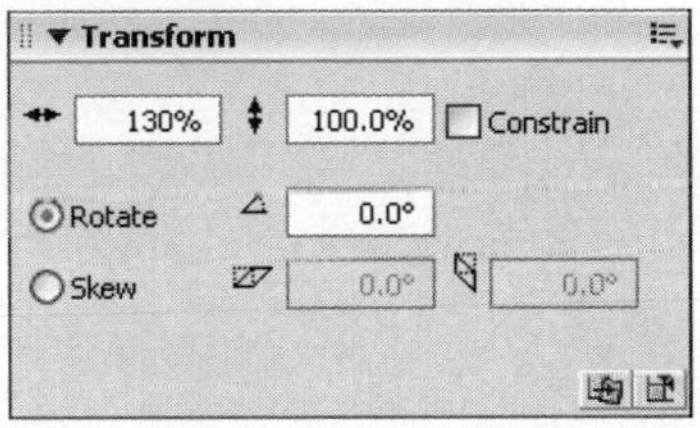

FIGURE 5-9
Text stretched to 130%

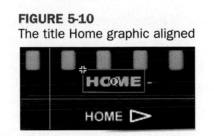

11. Use the Selection tool or the arrow keys to line up *HOME* directly above the HOME label visible from the Comp Image layer, as shown in Figure 5-10.

FIGURE 5-10
The title Home graphic aligned

12. Save and preview the document. Close the Preview window and remain in this screen for the next Step-by-Step.

Creating the Navigation Buttons

Buttons are similar to movie clip symbols, with independent Timelines containing four frames. When you select the Button behavior for a symbol, Flash creates the Timeline and the four frames. The first three frames display the button's three possible states, and the fourth frame defines the active area of the button. The Timeline doesn't play; it reacts to pointer movement and actions by jumping to the appropriate frame.

Each frame on the Timeline of a button symbol has a specific function:

- *Frame 1*: The Up state, representing the button's appearance whenever the pointer is not over the button.

- *Frame 2*: The Over state, representing the button's appearance when the pointer is over it.

- *Frame 3*: The Down state, representing the button's appearance as it is clicked.

- *Frame 4*: The Hit state, defining the area that responds to the mouse click. This area is invisible in the movie.

S TEP-BY-STEP 5.4

Creating Navigational Buttons

1. Click the **Page Name** layer. Click the **Insert Layer** button, and rename the new layer **Navigation**.

STEP-BY-STEP 5.4 Continued

2. Select the **Line** tool. In the Tools section of the toolbar, change the Stroke color to dark gray (**#666666**).

3. Click just below and to the left of the page name (below the word *Home* that you just placed) and drag to create a line over the gray line visible from the Comp Image layer, as shown in Figure 5-11. To draw a straight line, hold down the **Shift** key as you drag.

FIGURE 5-11
Creating a dividing line

4. Use the **Selection** tool to select the line. On the Property inspector, set the line's X value to **–20**.

5. Click the **Modify** menu, and click **Convert to Symbol** to open the Convert to Symbol dialog box.

6. Name the symbol **Navigation Divider**, select the **Graphic** behavior, and click **OK**.

7. Select the **Text** tool.

8. Set the keyboard to **Caps Lock**. On the Property inspector, set the following text attributes: **Arial**, **12**, **Bold**, and white (**#FFFFFF**).

9. While still in the Navigation layer, click the Stage below the orange *Home* title and key **HOME** (near the white Home text visible from the Comp Image layer).

> **Hot Tip** 🎯
>
> When you have several text items to create and then place – all with the same properties – you might find it easier to enter all your text items first and then switch to the Selection tool for placement of the text boxes.

10. Use the Selection tool (and arrow keys) to align the HOME text on top of the text from the Comp Image layer.

11. Use the Text tool again and key **FEATURED ARTIST**. Align it to its text from the Comp Image layer.

12. Add additional text objects for **GALLERY EVENTS** and **VISIT**, and align them appropriately, as shown in Figure 5-12.

FIGURE 5-12
Creating button labels

13. Save your changes and remain in this screen for the next Step-by-Step.

Applying Symbols to the Navigation Buttons

To make the navigation text look more like a set of buttons, you will insert arrow symbols next to each navigation label.

S TEP-BY-STEP 5.5

Creating Button Symbols

1. With the **Navigation** layer still selected, open the **File** menu, point to **Import**, click **Import to Library**, and select **navArrow.swf** from the **images** folder in your **build_GallerySanLuis** folder. Click **Open** (Windows) or **Import** (Macintosh). The navArrow symbol displays in the library as a graphic symbol.

2. Make sure the **Library** panel is open. Drag four instances of the **navArrow** symbol onto the Stage and align each of them to the right of the navigation labels (on top of the arrows visible from the Comp Image layer).

3. Click outside the Stage to make sure no arrows are selected. Hold down the **Shift** key and click the **HOME** label and its arrow to select both of them.

4. With both buttons selected, open the **Modify** menu, and click **Convert to Symbol**.

5. Name the symbol **Button Home** and set the Behavior to **Button**. Click **OK**. The label and arrow are now one instance of the Button Home symbol.

6. Repeat steps 3-5, selecting the other pairs of labels and arrows to create three more buttons named **Button Artist**, **Button Events**, and **Button Visit**.

7. Save your work and remain in this screen for the next Step-by-Step.

Hot Tip

You might also want to try selecting all the buttons and then clicking **Space evenly horizontally** (do not select Align To Stage on the Align panel).

    The buttons are now on the Stage. You will make them active in Lesson 6 when you create the pages to which they will link. First, however, you will put some of the layers into folders to clean up the Timeline.

Creating Layer Folders

    Most designers organize their work in a Flash document by separating objects on different layers. Often this results in a lot of layers, making it difficult to see all the layers in the movie without collapsing the Stage. You might have noticed that your Timeline is getting long and difficult to see. In Flash you can have layer folders for storing several layers that hold similar content. You are going to create two folders to sort the layers by Filmstrip and Navigation. These folders will help later when you are dividing the content that changes from page to page and the content that remains static.

STEP-BY-STEP 5.6

Creating Layer Folders

1. Move your pointer over the dividing bar between the Stage and the Timeline. When the pointer turns into a two-headed arrow, drag the dividing bar down to display the complete list of layers, as shown in Figure 5-13.

FIGURE 5-13
Dragging the Timeline divider to increase the Timeline area

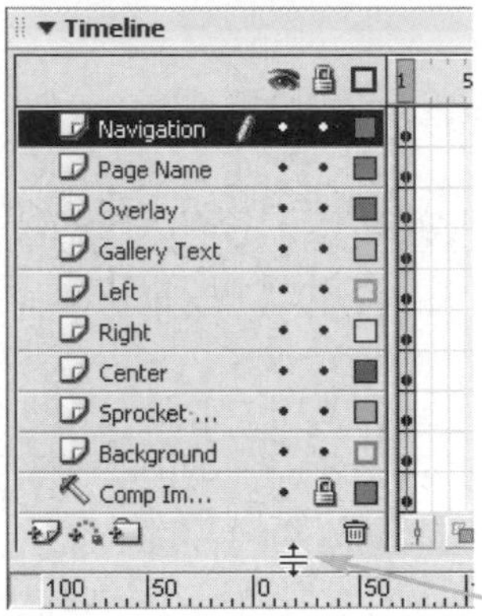

Double-headed arrow

2. Continue to drag down to allow space for two more layer items you will be adding.

3. Click the **Insert Layer Folder** button, located below the list of layers on the Timeline.

4. Double-click the **Folder 1** layer, rename the folder **Filmstrip**, and press **Enter** (Windows) or **Return** (Macintosh).

5. Hold down **Control** (Windows) or **Command** (Macintosh) and select the following layers: **Overlay**, **Gallery Text**, **Left**, **Right**, **Center**, **Sprocket Holes**, **Background**, and **Comp Image**.

6. Click and drag any one of the selected layers to move them all into the **Filmstrip** folder. All of the selected layers are moved.

7. Click the **Filmstrip** folder and then click the **Insert Layer Folder** button to create another layer folder above the **Filmstrip** folder. Rename it **Navigation**.

8. Drag the **Page Name** and **Navigation** layers into this **Navigation** folder.

9. Click the arrows next to the folders to expand or collapse their contents. With the folders collapsed, you have a much narrower Timeline. You can increase the area for the Stage by dragging the dividing line between the Timeline and the Stage.

10. Save your changes and remain in this screen for the next Step-by-Step.

Adding the Logo and Gallery Title Text

You've created and organized the filmstrip and navigation layers. Now it's time to finish the home page by creating the title and logo areas at the top of the page.

S TEP-BY-STEP 5.7

Adding the Logo and Gallery Title Text

1. Click in the **Navigation** layer folder and then click the **Insert Layer** button. Rename the new layer **Logo**.

2. Open the **File** menu, point to Import, click **Import to Library**, and double-click your **logo.swf** file in the **Images** folder (the one you created earlier). The logo appears in the library as a graphic symbol.

3. Click **Show as Outline** to the right of the Logo layer name, as shown in Figure 5-14, and then select the **Logo** layer.

FIGURE 5-14
Using the Show as Outline button with the Logo layer

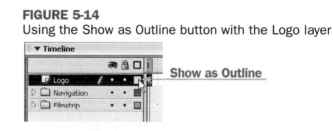

4. Drag an instance of the logo graphic onto the Stage near the logo image visible from the Comp Image layer.

5. Use the arrow keys to line up the arch outline of the logo graphic with the logo on the comp image, as shown in Figure 5-15.

FIGURE 5-15
Lining up the logo

6. Select the **Text** tool and set the font to **Arial** or **Helvetica**, the size to **14**, and the color to white.

7. Next to the logo and in the same layer, insert a text box and key **GALLERY SAN LUIS**.

8. Select **SAN LUIS** and change its font to **Arial Black**, **18**. (If you don't have Arial Black, make it Helvetica bold.)

STEP-BY-STEP 5.7 Continued

9. Use the Selection tool to deselect **SAN LUIS** and to select the entire text box.

10. Locate the Transform panel. If necessary, open the **Window** menu, point to **Design Panels**, and click **Transform** to open the Transform panel.

11. Change the horizontal Width to **130%**.

12. Use the Selection tool or the arrow keys to align the gallery name over the name visible from the Comp Image layer.

13. Use the Selection tool to select outside the Stage area. Select the **Text** tool and set the font to **Arial** or **Helvetica** and the size to **14**.

14. On the Stage, key **227 BOB ST SF CA** (note the two spaces between ST and SF and between SF and CA). Create another text box and key **415.555.2342**.

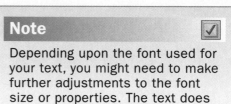

> **Note** ☑
>
> Depending upon the font used for your text, you might need to make further adjustments to the font size or properties. The text does not have to be an exact match— you just want it to be close.

15. Use the Selection tool and the Shift key to select both text boxes and then use the Transform panel to set the horizontal widths for the text boxes to **130%**.

16. Use the Selection tool and the arrow keys to align these two text boxes to the Comp Image layer.

17. With the **Logo** layer selected, click on the **Insert Layer** button, and then rename the new layer **Border**.

> **Note** ☑
>
> Insert these text boxes toward the top of the Stage. You don't have to be precise. You will soon align them to the comp image.

18. Select the **Rectangle** tool. Click in the gray area outside the Stage. On the Property inspector, set the stroke to white, the fill to none (the square with the red line through it), and the line width to **1.5**.

19. Draw a rectangle around the entire Stage. Don't worry about making it a perfect shape. You'll set it perfectly in the next step. You might need to zoom out to see the entire Stage.

20. With the Selection tool, double-click the rectangle to select it. On the Property inspector, set the W dimension to **779**, the H dimension to **437**, the X dimension to **0**, and the Y dimension to **0**.

21. With the rectangle still selected, open the **Modify** menu, and click **Convert to Symbol**.

22. In the Convert to Symbol dialog box, name the symbol **Page Border** and set the Behavior to **Graphic**. Click **OK**.

23. Open the **Control** menu, and click **Test Movie** to preview the document. You should see a white border showing the size of the final dimensions of your movie.

STEP-BY-STEP 5.7 Continued

24. Close the Preview window.

25. To see what the site will look like in a Web browser, open the **File** menu, point to **Publish Preview**, and then click **Default – (HTML)** to open the movie in your browser. You might have to switch windows to see the HTML page.

26. If you are satisfied with the look of the project, close your browser, and then delete the **Comp Image** layer by making sure it's unlocked and dragging it into the Trash, as illustrated in Figure 5-16.

FIGURE 5-16
Deleting the Comp layer

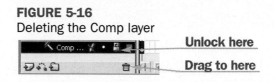

27. Save your work and then close the file and exit Flash.

SUMMARY

In this lesson, you learned to:

■ Create and configure text.

■ Line up objects with another layer.

■ Create a transparent overlay image.

■ Create navigation buttons.

■ Create Layer folders.

■ Insert Flash movies (documents with .swf extensions).

WORKING WITH MOVIE CLIPS

Gallery San Luis Web Site Progress

When you started designing the Gallery San Luis Web site in Lesson 4, you outlined the list of items the client wanted incorporated into the site. In both Lessons 4 and 5 you worked on specific tasks within that list. Following is a quick look at how the Gallery San Luis project has progressed thus far.

☑ A Home page that is both appealing and speaks photography.

❑ A Featured Artist page with a Photo Viewer and featured photographer information.

❑ Video interviews with the featured artist (optional).

❑ An animated Map page to indicate where the gallery is located.

❑ An Events page for requesting tickets for gallery events.

❑ Sound incorporated on buttons.

❑ Slick transitions between pages.

☑ An overall photography metaphor for the site.

Building Out from the Home Page

The next step in the project list is to build the Featured Artist's page within the home.fla document. Unlike building an HTML site in which you have a home page and three separate HTML pages for the Featured Artist, Gallery Events, and Visit content, you can create all the content for the site in one Flash movie document.

One way to meet the challenge is by creating four movie clip symbols within the home.fla document, one for each section of the Web site. Each of the movie clip symbols is based on the

61

content you've already created in the filmstrip area, because this is where new site content appears, as shown in Figure 6-1.

FIGURE 6-1
Changes to filmstrip content for Featured Artist page

Featured Artist Selection based on center film strip area of Home page. Three cells in filmstrip change accordingly.

Converting Layers to a Movie Clip Symbol

To create the four movie clips, you start by creating one movie clip symbol from all the layers in the Filmstrip folder. That gives you all the components you need to make the other movie clip symbols.

Flash makes it easy to convert a set of layers, with all their contents, into a single large movie clip symbol. You select and copy frames, insert a new movie clip symbol, and then paste the frames into the new movie clip.

STEP-BY-STEP 6.1

Creating a Movie Clip from Layers

1. Start Flash. Open the **home.fla** file you worked with in Lesson 5, which should be in the **build_GallerySanLuis** folder.

2. Make sure the **Timeline** is expanded so you can see all the Layers. If the Filmstrip folder is collapsed, expand it.

> **Note** ☑
>
> If you had problems with the project in the previous lesson, ask your instructor for the **home2.fla** sample solution file. Once you have opened this file, save it as **home.fla** followed by your initials in the main **build_GallerySanLuis** folder (overwriting the file with which you had problems) and proceed with this lesson.

STEP-BY-STEP 6.1 Continued

3. Drag in the first frame of the **Timeline** to select the first frames of the **Overlay**, **Gallery Text**, **Left**, **Right**, **Center**, **Sprocket Holes**, and **Background** layers shown in Figure 6-2.

> **Hot Tip** ⊚
>
> In addition to dragging to select, you can select multiple frames by clicking on the first frame you want to select, holding down the **Shift** key, and clicking on the last frame you want to select. You can also hold the **Ctrl** key (Windows) or **Command** key (Macintosh) to select several noncontiguous frames.

FIGURE 6-2
Selecting frames

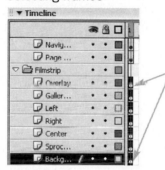

4. On the **Edit** menu, point to **Timeline**, and click **Copy Frames**.

5. Click the **Insert** menu, and click **New Symbol**.

6. Name the symbol **Fstrip Home**, select **Movie Clip** for the Behavior, and click **OK**. Notice that the Stage has changed. You are no longer in Scene 1. You are inside the Fstrip Home movie clip. You can tell what you are

> **Note** ☑
>
> If you just choose the Copy command on the **Edit** menu, you lose the layer structure and end up with all the elements on one layer.

editing by looking at the Information bar. When you were working on the original movie, the Information bar just displayed Scene 1. Now "Fstrip Home" appears next to Scene 1, as shown in Figure 6-3.

FIGURE 6-3
Fstrip Home movie clip

STEP-BY-STEP 6.1 Continued

7. Select **Layer 1**, open the **Edit** menu, point to **Timeline**, and then click **Paste Frames**. All the frames from the Home filmstrip are pasted, retaining their layer names and structure, as shown in Figure 6-4.

FIGURE 6-4
Pasting frames

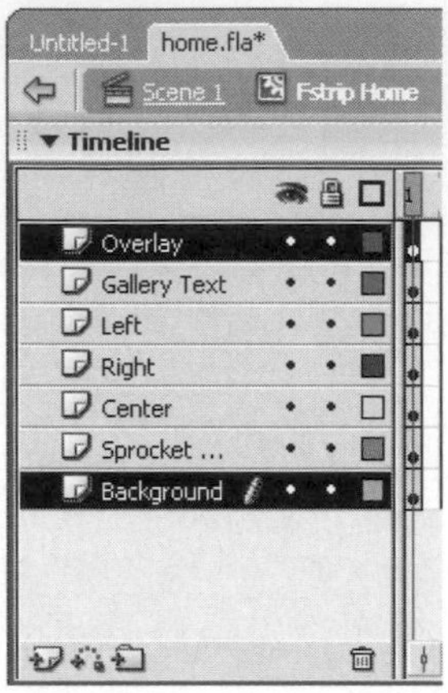

8. Save your document and remain in this screen for the next Step-by-Step.

Replacing Layers with a Movie Clip

Because you have created a movie clip of the Home filmstrip layers, you can now replace the original filmstrip layers in Scene 1 with the Fstrip Home movie clip. Using movie clips makes your **Timeline** much less complicated and animating the filmstrip much easier.

STEP-BY-STEP 6.2

Replacing Original Layers with a Movie Clip Symbol

1. On the left side of the Information bar, click **Scene 1** to return to the main movie **Timeline**.

2. Insert a new layer above the Overlay layer and rename it **Home**.

3. Make sure the Library panel is expanded and the Home layer is selected.

STEP-BY-STEP 6.2 Continued

4. With the Home layer selected, drag the Fstrip Home movie clip symbol from the library onto the Stage. An instance of the Fstrip Home movie clip appears on the Stage, as shown in Figure 6-5.

FIGURE 6-5
Movie clip symbol in frame 1 of the Home layer

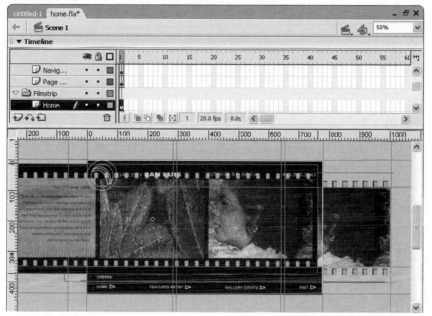

5. Because Fstrip Home is a movie clip, you can move the entire contents of the movie clip at once. Using the Selection tool and the arrow keys, position the Fstrip Home movie clip instance to align it with the original layers below it.

6. Click the **Overlay** layer and then scroll down the layer list. Hold down the **Shift** key and click the **Background** layer. All the original filmstrip layers are selected.

7. Drag the selected layers into the trashcan. This is a quick way to delete multiple layers.

8. Save the document and remain in this screen for the next Step-by-Step.

Hot Tip 🎯

One way to align exactly is to zoom in and line up the movie clip instance with the corners of the background layer.

Note ☑

The advantage of creating a movie clip for the home page film strip is that the filmstrip can all fit on one layer, which will save time when you animate it later.

Creating a New Movie Clip from Another Movie Clip Symbol

The Featured Artist section of the Gallery San Luis site includes three elements:

- An artist's biography in the left section.
- A Photo Viewer of the artist's work in the center section.
- A photograph of the artist in the right section.

Your first task is to create the artist's biography section, which is similar to the gallery text on the home page except that you will be aligning the text without a comp image to which to match it.

Because the Featured Artist section is similar to the home page, you can copy the Fstrip Home movie clip and edit the new symbol to contain the featured artist content.

You edit a symbol by changing the window from the Stage view to a view of only the symbol, using the symbol-editing mode.

STEP-BY-STEP 6.3

Duplicating a Symbol

1. Select the **Fstrip Home** movie clip in the library.

2. Click the **Options** button (upper-right corner of the Library panel). From the menu, choose **Duplicate**. The Duplicate Symbol dialog box opens.

3. Name the new symbol **Fstrip Artist** and click **OK**. The movie clip symbol Fstrip Artist is added to the library. No instances of this symbol will appear in the document until you drag the symbol onto the Stage.

4. Save your document and remain in this screen for the next Step-by-Step.

Symbol Editing

You have created the Fstrip Artist symbol from the Fstrip Home movie. Now you need to customize the content of the Fstrip Artist symbol so it contains the artist's biography and photographs. You can customize a library symbol by editing it.

A word of caution: When you edit a symbol, you change all its instances throughout a movie document. Also, after you exit symbol-editing mode, you cannot use the Undo command to undo changes you made to the symbol in the editing mode.

There are actually three symbol-editing modes in Macromedia Flash MX 2004. Table 6-1 lists when and how to use them.

TABLE 6-1
Symbol-editing modes

SYMBOL-EDITING MODES	PURPOSE	HOW TO BEGIN EDIT SESSION	HOW TO EXIT SYMBOL-EDITING MODE
Edit	Edit a symbol in isolation. You see only the symbol elements on the Stage.	Choose a symbol on the Stage and select Edit Symbols on the Edit menu, or double-click a symbol in the library.	Click the scene name on the Information bar at the top of the Stage.
Edit in Place	Edit a symbol while seeing it positioned on the Stage with the rest of the elements in the scene.	Choose a symbol on the Stage and select Edit in Place on the Edit menu, or double-click a symbol Instance on the Stage.	Click the scene name on the Information bar at the top of the Stage.
Edit in New Window	Edit a symbol in isolation. You can preview just the symbol (select Test Movie on the Control menu).	Choose a symbol on the Stage and select Edit Selected on the Edit menu, or right-click (Windows) or Ctrl-click (Macintosh) a symbol instance on the Stage and choose Edit in New Window.	Close the window.

S TEP-BY-STEP 6.4

Editing a Movie Clip Instance

1. Double-click the icon for the **Fstrip Artist** movie clip in the library. (Make sure you double-click on the icon, not the name.) The Fstrip Artist movie appears by itself on the Stage. You are now in symbol-editing mode. Notice that the Information bar has changed. It displays "Fstrip Artist" next to "Scene 1."

2. Select the **Overlay** layer and drag it to the trashcan. The Overlay layer is deleted from the Fstrip Artist symbol. There will be no overlay image for this page.

3. Select the purple background in the Left layer.

STEP-BY-STEP 6.4 Continued

4. On the Properties inspector, choose **Tint** from the **Color** menu.

5. Change the tint fill to green **(#99CC66)**. You can key this number directly into the Color Definition box, as shown in Figure 6-6. Make sure the Tint amount is set to 100%.

> **Note** ✓
>
> You are altering only one instance of the Home Left Background symbol. As long as you don't enter editing mode on an instance, you can change its size, transparency, or color without affecting other instances of that symbol.

FIGURE 6-6
Manually entering a fill color

Enter color value directly here, or select from the palette

6. Double-click the title text GALLERY SAN LUIS at the top of the left cell to enter text-editing mode. Select the text within the text box and key BIJI in all caps.

7. Select the text you just typed and set the following text attributes: **Arial Black** or **Helvetica Bold**, **14**, and right-aligned. Notice that the text boxes aren't symbols, so their font doesn't change.

8. Double-click the body text to enter text-editing mode. Select all the text within the box and then change the font to **14**-point **Arial**.

> **Important**
>
> Macintosh and Windows computers might display text differently in Flash movies. Specifically, some browsers display smaller text in Macintosh browsers. One way to avoid differing text displays is to break apart the text by clicking the **Modify** menu and then clicking **Break Apart** before you publish your movie. If you're developing on a Macintosh, keeping font sizes above 9 points is also helpful. This movie uses fonts of 12 points and larger, so you don't need to break it apart.

STEP-BY-STEP 6.4 Continued

9. Replace the text with the text shown in Figure 6-7.

FIGURE 6-7
Artist's biography text box

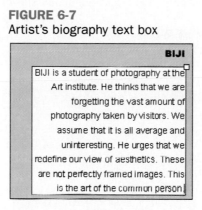

10. Save your document and remain in this screen for the next Step-by-Step.

Using the Align Panel

You can make sure objects on the Stage line up exactly with each other by using the Align panel. On the Align panel, you can align selected objects horizontally and vertically to each other or to the Stage.

S TEP-BY-STEP 6.5

Aligning Objects Accurately

1. Using the **Selection** tool, double-click the text describing Biji. The cursor blinks to indicate text-editing mode.

2. Drag the size handle in the upper-right corner to size the text box, as shown in Figure 6-8, if necessary.

3. Select the Selection tool. The text box is selected automatically.

4. Use the arrow keys to position the text until it is approximately in line with the title.

5. Hold down the **Shift** key and click the **BIJI** title. Both text boxes are selected.

6. If necessary, click the **Window** menu, point to **Design Panels**, and then click **Align** to open the Align panel. On the Align panel, click the **To stage** button to turn it off. (When you align to the Stage, objects align to the whole space on the Stage as well as to each other.)

STEP-BY-STEP 6.5 Continued

7. Click the **Align right edge** button (the third button in the top row of buttons under the Align label). The two text boxes align precisely along their right edges, as shown in Figure 6-8.

FIGURE 6-8
Aligning the text boxes

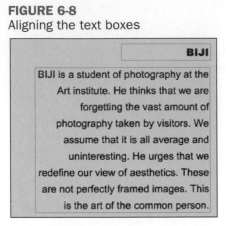

8. Save the document, close it, and then exit Flash.

Web Design Skills

You can use special "device fonts" in Flash as an alternative to embedding font information (for horizontal text only). Device fonts are not embedded in the Flash SWF file. Instead, the Macromedia Flash Player uses whatever font on the local computer most closely resembles the device font. Because device font information is not embedded, using device fonts yields a somewhat smaller Flash movie file size. In addition, device fonts can be sharper and more legible than embedded fonts at small point sizes (below 10 points). However, because device fonts are not embedded, if users do not have a font installed on their system that corresponds to the device font, text might look different than you expect on the user's system. The following table shows how Windows and Macintosh computers typically interpret device fonts.

DEVICE FONT TYPE	WINDOWS	MACINTOSH
_sans	Arial	Helvetica
_serif	Times New Roman	Times
_typewriter	Courier New	Courier

In general, device fonts work best on a page with few design elements and a lot of text, such as a print article. Device fonts would not be appropriate for a site with as many visual elements as the Gallery San Luis site.

SUMMARY

In this lesson, you learned to:

- Create a movie clip symbol out of existing layers and from another movie clip symbol.
- Work in symbol-editing mode to edit a movie clip instance.
- Edit and align text boxes.

CREATING BUTTONS

Creating a Photo Viewer

You have already created the artist's biography in the Featured Artist section. Now you're ready to create a Photo Viewer to display samples of the artist's work. To create the Photo Viewer, you insert a set of images into your document and create Macromedia Flash buttons that let users browse through the images.

You can use a single movie clip to store all the photos in different keyframes and then build buttons that will advance the movie to the next frame or move it back to the previous frame to browse the photos. Finally, you need to insert an instance of the Photo Viewer movie clip in the center cel of the Fstrip Artist movie clip, as shown in Figure 7-1.

FIGURE 7-1
Design of the Photo Viewer

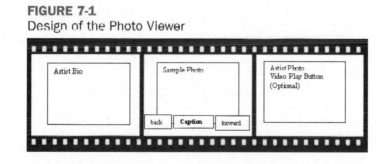

Importing a Sequence of Images

You can import one image at a time or, if you have a series of images that you want to appear in sequence, you can import a group of images simultaneously by giving them the same name followed by a numerical sequence, such as picture0, picture1, and so on. When you do this, all the images are imported as a sequence in the current layer. The images come in on individual frames. You will see only the first image because you are viewing only the first frame in the sequence. If you click on subsequent frames, you will see the subsequent images.

STEP-BY-STEP 7.1

Importing a Sequence of Images

1. Start Flash and open the **home.fla** movie you worked with in Lesson 6, which should be in the **build_GallerySanLuis** folder.

2. Make sure the Library panel is open.

3. On the Library panel, double-click the icon beside the symbol name **Fstrip Artist**. You are in symbol-editing mode for the Fstrip Artist movie clip symbol, which appears by itself on the Stage.

> **Note** ☑
>
> If you had problems with the previous lesson, ask your instructor for the **home3.fla** sample solution file. Once you open this file, save it as **home.fla** in your **build_GallerySanLuis** folder and proceed with this lesson.

4. Click the **Insert** menu, and then click **New Symbol**.

5. Name the movie **Artist Photo Viewer**, set the Behavior to **Movie clip**, and click **OK**. You are in symbol-editing mode for the Artist Photo Viewer movie clip symbol, which appears as a blank Stage.

6. Click the **File** menu, point to **Import**, and click **Import to Stage**, and open the **photographs** folder.

7. Double-click **picture0.jpg**. A dialog box appears, asking if you want to import a sequence of images.

> **Note** ☑
>
> The images in this file have already been optimized and sized to fit the middle cel of the filmstrip area.

8. Click **Yes**. All five images are imported as a sequence on Layer 1 because they have been named picture0.jpg through picture4.jpg.

9. Double-click the **Layer 1** title and rename it **Photos**, as shown in Figure 7-2.

FIGURE 7-2
The Photos layer

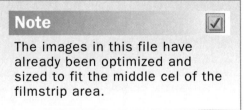

10. Save the document and remain in this screen for the next Step-by-Step.

Aligning Images

The photographs have been imported into the Artist Photo Viewer movie clip symbol slightly off center. You can center one or more images by using the Align panel.

S TEP-BY-STEP 7.2

Aligning Images to the Center of the Stage

1. Select frame **1** of the Photos layer and click the **Align** panel title bar if you need to expand the panel.

2. On the Align panel, make sure the **To stage** button is turned on. Then, as shown in Figure 7-3, click **Align horizontal center** and **Align vertical center** to align the photograph in frame 1 to the horizontal and vertical center of the Stage.

FIGURE 7-3
The Align panel

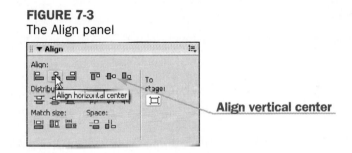

3. Click in frames **2** through **5** one at a time and repeat step 2 to align each of the other four photographs to the center of the Stage.

4. Save your work and remain in this screen for the next Step-by-Step.

Creating Navigation Between the Photographs

Although you could see each of the photographs by clicking frames on the Timeline, Web users will need buttons for browsing photographs. You need to create Forward and Back button symbols.

As you learned in Lesson 5, buttons are four-frame movie clips. Following is a review:

- *Frame 1*: The Up state, representing the button whenever the pointer is not over the button.

- *Frame 2*: The Over state, representing the button's appearance when the pointer is over it.

- *Frame 3*: The Down state, representing the button's appearance as it is clicked.

> **Note** ☑
>
> If the Align panel is not visible, open the **Window** menu, point to **Design Panels**, and then click **Align**.

- *Frame 4*: The Hit state, defining the area that will respond to the mouse click. This area is invisible in the movie.

The Forward and Back buttons you create will have color changes in the Over state and they will have a camera shutter sound and color changes in the Down state. First, however, you must configure the Up state of one button.

S TEP-BY-STEP 7.3

Creating a Button's Up State

1. Create a new layer above the Photos layer and name it **Navigation**. Click on frame **1** of the Navigation layer.

2. Select the **Rectangle** tool and draw a small rectangle near the bottom left of the picture.

3. Select the **Selection** tool, select the rectangle (by double-clicking), and set the following properties on the Property inspector:

   Width: **73**

   Height: **15**

   Stroke: **White**

   Fill: **Black**

4. Convert the rectangle to a symbol. In the Convert to Symbol dialog box, name the symbol **Back Button** and select **Button** as the behavior. Click **OK**.

5. Double-click the instance of the **Back Button** symbol on the Stage to enter symbol-editing mode. Notice that the symbol has its own Timeline, with individual frames for Up, Over, Down, and Hit.

6. Select the **Zoom** tool from the toolbox. Then click the rectangle on the Stage to make it larger and easier to edit.

7. To make editing easier, you can separate the elements of the button into separate layers. Double-click **Layer 1** and rename the layer **Box**. Add a layer above the Box layer and name it **Text**. Add a layer above the Text layer and name it **Sound**. The separate layers are shown in Figure 7-4.

FIGURE 7-4
Text and Sound layers added to the Back Button

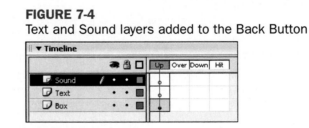

8. Click the **Up** frame of the Text layer and then select the **Text** tool.

9. Click on the rectangle, and on the Property inspector, set the text properties to **Arial Black** or **Helvetica Bold**, **10** pt., white, and left-aligned.

10. Key **Back**.

11. Select the **Selection** tool. With the text box still selected, hold down the **Shift** key and double-click the black and white rectangle. Both the text and the box are selected.

STEP-BY-STEP 7.3 Continued

12. On the Align panel, click the **To stage** button to turn it off. Then click **Align horizontal center** and **Align vertical center** to align the text and the button box, as shown in Figure 7-5.

13. Save your work and remain in this screen for the next Step-by-Step.

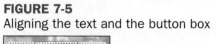

FIGURE 7-5
Aligning the text and the button box

Next, you create a button's Over state.

S TEP-BY-STEP 7.4

Creating a Button's Over State

1. Click the **Over** frame of the Text layer, click the **Insert** menu, point to **Timeline**, and then click **Keyframe**. By inserting a keyframe, you can change the look of this layer when the pointer is over the button, without changing the look of the Up state.

2. Select the **Selection** tool and click the text to select it.

3. On the Property inspector, change the text color to orange, **#FF9900**.

4. Click the **Down** frame of the Text layer, click the **Insert** menu, point to **Timeline**, and then click **Frame**. The orange text will now appear in the Down state of the button. The Hit state is invisible and thus does not need to be configured for text.

5. In the Box layer, click the **Over** frame. Click the **Insert** menu, point to **Timeline**, and then click **Keyframe**.

6. Save your work and remain in this screen for the next Step-by-Step.

Now you create a button's Down state.

S TEP-BY-STEP 7.5

Creating a Button's Down State

1. Insert keyframes on the Box layer's Down and Hit frames. The box is configured to show in the Up, Over, and Down states. The Hit state is set to make the area of the box the active area for the button.

2. Select the **Down** frame in the Box layer. With the **Selection** tool, double-click to select the box.

STEP-BY-STEP 7.5 Continued

3. On the Property inspector, change the fill color to white. The button is configured to turn white when a user clicks it, as shown in Figure 7-6.

FIGURE 7-6
Creating a Down state for the button

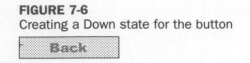

4. Click the **Down** frame of the Sound layer, click the **Insert** menu, point to **Timeline**, and then click **Keyframe**. A frame is created to hold a sound when the user clicks the button.

5. On the **Window** menu, point to **Other Panels, Common Libraries**, and then click **Sounds** to open the library's Sound panel. This panel contains sound clips that come with Flash and can be used for button clicks and other user interactions.

6. Scroll through the list of sounds and select the **Camera Shutter 35mm SLR** sound file. In the Preview window at the top of the library's Sound panel, click **Play**, as shown in Figure 7-7. The camera shutter sound plays.

FIGURE 7-7
Previewing a sound

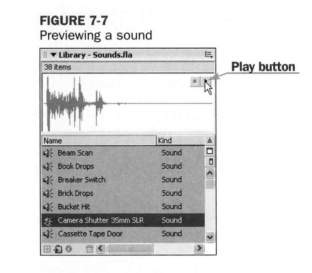

7. Make sure the **Down** state in the Sound layer is still selected, and drag an instance of the **Camera Shutter 35mm SLR** sound onto the Stage. An instance of the sound is inserted into the Down frame of the Sound layer of the Back Button symbol.

8. Click **Artist Photo Viewer** on the Information bar. You return to the symbol-editing mode of the Artist Photo Viewer movie clip.

9. To test the button, click the **Control** menu, and then click **Enable Simple Buttons**. Button sounds and states become active. You can no longer double-click a button to enter its editing mode.

10. Click the **Back** button. Its color changes on rollover. On click, it turns white and makes the camera shutter sound.

STEP-BY-STEP 7.5 Continued

11. Click the **Control** menu again, and click **Enable Simple Buttons** to toggle it off.

12. Save your work and remain in this screen for the next Step-by-Step.

Duplicating and Customizing a Button

You need a Forward button. Rather than start all over again, you can duplicate and customize the existing Back Button symbol and change the text to say "Forward."

S TEP-BY-STEP 7.6

Duplicating and Customizing a Button

1. Select the title bar for **Library – home.fla** to expand it and then click the **Back Button**.

2. On the library's Options menu, click **Duplicate**, as shown in Figure 7-8.

> **Note** ☑
>
> You can minimize the Library – Sounds.fla panel by selecting the title bar or you can close it by clicking on the Options menu and choosing **Close Panel**.

FIGURE 7-8
Duplicating a button symbol

3. Name the button **Forward Button** and click **OK**.

4. Make sure the Navigation layer is selected, and then drag an instance of the **Forward Button** symbol onto the Stage and drop it near the lower-right corner of the picture. The button appears on the Stage with its text still reading "Back."

STEP-BY-STEP 7.6 Continued

5. Double-click the instance to enter symbol-editing mode.

6. Change the button's text to **Forward** in the first Up frame of the Text layer by double-clicking (or dragging) the text to select it, deleting existing text, and replacing it with the new text.

7. With the text selected, select the **Selection** tool, hold down the **Shift** Key, and double-click the text box. Both the text and its box are selected.

8. On the Align panel, center the text in the box horizontally (vertical alignment is already okay).

9. Change and align the text in the Over state.

10. Click **Artist Photo Viewer** on the Information bar to return to the Stage for the Artist Photo Viewer movie clip.

11. Save your work and remain in this screen for the next Step-by-Step.

Creating Captions for Photographs

You want captions for photographs, so in the next Step-by-Step you create a caption box.

STEP-BY-STEP 7.7

Creating a Photograph Caption Box

1. Select the **Rectangle** tool and set the stroke to white and the fill to green, **#99CC66**.

2. Make sure the **Navigation** layer is selected and draw a rectangle between the two buttons, as shown in Figure 7-9. (Don't worry about the exact size or location of the rectangle. You will configure that later.)

FIGURE 7-9
Drawing the rectangle for the caption box

3. Select the **Selection** tool, and double-click the rectangle to select both fill and stroke.

4. On the Property inspector, set W: to **173** and H: to **15**.

5. Convert the rectangle to a graphic symbol and name it **Caption Box**. Click **OK**.

6. Position the Caption Box symbol between the two buttons.

7. Hold down the **Shift** key and select both buttons and the caption box.

STEP-BY-STEP 7.7 Continued

8. On the Align panel, toggle the **To stage** button on and click **Distribute horizontal center**, as shown in Figure 7-10.

FIGURE 7-10
Distribute horizontal center button

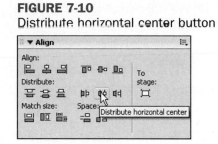

9. On the Align panel, toggle the **To stage** button off and click **Align vertical center**.

10. On the Property inspector, set Y: to **112**. The navigation elements are centered and lined up along the bottom of the photograph, as shown in Figure 7-11.

FIGURE 7-11
Aligned buttons and caption box

11. Save your work and remain in this screen for the next Step-by-Step

Creating Caption Text

When you create captions for the photographs, you need to add a separate text object to each frame that has a photograph in it.

STEP-BY-STEP 7.8

Creating Captions for the Photographs

1. Create a new layer above the Navigation layer and name it **Captions**.

2. Click in frame **1** of the Captions layer.

3. Select the **Text** tool and click inside the caption box. On the Property inspector, set the text properties to **Arial** or **Helvetica**, **10** pts., black, and left-aligned.

4. Key the following caption for the first photograph: **Looking down and around the Peaks.** (Be sure to include the period.)

STEP-BY-STEP 7.8 Continued

5. Click the **Selection** tool to select the text box.

6. On the Align panel, center the text horizontally to the Stage. Use the Selection tool to align the text vertically in the caption box, as shown in Figure 7-12.

> **Note** ☑
>
> You can also drag the elements by using the arrow keys on the keyboard.

FIGURE 7-12
Centered text in the caption box

Looking down and around the Peaks.

7. Click frame **2** of the Captions layer, click the **Insert** menu, point to **Timeline**, and then click **Keyframe**. The text box is copied to the caption for the second photo.

8. Insert keyframes on frames 3, 4, and 5 of the Captions layer.

9. Click each frame of the Captions layer and change the text in that frame to the following:

Frame 2: **Twin Peaks hugs her houses.**

Frame 3: **Grasses flowing down Twin Peaks.**

Frame 4: **Seeing is experiencing.**

Frame 5: **Life under the tower.**

10. Center the captions horizontally.

11. Click through the five frames of the Artist Photo Viewer and make sure the captions and pictures are all correct.

> **Note** ☑
>
> If a button disappears as you move through the photographs, make sure the buttons exist in frame 1 of the Navigation layer. You might have created the buttons on a keyframe of the Photos or Captions layers. If a button is in the wrong layer, cut it from that layer and paste it into frame 1 of the Navigation layer.

12. Save your work and remain in this screen for the next Step-by-Step.

Making the Photo Viewer Work

The last step in making the Photo Viewer work is to make the buttons work. In Flash, you make buttons work by using ActionScript to add "actions." ActionScript, the scripting language for Flash, lets you add interactivity to a movie. You use the Actions panel to write scripts with ActionScript. There are two areas where you can enter code:

■ *On an object*: A button or movie clip can contain ActionScript that does something (for example, stops the movie or turns off all sounds) when clicked or rolled over.

■ *On a frame*: Certain actions are performed (such as going to the beginning of the movie or stopping the movie) when the movie reaches a certain frame (which has to be a keyframe).

STEP-BY-STEP 7.9

Adding an Action to a Frame and a Button

1. Add a layer above the Captions layer and name it **Actions**.

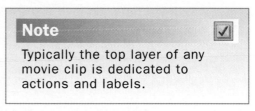

Note ✓

Typically the top layer of any movie clip is dedicated to actions and labels.

2. Select the first frame of the Actions layer and click the title bar of the Actions panel (or click the **Window** menu, point to **Development Panels**, and click **Actions**). The Actions panel expands and is titled *Actions – Frame*. Figure 7-13 is an example of the Actions panel in use.

FIGURE 7-13
Areas of the Actions panel

3. In the Actions toolbox on the left of the panel, click the **Global Functions** category if you need to expand the category.

4. Expand the **Timeline Control** category. Double-click the *stop* action shown in Figure 7-14.

FIGURE 7-14
Creating a *stop* action

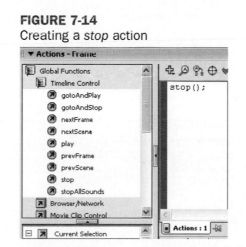

STEP-BY-STEP 7.9 Continued

5. Click the **Actions** panel title bar to collapse the panel.

6. To add an action to a button, click the **Back** button (with the Selection tool) and then click the **Actions** panel title bar to expand the panel.

7. Expand the Movie Clip Control category and double-click the *on* action in the Actions toolbox.

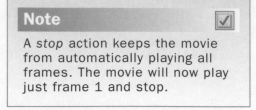

Note ☑

A *stop* action keeps the movie from automatically playing all frames. The movie will now play just frame 1 and stop.

The *on* action performs an action when a mouse *event* occurs. You can choose when the action will occur by making a selection from the menu of events, as shown in Figure 7-15. For example, clicking the Back button should take you to the previous frame when the button is *released*.

FIGURE 7-15
Menu showing events for the *on* action

8. Double-click **release**.

9. Click after the open curly bracket to place the insertion point.

10. Double-click the *prevFrame* action in the Actions toolbox (in the Timeline Control category). The Script pane now looks like Figure 7-16.

FIGURE 7-16
Previous Frame ActionScript

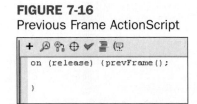

11. Collapse the Actions panel, click the **Forward** button, and then expand the Actions panel.

12. Double-click the *on* action, and then double-click **release** from the events menu.

STEP-BY-STEP 7.9 Continued

13. Click after the open curly bracket, and then double-click the *nextFrame* action (in the Timeline Control category).

14. Collapse the Actions panel.

15. Save the movie and close it by clicking on **Scene 1** on the Information bar. Remain in this screen for the next Step-by-Step.

Integrating a Movie Clip into Another Movie Clip

Now that you have a working Photo Viewer, you're ready to add it to the middle cel of the Featured Artist movie clip.

STEP-BY-STEP 7.10

Bringing a Movie Clip into Another Movie Clip

1. Double-click the **Fstrip Artist** movie clip in the library. It appears on the Stage in symbol-editing mode.

2. Select the **Center** layer.

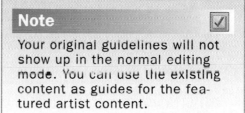

> **Note** ✓
>
> Your original guidelines will not show up in the normal editing mode. You can use the existing content as guides for the featured artist content.

3. Drag an instance of the **Artist Photo Viewer** symbol from the library onto the Stage, over the center image.

4. Zoom in and use the arrow keys to align the Artist Photo Viewer instance over the center image of the Fstrip Artist movie.

5. With the Artist Photo Viewer instance selected, click the **Edit** menu, and then click **Cut**. The movie clip is saved on the Clipboard.

6. Select the leaf image now visible in the center cel (an instance of Home Center) and delete it.

7. Click the **Edit** menu, and then click **Paste in Place**. The movie clip instance now resides in the Center layer of the Fstrip Artist movie clip symbol.

8. Save the movie and remain in this screen for the next Step-by-Step.

You're now ready for the last component of the Featured Artist section: the artist's picture.

S TEP-BY-STEP 7.11

Adding an Image to the Featured Artist Section

1. In the Fstrip Artist symbol-editing mode, select the **Right** layer.

2. Open the **File** menu, point to **Import**, and then click **Import to Stage**.

> **Note** ✓
> If you are not in the editing mode for the symbol, double-click the **Fstrip Artist** movie in the library.

3. Navigate to the **images** folder in your **build_GallerySanLuis** folder, select **artist.jpg**, and click **Open** (Windows) or **Import** (Macintosh). The artist's photo appears on the Stage in the Right layer.

4. Using the Selection tool, click the artist's photo to select it. On the Property inspector, change the size of W: to **345** and H: to **260**.

5. Use the Selection tool and the arrow keys to align the image directly on top of the image of the woman's face in the right cel.

6. With the artist's image selected, click the **Edit** menu, and then click **Cut**.

7. Delete the woman's face (instance of Home Right) from the right cel of the filmstrip.

8. On the **Edit** menu, click **Paste in Place**. The artist's image appears aligned in the Right layer.

9. Save the movie.

10. Click **Test Scene** from the **Control** menu and test it by paging through the images.

11. When you finish, close the viewer window, close the document, and exit Flash.

> **Note** ✓
> If you are asked to save changes to the Sounds.fla document, click No.

SUMMARY

In this lesson, you learned to:

- Import a sequence of images.
- Create button symbols to control photograph navigation.
- Add ActionScript to buttons and frames to control movement on the Timeline.
- Insert keyframes and frames.

MOTION TWEENING

OBJECTIVES

Upon completion of this lesson, you should be able to:

■ Insert motion tweens to create animated transitions between sections of the Web site.

■ Insert keyframes and frames to extend the Timeline.

■ Create frame actions to stop the movie clip.

■ Create button actions so users can navigate the Gallery site.

Gallery San Luis Web Site Progress

When you started designing the Gallery San Luis Web site in Lesson 4, you outlined the list of items the client wanted incorporated into the site. Let's take a quick look at how the Gallery San Luis project has progressed:

☑ A Home page that is both appealing and speaks photography.

☑ A Featured Artist page with a Photo Viewer and featured photographer information.

❏ Video interviews with the featured artist (optional).

❏ An animated Map page to indicate where the gallery is located.

❏ An Events page for requesting tickets for gallery events.

☑ Sound incorporated on buttons.

❏ Slick transitions between pages.

☑ An overall photography metaphor for the site.

Adding a Movie Clip Instance to a Macromedia Flash Document

In this lesson you will work on creating the slick transitions between pages. First, however, you must bring the Featured Artist section into the main Timeline.

It might seem a little strange that you have been building the Featured Artist section for a while now and still haven't seen it appear on the main Timeline. Think of it as if you're making a Hollywood film and have been working on a scene from the middle of the movie and now it's finally time to edit the scene into the overall movie. In this phase of the project, you incorporate the Featured Artist page onto the main Timeline with the home page.

Additionally, you need to create animated transitions between the sections of the Gallery San Luis site. You must use an animation that goes with the overall theme of photography. You must also be able to control the animation with the navigation buttons at the bottom of the page.

In going from one section of the site to the other, you will make the filmstrip movie clips slide back and forth, like film advancing in a camera. You will use the Timeline of the main movie to build this animation. This technique takes advantage of Macromedia Flash MX 2004's capability to stream—to load information in the background. You will place the home page at the beginning of the Timeline. Further down the Timeline are the other pages of the site, which can load in the background while the user is viewing the home page. The navigation buttons at the bottom of the page provide a means for moving down the Timeline to the Featured Artist section and other sections of the site, as shown in Figure 8-1.

FIGURE 8-1
Motion tweening transitions into the Artist section

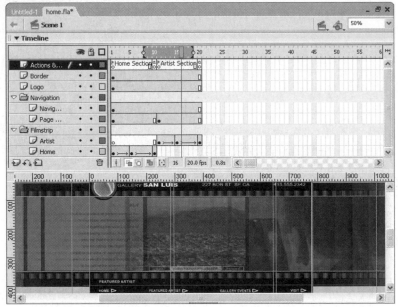

S TEP-BY-STEP 8.1

Inserting the Featured Artist Section

1. Start Flash and open the **home.fla** file you worked with in Lesson 7, which should be in the **build_GallerySanLuis** folder.

2. Make sure you're on the main Timeline (click on **Scene 1** on the Information bar if necessary).

3. Inside the **Filmstrip** folder on the Timeline, insert a new layer above the Home layer. Rename the layer **Artist**.

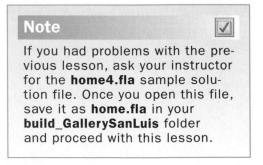

Note   ☑

If you had problems with the previous lesson, ask your instructor for the **home4.fla** sample solution file. Once you open this file, save it as **home.fla** in your **build_GallerySanLuis** folder and proceed with this lesson.

STEP-BY-STEP 8.1 Continued

4. Make sure the Library panel is open.

5. With the Artist layer still selected, drag an instance of the **Fstrip Artist** movie clip symbol from the Library to the Stage.

6. From the **View** menu, point to **Guides**, and then click **Show Guides** if the guides are not already turned on.

7. Use the Selection tool and the arrow keys to move the **Fstrip Artist** movie clip until it is within the vertical guides of the filmstrip area and the left cell is just to the right of the left border beyond the left edge of the Stage, as shown in Figure 8-2. You might need to zoom out to do this.

FIGURE 8-2
Lining up the Featured Artist movie clip

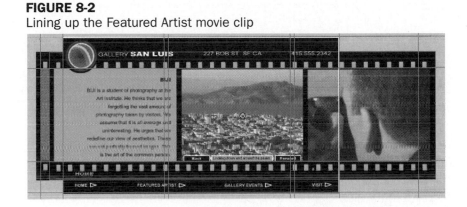

8. Click the **Control** menu, and then click **Test Movie**. The movie enters Preview mode. The Featured Artist section is lined up vertically inside the filmstrip border and extends off-stage to the right.

9. To test the Photo Viewer, click the **Forward** and **Back** buttons. It is okay that you can see the home page images behind the Featured Artist section. You will correct this later.

10. Close the Preview window and save the document. Remain in this screen for the next Step-by-Step.

Creating an Animated Transition Between Sections

The design of the Gallery San Luis Web site uses camera and filmstrip metaphors. You can apply this design in the transition between sections (also referred to as pages) of the Web site by moving the filmstrip back and forth like film advancing in a camera. You do this by creating an animation along the Timeline of the movie. Before you create the transitions, take a moment to get familiar with the basics of Flash animation.

Flash Animation

There are two methods for creating an animation sequence: in Flash: tweened animation and frame-by-frame animation. Frame-by-frame animation involves a series of keyframes with different images in every frame. Although this can be helpful with complex animations, Flash is capable of automatically creating animation by tweening images. The word **tween** comes from an animation technique in which an artist draws the starting point of a motion animation—such as a dog wagging its tail to the left—and the stopping point of the motion—a wag to the right. Then the artist has to draw all the stages *in be*tween to make it look like the tail is actually moving. In Flash, you set the starting and ending frames for an object on the Stage, and then Flash automatically fills in the frames between. There are two types of tweens in Flash: shape tweens and motion tweens.

Motion Tween

For a motion tween to work, you need two things:

■ A symbol (graphic, button, or movie clip)

■ Two keyframes containing the same symbol

In a motion tween, you can change the following properties:

■ Color (tint)

■ Alpha (fade)

■ Position

■ Size

Shape Tweening

A shape tween morphs one image into another. The major requirement for a shape tween is that both the start and ending images are NOT symbols but are bitmap images. Thus you must break apart any symbols in the beginning and end frames. *Note:* Shape tweens can be much more memory intensive than motion tweens.

For Shape tweening to work, you need two things:

■ A non-symbol object (shape drawn in Macromedia Flash or an imported bitmap image)

■ Two keyframes designating the start and end

In a shape tween, you can change the following properties.

■ Color (tint)

■ Alpha (fade)

■ Shape

In this project, you will use motion tweens to create transitions between the sections of the Gallery San Luis Web site. So far, the Gallery San Luis site's main movie exists only in frame 1. By adding keyframes down the Timeline, you can create a motion tween of the film advancing.

Planning a Motion Tween

Before you create a motion tween, you should come up with a general animation plan. Table 8-1 is an example.

TABLE 8-1
Example of animation plan

FRAME	1	5	10	11	14	20
Fstrip Home movie clip position	Far left	Far Right	Center	Not on Stage	Not on Stage	Not on Stage
Fstrip Artist movie clip position	Not on Stage	Not on Stage	Not on Stage	Far Right	Left	Center

Remember that your movie plays 20 frames per second. We choose fewer frames for the first part of our animation so it moves faster at the beginning. This technique creates a more fluid movement, imitating the way an object naturally slows down before it stops.

Creating a Motion Tween

When visitors arrive at the Gallery San Luis Web site, they see the home page. If they click the Featured Artist navigation button, the Featured Artist section (the Fstrip Artist movie clip symbol) slides into view. The transition between the home page and the Artist Section should resemble the way a filmstrip advances inside a camera. To create this animation, use a motion tween. Motion tweens are represented on the Timeline by light blue shading and a solid arrow, as shown in Figure 8-3.

FIGURE 8-3
A motion tween is represented on the Timeline by light blue shading and a solid arrow

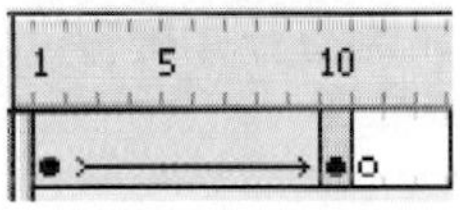

If you don't create the motion tweens correctly, you will get a dashed arrow instead of a solid arrow between the keyframes. Table 8-2 gives some troubleshooting causes and solutions for motion tweening.

TABLE 8-2
Motion tweening solutions

PROBLEM	SOLUTION
No keyframe at beginning or end of motion tween	Remove the motion tween on the Property inspector, click the Insert menu, and then click Keyframe in the appropriate frame. Add the motion tween again.
Instances in keyframes aren't the same	Remove the motion tween on the Property inspector. Click on the keyframe farther down the Timeline. Click the Insert menu, and click Clear Keyframe. Make sure the first keyframe has the correct instances in it. Insert a second keyframe and re-create the motion tween.

In the following Step-by-Step, you will add keyframes to the Artist layer. You will then adjust the horizontal position of the Fstrip Artist movie clip symbol in each keyframe and apply motion tweens to make the Artist Section appear to slide into view.

STEP-BY-STEP 8.2

Inserting Keyframes and Adding the Motion Tween

1. Click and drag frame **1** of the Artist layer to frame **11** of the same layer. The keyframe moves to frame 11, leaving blank frames in frames 1–10 of the Artist layer, as shown in Figure 8-4. Now the Featured Artist section won't be visible until the movie reaches frame 11.

FIGURE 8-4
Setting the Fstrip Artist movie at its starting point

2. Click frame **15** of the Artist layer, click the **Insert** menu, point to **Timeline**, and then click **Keyframe**.

3. Insert another keyframe in frame **20** of the Artist layer.

4. Click on the **Home** layer and insert keyframes at frames 5 and 10. The Timeline should now look like Figure 8-5.

> **Note** ☑
>
> A keyframe tells Flash that something is going to change in that frame without affecting the frames before it. You must insert a keyframe—not a regular frame—for motion tweening to work.

FIGURE 8-5
Keyframes added to the Timeline

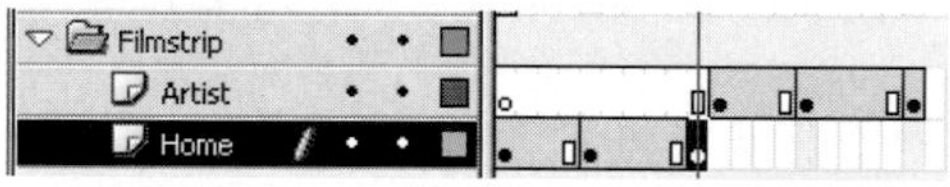

5. The next step is to show changes in the keyframes. Click frame **1** on the Home layer.

> **Note** ☑
>
> Holding the **Shift** key lets you drag something in a perfectly straight line so its vertical position doesn't change.

STEP-BY-STEP 8.2 Continued

6. Make sure the **Selection** tool is selected. Then hold down the **Shift** key and drag the **Fstrip Home** movie clip to the left until the left cel is off the Stage, as shown in Figure 8-6.

FIGURE 8-6
Sliding the filmstrip to the left

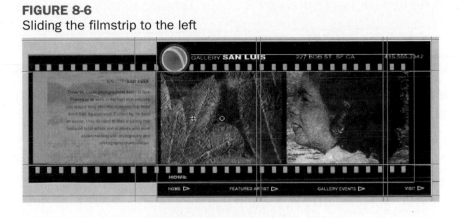

7. Click the keyframe in frame **5** of the Home layer.

8. Make sure the **Selection** tool is selected. Then hold down the **Shift** key and drag the filmstrip to the right until the right cel is to the right of the Stage. Don't worry about the positioning right now—you'll be able to tweak all these positions after you add motion tweening.

9. Click in frame **1** of the Home layer.

10. On the Property inspector, choose **Motion** from the **Tween** menu.

11. Click in frame **5** of the Home layer. On the Property inspector, add a motion tween for this frame. (Frame 10 is already in the correct stop position.)

12. Click in frame **11** of the Artist layer and (using the Shift key) slide the filmstrip to the right until the center cel is slightly off the Stage.

13. Click in frame **11** of the Artist layer and choose **Motion** from the **Tween** menu on the Property inspector.

14. Click in frame **15** of the Artist layer and (using the Shift key) slide the filmstrip to the left until the left cel is off the Stage.

15. Click in frame **15** of the Artist layer and choose **Motion** from the **Tween** menu on the Property inspector. The Timeline should look like Figure 8-7.

FIGURE 8-7
Timeline for the Home and Artist transitions

16. Test the movie. The filmstrips move across the Stage continuously, and the navigation and logo areas disappear after the first frame.

17. Close the test window and save the document. Remain in this screen for the next Step-by-Step.

Extending Layers Across the Timeline

You might have noticed that the logo and navigation areas of the Gallery site are not visible during the animation. These areas disappear as the motion tween starts, because their instance occupies only frame 1 of a document that is now 20 frames long. You can insert frames on these layers to extend the appearance of these areas on the Timeline so they continue to be visible.

S TEP-BY-STEP 8.3

Extending Layers Down the Timeline

1. Click in frame **20** of the Border layer, click the **Insert** menu, point to **Timeline**, and then click **Frame**. The Timeline for the Border layer is extended to frame 20. A small rectangle (the Instance box) appears in frame 20, indicating the end of the instance in a Timeline segment.

2. Insert frames in frame 20 of the Logo and Navigation layers.

3. Insert a keyframe in frame 11 of the Page Name layer. This allows you to change the title for the Featured Artist section. Frames 1–10 will contain the "Home" title, which switches to "Featured Artist" when the new section begins in frame 11.

4. In the Library, duplicate the Title Home symbol. Name the new symbol **Title Artist**.

5. Double-click the Title Artist symbol in the library to enter its symbol-editing mode.

6. In Title Artist symbol-editing mode, select the Text tool, and change the text to read **FEATURED ARTIST**. You might need to widen the text box to fit the title.

7. On the Information bar above the Timeline, click on **Scene 1** to return to the main Timeline.

8. Click frame **11** of the Page Name layer.

9. Drag an instance of the **Title Artist** graphic symbol onto the Stage and line up its left edge with the left edge of the HOME title, as shown in Figure 8-8.

FIGURE 8-8
Inserting the Featured Artist title

STEP-BY-STEP 8.3 Continued

10. With the Title Artist symbol selected, click the **Edit** menu, and then click **Cut**.

> **Note** ☑
>
> Because you inserted a keyframe in frame 11 of the Page Name layer, frames 1–10 still have the HOME title.

11. Click the **Title Home** instance in frame 11 of the Page Name layer. The instance has a blue outline, indicating it is selected.

12. Delete the **Title Home** instance from the Stage.

13. Click the **Edit** menu, and then click **Paste in Place**. An aligned instance of the Title Artist symbol appears on the Stage.

14. Click in frame **20** of the Page Name layer, click the **Insert** menu, point to **Timeline**, and then click **Frame**.

15. Test the movie. The border, logo, section title, and navigation buttons remain visible throughout the motion tween. The section title changes to Featured Artist during that motion tween.

16. Close the test window.

17. Save your changes and remain in this screen for the next Step-by-Step.

Adding Actions to the Main Navigation Buttons

You've added the Featured Artist movie clip to the main Timeline, and you've created animated transitions between the sections. However, a user still cannot move from Home to the Featured Artist section, because the buttons don't work. Currently the Home and Featured Artist sections play continuously.

Just as you did for the Photo Viewer buttons, you can add actions to the main navigation buttons at the bottom of the Stage for moving from section to section.

STEP-BY-STEP 8.4

Adding Button Actions to Control Movie Clips

1. Click the **Control** menu, click **Test Movie**, and roll your pointer over the site navigation buttons at the bottom of the Stage. The buttons are active only when the pointer is exactly over the letters of the words or the arrow. You need to configure Hit states for these buttons so the entire button area is clickable.

> **Note** ☑
>
> The rectangular area around the text is where the button becomes active when the user moves the pointer over it. You can choose any stroke and fill to show the Hit state, because the rectangle is not visible when the movie is played.

2. Close the Preview window.

3. Double-click the **Featured Artist** button (the one with the arrow next to it) to enter its symbol-editing mode. The button has only an Up state configured with the text and arrow symbol.

STEP-BY-STEP 8.4 Continued

4. Insert keyframes in both the Over and Hit frames, as shown in Figure 8-9. The Timeline now covers all four states.

FIGURE 8-9
Adding keyframe to the Down and Hit states of a button

5. Click in the **Hit** frame, select the **Rectangle** tool, and draw a rectangle over the text and arrow symbol to indicate the area where a user can click, as shown in Figure 8-10.

FIGURE 8-10
Drawing the Hit state

FEATURED ARTIST ▷

6. Click the frame for the **Over** state.

7. Select the **Selection** tool and click on the edge of the Stage to deselect all items on the Stage.

8. Click the **Featured Artist** button text to select it. On the Property inspector, change the text color to orange **(#FFCC00)**.

9. Select the arrow graphic next to the Featured Artist text. On the Property inspector, select **Tint** from the Color list. On the color picker, choose orange **(#FFCC00)**. The arrow changes to the same color as the text.

10. Add a new layer above Layer 1 and rename it **Sound**.

11. Create a keyframe in the Down frame and then, on the **Window** menu, point to **Other Panels, Common Libraries**, and then click **Sounds**.

12. Click the **Down** frame of the Sound layer, and drag the **Camera Shutter 35mm SLR** sound onto the Stage. The sound is inserted into the Down state.

13. Click on **Scene 1** on the Information bar to exit the symbol-editing mode for the Featured Artist button.

14. Save the document.

15. Repeat steps 3–14, this time editing the Home button and its arrow.

16. Test the movie and the buttons. You should get a satisfying camera-shooting sound when you click the buttons.

17. Close the Preview window and save your work. Remain in this screen for the next Step-by-Step.

Adding Navigation ActionScript to the Main Movie

As with the Photo Viewer in the Fstrip Artist movie clip, you need frame actions and button actions to control the main movie. In the following Step-by-Step, you add a *stop* action to the first frame so the movie doesn't automatically play all the frames on the Timeline. Then you add actions to the navigation buttons so that when you click a button, the animations end up at the initial frame of the selected section.

You also add labels to identify the frames within the movie. These labels can then be referenced in other ActionScript functions.

STEP-BY-STEP 8.5

Adding *Stop* Actions and Frame Labels

1. Insert a new layer above the Border layer and label it **Actions & Labels**.

2. Click frame **10** of the Actions & Labels layer, click **Insert**, point to **Timeline**, and then click **Keyframe**.

3. Insert another keyframe at frame 20 of the same layer. The keyframe is to hold a *stop* action for the Featured Artist section.

4. Expand the Actions panel.

5. If they're not already open, open the **Global Functions** category and then the **Timeline Control** category.

6. Double-click the *stop* action. The *stop* action appears on the Script pane and is added to frame 20 of the Actions & Labels layer.

7. Click the keyframe in frame **10** of the Actions & Labels layer.

8. From the Actions panel, add a *stop* action to this frame.

9. Click in frame **11** of the Actions & Labels layer, click **Insert**, point to **Timeline**, and then click **Keyframe**. You will add labels to frames 1 and 11 of the Actions and Labels layer.

10. Click the title bar of the Actions panel to collapse the panel.

11. Expand the Property inspector, if necessary.

12. Click frame **1** of the Actions & Labels layer. The Property inspector shows frame properties.

13. Click in the **Frame Label** text box and key **Home Section**.

STEP-BY-STEP 8.5 Continued

14. Click frame **11** of the Actions & Labels layer and key **Artist Section** in the Frame Label text box. Your Timeline should now look like Figure 8-11.

FIGURE 8-11
Labels identify the Home and Artist sections on the main Timeline

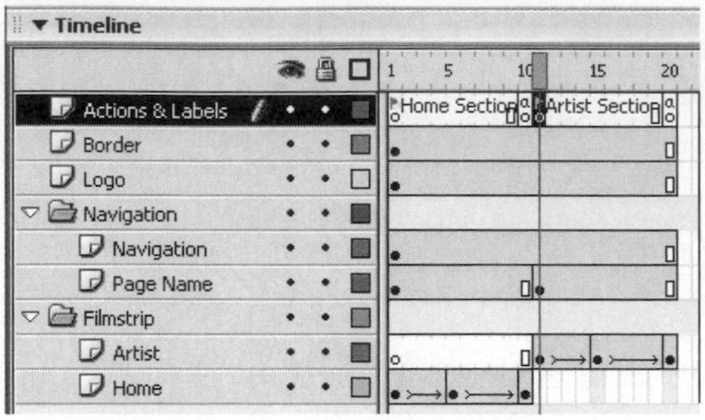

15. Test the movie. The movie plays and then stops at frame 10.

16. Close the Preview window and save your work. Remain in this screen for the next Step-by-Step.

Site Navigation Using the GotoAndPlay ActionScript

Currently there is no way to advance to the Featured Artist section. That's the next thing to add. To do this you will use the frame labels placed in the previous Step-by-Step combined with the GotoAndPlay ActionScript. Frame labels are easy to understand, and if you move the frame, the frame still has its name and thus the ActionScript doesn't have to change. For example, if you decide to drag the motion tweens to start on frames 5 and 15 instead of frames 1 and 10, all you have to do is drag the frames labeled Home Section and Artist Section. The ActionScript on the buttons remains the same.

S TEP-BY-STEP 8.6

Adding *gotoAndPlay* Actions for Site Navigation

1. Using the Selection tool, click the **Featured Artist** navigation button to select it. The button shows a blue outline.

2. Click the title bar of the Actions panel. The Actions panel appears. Its title bar reads *Actions - Button*.

3. Double-click the *on* action in the Movie Clip Control category. The *on* action appears on the Script pane. Double-click the **release** event.

4. Click after the open curly bracket and double-click the *gotoAndPlay* action. The *gotoAndPlay* action appears on the Script pane. The insertion point is between the parentheses. This is where you indicate which frame to go to when the button is clicked.

STEP-BY-STEP 8.6 Continued

5. Key "Artist Section" (make sure to include the quotation marks). The action script in the Script pane should look like Figure 8-12.

FIGURE 8-12
Actions applied to the Featured Artist navigation button

```
+ ⊘ ⅌ ⊕ ✓ ☰ ⍟
on (release) {gotoAndPlay("Artist Section");
}
```

6. Collapse the Actions panel by clicking its title bar.

7. Click the **Home** button.

8. Click the title bar of the Actions panel to expand it.

9. Double-click the *on* action, and then double-click the **release** event.

10. Click after the open curly bracket, double-click the *gotoAndPlay* action, and then key "**Home Section**" (be sure to include the quotation marks).

11. Collapse the Actions panel by clicking its title bar.

12. Test the movie and try both the Home button and the Featured Artist button. The buttons should now control the advance of the filmstrip.

13. Close the Preview window.

14. Adjust the horizontal position of the filmstrips in keyframes 1, 5, 11, and 15 to speed up or slow down their animations. You should also make sure the filmstrips don't slide too far off the Stage in the motion tweens.

> **Note** ☑
> Moving the filmstrips farther off the Stage results in faster animation because they have more distance to cover in the same amount of time.

15. When you are satisfied with the animations, save the movie. Then close the document and exit Flash.

SUMMARY

In this lesson, you learned to:

■ Insert motion tweens to create animated transitions between sections of the Web site.

■ Insert keyframes and frames to extend the Timeline.

■ Create frame actions to stop the movie clip.

■ Create button actions so users can navigate the Gallery San Luis Web site.

CREATING AN ANIMATED MAP

OBJECTIVES

Upon completion of this lesson, you should be able to:

- Create a mask to control the view of a large graphic.
- Create motion tweens that zoom in and shift position.
- Use the Pen tool to draw map highlights.
- Add sounds to animation.
- Use a *stop* action to control movie segments.

Gallery San Luis Web Site Progress

When you started designing the Gallery San Luis Web site in Lesson 4, you outlined the list of items the client wanted incorporated into the site. Let's take a quick look at how the Gallery San Luis project has progressed:

- ☑ A home page that is both appealing and speaks photography.
- ☑ A Featured Artist page with a Photo Viewer and featured photographer information.
- ❏ Video interviews with the featured artist (optional).
- ❏ An animated Map page to indicate where the gallery is located.
- ❏ An Events page for requesting tickets for gallery events.
- ☑ Sound incorporated on buttons.
- ☑ Slick transitions between pages.
- ☑ An overall photography metaphor for the site.

Creating the Visit Movie Clip

The Visit page of the Gallery San Luis Web site offers a handy animated tool for getting directions to the Gallery from four different starting points. As illustrated in Figure 9-1, after a user chooses a starting point in a drop-down menu, the section displays step-by-step directions and zooms into a section of a San Francisco map to show the route. The Visit page truly models how you can use Macromedia Flash MX 2004 to create complex graphics easily.

FIGURE 9-1
The Visit page

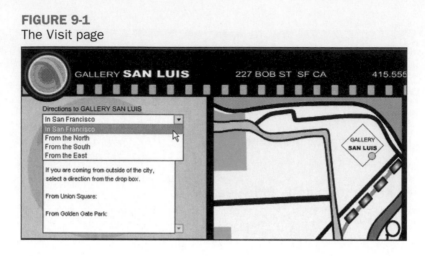

The Visit page features a single map that customizes its view depending on where Gallery visitors say they are coming from. On a typical HTML page, you would need four maps on four pages or one long page to scroll through to get different views of the appropriate map and directions. A much better design incorporates one image that can graphically shift to the correct area, depending on the starting point of the user.

Flash movie clip symbols can use the Timeline to fluidly move from one image to another. As seen on the main Timeline, ActionScript on frames and buttons can be used to control what point of the Timeline displays according to user selection. Thus you will be creating a map movie clip with four sections on the Timeline. The images will present animations indicating how to get to Gallery San Luis from the north, south, and east of San Francisco, as well as from within the city of San Francisco. You will have to create motion tweens for each of these sections and use a technique called masking to crop out the unneeded portions of the map for each direction. You will then add highway highlights by using the Pen tool.

The Fstrip Visit Movie Clip

Because the Visit page has three cels—directions, map, and a decorative image—you can use the Fstrip Artist movie clip as your starting point. You first modify it by deleting the Text layer and changing the background color of the left cel.

STEP-BY-STEP 9.1

Creating the Fstrip Visit Movie Clip

1. Start Flash and open the **home.fla** file you worked with in Lesson 8, which should be in the **build_GallerySanLuis** folder.

2. Click the **Window** menu, and then click **Library** to open the Library panel if it is not already open.

3. Select the **Fstrip Artist** movie clip in the library.

4. Open the Options menu from the Library panel and click **Duplicate**, as shown in Figure 9-2. The Duplicate Symbol dialog box opens.

> **Note** ☑️
>
> If you had problems with the previous lesson, ask your instructor for the **home5.fla** sample solution file. Once you open this file, save it as **home.fla** in your **build_GallerySanLuis** folder and proceed with this lesson.

FIGURE 9-2
Duplicating the Fstrip Artist movie clip symbol

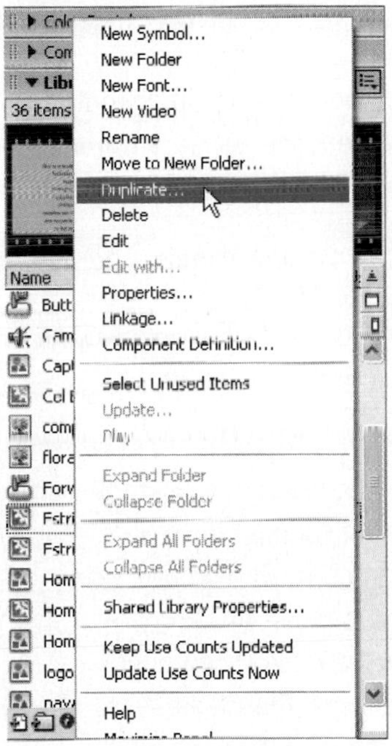

5. Name the new symbol **Fstrip Visit** and click **OK**. The movie clip symbol Fstrip Visit is added to the library. No instances of this symbol will appear in the movie document until you drag the symbol onto the Stage.

6. Double-click the icon for the **Fstrip Visit** movie in the library. The Fstrip Visit movie appears by itself on the Stage. You are now in symbol-editing mode.

7. Delete the **Gallery Text** layer by dragging it into the trashcan. You will not need text in the left cel.

8. Save the document and remain in this screen for the next Step-by-Step.

The Map Movie Clip

To add the map to the center cel, you create a new movie clip for the map. Then you import a map of San Francisco as a SWF document.

S TEP-BY-STEP 9.2

Creating the Map Movie Clip

1. Click the **Insert** menu, and then click **New Symbol**.

2. Name the symbol **Map**, select **Movie clip** as its Behavior, and click **OK**. You enter symbol-editing mode for the map symbol.

3. Rename Layer 1 **Map Image**.

4. Click the **File** menu, point to **Import**, and then click **Import to Library** to open the Import window.

5. Browse to the **images** folder and double-click **map_image.swf**.

6. Drag the map-image graphic symbol from the library onto the Stage to create an instance of the symbol in the Map movie clip. If a message appears warning that fonts are missing from your system, click **Use Default**.

7. Click the **Window** menu, point to **Design Panels**, and then click **Transform**. Or, click the Transform panel title bar to expand it.

8. Select the **Constrain** check box to keep the horizontal and vertical proportions of the graphic the same.

9. Double-click in the Height box on the Transform panel, key **400%**, and press **Enter** (Windows) or **Return** (Macintosh). The map graphic expands to a size where you can see specific streets. The image is 2880 × 2205.6 pixels (see the size on the Property inspector), much larger than the 360 × 260 center box of the filmstrip. That's OK. You'll use the Mask Layer feature to control how much of the map the user sees.

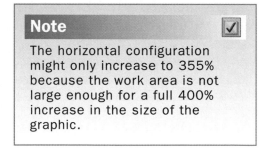

Note ☑

The horizontal configuration might only increase to 355% because the work area is not large enough for a full 400% increase in the size of the graphic.

10. Save your work and remain in this screen for the next Step-by-Step.

Creating Masks

Mask layers are an extremely useful design element in Flash. You can use a mask layer to create a hole through which underlying layers are visible. You can think of a mask as a viewing frame. Objects in layers within this viewing frame can be seen. Objects outside this viewing frame cannot be seen, as shown in Figure 9-3. You create objects on the mask layer that are the holes that show the layers below.

FIGURE 9-3
Masking illustrated

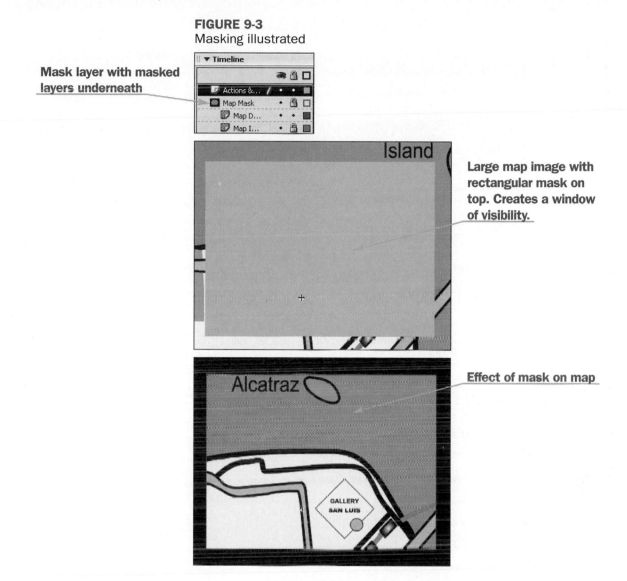

Mask layer with masked
layers underneath

Large map image with
rectangular mask on
top. Creates a window
of visibility.

Effect of mask on map

You can use a mask to show a selected part of the map in the center cel of the filmstrip. A 345 × 260 rectangular mask keeps the viewing area constant and correct for the center box of the Map movie clip. The mask remains stable while the map-image instance moves and zooms in and out beneath the mask.

Using an Animation Plan

To visualize the map animation before creating it, designers create an *animation plan*. The animation plan helps a designer visualize and lay out complex animation, often involving several graphic elements, size changes, and fading. The plan contains sketches or rough images of what the transformations will look like. It is similar to a storyboard for a cartoon or a film, but it also contains information on the numerical transformation and position changes of the map-image graphic.

The animation plan in Table 9-1 shows how the San Francisco map moves and resizes to show the different routes to the Gallery San Luis.

TABLE 9-1
Animation plan for map image

FRAME	SETTINGS	IMAGE
1: Gives Gallery Location	Position: Standard image size and position Size: (Transform Panel) = 400% Size: (Transform Panel) = 400%	
2–10: From North	Position: Center on bridge Size: (Transform Panel) = 400% to 200%	
11–20: From South	Position: Moves from center on bridge to center over highway Size: (Transform Panel) = 200% throughout	
21–30: From East	Position: Moves from left of peninsula to Bay Bridge Size: (Transform Panel) = 200% to 150%	
31–40: From Home	Position: Standard position over peninsula Size: (Transform Panel) = 200% to 400%	

Using a Mask and Motion Tweens

To build this plan, you first create a mask and then add the appropriate motion tweens to the Map Image layer.

S TEP-BY-STEP 9.3

Creating a Mask

1. If you are not in symbol-editing mode for the **Map** movie clip, double-click its icon in the library.

2. Click the **View** menu, point to **Magnification**, and then click **50%** (Windows) or zoom out to 50% (Macintosh). Using the Selection tool, drag the map until the upper-right corner of the San Francisco peninsula is visible on the Stage, as shown in Figure 9-4.

FIGURE 9-4
Upper-right corner of the San Francisco peninsula

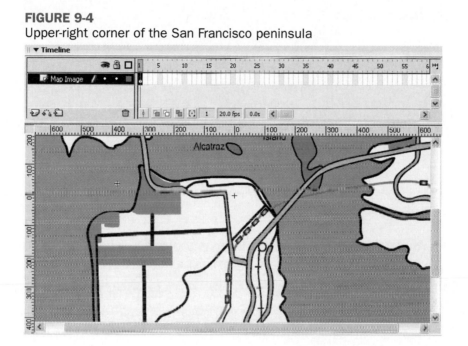

3. Create a layer above the Map Image layer and rename it **Map Mask**.

4. Select the **Rectangle** tool and change its Stroke to **None**. (*Note:* The image is easier to select when it is only a fill, with no stroke. The fill color of a mask doesn't matter; the rectangle only shows the shape of the mask area.)

5. Draw a rectangle over the map on the Map Mask layer. (Don't worry about the specific size or location at this point.)

6. Use the Selection tool to select the rectangle.

7. On the Property inspector, set W: to **345** and H: to **260**.

8. On the Align panel, make sure the To stage button is toggled on, and then click **Align horizontal center** and **Align vertical center**. The rectangle is centered on the Stage.

STEP-BY-STEP 9.3 Continued

9. Select the Map Image layer, and use the Selection tool and arrow keys to move the map until the upper-right corner of the San Francisco peninsula is within the rectangle, as shown in Figure 9-5.

FIGURE 9-5
Map lined up beneath the rectangle on the Mask Layer

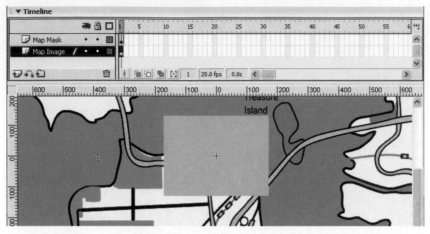

10. Click the **Map Mask** layer, click the **Modify** menu, point to **Timeline**, and then click **Layer Properties** to open the Layer Properties dialog box.

11. Select **Mask** from the Type category in the Layer Properties dialog box and click **OK**. The mask layer has a mask icon, but the Map Image layer is not masked. To mask a pre-existing layer, you must drag it below the mask layer.

12. Drag the **Map Image** layer above the Map Mask layer. Then drag it below the Map Mask layer. The Map Image layer is masked, as shown in Figure 9-6.

FIGURE 9-6
Masking the Map Image layer

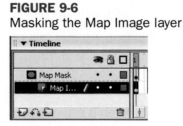

STEP-BY-STEP 9.3 Continued

13. Click the padlock icon above the layers to lock all the layers in this movie. When you lock the layers, the mask effect becomes visible on the Stage, as shown in Figure 9-7.

FIGURE 9-7
The mask in effect

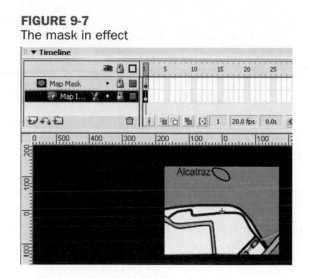

14. Save the document. Remain in this screen for the next Step-by-Step.

Working with Masks

You can use the outline feature of layers to help you work with masks. With the Mask layer set to Outline mode, you can tell where the mask is and can work with the masked layers below it.

STEP-BY-STEP 9.4

Keeping a Mask in View

1. Click the padlock icon on the Map Image layer to unlock the layer.

STEP-BY-STEP 9.4 Continued

2. Click the **Outline View** box on the Map Mask layer, as shown in Figure 9-8. The outline of the mask appears and the layer remains locked.

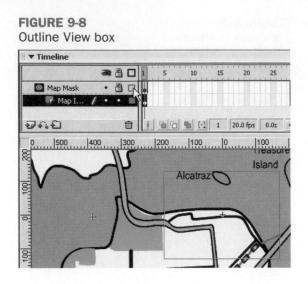

FIGURE 9-8
Outline View box

3. Save the document and remain in this screen for the next Step-by-Step.

Animating the Map

You have created a mask layer that shows the right amount of the map. Now you need to change the map to the right size and position it beneath the mask so it shows the roads and streets that are listed in the directions.

Setting Up the Timeline

This animation is similar to the animation that changes the filmstrip between sections of the Gallery site. You use keyframes along the Timeline to indicate when the map view changes, as shown in Figure 9-9. In each keyframe, you position the map under the mask and resize it to show the San Francisco area described in one of the sets of directions.

FIGURE 9-9
The Timeline configured for animation

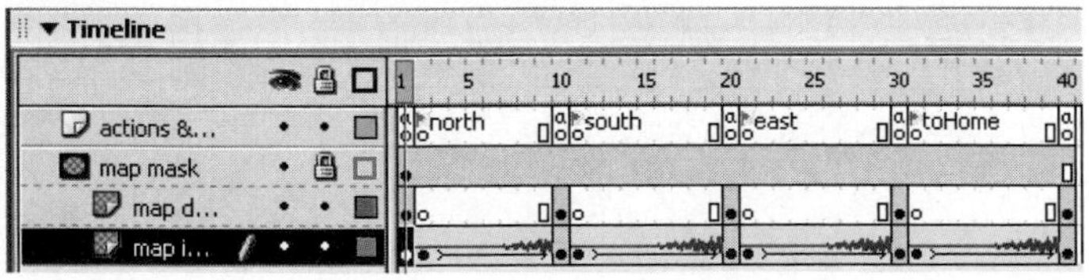

S TEP-BY-STEP 9.5

Setting Up the Timeline for Animation

1. On the Map Image layer, click frame **2**, click the **Insert** menu, point to **Timeline**, and then click **Keyframe**.

2. Insert keyframes in frames **11**, **21**, **31**, and **40** on the Map Image layer. These keyframes will be the starting points of the various motion tweens indicated in the animation plan.

3. Click frame **40** of the Map Mask layer, click **Insert**, point to **Timeline**, and then click **Frame**. The mask is extended to be visible in all the frames of the Map Image layer.

4. Click the **Map Mask** layer and then click the **Insert Layer** button. Rename the new layer **Actions & Labels**. This layer will be important when you are creating ActionScript for the map.

5. Insert keyframes in frames **2**, **10**, **11**, **20**, **21**, **30**, **31**, and **40** of the Actions & Labels layer.

6. Click frame **2** on the Actions & Labels layer. On the Property Inspector, label frame 2 **north**, as shown in Figure 9-10.

FIGURE 9-10
Labeling frames on the Property inspector

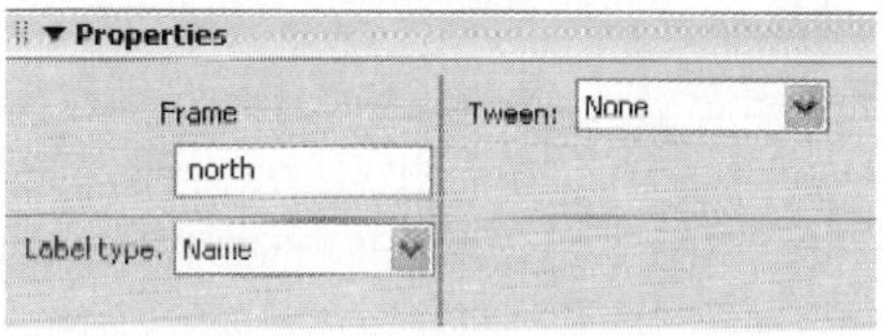

7. On the Actions & Labels layer, name the following frames (remember that the names are case-sensitive):
   Frame 11: **south**
   Frame 21: **east**
   Frame 31: **toHome**

8. Save your work and remain in this screen for the next Step-by-Step.

Animating the Map Image

The animation plan will guide you as you animate the map for different driving directions. Recall that the map mask stays in one place while the map image below it moves, increasing and decreasing in size as necessary. The first animation, for directions coming from north of San Francisco, is in frames 2–10 on the Map Image layer.

S TEP-BY-STEP 9.6

Animating the Map Image Layer

1. Click frame **2** on the Map Image layer. This selects the instance of the map in frame 2.

2. Using the arrow keys, slide the map image until the mask outline is over the northwest tip of the San Francisco peninsula, as shown in Figure 9-11.

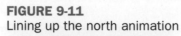
FIGURE 9-11
Lining up the north animation

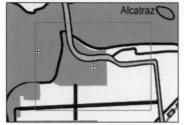

3. Click frame **10** on the Map Image layer, click **Insert**, point to **Timeline**, and then click **Keyframe**. An endpoint is created for a motion tween to zoom into the map.

4. Make sure the **Transform** panel is expanded (click the title bar of the panel if necessary).

5. Make sure the **Constrain** option is checked. Double-click in the Height box, key **200%**, and then press **Enter** (Windows) or **Return** (Macintosh). You might need to zoom out and scroll to locate the map after it has been sized. If the new size of the map does not match Figure 9-12, repeat this step.

6. Use the Selection tool and the arrow keys to slide the map until the Golden Gate Bridge is in the center of the mask, as shown in Figure 9-12.

FIGURE 9-12
Lining up the north animation over the bridge

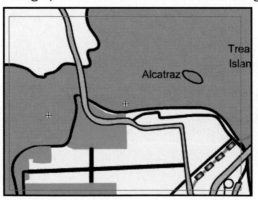

STEP-BY-STEP 9.6 Continued

7. Click frame **2** on the Map Image layer. On the Property inspector, create a motion tween.

8. Click and drag the playhead (the red rectangle at the top of the Timeline) from frame **2** to frame **10** or press **Enter** (Windows) or **Return** (Macintosh) to inspect the motion tween. Notice that this tween does not shift position; instead, it changes the size of the map, creating a zoom effect.

9. Click frame 11 on the Map Image layer. On the Transform panel, make sure **Constrain** is checked and change the dimensions to **200%**. (Again, you might have to do this twice to achieve the map size shown in Figure 9-13.)

10. Using the **Selection** tool and arrow keys, slide the map until the middle of the San Francisco peninsula is centered in the mask, as shown in Figure 9-13.

FIGURE 9-13
Lining up the beginning of the south animation

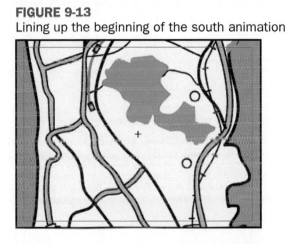

11. Click frame **20** on the Map Image layer, click **Insert**, point to **Timeline**, and then click **Keyframe**. An endpoint is created for a motion tween to zoom up from the south.

STEP-BY-STEP 9.6 Continued

12. Using the **Selection** tool, select the map and slide it until the upper-right side of the San Francisco peninsula is centered in the mask, as shown in Figure 9-14.

FIGURE 9-14
Lining up the end of the south animation

13. Click frame **11** on the Map Image layer. On the Property inspector, create a motion tween.

14. Click and drag the playhead from frame **11** to frame **20** or press **Enter** (Windows) or **Return** (Macintosh) to inspect the motion tween.

15. Click frame **21** on the Map Image layer. Slide the map until the upper-left side of the San Francisco peninsula is centered in the mask, as shown in Figure 9-15.

FIGURE 9-15
Lining up the beginning of the east animation

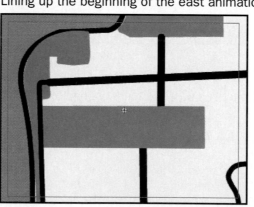

16. Click frame **30** on the Map Image layer, click **Insert**, point to **Timeline**, and then click **Keyframe**. An endpoint is created for a motion tween to zoom from west to east.

17. Click the map to select it.

18. On the Transform panel, make sure **Constrain** is checked and change the dimensions to **150%**. (You might have to enter the desired value twice.)

STEP-BY-STEP 9.6 Continued

19. Click on the map and then slide it until the Bay Bridge is centered in the mask, as shown in Figure 9-16. (*Hint*: Make sure you don't show the edge of the map where the bay is cut off.)

FIGURE 9-16
Lining up the end of the south animation

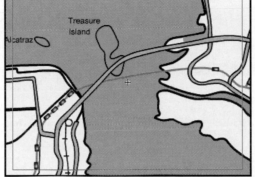

20. Click frame **21** on the Map Image layer. On the Property inspector, create a motion tween.

21. Click and drag the playhead from frame **21** to frame **30** or press **Enter** (Windows) or **Return** (Macintosh) to inspect the motion tween.

22. Click frame **31** on the Map Image layer. On the Transform panel, make sure **Constrain** is checked and change the dimensions to **200%**. (Repeat if necessary.) Frame 31 is configured to be the starting point of a zoom.

23. Slide the map until the upper-right side of the San Francisco peninsula is centered in the mask, as shown in Figure 9-17.

FIGURE 9-17
Lining up the beginning of the toHome animation

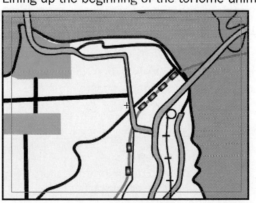

24. Click frame **40** in the Map Image layer. Note that the endpoint is already configured.

25. Click frame **31** in the Map Image layer and, on the Property inspector, create a motion tween.

STEP-BY-STEP 9.6 Continued

26. Click and drag the playhead from frame **31** to frame **40** or press **Enter** (Windows) or **Return** (Macintosh) to inspect the motion tween. The Timeline for the Map movie clip symbol should now look like Figure 9-18.

FIGURE 9-18
Timeline for the Map Image layer

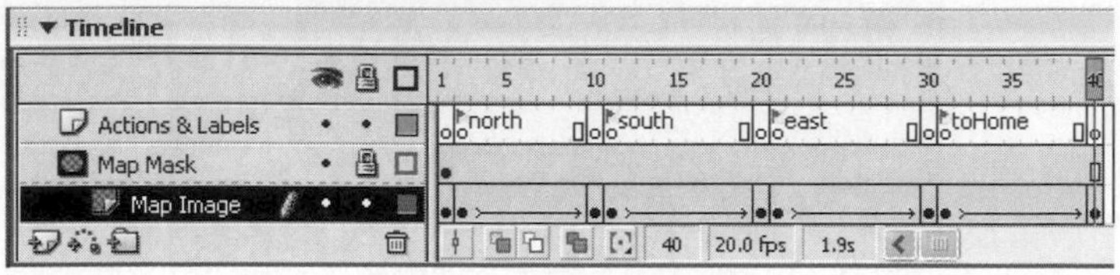

27. Save the document and remain in this screen for the next Step-by-Step.

Adding a Graphic

Next, add a graphic to indicate the specific location of Gallery San Luis.

STEP-BY-STEP 9.7

Adding a Gallery Location Graphic

1. Click the **Map Image** layer and insert a new layer above it. Rename the layer **Map Details**. The layer appears masked by the map mask.

2. Lock the **Map Image** layer. You might want to zoom in on this area for the detailed drawing steps to follow.

3. Select the **Rectangle** tool. Change its Stroke to **black** and its Fill to **None**.

4. In the first frame of the Map Details layer, hold down the Shift key and draw a square that is approximately the size and location shown in Figure 9-19. (After you have drawn the rectangle, select it and you can view and edit its size on the Property inspector.) A square appears on the map, indicating the location of the gallery, as shown in Figure 9-19.

> **Did You Know?**
>
> If you're not satisfied with what you draw, use the **Undo** command on the **Edit** menu and do it again.

FIGURE 9-19
Map detail of the gallery's location

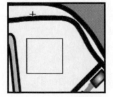

STEP-BY-STEP 9.7 Continued

5. Using the Selection tool, double-click to select the square.

6. On the **Transform panel**, select the **Rotate** option, and enter **45** in the Rotation box. Press **Enter** (Windows) or **Return** (Macintosh). The box rotates 45 degrees.

7. Select the **Oval** tool. Make sure the Stroke color is **black** and the Fill is orange (**#FFCC33**).

8. Create a small circle on the lower-right side of the box, as shown in Figure 9-20. You can hold down **Shift** while drawing to draw a perfect circle. If the circle is not placed as shown in the figure, use the Selection tool to select it and then drag it, or use the arrow to move it to the desired location.

> **Note** ☑
>
> An interesting aspect of objects drawn in Flash is that they can erase each other. For example, if you drag the circle away from the square, a piece of the square is missing. You can avoid this effect by converting drawn objects into symbols, but because you are drawing so little and will actually be deleting part of the square in later frames, you don't need to turn these objects into symbols.

FIGURE 9-20
Box with circle indicating gallery location

9. Insert keyframes at frames **10**, **20**, **30**, and **40** of the Map Details layer. You have created keyframes for details specific to the direction from which visitors are coming. (Creating these keyframes places the graphic you have just created in each of those frames. You will edit these later.)

10. Click frame **1** on the Map Details layer.

11. Select the **Text** tool, and key the following in the middle of the square, applying the formats indicated, as shown in Figure 9-21:

Line 1: **GALLERY** (Arial, 9 pt., all caps, centered, black color)

Line 2: **SAN LUIS** (Arial Black or Helvetica bold, 9 pt., all caps, centered, black color)

FIGURE 9-21
Text box for gallery location

STEP-BY-STEP 9.7 Continued

12. Drag the playhead over frames 2–10. The location graphic stays in place as the map moves. To remove the location graphic during the animation, you can insert a blank keyframe in frame 2 of the Map Details layer.

Note ☑

If the text does not fit within the box, you can resize the box (using the Property inspector) so that the text does fit.

13. Click frame **2** on the Map Details layer, click **Insert**, point to **Timeline**, and then click **Blank Keyframe**.

14. Drag the playhead over frames 2–10 again. The location graphic no longer interferes with the moving map.

15. Save the document and remain in this screen for the next Step-by-Step.

Using the Pen Tool

Adding Highlights

Next you will add features to indicate the specific routes to Gallery San Luis by using the Pen tool to trace along the route from each starting point. The routes are stored in different keyframes on the Map Details layer.

S TEP-BY-STEP 9.8

Adding Highway Highlights

1. Click frame **10** on the Map Details layer.

2. Using the Selection tool, click the blue background of the map to deselect the location graphic.

3. Double-click the circle to select it. Drag the circle to the approximate location of the gallery, as shown in Figure 9-22.

FIGURE 9-22
Dragging the location point

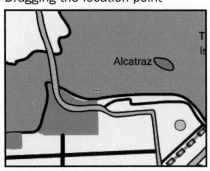

STEP-BY-STEP 9.8 Continued

4. Select the sides of the box graphic and delete them.

5. Select the **Pen** tool and change the Stroke to orange (**#FFCC00**) and a stroke height of 5.

6. Click just above the gray road at the top of the graphic. A point is created to start the pen line.

7. Click again at each point where the road bends and then off the road at the circle indicating the gallery location.

8. Double-click just to the left of the gallery circle to end the line. (If the circle changes colors, use the **Undo** command on the **Edit** menu to turn it back to its original color without erasing the line.)

9. If the line is not thick enough to show up well, select the **Selection** tool and double-click the line to select it. On the Property inspector, increase the stroke height.

10. Click frame **11** on the Map Details layer, click **Insert**, point to **Timeline**, and then click **Blank Keyframe**. Now the highlight will pop up only at the end of the north animation.

11. In frames **20** and **30**, repeat steps 2–10 to move the location circle and highlight the highway, as shown in Figures 9-23 and 9-24.

FIGURE 9-23
Map details for south

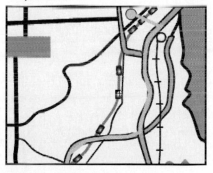

FIGURE 9-24
Map details for east

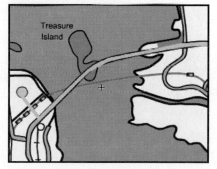

12. Click frame **1** on the Map Detail layer to select the text boxes and the rectangle/circle. Click the **Edit** menu, and then click **Copy**. This will make a nice addition to frame 40.

STEP-BY-STEP 9.8 Continued

13. Click frame **40** on the Map Details layer, and then click **Paste in Place** on the **Edit** menu.

14. Step through the document by using the playhead or the comma and period keys to move frame by frame through the animation.

15. Save the document and remain in this screen for the next Step-by-Step.

Adding Sound

To enhance the animation, you can add sounds. Flash has an entire library of sounds to choose from.

S TEP-BY-STEP 9.9

Adding Sound to the Transitions

1. On the **Window** menu, point to **Other Panels**, **Common Libraries**, and then click **Sounds**.

2. Make sure the **Map Image** layer is unlocked.

3. Select frame **2** on the Map Image layer.

4. Select the **Beam Scan** sound from the Sounds library and drag it onto the Stage. The sound is inserted into frame 2 of the Map Image layer.

5. Drag the **Beam Scan** sound into frames **11**, **21**, and **31** on the Map Image layer.

6. Press **Enter** (Windows) or **Return** (Macintosh) to play and pause the map animation. The animations should run with the sounds.

7. Save the document and remain in this screen for the next Step-by-Step.

> **Hot Tip**
>
> You can also use the caret keys to slowly advance forward and back through the animations to test them.

Adding an Action

You might have noticed that the movie plays all the map directions continuously. To divide the movie into segments that just play when people want specific directions, you can add *stop* actions on the Actions & Labels layer.

STEP-BY-STEP 9.10

Adding *stop* Actions to the Map Movie Clip

1. Click frame **1** on the Actions & Labels layer.

2. Expand the **Actions** panel and double-click **stop** in the Timeline Control category. A *stop* action is added to the first frame on the Actions & Labels layer.

3. Add *stop* actions to frames **10**, **20**, **30**, and **40** on the Actions & Labels layer.

4. Collapse the Actions panel.

5. Save the document. Then close it, and exit Flash.

SUMMARY

In this lesson, you learned to:

- Create a mask to control the view of a large graphic.
- Create motion tweens that zoom in and shift position.
- Use the Pen tool to draw map highlights.
- Add sounds to animation.
- Use a *stop* action to control movie segments.

INTEGRATING COMPONENTS AND DYNAMIC TEXT BOXES WITH THE ANIMATED MAP

OBJECTIVES

Upon completion of this lesson, you should be able to:

- Add controls to the map.
- Use Flash components to build a combo box for directions to the Gallery.
- Configure a dynamic text box to hold directions sent from ActionScript.
- Work with ActionScript to process a user selection.
- Integrate and animate the Visit section onto the main Timeline.

Creating Controls for the Animated Map

Figure 10-1 shows the Timeline for an animated map with four sections of motion tweens. These are the motion tweens you created for the Map movie in the previous lesson. There are actually five states for the animated map:

- A starting point showing the Gallery location
- Coming from the north
- Coming from the south
- Coming from the east
- Coming from the city of San Francisco

FIGURE 10-1
Motion tweens in Map movie clip

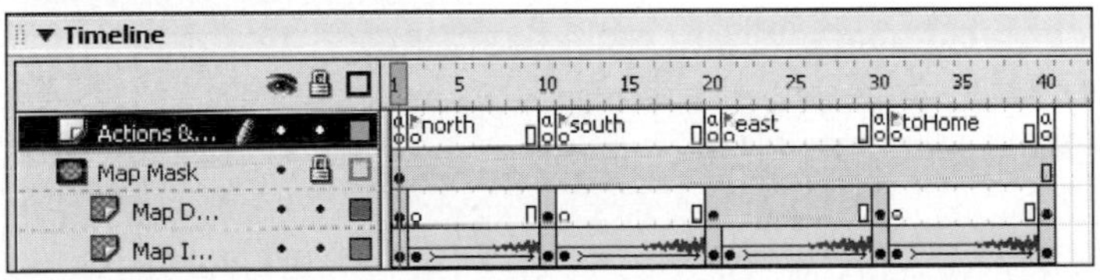

Users need a way to control when each section activates. You could create four buttons to the left of the map, but that would leave little room to add directions from the various points. A solution to this design problem is to create a combo box to the left of the map. You should be familiar with the combo box control, which is a common item you see in dialog boxes. A combo box consists of a text box in which the user can key information along with a drop-down list box that contains options the user can select.

When users select the appropriate direction option in the combo box, their selection sends the map animation to the corresponding frame and populates a text box with driving directions, as shown in Figure 10-2.

FIGURE 10-2
Combo box driving content and animation

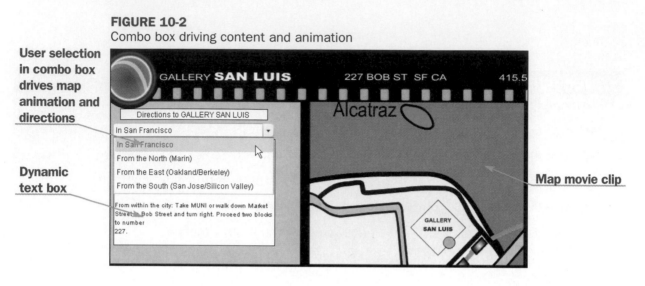

User selection in combo box drives map animation and directions

Dynamic text box

Map movie clip

Similar to creating the Map movie clip, you can create a new movie clip symbol for the driving directions and work on it in symbol-editing mode before integrating it into its cel in the Fstrip Visit movie clip.

STEP-BY-STEP 10.1

Creating the Directions Movie Clip

1. Start Macromedia Flash MX 2004 and open the **home.fla** file you worked with in Lesson 9, which should be in the **build_GallerySanLuis** folder.

2. Make sure the Library panel is open.

3. Select the **Cel Background** movie clip and then choose **Duplicate** from the Library options menu. The Duplicate Symbol dialog box opens.

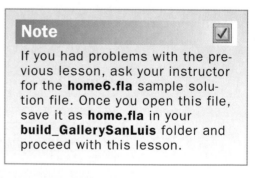

Note ✓

If you had problems with the previous lesson, ask your instructor for the **home6.fla** sample solution file. Once you open this file, save it as **home.fla** in your **build_GallerySanLuis** folder and proceed with this lesson.

4. Name the new symbol **Directions Movie** and click **OK**. The symbol is in the library.

5. Double-click the icon beside the **Directions Movie** symbol in the library to enter symbol-editing mode.

STEP-BY-STEP 10.1 Continued

6. Make sure the gray rectangle is centered vertically and horizontally on the Stage and lock the **Background** layer.

7. Insert a layer above the Background layer and rename it **Combo Box**.

8. Save the document and remain in this screen for the next Step-by-Step.

Working with Flash Components

Flash features ready-made movie clips called *components*. Components are like templates for creating commonly used movie clip controls such as check boxes, drop-down menus, and buttons. You can use components to quickly develop complex items such as multiple-choice quizzes, e-mail forms, or—for this project—a drop-down list box that contains options for driving directions to Gallery San Luis. You find components on the Components panel (accessed through the Window menu) shown in Figure 10-3, which is like a library for components.

> **Hot Tip** ◎
>
> Macromedia has more components available on its Web site at *www.macromedia.com/ devnet/mx/flash*. When you download new components, they appear as menu items on the Components panel.

FIGURE 10-3
The Components panel

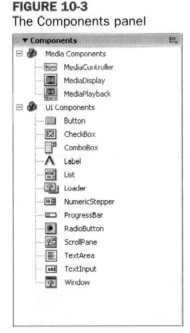

S TEP-BY-STEP 10.2

Inserting and Configuring a Component

1. Click the **Components** panel title bar to expand the panel. If the Components panel is not in your panel set, click the **Window** menu, point to **Development Panels**, and then click **Components**.

2. Drag an instance of the **ComboBox** component onto the Stage. The ComboBox component is in the UIComponents folder of the Components panel. The Stage will look similar to Figure 10-4.

FIGURE 10-4
The ComboBox component added to the Stage

3. The Property inspector enables quick customization of the look and content of a component. Click the Parameters tab. This is where you add labels for the combo box items, as shown in Figure 10-5. Leave the *editable* line set to false because users will have no need to change or copy the menu items.

FIGURE 10-5
Property inspector for the ComboBox

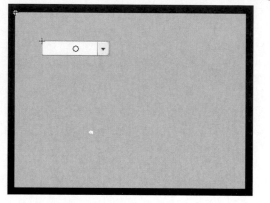

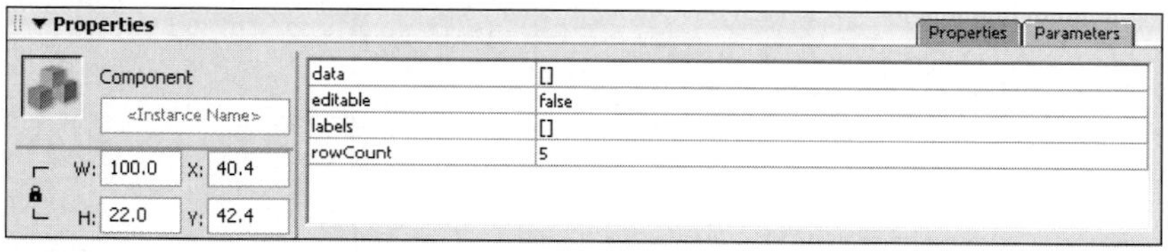

4. Click the **labels** row and then click the magnifying glass to open the Values dialog box.

5. Click the Add (**+**) button to add a line of text to the combo box. A line appears with the value of *defaultValue*.

6. Key **In San Francisco** for the line value.

STEP-BY-STEP 10.2 Continued

7. Use the Add (+) button to add the following lines to the combo box, as shown in Figure 10-6. (Note that Macintosh users will not see the line numbers.)

   Line 1: **From the North (Marin)**

   Line 2: **From the East (Oakland/Berkeley)**

   Line 3: **From the South (San Jose/Silicon Valley)**

FIGURE 10-6
Component labels added

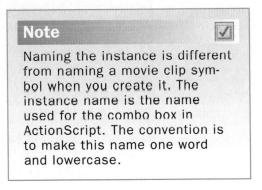

8. Click **OK** to close the Values dialog box and enter the lines and values you created.

9. Leave the Data row empty (no values are associated with the text in the combo box) and the rowCount (number of items to display before adding a scroll bar) at **5**.

10. On the Property inspector, click in the Instance Name box and key **combo**.

11. Make sure the constrain padlock icon is unlocked and set the width of the combo box to **260**. Leave the height set to **22**.

12. On the Align panel, make sure the **To stage** button is set to On, and then click **Align horizontal center**. The combo box moves to the center of the Stage.

> **Note** ☑
>
> Naming the instance is different from naming a movie clip symbol when you create it. The instance name is the name used for the combo box in ActionScript. The convention is to make this name one word and lowercase.

13. Save your changes and remain in this screen for the next Step-by-Step.

Labeling a Component

You can insert a title above the combo box so users know what it is for.

S TEP-BY-STEP 10.3

Inserting a Title Above the Combo Box

1. Insert a new layer above the Combo Box layer and name it **Text**.

2. Select the **Text** tool and click to add a text box just above the combo box.

3. Set the font to **Arial**, **12** pt., **centered**, black text, center aligned, and key **Directions to GALLERY SAN LUIS**.

4. Click the **Selection** tool. On the Align panel, align the text box to the horizontal center of the Stage.

5. Use the Selection tool and the arrow keys to select and vertically align the text box and combo box as shown in Figure 10-7.

FIGURE 10-7
The text box and combo box aligned

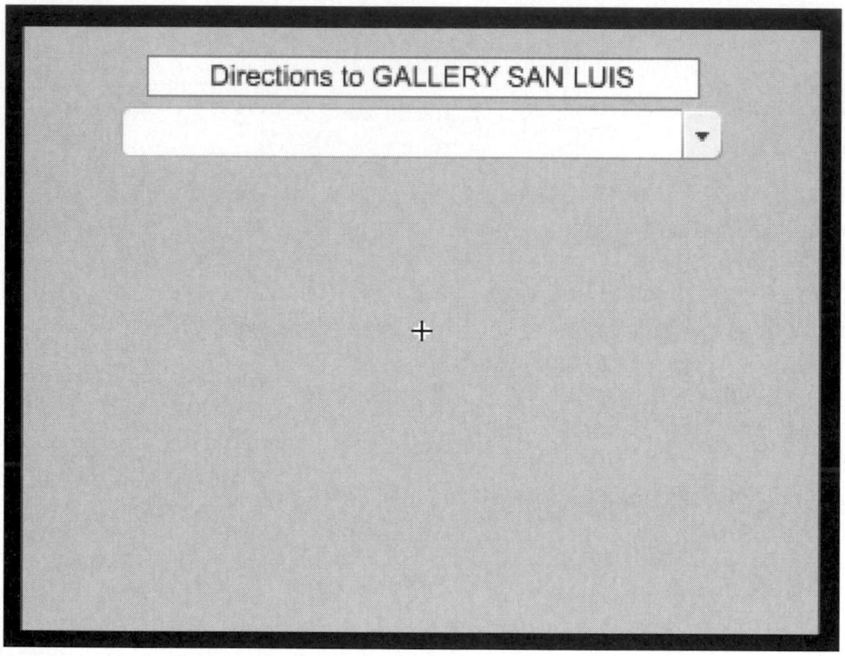

6. Save the document and remain in this screen for the next Step-by-Step.

Working with Dynamic Text

The next challenge is to create one text box that can hold different driving directions based on the user's selection from the combo box. You could make a big text box that users would have to scroll through to find the appropriate driving directions, but that would be difficult for users to navigate and it would defeat the purpose of the combo box. Instead you will use a dynamic text box that changes its text depending on what direction a user picks from the combo box. A dynamic text box gets its text from ActionScript, a database, or another external text source. Dynamic text boxes are typically used on the Web to hold information that is constantly changing, such as sports scores or stock prices. Creating a dynamic text box is easy—you use the now familiar Text tool.

S TEP-BY-STEP 10.4

Creating a Dynamic Text Box

1. Make sure you are on the Text layer, and select the **Text** tool.

2. Click below the combo box and drag to create a text box approximately the same width as the combo box, as shown in Figure 10-8.

FIGURE 10-8
The text box inserted

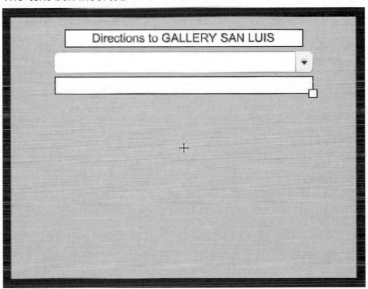

3. On the Property inspector, select the following settings:

Text type: **Dynamic Text** (from Static Text)

Font: **Arial**

Size: **11 pts.**

Alignment: **Left**

Line type: **Multiline**

Text options (the buttons to the right of the Line type): **Selectable** (this allows users to copy directions from this box), **Render text as HTML**, and **show border around text**.

STEP-BY-STEP 10.4 Continued

4. Click the **Format** button and set the following in the Format Options dialog box:
Line Spacing: **2 pt.**
Left Margin: **5 px.**
Right Margin: **5 px.**

5. Click **OK** (Windows) or **Done** (Macintosh) to close the Format Options dialog box.

6. In the Var (Variable) box, key **directions**. Setting a variable name tells Flash which text box will receive the text for the selected directions. This is different from the instance name in that the instance name is used in ActionScript to control the entire text box (its position, color, and such), not its contents. Variables are discussed in more detail later in this lesson.

7. Double-click in the text box, and then drag the handle (the box in the lower-right corner) of the text box to stretch the box to near the bottom of the background.

8. Click the **Selection** tool, which selects the text box. Then, on the Property inspector, set W: to **260** and H: to **170**. Adjust the position of the box as needed to line up under the combo box.

9. Save the document and remain in this screen for the next Step-by-Step.

Tying It All Together with ActionScript

The three interacting components are now in place:

- The combo box, named *combo*, which holds four possible directions from which the user can select.

- The dynamic text box, which is named with the variable *directions* for its contents.

- The Map movie clip, which is configured with four animations: east, south, north, and toHome (San Francisco) directions.

To tie these three elements together, you create ActionScript in a frame of the Directions Movie movie clip.

STEP-BY-STEP 10.5

Creating ActionScript for the Directions Movie Clip

1. Create a new layer above the Text layer and rename it **Actions**.

STEP-BY-STEP 10.5 Continued

2. Expand the Actions panel. You might also want to drag the top border of the panel to lengthen the Script pane, as shown in Figure 10-9.

FIGURE 10-9
Resizing the Actions panel

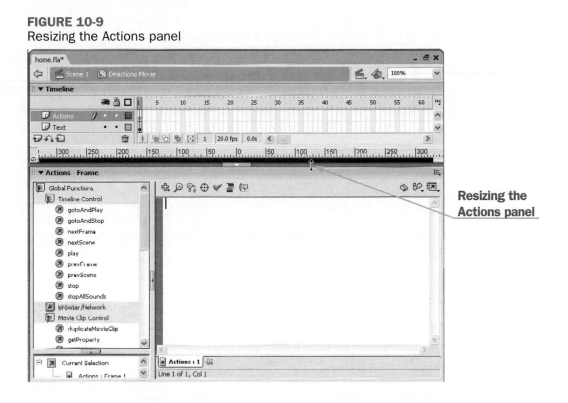

Resizing the
Actions panel

3. Click in the Script pane and key // **Create variables for the four different directions text.** Press **Enter** (Windows) or **Return** (Macintosh). This is just a comment, which merely explains the scripting that follows. It does not affect the final document; it's more of a note to the reader.

4. Key **sf = "Gallery SAN LUIS is located at 227 Bob Street in the South Beach neighborhood of San Francisco, California.

If you are coming from outside the city, select a direction from the drop box above.

From within the city: Take MUNI or walk down Market Street to Bob Street and turn right. Proceed two blocks to number 227."**

STEP-BY-STEP 10.5 Continued

5. Follow Table 10-1 to check the variable you just created and to enter the variables for north, east, and south.

TABLE 10-1
Variable values

VARIABLE NAME (case-sensitive)	VALUE indicates a line break. This is HTML scripting and will work because you set the dynamic text box to display as HTML.
sf	Gallery SAN LUIS is located at 227 Bob Street in the South Beach neighborhood of San Francisco, California. If you are coming from outside the city, select a direction from the drop box above. From within the city: Take MUNI or walk down Market Street to Bob Street and turn right. Proceed two blocks to number 227.
north	From Marin: Take the Golden Gate bridge to San Francisco. Get off at the Bob Street exit and follow the signs to our rooftop parking facility.
east	From Oakland or Berkeley: Take the Bay Bridge to San Francisco. Get off at the Bob Street exit.
south	From San Jose or Silicon Valley: Take 280 North to San Francisco. Get off at the Bob Street exit.

6. When you finish creating the four variables, add a new comment. Key **// Sets the default value for the dynamic text box variable "directions."** Press **Enter** (Windows) or **Return** (Macintosh).

7. Key **directions = sf;**

8. Press **Enter** (Windows) or **Return** (Macintosh).

> **Hot Tip**
>
> Seeing all the text in the Script pane might be difficult. Use the arrow keys to scan the text for errors after typing. Or click the View Options button above the Script pane, and click Word Wrap.

9. To add another comment, key **// Create a function to take a user's selection from the combo box, set the correct directions in the text box, and send the map animation to the correct frame.**

10. Press **Enter** (Windows) or **Return** (Macintosh).

11. Save your work and remain in this screen for the next Step-by-Step.

Web Design Skills

Variables are amazingly useful in ActionScript and many other scripting languages. They are short words that can refer to a larger amount of information or a calculation. You know it's time to start using variables when you have certain objects in your movie that need to change to specific values with user input. For example, a movie clip of a shirt might have a color variable that changes based on a user's selection, or a space-ship movie clip could have a speed variable that increases as a thrust button is pressed. In your Fstrip Visit movie clip, you will use the variables listed below.

VARIABLE NAME	CREATED	USE/VALUES
sf, north, south, east	In Actions layer of the Directions Movie movie clip	Holds text to describe how to get to Gallery San Luis from different points in the city. Example: north = *From Marin: Take 280 North to the...*
active	In Actions layer of the Directions Movie movie clip	Gets a value from 0 to 3 when user clicks an item in the combo box. Example: When user clicks From Berkeley in combo box, active = 2. (You will add this in Step-by-Step 10.6.)
directions	On Property inspector for the dynamic text box	Takes on the value of various variables representing driving directions. directions = sf *Directions* is equal to another variable that has a text value. Thus you don't see quotes around sf. The statement *directions = "sf"* would set the variable directions equal to the text "sf" and fill the dynamic text box with "sf."

Creating the ActionScript

There are a couple of ways to get the ActionScript for the map to work, but one of the most common is to search a reference Web site such as *www.macromedia.com/devnet/mx/flash* or *www.flashkit.com* for preconfigured scripts. On these sites you can find ActionScript for common objects such as combo boxes. When you download a preconfigured ActionScript, you will usually have to customize certain variables and path names to your document. An example ActionScript that meets your needs for this project is supplied with the data files for this unit. This script is given to you in a generic form as you might find it on a Web site. You will copy this ActionScript and paste it into the Script pane. Then you will have to edit it to meet your needs, just as you would a downloaded script.

S TEP-BY-STEP 10.6

Creating ActionScript from an External Source

1. Open a text-editing program such as WordPad, Notepad, or TextEdit.

2. Choose **Open** from the **File** menu and navigate to the **scripts** folder (in your **build_GallerySanLuis** folder). Select the **visitScript.txt** file and click **Open**.

3. Select all the text in the file, click the **Edit** menu, and then click **Copy**.

4. Close the text editor and switch to Macromedia Flash. Click the Script pane on the Actions panel to activate it.

5. **Right-click** (Windows) or **Control-click** (Macintosh) in the Script pane after the last comment and choose **Paste**.

6. The script is inserted into the Script pane in generic form. You will now customize the script.

7. Click the **Replace** button at the top of the Script pane, as shown in Figure 10-10. The Replace dialog box opens. Here you can replace all general names with the proper names from your file.

FIGURE 10-10
The Replace button

8. In the *Find what* text box, key **componentName**. This is the general name from which a component gets data. In our case, the component name is *combo*.

9. In the *Replace with* text box, key **combo**.

10. Click **Match case** to select it, and then click **Replace All**, as shown in Figure 10-11.

FIGURE 10-11
The Replace dialog box

Replace	☒
Find what:	componentName	Find Next
Replace with:	combo	Replace
☑ Match case		Replace All
		Close

11. When the search and replace is complete, click **OK** in the message box that appears indicating that the process has finished.

STEP-BY-STEP 10.6 Continued

12. Repeat steps 8–11 to replace the items listed in Table 10-2.

TABLE 10-2
Customizing script code

ITEM	REPLACE WITH	REASON
name	change	function from the parameters set for the combo box
text	directions	variable for the dynamic text box (*Note*: Do not use the Replace All option for this item. The word text is used in the comments and you do not want to replace it there.)
var1	sf	variable for directions from San Francisco
var2	north	variable for directions from North of San Francisco
var3	east	variable for directions from East of San Francisco
var4	south	variable for directions from South of San Francisco
part1	toHome	frame in the Map movie where the San Francisco animation starts
part2	north	frame in the Map movie where the North animation starts
part3	east	frame in the Map movie where the East animation starts
part4	south	frame in the Map movie where the South animation starts
path	_parent.map	path name _parent.map directs the ActionScript one level up (parent level) to the Fstrip Visit movie clip and then into the Map movie. Once there, the gotoAndPlay function directs the Map movie to a specific frame.

13. When you have replaced all the text, click **Close** to close the Replace dialog box.

STEP-BY-STEP 10.6 Continued
_____

14. Inspect your text to make sure it looks like Figure 10-12.

FIGURE 10-12
Completed ActionScript

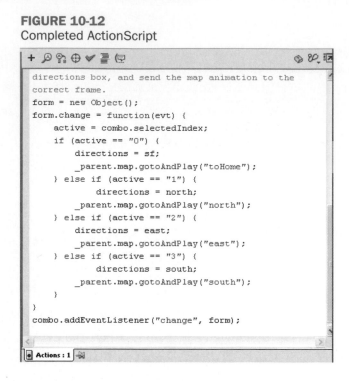

```
directions box, and send the map animation to the
correct frame.
form = new Object();
form.change = function(evt) {
    active = combo.selectedIndex;
    if (active == "0") {
        directions = sf;
        _parent.map.gotoAndPlay("toHome");
    } else if (active == "1") {
            directions = north;
        _parent.map.gotoAndPlay("north");
    } else if (active == "2") {
        directions = east;
        _parent.map.gotoAndPlay("east");
    } else if (active == "3") {
            directions = south;
        _parent.map.gotoAndPlay("south");
    }
}
combo.addEventListener("change", form);
```

15. Collapse the Actions panel.

16. Click on **Scene 1** on the Information bar to close the Directions Movie movie clip.

17. Save the document and remain in this screen for the next Step-by-Step.

Finishing the Fstrip Visit Movie Clip

You have almost finished the visit section of the site. You need to update the right cel, and then you will integrate the entire movie clip into the main site.

S TEP-BY-STEP 10.7
_____

Filling the Right Cel of the Fstrip Visit Movie Clip

1. On the Library panel, double-click the icon beside the **Fstrip Visit** movie clip to open it in symbol-editing mode.

2. Click the image in the right cel. Click **File,** point to **Import,** and then click **Import to Stage.**

3. Navigate to the **images** folder, and double-click **grasses.jpg**. The grasses.jpg image is imported into the Fstrip Visit movie clip on the Right layer. On the Property inspector, change the size of W: to **345** and H: to **260**.

STEP-BY-STEP 10.7 Continued

4. Line up the grasses.jpg image over the artist.jpg image on the Right layer.

5. Click the **Edit** menu, and then click **Cut** to place the grasses.jpg file on the Clipboard.

6. Delete the **artist.jpg** image from the right cel, click the **Edit** menu, and then click **Paste in Place**. The grasses.jpg file is pasted in the correct location on the Right layer.

7. Repeat steps 4–6 for the following items:

   Map movie clip: Drag from the library and replace image on the Center layer.

   Directions Movie movie clip: Drag from the library and replace the background on the Left layer.

   The Fstrip Visit movie clip should now look like Figure 10-13.

FIGURE 10-13
Fstrip Visit movie clip configured correctly

8. Click the **Map** instance on the Center layer.

9. Make sure the Property Inspector is expanded, and enter **map** in the Instance Name text box. The path name you configured in the ActionScript for the Directions Movie now has the correct target. (Although the symbol has been named *map*, this name is not recognized in ActionScript. You must give an instance an instance name to target it in ActionScript.)

10. On the Information bar, click **Scene 1**.

11. Save the document and remain in this screen for the next Step-by-Step.

Integrating the Fstrip Visit Movie Clip onto the Main Timeline

Most of the following steps will be familiar from Lesson 8. You can try doing this section on your own for a challenge.

S TEP-BY-STEP 10.8

Creating a Motion Tween for the Fstrip Visit Section

1. Inside the **Filmstrip** folder on the Timeline, insert a new layer above the Artist layer. Rename the new layer **Visit**.

2. With the **Visit** layer selected, select the **Fstrip Visit** movie clip symbol from the Library panel and drag an instance of it onto the Stage.

3. On the **View** menu, point to **Guides**, and then click **Show Guides** if necessary to turn the guides on.

4. Drag the **Fstrip Visit** movie clip until it is within the vertical guides of the filmstrip area. (You might need to zoom out to see the guides better.)

5. To adjust the horizontal placement of the Fsrip Visit movie clip, use the arrow keys on the keyboard to slide the movie clip horizontally until the left edge of the left cel is just beyond guide line, as shown in Figure 10-14.

FIGURE 10-14
Aligning the Fstrip Visit movie clip on the main Stage

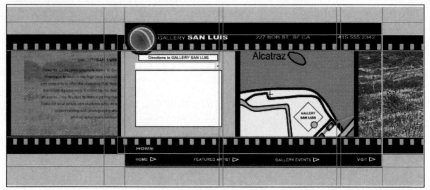

6. Click and drag frame **1** of the Visit layer to frame **21** of the same layer.

7. Click frame **25** of the Visit layer, click **Insert**, point to **Timeline**, and then click **Keyframe**.

8. Click frame **30** of the Visit layer, click **Insert**, point to **Timeline**, and then click **Keyframe**.

9. Click frame **21** of the Visit layer.

10. Using the Selection tool, hold down **Shift** and drag the **Fstrip Visit** movie clip to the left until the left cel is off the Stage. (Holding down the **Shift** key lets you drag something in a perfectly straight line so its vertical position doesn't change.)

11. Click the keyframe in frame **25** of the Visit layer.

12. Hold down **Shift** and drag the filmstrip to the right until the right cel is to the right of the Stage.

STEP-BY-STEP 10.8 Continued

13. Click frame **21** of the Visit layer.

14. On the Property inspector, choose **Motion** from the **Tween** menu.

15. Click frame **25** of the Visit layer. On the Property inspector, add a motion tween there.

16. Save your work and remain in this screen for the next Step-by-Step.

> **Note** ☑
>
> Because you inserted keyframes in frames 11 and 21 of the Page Name layer, frames 1–10 still have the HOME title and frames 11–20 still have the FEATURED ARTIST title.

Extending Layers

Now you want to extend the other layers.

STEP-BY-STEP 10.9

Extending the Other Layers

1. Click frame **30** of the Border layer, click **Insert**, point to **Timeline**, and then click **Frame**.

2. Insert frames in frame **30** of the Logo and Navigation layers.

3. Insert a keyframe in frame **21** of the Page Name layer.

4. In the library, duplicate the **Title Home** symbol. Name the new symbol **Title Visit**.

5. Double-click the symbol in the library to enter its symbol-editing mode.

6. Change the text to read as follows: **VISIT THE GALLERY Mon–Wed 11 a.m. – 6 p.m. Fri–Sun 11 a.m. – 8 p.m.** You might need to widen the text box. The text should all fit on one line.

7. On the Information bar at the top of the Stage, click **Scene 1** to return to the main Timeline.

8. Click frame **21** of the Page Name layer.

9. Drag an instance of the **Title Visit** graphic symbol onto the Stage and position it so its left edge lines up vertically and horizontally with the left edge of the Featured Artist title. You may need to Zoom in to do this.

10. With the **Title Visit** symbol selected, click **Cut** on the **Edit** menu.

11. Select the **Title Artist** instance and delete it from the Stage.

12. On the **Edit** menu, click **Paste in Place**. An aligned instance of the Title Visit symbol appears on the Stage.

13. Click frame **30** of the Page Name layer, click **Insert**, point to **Timeline**, and then click **Frame**.

14. Save your changes and remain in this screen for the next Step-by-Step.

Configuring the Visit Button

To continue, you now want to configure the Visit button.

S TEP-BY-STEP 10.10

Configuring the Visit Button

1. Using the Selection tool, double-click the **Visit** button (on the Stage) to enter its symbol-editing mode. The button has only an Up state, configured with the text and an arrow symbol.

2. Insert keyframes in both the **Over** and **Hit** frames. The Timeline now covers all four states.

3. Click in the **Hit** frame, select the **Rectangle** tool, and draw a rectangle over the text and the arrow symbol to indicate the area where a user can click.

4. Click the frame for the **Over** state.

5. Select the **Selection** tool, and click on the edge of the Stage to deselect the objects.

6. Click the **Visit** text to select it. On the Property inspector, change its color to orange (**#FFCC00**).

7. Select the arrow graphic. On the Property inspector, change the Color selection to **Tint**.

8. On the Color Picker, choose orange (**#FFCC00**). The arrow changes to the same color as the text.

9. Add a new layer above Layer 1 and rename it **Sound**.

10. Create a keyframe in the **Down** frame and then, on the **Window** menu, point to **Other Panels**, **Common Libraries**, and then click **Sounds**.

11. Make sure the **Down** frame of the Sound layer is selected, and then drag the **Camera Shutter 35mm SLR** sound onto the Stage. The sound is inserted into the Down state and the Hit state.

12. Click **Scene 1** on the Information bar to exit the symbol-editing mode for the Visit button.

13. Save your changes and remain in this screen for the next Step-by-Step.

Adding Actions and Frame Labels

The last thing you need to do is add actions and frame labels.

STEP-BY-STEP 10.11

Adding Stop Actions, Frame Labels, and Goto Actions

1. Insert a keyframe in frame **30** of the Actions & Labels layer. The keyframe is to hold a *stop* action for the Visit section.

2. Expand the Actions panel. Open the **Global Functions** category and then the **Timeline Control** category, if they're not already open.

3. Double-click the *stop* action. The *stop* action appears in the Script pane and is added to frame 30 of the Actions & Labels layer.

4. Collapse the Actions panel.

5. Click frame **21** of the Actions & Labels layer, click **Insert**, point to **Timeline**, and then click **Keyframe**. A keyframe is added to hold the label for the Visit section.

6. Make sure the Property inspector is expanded.

7. In the Frame Label text box, key **Visit Section**.

8. Click the **Visit** button to select it. The text and arrow show a blue outline.

9. Click the title bar of the **Actions** panel to open the Actions panel.

10. Double-click the *on* action in the Movie Clip Control category (within the Global Functions category). Double-click the **release** event.

11. Click after the open curly bracket, and then double click *gotoAndPlay* in the Timeline Control category. Type **"Visit Section"** (be sure to include the quotes). It's case-sensitive, so don't forget the capital letters. Your ActionScript should look like Figure 10-15.

FIGURE 10-15
ActionScript for the Visit button

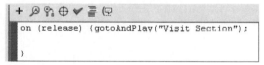

```
on (release) (gotoAndPlay("Visit Section");

}
```

12. Collapse the **Actions** panel.

13. Test the movie. Try all the buttons and test the Visit section. The directions combo box should drive the text box and animated map in the Visit section. The navigation buttons should control the advance of the filmstrip.

14. Save the document and then close it. Exit Flash.

SUMMARY

In this lesson, you learned to:

- Add controls to the animated map.
- Use Flash components to build a combo box for directions to the Gallery.
- Configure a dynamic text box to hold directions sent from ActionScript.
- Work with ActionScript to process a user's selection.
- Integrate and animate the Visit section onto the main Timeline.

BUILDING THE EVENTS COMPONENTS

Gallery San Luis Web Site Progress

When you started designing the Gallery San Luis Web site in Lesson 4, you outlined the list of items the client wanted incorporated into the site. Let's take a quick look at how the Gallery San Luis project has progressed:

- ☑ A Home page that is both appealing and speaks photography.
- ☑ A Featured Artist page with a Photo Viewer and featured photographer information.
- ☐ Video interviews with the featured artist (optional).
- ☑ An animated Map page to indicate where the gallery is located.
- ☐ An Events page for requesting tickets for gallery events.
- ☑ Sound incorporated on buttons.
- ☑ Slick transitions between pages.
- ☑ An overall photography metaphor for the site.

Designing the Events Section

Gallery San Luis has monthly show openings (free parties) to welcome the work of a new artist. They would like people to easily get information about these events on their Web site and sign up to attend them. The challenge is to design a Macromedia Flash MX 2004 form that lets users browse through upcoming events and then submit their names and e-mail addresses for the events that interest them. Users must be able to quickly view a sample of different artists' work in the three-cel design of the site.

As illustrated in Figure 11-1, in the left cel will be a narrow Event Picker, presenting three thumbnail (small) images of artists' work. Clicking these images will create an enlargement of the artist's work in the center cel and populate a dynamic text box with information about the gallery event. In the right cel, the design calls for a form where users can input contact information, select events that interest them, and send a note with their preferences to the gallery.

FIGURE 11-1
Design outline for the Fstrip Events movie

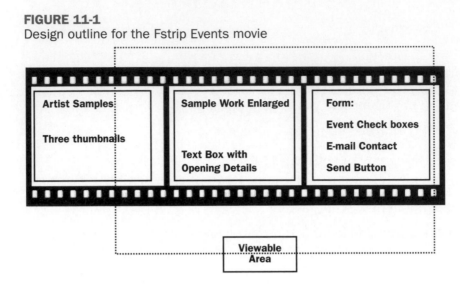

Designing the Artist's Work Sampler

As noted in the design outline, small thumbnail-image buttons in the left cel bring up enlargements of these images in the center cel when a user clicks. From a Flash design perspective, bringing in separate images for the thumbnails and the enlargements would take up too much memory. There are two solutions to this problem:

■ Use the same image for both the thumbnail and the enlargement. Rather than having two versions (a standard size and a thumbnail size) of the images, use the Flash Transform panel to create the thumbnails.

■ Load the images into Flash dynamically. Instead of importing the images into the Flash Library and increasing the file size, use the loadMovie ActionScript command and keep the files in the images folder.

To make the first solution possible, you can create movie clips that automatically shrink the images when they arrive in the left cel. This technique saves time and creates smaller, faster SWF (Flash) files. First you need a movie clip for the left cel. Then you will create the thumbnail images for the left cel and configure the left and center cels with buttons and ActionScript so the thumbnails bring up enlarged images of the artist's work and descriptions of their gallery event(s).

S TEP-BY-STEP 11.1

Creating a Movie Clip for the Thumbnails

1. Start Flash and open the **home.fla** file you worked with in Lesson 10, which should be in the **build_GallerySanLuis** folder.

2. Open the Library panel if it is not already open.

3. Select the **Cel Background** movie clip and then choose **Duplicate** from the Library **Options** menu. The Duplicate Symbol dialog box opens.

4. Name the new symbol **Events Left** and click **OK**. The symbol is in the library.

5. Double-click the icon beside the **Events Left** symbol in the library to enter symbol-editing mode.

6. Lock the **Background** layer.

7. Save your work and remain in this screen for the next Step-by-Step.

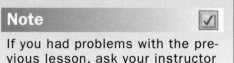

> **Note** ☑
>
> If you had problems with the previous lesson, ask your instructor for the home7.fla sample solution file. Once you open this file, save it as home.fla in your build_GallerySanLuis folder and proceed with this lesson.

Creating Thumbnail Images for the Left Cel

You want to create buttons that represent each thumbnail image. As you create the buttons, you need to be aware of their registration points. The registration point determines where an exterior image will load into the button. An image starts loading at its upper-left corner (not from the center point out). You must place the registration point in the upper-left corner if you want the loaded image to be centered over the button.

The next Step-by-Step creates the thumbnail buttons into which the images will be loaded.

S TEP-BY-STEP 11.2

Creating Thumbnail Buttons

1. Insert a new layer above background and rename it **Buttons**.

2. With the **Buttons** layer highlighted, select the **Rectangle** tool and draw a white (both stroke and fill) rectangle.

3. Select the **Selection** tool and double-click the white rectangle to select it.

4. On the Property inspector, change the white rectangle's W: setting to **345** and H: to **260**. You will later use the Transform panel to reduce these buttons to thumbnail size.

STEP-BY-STEP 11.2 Continued

5. Convert the rectangle to a button symbol (**Convert to Symbol** on the **Modify** menu) and name it **Thumbnail**. Configure its registration point to the upper-left corner, as shown in Figure 11-2. Click **OK**.

FIGURE 11-2
Creating a symbol with its registration point in the upper-left corner

6. On the Property inspector, name the instance of the Thumbnail symbol **Thumb1**.

7. On the Transform panel, constrain the proportions and size the button to **20%**. The instance size should be W: **69** and H: **52**. If it is not, use the Property inspector to adjust the size. This will also automatically reduce to 20% any images imported into the Thumb1 instance.

> **Note** ☑
>
> Because you are not changing any text or images within the symbol, you can copy and paste it. You could not use copy and paste to create the site navigation buttons in Lesson 5 because you were actually changing the text within the buttons.

8. Copy the **Thumb1** symbol and paste two copies on the Stage. You now have thumbnails for three artist samples.

9. On the Property inspector, name the second and third instances **Thumb2** and **Thumb3**.

10. Drag the three thumbnail instances to the right side of the gray background area. Be sure to place Thumb1 at the top, Thumb2 in the middle, and Thumb3 at the bottom. Hold down **Shift** and click to select all three.

11. On the Align panel, toggle **To stage** to off.

12. Click **Space evenly vertically** and **Align left edge**.

STEP-BY-STEP 11.2 Continued

13. Use the arrow keys to move the three instances until they appear to be spaced approximately like those in Figure 11-3.

FIGURE 11-3
Lining up the instances

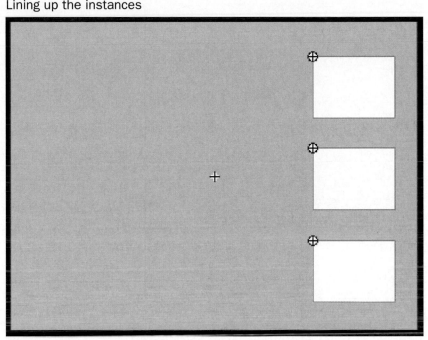

14. Insert a layer above the Buttons layer and rename it **Text**.

15. On the Text layer, create three text boxes for the following captions in **Static Text**, **Arial**, **11** pt., black, and center-aligned:

Thumb1: **BiJi**

Thumb2: **Marla Rejas**

Thumb3: **Palo Reni**

STEP-BY-STEP 11.2 Continued

16. Using the Selection tool, drag the captions below the boxes, as shown in Figure 11-4.

17. Hold down the **Shift** key, and select the three text boxes. On the Align panel, click the **Align horizontal center** button. The text boxes should appear as shown in Figure 11-4.

FIGURE 11-4
Aligned button text

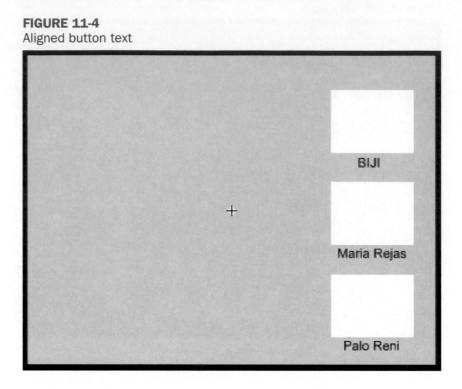

18. Save your work and remain in this screen for the next Step-by-Step.

Configuring the Left Cel with ActionScript

You can use the loadMovie command to load SWF files, MP3 files, or JPEG files into a level or target in a Flash movie. In this case you will be loading JPEG files into button targets. The target name comes from the instance names: Thumb1, Thumb2, and Thumb3.

STEP-BY-STEP 11.3

Loading Thumbnail Images by Using ActionScript

1. Insert a layer above the Text layer and rename it **Actions**.

2. Click the first frame on the Actions layer and open the **Actions** panel.

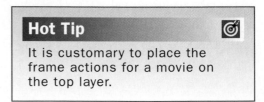

Hot Tip

It is customary to place the frame actions for a movie on the top layer.

STEP-BY-STEP 11.3 Continued

3. On the Actions panel, click on the **Global Functions** category to expand it (if it is not already), and then click the **Browser/Network** category to expand it.

4. Double-click **loadMovie**.

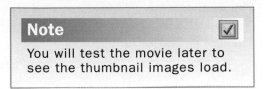

> **Note** ☑
>
> You will test the movie later to see the thumbnail images load.

5. In the parentheses next to the loadMovie function in the Script pane, key **"images/event1.jpg"**, **"Thumb1"**

6. Click after the semicolon and press **Enter** (Windows) or **Return** (Macintosh).

7. Double-click loadMovie again and key **"images/event2.jpg", "Thumb2"**

8. Click after the semicolon and press **Enter** (Windows) or **Return** (Macintosh).

9. Double-click loadMovie again and key **"images/event3.jpg", "Thumb3"**

10. Save your work and remain in this screen for the next Step-by-Step.

Integrating the Events Section onto the Main Timeline

From a design perspective, building a movie clip without seeing it in the Preview window can be hard. Although you are only halfway finished with the Events Left movie clip, you might want to integrate it onto the main Timeline. This will let you test the functionality of the cels as you build them out.

Creating a Partial Movie Clip

The first step is to create a partially finished Fstrip Events movie clip. Then you will integrate it onto the main Timeline.

Web Design Skills

Next to audio and video, imported JPEGs and GIFs can pump up a Flash file's size, greatly increasing download times over the Internet. Although you should always optimize your images (high quality balanced with small file size) before bringing them into Flash, the major question is whether to use the Import function or the loadMovie command. Your decision should rest on design needs. If you need to see and/or animate the image in Flash, use the Import command. But if you simply need to bring a picture into a fixed area and keep file size to a minimum, use loadMovie.

STEP-BY-STEP 11.4

Creating a Movie Clip for the Events Section

1. In the Library, select the **Fstrip Visit** movie clip symbol and duplicate it.

2. Name the new movie **Fstrip Events** and then click **OK**.

3. Double-click the **Fstrip Events** movie clip to enter symbol-editing mode.

4. Collapse the Actions panel so you can see the Stage. Select the **Left** layer. Drag the **Events Left** movie clip from the Library over the left cel.

5. Use the arrow keys to line up the movie clip over the object in the left cel.

6. Click **Cut** on the **Edit** menu to place the Events Left movie clip on the Clipboard.

7. Delete the object from the left cel.

8. Click **Paste in Place** on the **Edit** menu. The Events Left movie clip is in the left cel, as shown in Figure 11-5.

FIGURE 11-5
Left cel configured for Fstrip Events

9. Click the **View** menu, point to **Snapping**, and make sure **Snap to Objects** is selected (note the check mark next to the option).

10. Select the image in the center cel.

11. Select the **Rectangle** tool and set the stroke and fill colors to gray (**#CCCCCC**).

12. Position the pointer on the upper-left corner of the center image, and then drag diagonally to the lower-right corner of the center image. A gray rectangle is drawn behind the center image, snapped to its size.

13. Use the Selection tool to select the center image of the map and delete it. The gray rectangle remains on the Center layer, properly aligned in its cel.

14. Double-click the gray rectangle on the center layer.

15. Click the **Modify** menu, and then click **Convert to Symbol**.

STEP-BY-STEP 11.4 Continued

16. Confirm that the registration point is set to the upper-left corner, as shown in Figure 11-6.

FIGURE 11-6
Registration point set to upper-left corner

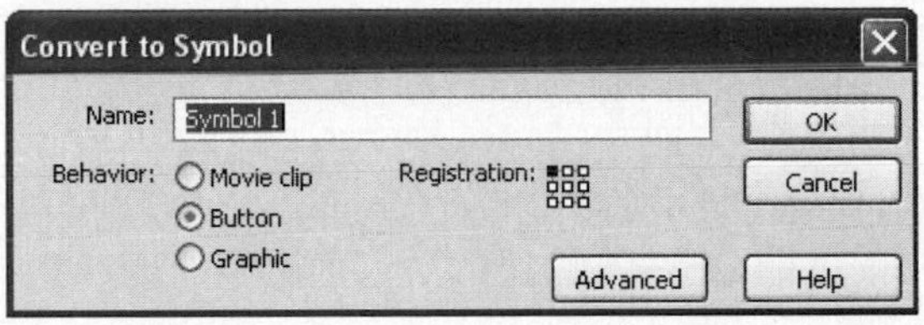

17. Name the symbol **Event Center**, select the **Movie clip** behavior, and click **OK**. The movie clip is selected on the Center layer.

18. On the Property inspector, key **center** as the instance name. You give the movie clip a name so the loadMovie command can target it. (The instance name is case-sensitive and will be in lowercase when it is called later.)

19. Save the document and remain in this screen for the next Step-by-Step.

> **Note** ☑
>
> The registration point determines from what point objects load into the movie clip. Because you will be bringing JPEGs into this center cel and a JPEG's registration point is automatically set to the upper-left corner, the registration point of the Events Center movie clip must also be in the upper-left corner to center the JPEG in the cel.

Integrating the Partial Movie Clip onto the Timeline

Now you are ready to create the Events section on the main Timeline. This section will have a moving filmstrip introduction like the other sections.

STEP-BY-STEP 11.5

Creating the Events Section on the Main Timeline

1. Click **Scene 1** on the Information bar to return to the main Timeline.

2. Inside the Filmstrip folder on the Timeline, insert a new layer above the Visit layer and rename it **Events**.

3. With the Events layer selected, select the **Fstrip Events** movie clip symbol on the Library panel and drag an instance of it onto the Stage.

4. Make sure guides are turned on. (On the **View** menu, point to **Guides**, and click **Show Guides**.)

5. Drag the **Fstrip Events** movie clip until it is within the vertical guides of the filmstrip area.

STEP-BY-STEP 11.5 Continued

6. To adjust the horizontal placement, use the arrow keys to move the movie clip horizontally until the three thumbnail images in the Fstrip Event's left cel are just to the right of the left Stage border, as shown in Figure 11-7.

FIGURE 11-7
Aligning the Fstrip Events movie clip in the main movie

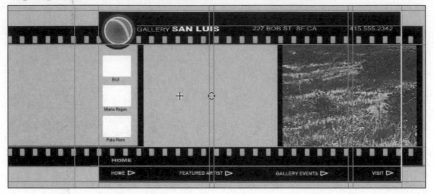

7. Drag frame **1** of the Events layer to frame **31** of the same layer, as shown in Figure 11-8.

FIGURE 11-8
Moving the Fstrip Events movie clip to the starting point

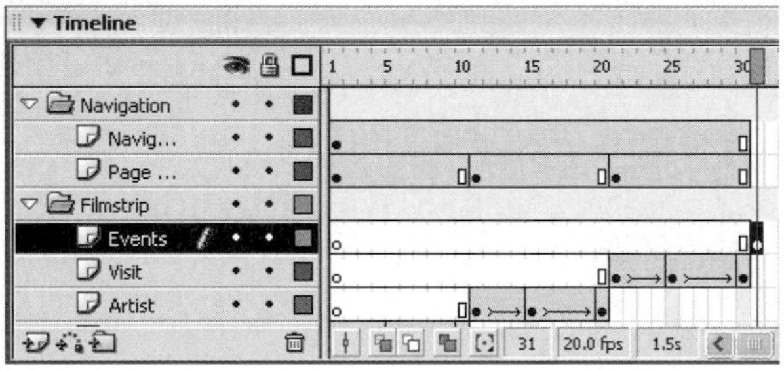

8. Click frame **35** of the Events layer, click the **Insert** menu, point to **Timeline**, and then click **Keyframe**. Click frame **40** of the same layer, click **Insert**, point to **Timeline**, and then click **Keyframe** again.

9. Click frame **31** on the Events layer and select the Selection tool. Then hold down the **Shift** key and drag the **Fstrip Events** movie clip to the left until the left cel is just off the Stage.

10. Click the keyframe in frame **35** of the Events layer. Then hold down **Shift** and drag the filmstrip to the right until the right cel is just to the right of the Stage.

11. Click frame **31** of the Events layer. On the Property inspector, choose **Motion** from the **Tween** menu.

12. Click frame **35** of the Events layer. On the Property inspector, add a motion tween between frames 35 and 40. Remain in this screen for the next Step-by-Step.

Extending Layers and Creating a Title Symbol

Now that you have begun the creation of a movie clip for the Events section and placed it on the main Timeline, you need to extend the other layers to the same frame as the Events section. You also need to create a new Title symbol for the Events section. You will do this by duplicating an existing symbol, editing it, and then placing it in the main Timeline.

S TEP-BY-STEP 11.6

Extending the Other Layers and Creating a Title Symbol

1. Click frame **40** of the Border layer, click **Insert**, point to **Timeline**, and then click **Frame**.

2. Click frame **40** of the Logo layer, click **Insert**, point to **Timeline**, and then click **Frame**.

3. Click frame **40** of the Navigation layer, click **Insert**, point to **Timeline**, and then click **Frame**.

4. Insert a keyframe in frame **31** of the Page Name layer.

5. In the Library, duplicate the **Title Home** symbol. Name the new symbol **Title Events**.

6. Double-click the **Title Events** symbol in the library to enter its editing mode.

7. Change the text to **GALLERY EVENTS**.

8. On the Information bar, click **Scene 1** to return to the main movie Stage.

9. Click frame **31** of the Page Name layer.

10. Drag an instance of the **Title Events** graphic symbol onto the Stage and line up its left edge with the left edge of the Visit title, as shown in Figure 11-9.

FIGURE 11-9
Lining up the Events title

11. With the **Title Events** symbol selected, select **Cut** on the **Edit** menu.

12. Delete the **Title Visit** instance in frame **31** of the Page Name layer.

13. Select **Paste in Place** on the **Edit** menu. An aligned instance of the Title Events symbol appears on the Stage.

STEP-BY-STEP 11.6 Continued

14. Click frame **40** of the Page Name layer, click **Insert**, point to **Timeline**, and then click **Frame**. Your Timeline should look like Figure 11-10.

FIGURE 11-10
The Timeline with an Events section

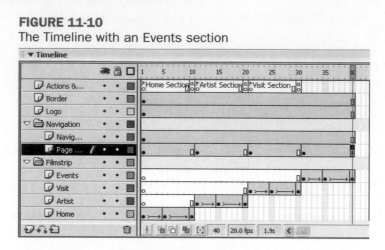

Configuring the Gallery Events Button

Now that there is a movie clip for the Gallery Events (even if it is only partially completed), you can configure the Gallery Events button to link it to the clip.

STEP-BY-STEP 11.7

Configuring the Gallery Events Button

1. Using the Selection tool, double-click the **Gallery Events** button instance (not the Gallery Events title you just placed) on the Stage to enter its symbol-editing mode. The button has only an Up state, configured with the text and an arrow symbol.

2. Insert keyframes in both the **Over** and **Hit** frames. The Timeline now covers all four states.

3. Click in the **Hit** frame, select the **Rectangle** tool, set the stroke and fill colors to None, and draw a rectangle over the text and the arrow symbol to indicate the area where a user can click.

4. Click the frame for the **Over** state.

5. Click the **Edit** menu, and then click **Deselect All**. You are now ready to edit the button text for rollover effects.

6. Using the Selection tool, click the **Gallery Events** text to select it. On the Property inspector, change the color of the text to orange (**#FFCC00**).

STEP-BY-STEP 11.7 Continued

7. Select the arrow graphic. On the Property inspector, change the color selection to **Tint**.

8. On the color picker, choose orange (**#FFCC00**). The arrow changes to the same color as the text. The Tint Amount should be set to 100%.

9. Add a new layer above Layer 1 and rename it **Sound**.

10. Insert a keyframe in the **Down** frame and then, on the **Window** menu, point to **Other Panels**, click **Common Libraries**, and then click **Sounds**.

> **Note** ☑
>
> When you test the Gallery Events button, you should see the text color change and hear the camera shutter sound when you click. However, you do not see any of the gallery events because you have not linked these to the buttons yet.

11. Click the **Down** frame of the Sound layer and drag the **Camera Shutter 35mm SLR** sound onto the Stage. The sound is inserted into the Down state of the button.

12. Click **Scene 1** on the Information bar to exit the symbol-editing mode for the Gallery Events button.

13. Click the **Control** menu, and then click **Test Movie**.

14. Roll the pointer over the Gallery Events button and click the button to test it.

15. Close the Preview window and save the document. Remain in this screen for the next Step-by-Step.

ActionScript for the Events Section

In the next two Step-by-Steps, you will add the ActionScript for *stop* actions and frame labels as well as for the *goto* actions that drive the navigation for the Events section.

STEP-BY-STEP 11.8

Adding *stop* Actions and Frame Labels

1. Click frame **40** of the Actions & Labels layer, click **Insert**, point to **Timeline**, and then click **Keyframe**. The keyframe is to hold a *stop* action for the Gallery Events section.

2. Expand the **Actions** panel. Make sure the **Global Functions** category and the **Timeline Control** category are open.

3. Double-click the **stop** action.

4. Collapse the Actions panel.

5. Click frame **31** of the Actions & Labels layer, click **Insert**, point to **Timeline**, and then click **Keyframe**. A keyframe is added to hold the label for the Events section.

STEP-BY-STEP 11.8 Continued

6. Make sure the Property inspector is expanded.

7. In the Frame Label text box, key **Events Section**. Press **Enter** (Windows) or **Return** (Macintosh). The label, Events Section, appears in frame 31 on the Actions & Layers layer.

8. Save your work and remain in this screen for the next Step-by-Step.

S TEP-BY-STEP 11.9

Adding *goto* Actions for Section Navigation

1. Using the Selection tool, click the **Gallery Events** button to select it. (The button shows a blue outline.)

2. Click the **Actions** title bar to expand the panel.

3. Double-click the **on** action in the Movie Clip Control category, and then double-click the **release** event.

4. Click after the open curly bracket, and then double-click the **gotoAndPlay** action from the Timeline Control category. Key **"Events Section"** (be sure to include the quotation marks). The actions appear in the Script pane, as shown in Figure 11-11.

FIGURE 11-11
Actions for the Gallery Events button

```
on (release) {gotoAndPlay("Events Section");

}
```

5. Collapse the Actions panel by clicking its title bar.

6. Test the movie and test the navigation buttons. Each navigation button now advances the movie to a different section on the main Timeline.

7. Close the Preview window and save the document. Remain in this screen for the next Step-by-Step.

Finishing the Artists' Work Sampler

Now that the Fstrip Events movie is on the main Timeline, you can test it to make sure its images and script are working properly. The next step in the construction of the Events section is to add a description box in the center cel, giving users information on specific events and navigation features of the section. This description box will be a dynamic text box so its content can change as users click on different events.

STEP-BY-STEP 11.10

Creating a Dynamic Text Box

1. Click frame **40** of the Events layer to select the **Fstrip Events** movie clip.

2. Using the Selection tool, double-click the center cel on the Stage. The Fstrip Events movie clip enters editing mode.

3. Insert a new layer above the Left layer and name it **Event Description**.

4. Select the **Text** tool and drag to make a text box approximately the width of the center cel.

5. On the Property inspector, set the properties shown in Table 11-1.

TABLE 11-1
Text box parameters

PROPERTY	SETTING	COMMENT
Text Type	Dynamic Text	ActionScripting will fill in the contents.
Font	11 pt. Arial, left aligned, blue (#000099)	
Format	Line Spacing 3 pt. Left Margin 12 px	
Lines	Multiline	Text box can include more than one line.
Selectable	Toggled Off	
Render text as HTML	Toggled On	Provides consistency in how the text is displayed.
Show Border Around Text	Toggled On	Adds white background and border for text readability.
Var (case sensitive)	description	Variable that will designate what text is in the box.

6. Click the **Selection** tool and double-click the text box to enter text-editing mode.

STEP-BY-STEP 11.10 Continued

7. Drag the corner size handle until the box is the width of the center cel and approximately 50 pixels high, and position the text box at the bottom of the center cel, as shown in Figure 11-12. You don't want to change the size on the Property inspector, because the text will become distorted.

FIGURE 11-12
Sizing the Description dynamic text box

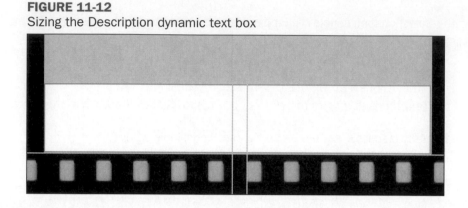

8. Save the document and remain in this screen for the next Step-by-Step.

Adding ActionScript and Button Functionality to the Event Picker

The left and center cels of the Events section now need ActionScript to add descriptive text and images to the center cel. This ActionScript will be associated with the three thumbnail images in the left cel, because these will be the triggers for different events.

Loading images into the thumbnail buttons means they can't be easily scripted for sound effects and loading commands. The best solution to this problem is to insert another set of invisible buttons on top of the thumbnail buttons to hold the scripting and sound functionality. Invisible buttons have graphic elements only in the Hit state and appear on the Stage as semi-transparent aqua-colored objects. They will not show up in the published file.

Web Design Skills

In Flash, you can give button functionality to movie clips. Instead of adding invisible buttons as in the following example, you could put ActionScript on the thumbnail movie clips with onPress commands to load images and change dynamic text. Here's an example:

OnPress (gotoAndPlay _root (15))

This ActionScript can get a little complicated and labor-intensive, especially if you want to add rollover and click sounds.

S TEP-BY-STEP 11.11

Creating Invisible Buttons

1. Using the Selection tool, double-click the **Events Left** movie clip symbol in the library to enter its editing mode.

2. Insert a new layer above the Buttons layer and name it **Invisible Buttons**.

3. Draw a rectangle in any color on the Stage on the Invisible Buttons layer.

4. Click the **Selection** tool and then double-click to select the rectangle and its border.

5. On the Property inspector, change the rectangle's W: setting to **69** and H: to **52**.

6. On the **Modify** menu, click **Convert to Symbol**.

7. Name the symbol **Invisible Button**, set the behavior to **Button**, and then click **OK**.

8. Double-click the button on the Stage to enter its editing mode.

9. Click the **Up** keyframe and drag it to the **Hit** frame, as shown in Figure 11-13. The Up, Over, and Down states are now empty.

FIGURE 11-13
Leave only the Hit state

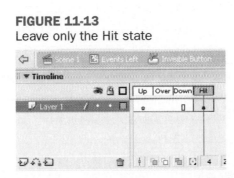

10. Add a new layer above Layer 1 and name it **Sound**.

11. Create a keyframe in the **Down** frame of the Sound layer and then expand the **Library-Sounds** panel.

12. With the **Down** frame on the Sound layer selected, drag the **Polaroid Shutter** sound onto the Stage. The sound is inserted into the Down state.

13. Click **Events Left** on the Information bar. The button appears as a semitransparent aqua shape.

14. Click **Copy** on the **Edit** menu, and then click **Paste in Center** on the **Edit** menu two times. Two more instances of the button appear on the Stage.

> **Note** ☑
>
> Keep in mind that the URL you place in the loadMovie ActionScript is always in reference to the directory or drive in which the Flash file is being saved. In our case, the home.fla file is being saved in the build_GallerySanLuis folder. As long as the images folder that is referenced is also in that folder, the ActionScript will be able to locate the graphics indicated. This method allows entire Flash sites to be moved from location to location without breaking links—as long as all of the files stay in the same relative location.

STEP-BY-STEP 11.11 Continued

15. Drag the button instances over the three white movie boxes.

16. Select the invisible button over the BIJI button and click the **Actions** panel title bar to expand the Actions panel.

17. Configure the ActionScripting on the buttons as shown in Table 11-2. Remember to select each button before entering the ActionScript. (*Hint:* You might want to copy and paste the BIJI script onto the other buttons and then customize it.)

TABLE 11-2
ActionScripts for buttons

BUTTON	ACTIONSCRIPT

BIJI	on (release) {
	loadMovie("images/event1.jpg", "_parent.center");
	_parent.description = "BIJI's opening will feature San Francisco vistas. He will be dressed as a tourist. Bring your own Burmudas at 7p.m., April 5.";
	}

Maria Rejas	on (release) {
	loadMovie("images/event2.jpg", "_parent.center");
	_parent.description = "Maria will be showing some of the plant photos under black light. Wear bright colors to the opening on May 7th at 6p.m.";
	}

Palo Reni	on (release) {
	loadMovie("images/event3.jpg", "_parent.center");
	_parent.description = "Palo's opening reception will feature mixed media photography and Afro-Brazilian music. Reception starts at 8p.m. on June 10th.";
	}

18. Collapse the Actions panel. Save and test the movie. The Gallery Events button should bring up working thumbnail images.

19. Click **Scene 1** on the Information bar to return to the main movie. Remain in this screen for the next Step-by-Step.

> **Hot Tip** ◎
>
> As you create these ActionScripts, you might need to resize some panels and collapse others so you can see and select the buttons while still having access to the Actions panel.

Creating a Form in Flash

Forms in Flash have been made fairly simple with components. As you might recall from the Visit sections, components are like templates for creating commonly used movie clips such as check boxes, drop-down menus, and buttons. The major challenge when creating an e-mail form for the gallery events is converting the user information from check boxes and input text boxes.

This challenge is met by some serious ActionScripting. To make it simpler, you will import the ActionScript for the form from a text file.

As you might have guessed, the form will fall into the right box when a user clicks on Gallery Events. It will be a separate movie loaded into the main movie.

STEP-BY-STEP 11.12

Designing the Form

1. Expand the **Library** panel and select the **Cel Background** movie.

2. Duplicate the movie and name the new movie **Events Right**.

3. Double-click the **Events Right** movie clip to enter its editing mode.

4. Insert a new layer above the Background layer and name it **Arch Shadow**.

5. With the Arch Shadow layer selected, import the file **arch.swf** from the **images** folder to the Stage.

6. Convert the arch.swf image into a movie clip symbol and name it **Arch Shadow**. The image looks pretty good, but the bottom of the arch is sticking out of the circle, as shown in Figure 11-14.

FIGURE 11-14
The Arch image

Arch extended
beyond the circle

7. Insert a new layer above the Arch Shadow layer and rename it **Mask**. You will use the Mask layer to crop the Arch image.

8. Hold down **Shift** and use the **Oval** tool to draw a black circle (you have to change the fill and stroke colors) on the Mask layer a little smaller than the circle behind the arch, as shown in Figure 11-15.

FIGURE 11-15
Arch image with a small circle on top

STEP-BY-STEP 11.12 Continued

9. Using the Selection tool, double-click the black circle. Then use the arrow keys to center the circle over the arch image, as shown in Figure 11-16.

FIGURE 11-16
Mask centered over image

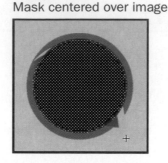

10. With the Mask layer selected, click **Modify**, point to **Timeline**, and then click **Layer Properties**.

11. In the Layer Properties dialog box, select **Show** and **Lock**.

12. Select **Mask** for the type and select **View layer as outlines**. Then click **OK**. The mask appears as an outline over the arch image.

13. If the **Mask** layer is locked, unlock it. Drag the **Arch Shadow** layer above the Mask layer, and then drag it back below the Mask layer.

14. Select the first frame of the Arch Shadow layer. Then hold down **Shift** and select the first frame of the Mask layer. Both the mask and the arch image are selected.

15. On the Transform panel, constrain the proportions and increase to **350%**.

16. Drag the image to the left center of the Stage, as shown in Figure 11-17. (The positioning does not have to be precise; this will be a background image.)

FIGURE 11-17
Enlarged arch image centered left on the Stage

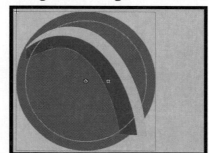

17. Click the **Arch Shadow** layer, and then click on the arch to select the instance of the Arch Shadow. On the Property inspector, change the color to **Alpha**, **20%**.

18. Save the document and remain in this screen for the next Step-by-Step.

Now you are ready to create the form items.

S TEP-BY-STEP 11.13

Creating Form Items

1. Insert a new layer above the Mask layer and name it **Text**.

2. Lock the **Mask**, **Arch Shadow**, and **Background** layers.

3. Select the **Text** tool and create a text box at the top of the Stage. Set the following text attributes:
   Static Text
   Arial, **11** pt., black
   Left-aligned
   Left margin: **0**

4. Key **NOTIFY ME OF GALLERY SAN LUIS EVENTS**.

5. Select the **SAN LUIS EVENTS** text and change its font to **Arial Black**.

6. Click the size handle on the text box and drag horizontally until all the text is on one line, as shown in Figure 11-18.

   FIGURE 11-18
   Dragging the text box handle

   NOTIFY ME OF GALLERY **SAN LUIS EVENTS**

7. Click the **Selection** tool to select the text box.

8. Align the text box to X: **–161** and Y: **–122**.

9. Click the **Text** tool again and create a static text box in **Arial**, **9** pt., left-aligned, and black that says **Name**.

10. Create another text box below the Name box, dragging its size handle to make it about as long as the title. Users can enter their names in this box.

11. On the Property inspector, change the Text Type to **Input Text**.

STEP-BY-STEP 11.13 Continued

12. Click the **Selection** tool to select the text box, and then use the Property inspector to apply the settings shown in Table 11-3.

TABLE 11-3
Property settings for Name text box

AREA	SETTING	COMMENTS
Type	Input Text	Users can enter information into the text box.
Font	10 pt. Arial, left aligned, black	
Line	Single Line	Limits the amount of text for the name.
Render text as HTML	Toggled Off	You cannot generate e-mail from HTML input.
Show Border Around Text	Toggled On	Important. Lets you see the text box for entering information.
Var	userName	The variable will be used in creating content for the e-mail form.
Maximum Characters	100	Limits the number of letters allowed in the box to 100.
Height (H:)	19	

13. Select and then drag the **Name** box or the **Input Text** box until they are close to one another vertically. (You will align all boxes on this form horizontally a little later.)

14. Hold down **Shift** and select both the **Name** and **Input Text** boxes.

15. Click **Copy** on the **Edit** menu.

16. Click **Paste in Center** on the **Edit** menu.

STEP-BY-STEP 11.13 Continued

17. Change the new static text field from Name to **E-mail**. (Resize the box if necessary to fit all the text on one line.)

18. Align the new text fields under the Name fields, as shown in Figure 11-19.

FIGURE 11-19
Copied text fields

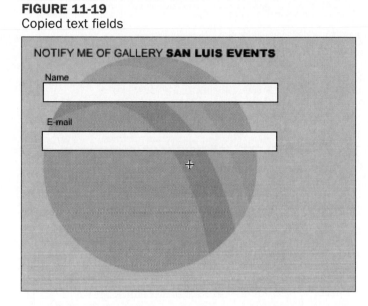

19. Select the second input text field, and then on the Property inspector, change the Var field to **userEmail**.

20. Save your work and remain in this screen for the next Step-by-Step.

Adding a Check Box

After viewing the images and descriptions of the various upcoming Gallery openings, users can check off which events they are interested in attending and send an e-mail message to the Gallery requesting an invitation and a reminder for the event. From the Components panel, you will build check boxes for the events and then a submit button for the form.

STEP-BY-STEP 11.14

Adding a Check Box

1. Expand the Components panel and drag the **CheckBox** component onto the Stage below the input boxes, as shown in Figure 11-20. If a message appears indicating the component already exists, select Use existing component, and click OK.

FIGURE 11-20
A check box on the Stage

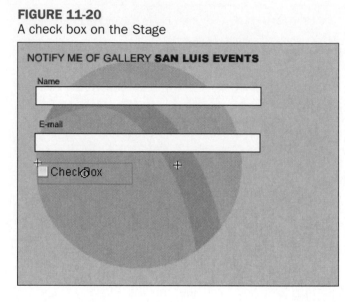

2. In the Label text box on the Property inspector, key **BIJI Opening, Friday April 5, 7 p.m.** (including the periods in "p.m.").

3. Set W: to **290** and H: to **18**.

4. Key **cb1** for the Instance Name, as shown in Figure 11-21.

> **Note** ☑
>
> If you see a message box indicating that a component with the same name already exists, select Replace existing component and then click OK.

FIGURE 11-21
Setting the check box instance name

▼ Properties			Properties	Parameters
Component	icon			
cb1	label	BIJI Opening, Friday April 5, 7 p.m.		
	labelPlacement	right		
W: 290.0 X: -147.7	selected	false		
H: 18 Y: -1.6	toggle	false		

5. With the check box selected, click **Copy** on the **Edit** menu.

6. Paste three more instances of the check box on the Stage.

STEP-BY-STEP 11.14 Continued

7. Place the instances below the top check box and label them on the Property inspector as follows:

   cb2: Maria Rejas Opening, Thursday, May 6, 6 p.m.

   cb3: Maria Rejas Silent Auction, Monday, May 20, 5 p.m.

   cb4: Palo Reni Opening, Friday, June 3, 8 p.m.

8. Click the keyframe on the Text layer to select all the text items.

9. On the Align panel, toggle **To stage** to Off and align the left edge of the text boxes.

10. Select the four check boxes and then choose **Space evenly vertically** on the Align panel. The Events Right cel should look similar to Figure 11-22.

FIGURE 11-22
Text and check box alignment

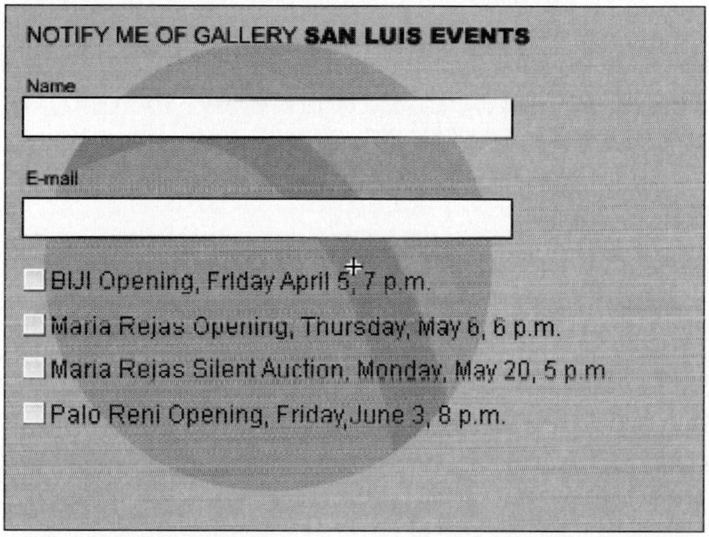

NOTIFY ME OF GALLERY **SAN LUIS EVENTS**

Name

E-mail

☐ BIJI Opening, Friday April 5, 7 p.m.

☐ Maria Rejas Opening, Thursday, May 6, 6 p.m.

☐ Maria Rejas Silent Auction, Monday, May 20, 5 p.m.

☐ Palo Reni Opening, Friday, June 3, 8 p.m.

11. Save the document and remain in this screen for the next Step-by-Step.

Sending Data from a Flash Site

The basis of e-commerce and the Internet in general is the power to communicate and to connect people to the things they want. Small businesses love the new channel of sales and feedback they can get from the Internet. The technical trick is in making information easy to send and receive. Some Web sites use server-side software to send information (order forms, polls, and such). You can also send information by e-mail.

E-mail links work pretty much the same in Flash as they do on an HTML page, with a *mailto: name@service.com* statement that tells the browser to bring up a new e-mail message to that address. The challenge of the Events form isn't just to bring up the e-mail message but to populate (fill in) the Subject and Body of the message with information from the fill-in and check boxes. You do this by using a script. Like any script you might get from a book or a Macromedia Flash support Web site, some customization is involved (for example, the e-mail address for the Gallery and the names of check and fill-in boxes). To call up the script, you use the Button component.

STEP-BY-STEP 11.15

Creating a Submit Button

1. Select the **Text** layer.

2. Drag the **Button** component from the Components panel to the Stage under the bottom check box, as shown in Figure 11-23. If a message appears indicating the component already exists, select **Use existing component**, and click **OK**.

FIGURE 11-23
Putting a push button on the Stage

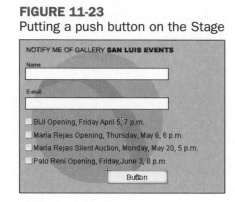

3. In the Label area of the Parameters tab on the Property inspector, enter **Notify Me**.

4. In the Instance Name text box, enter **submitBtn**. Your choices should look like those in Figure 11-24.

FIGURE 11-24
Button parameters

▼ Properties			Properties	Parameters
Component	icon			
submitBtn	label	Notify Me		
	labelPlacement	right		
W: 100.0 X: -22.6	selected	false		
H: 22.0 Y: 88.3	toggle	false		

5. Create a new layer above the Text layer and rename it **Actions**.

6. Select the first frame of the Actions layer and open the **Actions** panel.

7. On the Actions panel, click the **Options** menu in the upper-right corner and choose **Import Script**. If you cannot see the Options button on the Actions panel, undock the panel.

8. Browse to the **scripts** folder and double-click the **eventsScript.as** file. The script is imported into the first frame of the Actions layer.

9. Browse through the script and find the script that reads as follows:

```
getURL("mailto:you@youraddress.com?subject=" add subject add "&body=" add body);
```

STEP-BY-STEP 11.15 Continued

10. Replace you@youraddress.com with **events@gallerysanluis.org**. (The rest of the line of script remains the same.)

11. Save the document and remain in this screen for the next Step-by-Step.

> **Note** ☑️
>
> In a generic script, items such as e-mail addresses need to be customized.

Your last task in this lesson is to integrate the form into the Fstrip Events movie.

S TEP-BY-STEP 11.16

Integrating the Form into the Fstrip Events Movie

1. Double-click the **Fstrip Events** movie clip in the library to enter symbol-editing mode.

> **Note** ☑️
>
> You will be setting the default value for the dynamic text box, which is a description of how to work in the Events section.

2. Make sure the **Actions** panel is collapsed, and select the right cel on the Stage. The **Right** layer is selected.

3. Drag an instance of the **Events Right** movie clip onto the Stage.

4. Drag the **Events Right** movie clip over the image in the right cel, and select **Cut** on the **Edit** menu.

5. Delete the image from the right cel.

6. On the **Edit** menu, click **Paste in Place**. The form is aligned in the right cel of the Fstrip Events movie clip.

7. Insert a new layer above the Event Description layer and rename it **Actions**.

8. Select the first frame of the Actions layer and expand the **Actions** panel.

9. Click in the Script pane.

10. Key **set ("description", "Click on an image to the left for information on artist's opening. Fill out the form to the right to get on the invite list for these events.");**

The ActionScript you just entered should look like Figure 11-15.

FIGURE 11-25
Set variable action

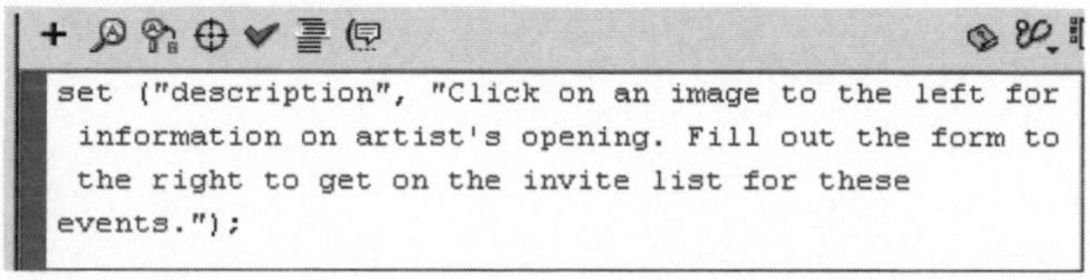

```
+  🔎 🐾 ⊕ ✔ ☰ 🗐                    ⊚ 🐾 ▤
set ("description", "Click on an image to the left for
 information on artist's opening. Fill out the form to
 the right to get on the invite list for these
 events.");
```

STEP-BY-STEP 11.16 Continued

11. Collapse the **Actions** panel, click **Scene 1** to return to the main Timeline, and then save the document.

12. Test the form in a browser by opening the **File** menu and pointing to **Publish Preview** and then clicking **Default**. The Flash document will appear in your default browser.

13. Close your browser, close the document, and exit Flash.

> **Note** ☑
>
> Try submitting the e-mail form with no name given, with no e-mail address, and/or with an improper e-mail format. You should get warning messages. If you fill everything and no e-mail is generated, you need to configure your browser to connect to your e-mail program (such as Outlook, Outlook Express, or Eudora).

SUMMARY

In this lesson, you learned to:

■ Import JPEG images into a Flash file dynamically.

■ Create invisible buttons for functionality.

■ Configure the registration point of a movie clip symbol.

■ Import script from a Script file.

■ Use check boxes and input text boxes to create an e-mail form.

VIDEO IN MACROMEDIA FLASH (OPTIONAL)

OBJECTIVES

Upon completion of this lesson, you should be able to:

- Import video into Flash.
- Create a new scene for a preloader.
- Develop the ActionScript and loading animation for a preloader.
- Create buttons to control video in Flash.
- Configure ActionScript to control the Timeline of another movie.
- Use the loadMovie command and a blank movie target to bring the video SWF into the main movie.

Gallery San Luis Web Site Progress

When you started designing the Gallery San Luis Web site in Lesson 4, there was a list of items the client wanted incorporated into the site. Let's take a quick look at how the Gallery San Luis project has progressed:

- ☑ A Home page that is both appealing and speaks photography.
- ☑ A Featured Artist page with a Photo Viewer and featured photographer information.
- ❑ Video interviews with the featured artist (optional).
- ☑ An animated Map page to indicate where the gallery is located.
- ☑ An Events page for requesting tickets for gallery events.
- ☑ Sound incorporated on buttons.
- ☑ Slick transitions between pages.
- ☑ An overall photography metaphor for the site.

Importing Video into Flash

Macromedia Flash MX 2004 supports complete integration of video. Unlike some Web sites in which video is shown in a pop-up window, the Gallery San Luis site will have video integrated into its design, as shown in Figure 12-1. You will import a previously edited video of the artist, Biji, explaining his work.

FIGURE 12-1
The artist video playing in the Artist section

Design Challenge

Because a video is a large file, it can greatly increase the file size of your SWF and slow down load time over the Internet. Another difficulty in incorporating the video in our particular case is that it will sit in the right cel, which is off the Stage. To show the video, the Play button must not only start the video but bring the right cel fully onto the Stage. The Stop button must then stop the movie and return the right cel to its original position.

> **Did You Know?**
>
> Software such as DigiDesign Final Cut Pro and Adobe Premiere can be used to edit video.

Solution

A solution to the size problem is to place the video in a separate SWF file with a preloader built in and then use the loadMovie command to import this SWF file into a blank movie in the left cel of the Artist section. For the Play/Stop button, you will use the *with* command in ActionScript, which gives you control over more than one Timeline with a single button. The first step is to create a SWF file to hold the video. Then you create the Play/Stop button and its ActionScript. Finally, you create the preloader for this video SWF and integrate it into home.fla with the loadMovie command.

S TEP-BY-STEP 12.1

Creating a SWF file for the Video

1. Start Flash and create a new document.

2. Save the document in the **build_GallerySanLuis** folder and name it **bijivideo.fla**.

3. Select **Document** from the **Modify** menu. In the Document Properties dialog box, set the width to **345** and the height to **260** (leave the frame rate at 12 fps) and click **OK**.

4. Rename Layer 1 to **Video**.

5. Save the document and remain in this screen for the next Step-by-Step.

Embedding a Video

In the next Step-by-Step, you will import and embed an existing video into the Flash document you just created. Although embedding a video creates a larger SWF (Flash file), you can control the appearance of the video better because you can see it on the Stage. This saves time and usually improves the layout for the video in Flash.

> **Note** ☑
>
> The video that has been created for importing in Step-by-Step 12.2 has the extension .mov. To import this file, you must have QuickTime installed on your computer and an association set for QuickTime to run automatically for MOV file types. If you do not have QuickTime installed, you can download it from the Apple Web site: www.apple.com.

S TEP-BY-STEP 12.2

Importing Video into a Document

1. With the **Video** layer selected, click the **File** menu, point to **Import**, and then click **Import to Stage**.

STEP-BY-STEP 12.2 Continued

2. Browse to the **video** folder and choose **bijiSpeaks.mov**. Then click **Open** (Windows) or **Import** (Macintosh) to open the Video Import Wizard shown in Figure 12-2. The Embed video in Macromedia Flash document option is selected.

FIGURE 12-2
The Video Import Wizard

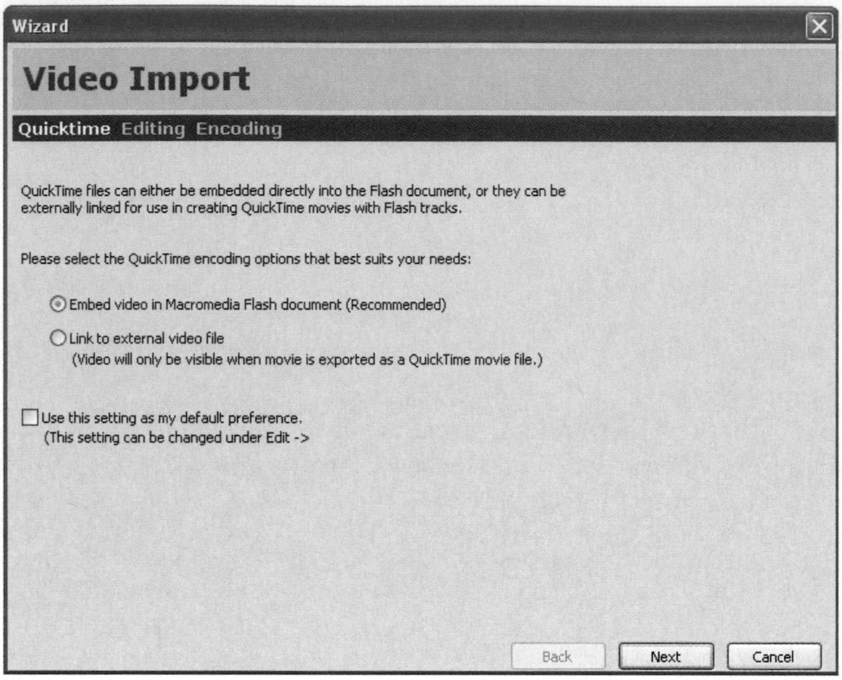

STEP-BY-STEP 12.2 Continued

3. Click **Next** to embed the video in Macromedia Flash. The second step of the Wizard appears, as shown in Figure 12-3.

FIGURE 12-3
The second step of the Import Wizard

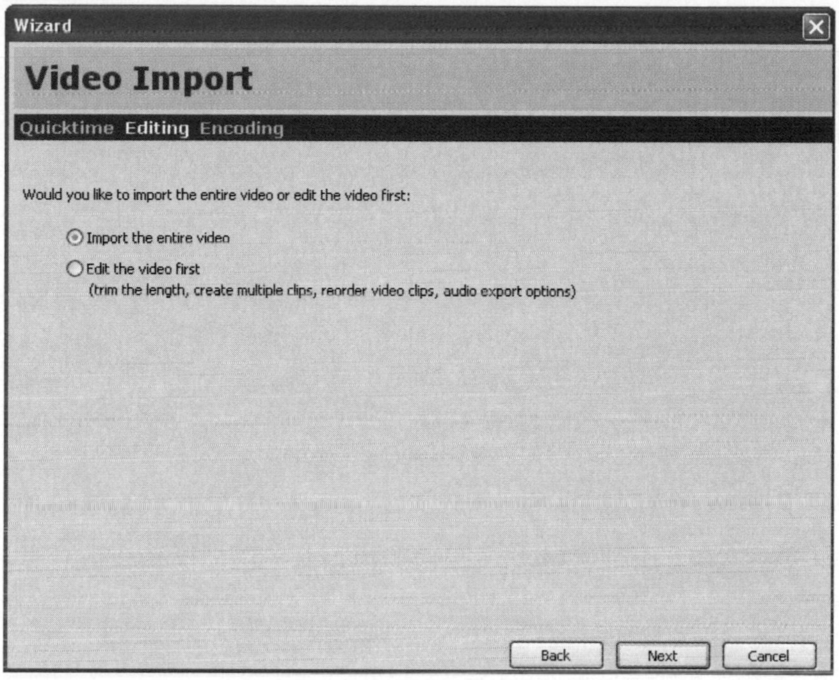

STEP-BY-STEP 12.2 Continued

4. Confirm that **Import the entire video** is selected, and then click **Next**. The next step is to select compression settings for the video, as shown in Figure 12-4. This is determined by the most common type of Internet connection used by the visitors to your site.

FIGURE 12-4
The Import Video Settings dialog box

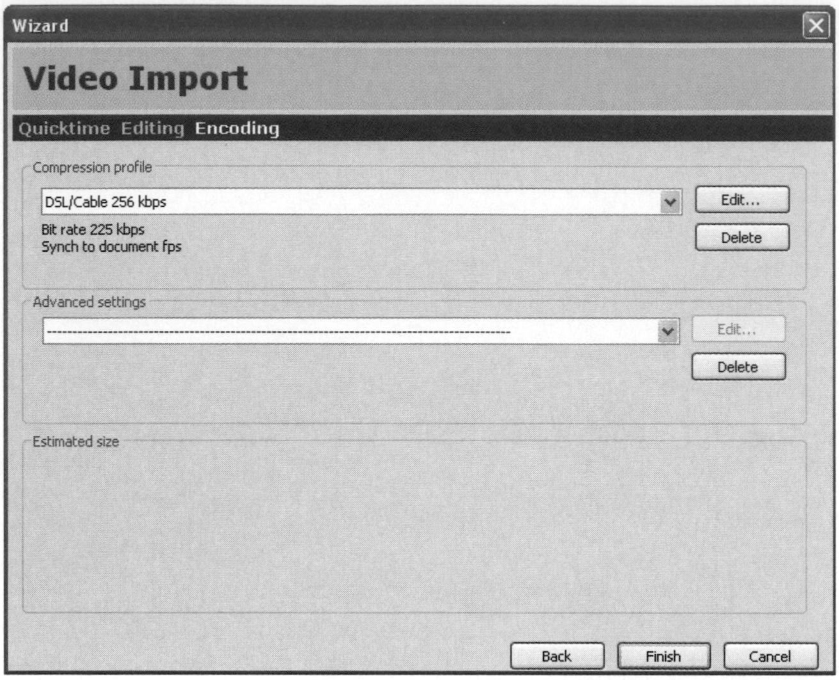

5. Click **Finish** to accept the default settings. The video is imported.

6. When the frame length warning appears, click **Yes** to insert the correct number of frames for the video to play.

7. Select the video on the Stage. On the Property inspector, make sure the video is lined up to X:**0**, Y:**0**.

8. Select the video on the Stage and press **Enter** (Windows) or **Return** (Macintosh) to play the video. (You won't hear the sound at this point.)

9. Save the document and remain in this screen for the next Step-by-Step.

Did You Know?

By default, Flash imports and exports video by using the Sorenson Spark codec, a compression/decompression formula that controls how multimedia files are compressed and decompressed during import and export. If QuickTime 4 is installed on your computer, Flash supports AVI, MPEG, MPG, MOV, and DV video formats.

Creating On-Screen Buttons

In the next two Step-by-Steps you will create the on-screen buttons that will, when pressed, cause the video to play or to stop playing. As you have done with other navigation buttons, you will first create the buttons and configure their various states. Then, in later Step-by-Steps, you will add the ActionScript that actually controls the video playback.

S TEP-BY-STEP 12.3

Creating a Play Button for the Video

1. Insert a layer above the Video layer and rename it **Buttons**. You now have a layer for the Play Video and Stop Video buttons.

2. Select the **Rectangle** tool.

3. In the Options area of the toolbar, click the **Round Rectangle Radius** button shown Figure 12-5.

FIGURE 12-5
The Round Rectangle Radius button

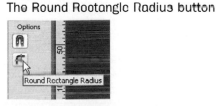

4. In the Rectangle Settings dialog box, set the corner radius to **30** points and click **OK**.

5. In the upper-left corner of the video, draw a rectangle as shown in Figure 12-6. Using the Selection tool, double-click the rectangle and change the stroke and fill to black.

FIGURE 12-6
Play Button position

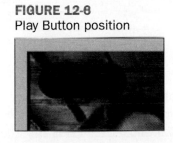

6. With the rectangle still selected, choose **Convert to Symbol** from the **Modify** menu. Name the symbol **Play Video**, set the Behavior to **Button**, and then click **OK**.

7. Double-click the button instance on the Stage to enter symbol-editing mode.

8. Insert a keyframe in the **Over** state.

> **Note** ☑
>
> The exact position of the rectangle isn't important, but make it large enough to hold two readable words, one on top of the other. The width should be at least 55 and the height at least 35.

STEP-BY-STEP 12.3 Continued

9. On the toolbar, change the fill color to beige (**#CCCC99**) as in Figure 12-7.

FIGURE 12-7
Choosing a color for the Over state

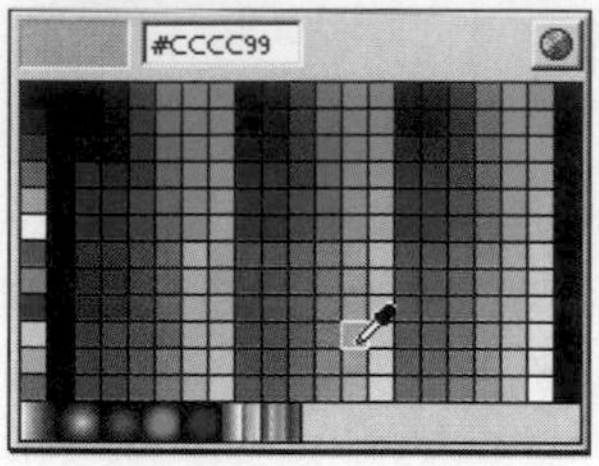

10. Insert a keyframe in the **Hit** state. The hit area is set to the entire button.

11. Insert a new layer above Layer 1 and rename it **Text**.

12. Select the **Text** tool and click on the button to begin a new text box. On the Property inspector, set the following text attributes: **Static Text**, **Arial**, **12** pts., white, bold, centered.

13. Key **Play Video**. Press **Enter** (Windows) or **Return** (Macintosh) after "Play" so the label will be on two lines, as shown in Figure 12-8.

FIGURE 12-8
Adding the button text

14. Use the Arrow keys or the Align panel to center the text on the button. Make sure the button is large enough to hold the text.

15. Add a layer above the Text layer and rename it **Sound**.

16. On the Sound layer, insert a keyframe in the **Down** state.

17. Click the **Window** menu, point to **Other Libraries**, **Common Libraries**, and then click **Sounds**. Drag an instance of the **Polaroid Shutter** sound onto the Stage, as shown in Figure 12-9. A shutter sound will play when users click the Play Video button.

> **Note** ☑
>
> Selecting both the text and the button on the Stage can be a little difficult. The best way to select them both is by shift-clicking the first keyframes of Layer 1 and the Text layer.

FIGURE 12-9
Inserting a Polaroid Shutter sound

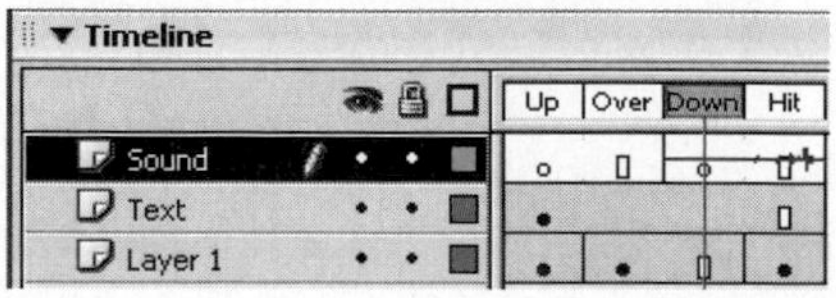

STEP-BY-STEP 12.3 Continued

18. On the Information bar at the top of the Stage, click **Scene 1** to return to the movie clip instance.

19. Save the document and remain in this screen for the next Step-by-Step.

Obviously, the Play Video button you just created will appear in the right cel when the Featured Artist section is opened. Once the video starts playing, you want the Stop Video button to appear.

S TEP-BY-STEP 12.4

Creating a Stop Video Button

1. From the library, select the **Play Video** button.

2. Use the options menu in the upper-right corner of the library to duplicate the symbol.

3. Name the new button symbol **Stop Video**, and then click **OK**.

4. Insert a keyframe into frame **2** of the Buttons layer of the main Timeline, as shown in Figure 12-10.

FIGURE 12-10
Creating a keyframe for the Stop Video button

5. Select the instance of the **Play Video** button on the Stage and note its X and Y coordinates on the Property inspector.

6. Delete the instance of the **Play Video** button on the Stage in frame 2.

7. Drag the **Stop Video** symbol from the library onto the Stage in frame 2 of the Buttons layer.

8. On the Property inspector, enter the X and Y coordinates from the Play Video button. The Stop and Play Video buttons are now in the same position on the Stage.

9. Double-click the instance of the **Stop Video** button on the Stage.

STEP-BY-STEP 12.4 Continued

10. Double-click the text on the button and change Play to **Stop**, as shown in Figure 12-11.

FIGURE 12-11
Configuring the Text for the Stop Video button

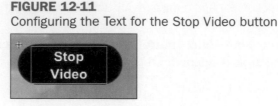

11. On the Information bar, click **Scene 1** to return to the movie clip instance.

12. Click on frame **1** and play the movie by pressing **Enter** (Windows) or **Return** (Macintosh). Notice how the buttons change as the movie progresses.

13. Save the document and remain in this screen for the next Step-by-Step.

Controlling Video Playback

The buttons need ActionScript to work properly. The Timeline also needs some ActionScript so the video doesn't start playing before the Play Video button is clicked.

A *with* command lets you target other movie clips or objects on the Stage. The Biji Video movie clip you are designing will eventually be located in the right cel of the Fstrip Artist movie. However, the Fstrip Artist movie ends its motion tween with the right cel barely visible, as shown in Figure 12-12A. You can use a *with* command to send the main Timeline of home.fla back to frame 15, where the right cel is entirely visible. You will later label frame 15 "Video" for further clarity when you configure home.fla to load the video at the end of this lesson, as shown in Figure 12-12B.

FIGURE 12-12A
The movie clip with the right cel barely visible

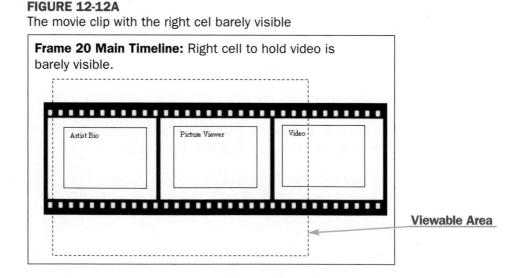

FIGURE 12-12B
The movie clip with the right cel entirely visible

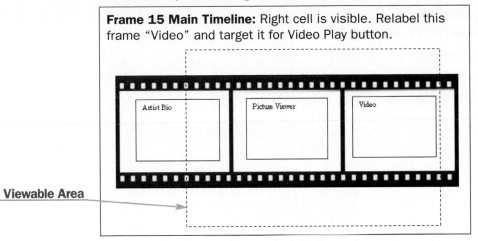

Frame 15 Main Timeline: Right cell is visible. Relabel this
frame "Video" and target it for Video Play button.

Viewable Area

STEP-BY-STEP 12.5

Creating ActionScript to Control Video Playback

1. Insert a layer above the Buttons layer and rename it **Actions**.

2. Select the first frame of the Actions layer and, on the Property inspector, label it **StartVideo**. This will
   create a target frame for the preloader developed later in this lesson.

3. Click on the **Actions** title bar to expand the Actions panel. In the Timeline Control category of the
   Global Functions category, double-click **stop**. A *stop* action is added to the first keyframe of the Actions
   layer. The video will no longer run automatically.

4. Scroll on the Timeline to the end of the movie clip and insert a keyframe in the last frame of the Actions
   layer, as shown in Figure 12-13.

FIGURE 12-13
Inserting a keyframe in the last frame of the Actions layer

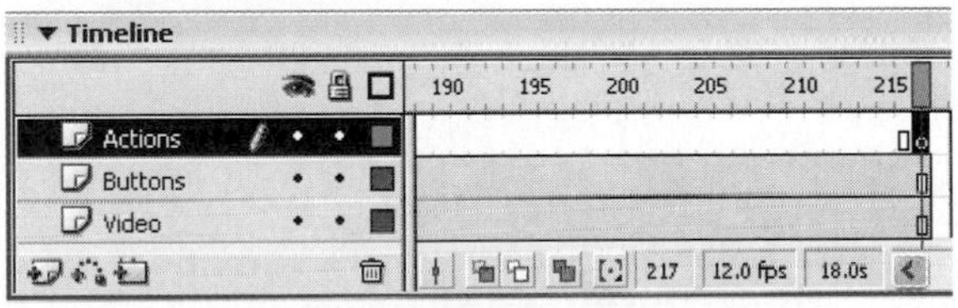

5. With this keyframe selected, double-click **gotoAndPlay** in the Timeline Control category.

6. Key **1**. When the movie reaches the last keyframe, it will go to and play frame 1.

7. Collapse the Actions panel. Select the instance of the **Play Video** button on the Stage in frame 1 of
   the Buttons layer.

8. Expand the **Actions** panel.

STEP-BY-STEP 12.5 Continued

9. Add the following ActionScript to the Script pane, as shown in Figure 12-14:

```
on(release){
gotoAndPlay(2);
with (_root){
gotoAndStop("Video");
}
}
```

FIGURE 12-14
Action Script for the Play Video button

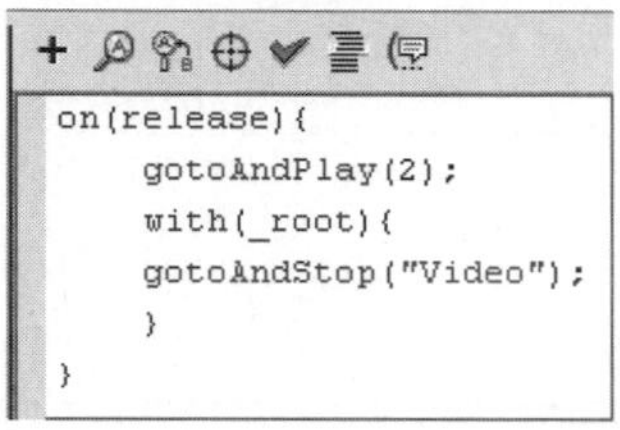

```
on(release){
    gotoAndPlay(2);
    with(_root){
    gotoAndStop("Video");
    }
}
```

10. When the Play Video button is pressed and released, the playhead will go to and play frame 2 and will go to and stop on the frame labeled "Video" in the main Timeline.

> **Note** ✓
> Playing from the Video frame of the main Timeline slides the video back to its resting point, Stage right.

11. Collapse the **Actions** panel.

12. Select frame **2** of the Buttons layer and click the **Stop Video** instance on the Stage.

13. Expand the **Actions** panel and add the following ActionScript to the Script pane, as shown in Figure 12-15:

```
on(release){
gotoAndPlay(1);
with (_root){
gotoAndStop("Video");
}
}
```

FIGURE 12-15
ActionScript for the Stop Video button

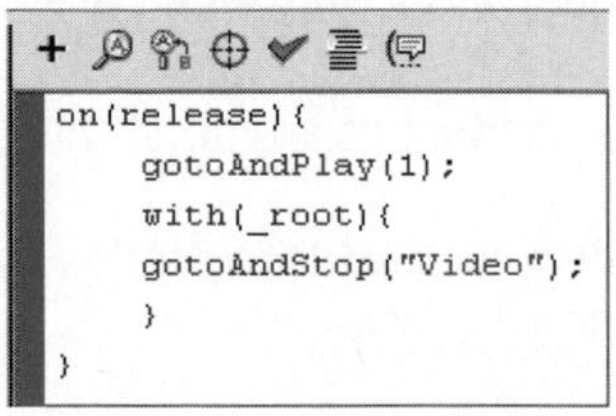

```
on(release){
    gotoAndPlay(1);
    with(_root){
    gotoAndStop("Video");
    }
}
```

14. Collapse the **Actions** panel, save the document and remain in this screen for the next Step-by-Step.

Creating Preloader Controls for a Movie

Because large Flash movies can take a while to load on the Internet (depending on connection and processor speed), many movies use a preloader: a short animation indicating that the main movie is loading. When the main movie is fully loaded (or partially loaded, depending on the designer's preference), the preloader automatically moves to the first frame of the main movie. There are three primary steps for creating a preloader:

■ Create a new scene for the preloader (completed in Step-by-Step 12.6)

■ Insert ActionScript to constantly check the load status of the main movie (completed in Step-by-Step 12.7)

■ Create an animation or load bar indicating that the preloader is working (completed in Step-by-Step 12.8)

Currently, bijivideo.swf is approximately 550 KB—fairly large for a Flash movie. A user trying to view this file over the Internet with a 56K modem would see a black screen for a while, unaware that the video is loading. The following sections walk you through the creation of a preloader for bijivideo. You might also want to create a preloader for home.fla.

A scene in Flash enables designers to organize content thematically. Each scene has its own Timeline and automatically jumps to the next scene when its Timeline or scripting loop ends.

S TEP-BY-STEP 12.6

Creating a New Scene for a Preloader

1. Click the **Window** menu, point to **Design Panels**, and then click **Scene**. The Scene panel opens, with Scene 1 selected.

2. Click the **Add scene** (+) button at the bottom of the panel.

3. Double-click **Scene 2** and rename it **Preloader**, as shown in Figure 12-16.

FIGURE 12-16
Naming the Preloader scene

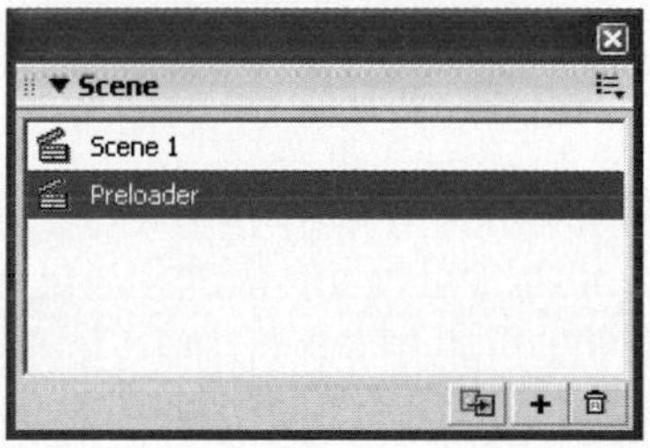

4. Drag the **Preloader** scene above Scene 1 so it will play before Scene 1.

5. Rename Scene 1 **Video**.

STEP-BY-STEP 12.6 Continued

6. Select the **Preloader** scene and close the **Scene** panel. You are presented with a blank Stage in the Preloader scene.

7. Save your work and remain in this screen for the next Step-by-Step.

STEP-BY-STEP 12.7

Writing the ActionScript for the Preloader

1. Double-click **Layer1** and rename it **Actions**.

2. Click the first keyframe of the Actions layer and, on the Property inspector, label it **Start**.

3. Click frame **3** of the Actions layer and insert a Keyframe.

4. With frame **3** selected, expand the **Actions** panel. Frames 1 and 2 will be the beginning of a loop that constantly checks the loading status of the movie. In frame 3 you need to enter the ActionScript that does the checking.

5. Enter the following ActionScript in the Script pane, as shown in Figure 12-17:

    if (_framesloaded >= _totalframes){
    gotoAndPlay("Video", "StartVideo");
    } else {
    gotoAndPlay("Start");
    }

FIGURE 12-17
Final script for the preloader

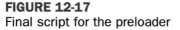

```
if (_framesloaded >= _totalframes){
gotoAndPlay("Video", "StartVideo");
} else {
gotoAndPlay("Start");
}
```

The *gotoAndPlay* action is set below the *if* statement, meaning that if all the frames of the entire movie are loaded, the movie will go to the first frame of the Video scene. The *else* action sets the action for when the *if* condition is not met. The second *gotoAndPlay* action is set for the *else* statement, meaning that if all the frames of the entire movie are not loaded, the scene loops back to the first frame and plays again until all the movie frames are loaded.

> **Did You Know?**
>
> The *if* statement sets up a conditional loop: If something is true, perform action X; if not true, perform action Y. In this case, the *if* statement will check to see if the video is loaded. If the video is loaded, the *if* statement will go to the video scene; if it's not loaded, the *if* statement will continue checking.

6. Collapse the **Actions** panel, save the document, and remain in this screen for the next Step-by-Step.

S TEP-BY-STEP 12.8

Creating an Animated Message for the Preloader

1. Insert a new layer and rename it **Animation**. Drag the Actions layer above the Animation layer.

2. Select frame **1** of the Animation layer, select the **Text** tool, and click on the Stage to create a text box with the following attributes: **Static Text**, **Arial**, **24** pt., white, bold, and left-aligned. Key **Loading Video**, as shown in Figure 12-18. If you cannot see the white text, you might need to change the Background color of your document to black.

FIGURE 12-18
Text for the preloading animation

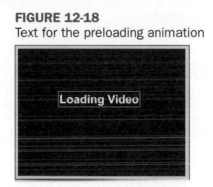

3. Use the **Selection** tool to select the text box.

4. Choose **Convert to Symbol** from the **Modify** menu.

5. Name the new symbol **Loading Text**, set its Behavior to **Movie clip**, and then click **OK**.

6. On the Align panel, toggle the **To stage** button to **On** and click **Align horizontal center** and **Align vertical center**.

7. Double-click the **Loading Text** instance on the Stage to enter symbol-editing mode.

   Now create a short animation to remind viewers that the Macromedia Flash Player is loading content.

8. Insert keyframes in frames **2**, **3**, and **4** of Layer1 in the Loading Text symbol.

9. Click frame **2**, select the Text tool, and click in the text box to edit it. Add a period (**.**) at the end of the text, as shown in Figure 12-19.

FIGURE 12-19
Adding a period to the Video Loading text

STEP-BY-STEP 12.8 Continued

10. Click frame **3**, select the Text tool, and click in the text box to edit it. Add two periods (**..**) at the end of the text.

11. Click frame **4**, and click in the text box to edit it. Add three periods (**...**) at the end of the text.

12. Select the **Selection** tool and click elsewhere on the Stage. Press **Enter** (Windows) or **Return** (Macintosh) to play the text animation.

13. On the Information bar, click **Preloader** to exit symbol-editing mode.

> **Note** ☑
>
> The SWF is already stored on your computer. The preloader will play only briefly because the entire SWF doesn't require any load time. If you want to see the preloader in action, you must post the file to the Internet and view it with a fairly slow modem connection.

14. Select **Test Scene** from the **Control** menu. You can see the preloader animation.

15. Close the preview window.

16. Select **Test Movie** from the **Control** menu. Try the Play Video and Stop Video buttons.

17. Close the preview window and save the document. Then close **bijivideo.fla** but leave Flash open for the next Step-by-Step.

Loading bijivideo.swf into the Gallery San Luis Web Site

To load the video into the Featured Artist section of home.fla, you can use the *loadMovie* action, which loads a SWF file into a level or target in a document. To locate the video precisely in the right cel of the Featured Artist section, you will use a blank movie called "Holder" as the target for loading bijivideo.swf.

S TEP-BY-STEP 12.9

Creating a New Right Cel for the Featured Artist Section

1. Open **home.fla**.

2. Make sure the Library panel is open. Duplicate the **Cel Background** movie.

3. Name the new symbol **Video Biji** and click **OK** to save the symbol in the library.

4. Double-click the **Video Biji** symbol in the library to enter symbol-editing mode.

> **Note** ☑
>
> If you had problems with the previous lesson, ask your instructor for the **home8.fla** sample solution file. Once you open this file, save it as **home.fla** in your **build_GallerySanLuis** folder and proceed with this lesson.

STEP-BY-STEP 12.9 Continued

5. Add a new layer above the Background layer and rename it **Video**.

6. Save the document and remain in this screen for the next Step-by-Step.

S TEP-BY-STEP 12.10

Creating a Blank Movie to Hold bijivideo.swf

1. Select **New Symbol** from the **Insert** menu.

2. Name the symbol **Holder**, set the Behavior to **Movie clip**, and then click **OK**. The Holder symbol is inserted in the library and you are in its symbol-edit mode.

3. Double-click the **Video Biji** movie clip symbol to enter its symbol-editing mode.

4. Select the first frame of the Video layer and drag an instance of the **Holder** movie clip symbol onto the Stage. A white dot with a center cross appears on the Stage on the Video layer.

5. On the Property inspector, give the instance of Holder the instance name **holder**. The movie clip can now be targeted as a holder in ActionScript.

6. Use the Selection tool to drag the **Holder** instance to the upper-left corner of the background rectangle. Zoom in to locate the instance precisely in the corner, as shown in Figure 12-20.

FIGURE 12-20
Aligning the Holder movie clip instance

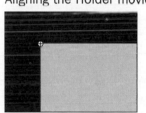

7. Insert a new layer above the Video layer and rename it **Actions**.

8. Click the first frame of the Actions layer and expand the **Actions** panel.

STEP-BY-STEP 12.10 Continued

9. Make sure the **Global Functions** category is expanded and click the **Browser/Network** subcategory to expand it.

10. Double-click the **loadMovie** command. Key **"bijivideo.swf","holder"** as shown in Figure 12-21.

> **Note** ☑
>
> Both home.fla and bijivideo.swf must be in the same folder (build_GallerySanLuis) for this URL in step 10 to work.

FIGURE 12-21
Configuration for the loadMovie command

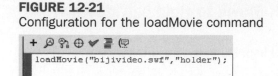

```
loadMovie("bijivideo.swf","holder");
```

11. Save the document and collapse the **Actions** panel. Remain in this screen for the next Step-by-Step.

STEP-BY-STEP 12.11

Inserting the Video Biji Movie Clip into the Fstrip Artist Movie Clip and Main Timeline

1. On the Library panel, double-click the **Fstrip Artist** movie clip to enter its symbol-editing mode. (If you zoomed in for the previous Step-by-Step, you will need to zoom out now.)

2. Select the **Right** layer and drag an instance of **Video Biji** onto the Stage. An instance of Video Biji is inserted into the Right layer of the Fstrip Artist movie clip symbol.

3. Line the instance up over the image in the right cel and choose **Cut** from the **Edit** menu. The Video Biji movie clip is placed on the Clipboard.

4. Delete the image in the right cel and then choose **Paste in Place** from the **Edit** menu. The Video Biji movie clip is centered in the right cel.

5. In the Scene Selector at the top of the Stage, click **Scene 1** to return to the main Timeline, as shown in Figure 12-22.

FIGURE 12-22
Using the Scene Selector to return to the main Timeline

6. Click frame **15** of the Artist layer.

STEP-BY-STEP 12.11 Continued

7. On the Property inspector, key **Video** in the Frame Label box, as shown in Figure 12-23. The ActionScript for the Play and Stop Video buttons will now work.

FIGURE 12-23
Naming the Video frame referred to by the Video Stop/Play buttons

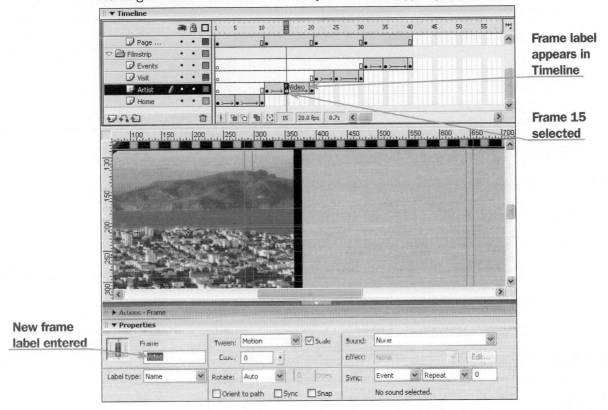

Frame label appears in Timeline

Frame 15 selected

New frame label entered

STEP-BY-STEP 12.11 Continued

8. Test the movie. Go to the Featured Artist section. The Play Video button brings the video cel onto the Stage and plays the video. The Stop Video button returns the video to frame 1 of the video and stops the video, as shown in Figure 12-24.

FIGURE 12-24
The Biji video playing as an integrated unit

9. Close the preview window. Save the document, close it, and exit Macromedia Flash.

SUMMARY

In this lesson, you learned to:

- Import video into Flash.

- Create a new scene for a preloader.

- Develop the ActionScript and loading animation for a preloader.

- Create buttons to control video in Flash.

- Configure ActionScript to control the Timeline of another movie.

- Use the loadMovie command and a blank movie target to bring the video SWF into the main movie.

PUBLISHING A MACROMEDIA FLASH MOVIE

OBJECTIVES

Upon completion of this lesson, you should be able to:

- Make Flash content accessible.
- Add named anchors for browser navigation capabilities.
- Publish a Flash movie for a Web site.

Gallery San Luis Web Site Progress

When you started designing the Gallery San Luis Web site in Lesson 4, you outlined the list of items the client wanted incorporated into the site. You have now finished all the sections for the Gallery San Luis site:

- A Home page that is both appealing and speaks photography.
- A Featured Artist page with a Photo Viewer and featured photographer information.
- Video interviews with the featured artist (optional).
- An animated Map page to indicate where the gallery is located.
- An Events page for requesting tickets for gallery events.
- Sound incorporated on buttons.
- Slick transitions between pages.
- An overall photography metaphor for the site.

What remains to be done is the final work to fine-tune this site. We will make this site accessible to users with a variety of disabilities. We will add named anchors to enhance browser functionality, and we will publish the Flash site that we have created.

Creating Accessibility

Accessibility refers to making Web content that is usable for people with visual, auditory, and other disabilities. For example, you can make images that people can read by using screen-reader software that reads aloud the content of a page. A screen reader, for example, would take the portion of the Events section shown in Figure 13-1 and read it to the user as "Notify me of Gallery San Luis events. Text Field, Name."

FIGURE 13-1
Sample form to be read by a screen reader

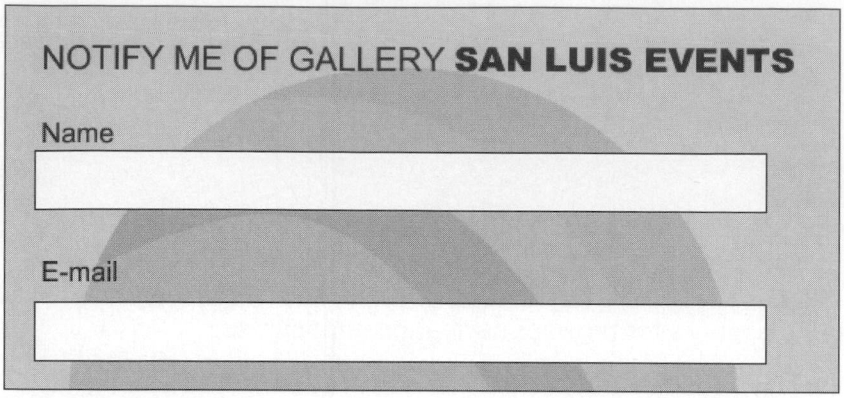

NOTIFY ME OF GALLERY **SAN LUIS EVENTS**

Name

E-mail

This section focuses on making the Macromedia Flash MX 2004 site work with a screen reader.

By default, the following items are accessible in Flash: text, buttons, and movie clips. This means all static, input, and dynamic text boxes will be read in their entirety, and the instance names of movie clips and button instances will be read by the screen reader. However, certain components and arrangements can be difficult for a screen reader to deal with. The following exercises help you find those difficult areas and change them appropriately, making the site as positive an experience as possible for everyone.

Adding Accessibility to a Site

Although it is best to design your site for accessibility in the beginning and add accessibility labels as you build, it is not too late to fine-tune the Gallery San Luis site for accessibility. Before dealing with areas of the site individually, you can configure the entire site for accessibility on the Accessibility panel.

S TEP-BY-STEP 13.1

Adding Overall Accessibility to a Site

1. Start Flash and open the **home.fla** file you worked with in Lesson 12 (or Lesson 11, if you have not completed the optional exercises in Lesson 12).

2. Open the **Edit** menu, and click **Deselect All** if it is available. (If it is not available, it means nothing is selected.) The entire movie is now the object of the Accessibility panel.

Note ✓

If you had problems with the Lesson 12 exercises, ask your instructor for the home8video.fla sample solution file. If you did not complete Lesson 12 and you had problems with Lesson 11, ask your instructor for the home8.fla sample solution file. Once you open the file supplied by your instructor, save it as **home.fla** in your **build_GallerySanLuis** folder and proceed with this lesson.

STEP-BY-STEP 13.1 Continued

3. On the Property inspector, click the **Edit accessibility settings** button, as shown in Figure 13-2.

FIGURE 13-2
The Edit accessibility settings button

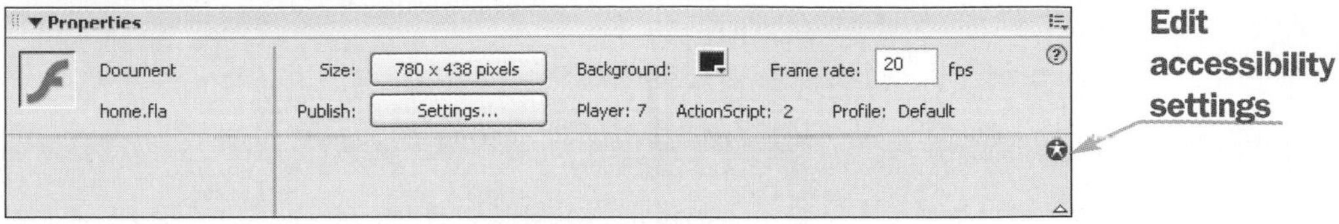

4. In the Accessibility dialog box, check the check boxes described below:

Make Movie Accessible: Exposes the movie to screen readers. The screen reader can read all static text, input text, and dynamic text fields. Buttons and movie clips will be read according to their instance names.

Make child objects accessible: Exposes all sub-movies (such as the Fstrip movies and the Map movie) to the screen reader.

Auto label: Automatically labels buttons with the text that appears inside them.

5. Key **Gallery San Luis Web Site** in the Name box. (When creating your own Web site names, be sure the name you choose is simple and informative.)

6. In the Description box, key **Gallery San Luis is a photography gallery located in San Francisco. It specializes in student and experimental work.** A screen reader will read this description after reading the title of the page.

7. Save the document and remain in this screen for the next Step-by-Step.

Removing Confusing Text from Accessibility

A screen reader can now read all the text boxes in the Home section plus the buttons at the bottom. However, screen readers typically read a page in columns; thus the phone number in the upper-right corner will be read toward the end of the page, potentially confusing a user with a screen reader. You can fix this by changing the Read options on the Accessibility panel for that particular object.

STEP-BY-STEP 13.2

Deactivating Disruptive Text

1. Use the Selection tool to select the phone number in the upper-right corner of the screen.

2. Click the **Modify** menu, and click **Convert to Symbol**. The text must be a symbol to control its accessibility options. Otherwise, the text is automatically read.

3. Name the symbol **phone** and make it a movie clip symbol. Then click **OK**.

STEP-BY-STEP 13.2 Continued

4. On the Accessibility panel, deselect **Make Object Accessible**, as shown in Figure 13-3. (If the Accessibility panel is not already open, click its button on the Property inspector.) This single object is now not accessible; the rest of the site remains accessible.

FIGURE 13-3
Object made inaccessible

To ensure that the phone number can still be read by a screen reader, you can type it into the overall document description.

5. Click in a blank area away from the Stage to deselect everything.

6. In the Description box of the Accessibility panel, edit the text as follows:

Gallery San Luis is a photography gallery located in San Francisco. The phone number is 415-555-2342. The Gallery specializes in student and experimental work.

7. Save the document and remain in this screen for the next Step-by-Step.

Removing "Noise" from an Object

The Visit section could be rather confusing for someone using a screen reader. Because you selected Make Child Objects Accessible, the map instance will actually recite "Alcatraz, Treasure Island" and all the other objects named on the map. Because this is not information the user needs at that particular moment, this is referred to as a "noisy" object. To avoid this confusion, you can suppress the child objects just for the Map movie clip and give it a general description.

STEP-BY-STEP 13.3

Fixing a "Noisy" Object

1. Click frame **30** of the Visit layer.

2. Double-click the **Fstrip Visit** movie clip instance to enter symbol-editing mode.

3. Select the **Map** movie clip instance in the center cel.

4. On the Accessibility panel, select **Make Object Accessible** and then make sure **Make child objects accessible** is not selected. Now the screen reader will ignore the labels on the map.

5. In the name box, key **Animated Map of San Francisco**.

6. In the Description box, key the following, as shown in Figure 13-4:

> **Map moves with directions selected. Refer to the Directions text box for driving directions to the Gallery.**

FIGURE 13-4
Map accessibility settings

7. Close the Accessibility dialog box, save the document, and remain in this screen for the next Step-by-Step.

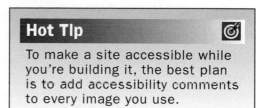

Hot Tip

To make a site accessible while you're building it, the best plan is to add accessibility comments to every image you use.

Adding Named Anchors for Enhanced Browser Functionality

As the design currently stands, a browser would read the entire Gallery San Luis site as one page, even though it has four sections to it, as shown in Figure 13-5. Thus users could not use the browser's bookmark (Favorites) features for specific sections (such as the Visit section) and could not use the browser's Forward and Back buttons.

FIGURE 13-5
Browser sees site as one page

The Back button cannot be used to return to the Home Section from the Featured Artist Section

Favorites can only mark one page for the entire site

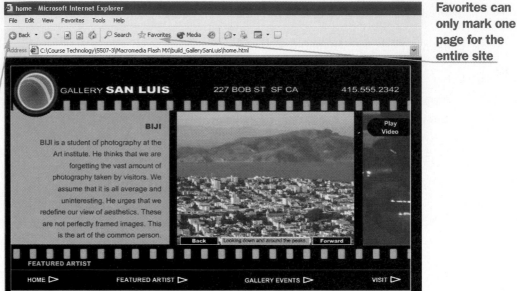

Some of the problems this presents are:

■ Favorites can mark only one page for the entire site.

■ The Back button is not activated to return to the Home section from the Featured Artist section.

To correct this, Flash has a named anchor feature you can use to mark frames on the Timeline as navigation and bookmarking points of reference. You create named anchors on the Property inspector. You must, however, label the frame before naming the anchor.

STEP-BY-STEP 13.4

Creating Named Anchors

1. Click **Scene 1** on the Information bar. You return to the main Timeline.

2. Select frame **10** of the Actions & Labels layer. There is a *stop* action in this frame, indicated by an "a" on the Timeline.

3. On the Property inspector, key **Home** in the Frame Label text box and select **Anchor** as the Label Type, as shown in Figure 13-6.

FIGURE 13-6
Labeling a named anchor

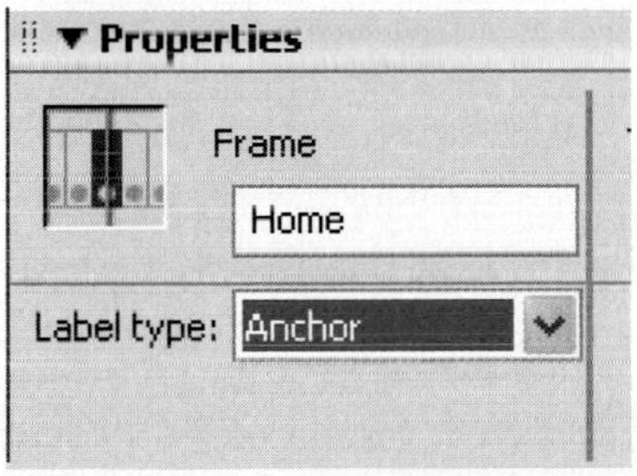

4. Add named anchors to the following frames on the Actions & Labels layer:

Frame 20: **Artist**

Frame 30: **Visit**

Frame 40: **Events**

> **Note** ☑
>
> You have to configure the publish settings before you can test the named anchors.

5. Save the document and remain in this screen for the next Step-by-Step.

Publishing in Flash

Gallery San Luis is Flash content designed to be a Web site. Web sites are viewed through browsers that require HTML, which opens Flash documents by using the Macromedia Flash Player. Flash can create the HTML page for you automatically through the Publish Settings dialog box. In fact, every time you select the Publish Preview and Default commands on the File menu, you create an HTML page to hold your Flash file (SWF).

> **Note** ☑
>
> The Publish command creates a SWF file and an HTML file based on the FLA file. Notice that an additional tab appears when you click HTML.

You might have noticed that the Gallery site displays in the upper-left portion of the Web page when you publish it, as shown in Figure 13-7. In the Publish Settings dialog box, you can configure the HTML page to expand the site in the browser window and activate the named anchors.

FIGURE 13-7
Site stuck in corner of the browser

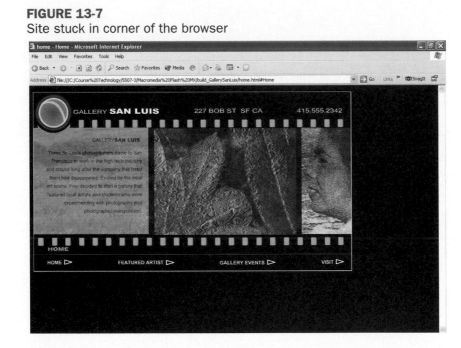

S TEP-BY-STEP 13.5

Configuring the Publish Settings

1. On the **File** menu, click **Publish Settings** to open the Publish Settings dialog box. Make sure the **Flash** and **HTML** check boxes on the Formats tab are selected. Make sure the filename for the HTML file is **index.html.** The dialog box should look like Figure 13-8.

> **Note** ✓
>
> The default name for a home page in most browsers is *index.html.* The *Web Design Skills* special feature at the end of this lesson discusses other file types you can create from a FLA file.

FIGURE 13-8
Initial publish settings

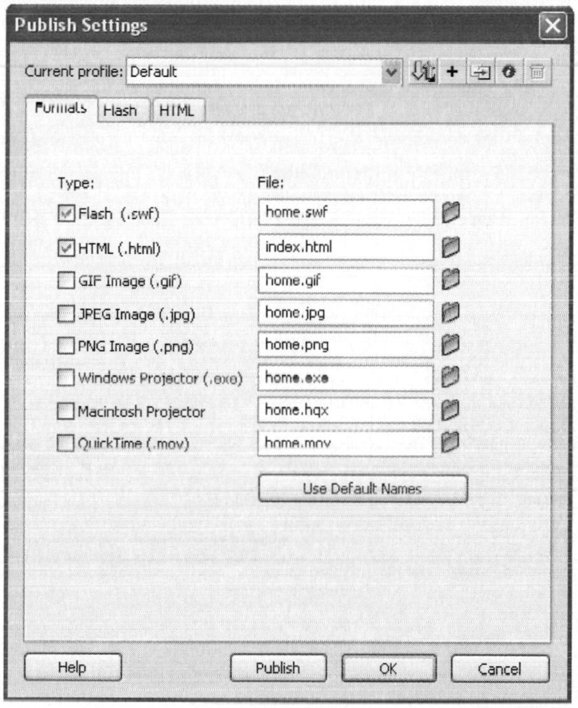

2. Click the **Flash** tab at the top of the dialog box. Set the version to **Flash Player 7**. (The HTML generated by Flash contains scripting to automatically route users to the Macromedia Flash Player download page if they don't have the latest version.) Confirm that ActionScript setting is **ActionScript 2.0**. Confirm that JPEG quality is set to **80**.

> **Note** ✓
>
> The quality setting of 80 is a nice balance between quality and size of JPEG files. You might want to play with increasing and decreasing this number and noting the resulting file size and quality changes.

STEP-BY-STEP 13.5 Continued

3. Confirm that the sound is set to **MP3**, **16 kbps**, **Mono**. See Figure 13-9 for reference. (Again you might want to increase or decrease the sound quality and check out the resulting file size. You don't have any Audio Stream in the Gallery San Luis site. All the sounds are Event sounds, which means they play independently of the Timeline.)

FIGURE 13-9
Flash publish settings

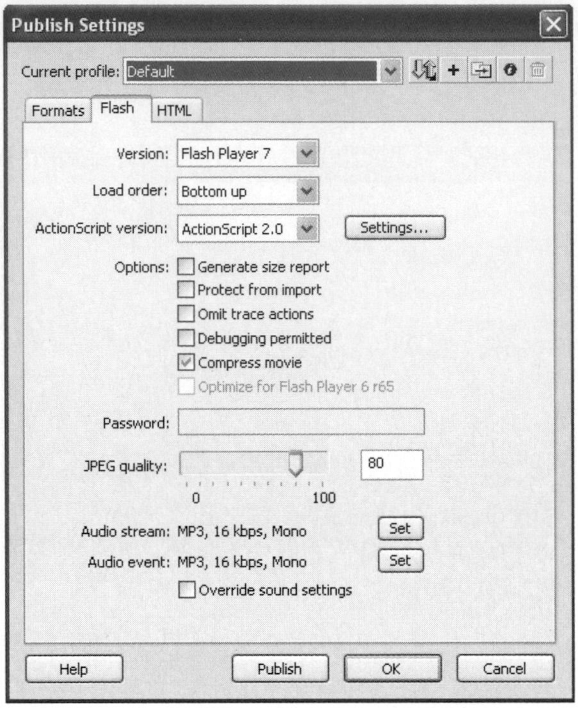

STEP-BY-STEP 13.5 Continued

4. Click the **HTML** tab. Change the Template to **Flash with Named Anchors**. (This configures the HTML to note the named anchors you inserted for each section.) Select **Percent** from the Dimensions list box and confirm that the Width and Height are both **100** (the movie will automatically resize to fill the browser window). Set the Flash alignment to **Center** for both Horizontal and Vertical. When you finish, the dialog box should look like Figure 13-10. Click **OK**.

> **Note** ☑️
>
> Because you configured the movie for 800 x 600 or 1024 x 768 resolution monitors, using percentage dimensions will work well. If the movie dimensions vary greatly from the resolution settings, the percentage dimensions can cut off part of your movie.

FIGURE 13-10
HTML publishing settings

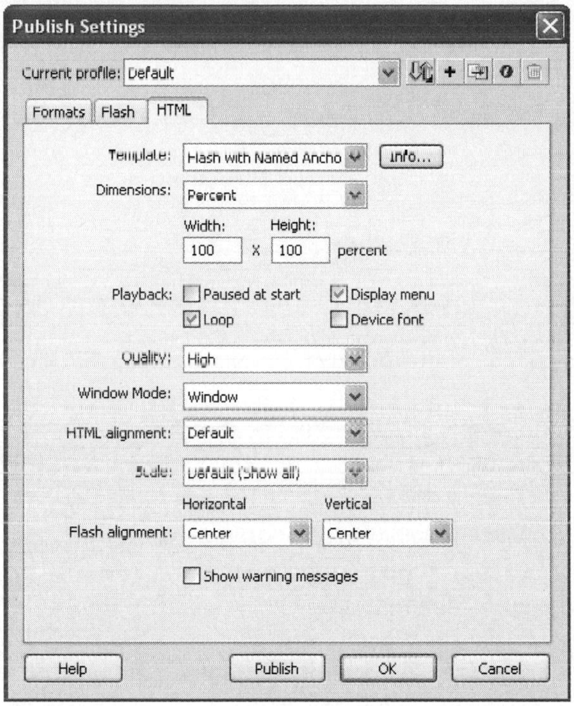

```
Publish Settings                                    [X]

Current profile: Default          [v] [🔧] [+] [🔃] [❸] [🗑]

[ Formats ] [ Flash ] [ HTML ]

        Template:  [Flash with Named Ancho v]  [ Info... ]

      Dimensions:  [Percent                   v]

                    Width:       Height:
                    [100]    X   [100]      percent

        Playback:  [ ] Paused at start    [✓] Display menu
                   [✓] Loop               [ ] Device font

         Quality:  [High                       v]

    Window Mode:   [Window                     v]

 HTML alignment:   [Default                    v]

          Scale:   [Default (Show all)         v]

                    Horizontal      Vertical
 Flash alignment:  [Center      v]  [Center      v]

                   [ ] Show warning messages

[ Help ]           [ Publish ]   [ OK ]   [ Cancel ]
```

5. On the **File** menu, point to **Publish Preview**, and then click **Default - (HTML)**.

STEP-BY-STEP 13.5 Continued

6. View the site in your browser (your browser window will open automatically). The site fills the screen, as shown in Figure 13-11.

FIGURE 13-11
Gallery San Luis published to 100% of the screen

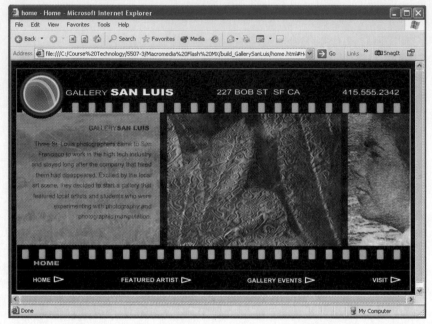

7. Shrink or expand the browser window and notice that the site shrinks or expands with it.

8. Test the buttons, form, and animated Visit page. Notice that you can use the browser's Forward and Back buttons and bookmark features.

9. Click the **View** menu, and then click **Source**. Note the HTML that directs users to *www.macromedia. com/go/getflashplayer* if they don't have the correct Flash Player version.

10. Close the source document and the browser. Return to Flash and save the document.

> **Note** ☑
>
> You would post the HTML and SWF files to the Internet to create the site. The FLA files remain local. You would also post the images folder (and any movies or other files loaded into the site) to the Internet because some photos are being dynamically pulled from that folder. In general, concentrating all pages on the Web site in one Flash document means you have significantly fewer files in your site folder.

STEP-BY-STEP 13.5 Continued

11. Navigate to the **build_GallerySanLuis** folder and note the file sizes of the HTML, SWF, and FLA files, as shown in Figure 13-12.

FIGURE 13-12
File sizes for HTML, SWF, and FLA files

index.html	1 KB	HTML Document
home.swf	296 KB	Flash Movie
home.fla	2,720 KB	Flash Document

12. Switch back to Flash, close the document, and exit Flash.

Web Design Skills

OTHER TYPES OF FILES GENERATED BY A FLA

The Formats tab of the Publishing Settings dialog box indicates many types of files you can generate from a FLA file. The illustration below should give you an idea of their variety and ways to create them.

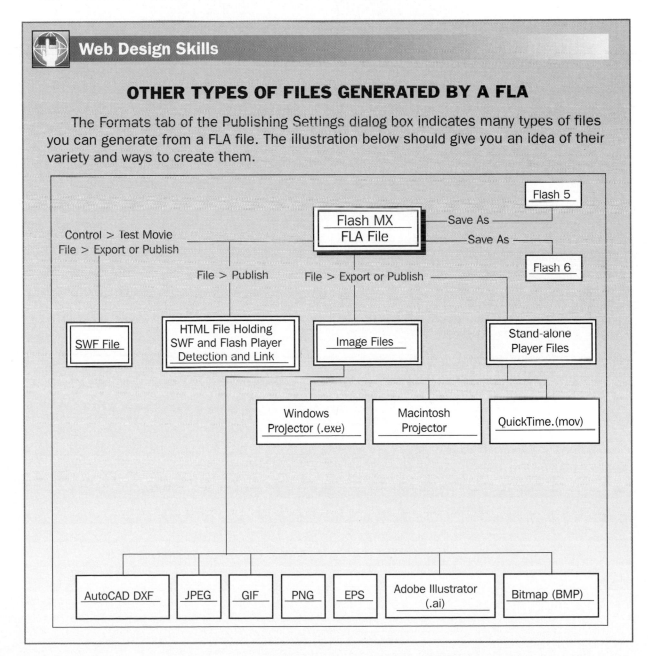

SUMMARY

In this lesson, you learned to:

- Make Flash content accessible.
- Add named anchors for browser navigation capabilities.
- Publish a Flash movie for a Web site.

MACROMEDIA FREEHAND MX

Project

INTRODUCING MACROMEDIA FREEHAND MX

OBJECTIVES

Upon completion of this lesson, you should be able to:

- Create a logo by using tools available in FreeHand.
- Create pages in which to place your graphics.
- Use page rulers and guides.
- Use panels and panel groups.

Introduction to FreeHand

This lesson is the first step to becoming familiar with the Macromedia FreeHand MX user interface and some of its basic features. We will discuss opening files; reestablishing links; choosing toolbars, guides, and views; selecting objects; and using panels—and then use these tools to create a simple logo.

STEP-BY-STEP 1.1

Getting Started

1. Launch FreeHand. Click the **File** menu, and then click **Open**. Select the **Andes_Storyboard.fh11** file from the data files supplied for this project, and click **Open** (Windows) or **Choose** (Macintosh). If you see a message saying that the original printer is not available, select a new printer, and click **OK**.

   This document contains artwork—both vector graphics and placed TIFF images created in programs such as Photoshop. Whenever you open a FreeHand document, if the links to images within the document are broken, you will be prompted to locate (or re-link) these images on your hard drive. Broken links can happen when the FreeHand file or images are moved, renamed, or copied to a different folder or hard drive.

2. If you have broken image links, you will see the Locate File window. Locate the folder named **L1_Images** in the data files for this project, and open it.

3

3. Navigate to find and select **USA.jpg**. You can tell this is the file FreeHand is looking for because the filename is indicated in the title bar of the Locate File window (Windows) or at the top of the Locate File window (Macintosh).

4. Select Search the Current Folder for Missing Links, also found at the bottom of the window, and then click **Open** (Windows) or **Choose** (Macintosh). Remain in this window for the next Step-by-Step.

> ### Did You Know?
>
> With FreeHand, you can search for missing links in a folder. This handy option prevents the need for you to re-link every placed image in your document individually.

Now that the document is open, let's examine the interface. At the top of the screen you will see the title bar and the menu bar. These two items are always visible in your display window.

If you don't see the Main toolbar just below the menu bar, select the Window menu, point to Toolbars, and then select Main. The Main toolbar contains a series of icons or buttons that perform various functions in FreeHand. You can open and save documents, print documents, open panels, and work with objects. Some of the icons on these buttons are very similar to icons you have seen in other programs. Figure 1-1 displays the basic default tools available on the toolbar. You will use some of these buttons later when you examine other parts of FreeHand.

> ### Note
>
> Placing the mouse over a button triggers a tooltip, a pop-up description of the button's function. Try reviewing some of the descriptions as you continue with this project.

FIGURE 1-1
The Main toolbar and the Text toolbar

Title bar

Menu bar

Main toolbar

Text toolbar

Toolbars, Rulers, and Guides

If you look at Figure 1-1 again, you will see that it also shows the Text toolbar below the Main toolbar. This toolbar does not open by default but is one you might find yourself using a great deal if you need to add and edit text. To display the Text toolbar, click the Window menu, point to Toolbars, and then click Text.

At the bottom of your FreeHand window you will see the Status toolbar (Windows) similar to that shown in Figure 1-2. (The same information can be found in the lower-left corner of the Document window on Macintosh systems.) This toolbar, which appears by default, provides information concerning the current document and enables you to make adjustments to the document. If your display does not show the Status toolbar, you can open it by choosing Toolbars from the Window menu and then clicking Status.

FIGURE 1-2
The Status toolbar

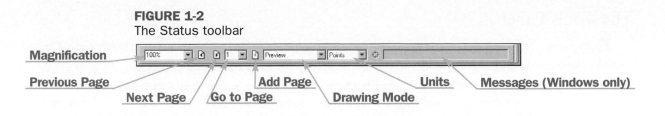

Two other tools you might find useful as you work are the rulers and the guides. These can help you accurately place objects on your page and also align multiple objects. Rulers appear at the edges of your FreeHand Document window—one along the top of the Document window and one along the left side of the Document window. To display the rulers, click the View menu, point to Page Rulers, and click Show. The rulers show the current default unit of measurement, found on the Status toolbar (Windows) or in the lower-left corner of the Document window (Macintosh).

Guides are blue lines that appear to be on the document itself, but, like rulers, they do not print. You can choose to view guides or to hide them by using a toggle available through the View menu. To display or hide guides in a document, click the View menu, point to Guides, and then click Show. (You can also show and hide guides by using the Layers panel, which you will learn about later in this project.) Once you have placed guides in your document, you can choose to snap objects to those guides. You can also toggle this feature on and off through the View menu. To toggle snapping to guides on or off, click the View menu, point to Guides, and then click Snap to Guides. Snapping enables you to automatically align an object to a guide. When an object is dragged near a guide, it magically "snaps" and sticks to the guide for exact placement.

STEP-BY-STEP 1.2

Using Page Rulers and Guides

1. Click the **View** menu, point to **Page Rulers**, and then click **Show** to display the page rulers.

2. To change the unit of measurement of the document to pixels, click the **Units** pop-up menu on the Status toolbar and choose **Pixels**.

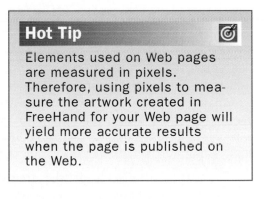

Hot Tip

Elements used on Web pages are measured in pixels. Therefore, using pixels to measure the artwork created in FreeHand for your Web page will yield more accurate results when the page is published on the Web.

3. Move the pointer over the left or top ruler. Click and drag out onto the page to create a guide. (You must move the guideline over a document page. You cannot place it in the blank areas around the document pages.) When the guide is in the location you want, release the pointer. Note the light blue line that has been added in the location where you release. Also note the other light blue lines already placed in this document.

4. Click the **Edit** menu, and then click **Undo Add Guide** to remove the guide you added. Remain in this screen for the next Step-by-Step.

The Tools Panel

Now take a look at the Tools panel shown in Figure 1-3. If the Tools panel is not visible, you display it by clicking the Window menu and then Tools.

As the name implies, the *Tools panel* is the main working set of tools in FreeHand. You can use the tools to create, select, and modify graphics; create and edit text; zoom in and out; select and trace placed bitmap graphics; complete perspective renderings; and more. FreeHand offers three tools for selecting objects: the Pointer tool, the Subselect tool, and the Lasso tool.

FIGURE 1-3
The Tools panel contains tools used to select, manipulate, and create objects

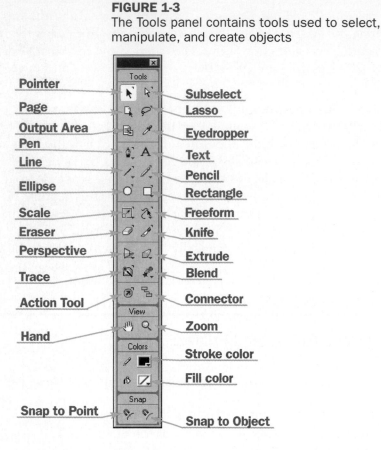

You can use the Pointer tool to select items by clicking on them. When an object is selected, you will see control points at the corners of the object. You can also select multiple objects or groups by dragging the pointer over a region of the document. When you do this, a dotted-line rectangle called a *marquee* appears as you drag. Any objects within the marquee when you release the pointer will be selected. Objects or groups must fall completely inside the marquee to be selected.

With the Subselect tool (the arrow to the right of the Pointer tool), you no longer select objects as a group but rather select only parts of objects. The Subselect tool lets you select objects within groups or within composite paths.

The Lasso tool allows you greater flexibility in the objects you select. You can use the Lasso tool to select objects or groups within a free-form selection area. As with the Pointer tool, objects or groups must fall completely inside the marquee to be selected.

S TEP-BY-STEP 1.3

Selecting Objects

1. Select the **Pointer** tool at the top of the Tools panel.

2. Experiment by selecting various objects on the page. Move the pointer over an object or group and click to select.

3. Experiment with selecting a group of items:
   a. Place the pointer at one of the corners of the objects you want to select.
   b. Hold down and drag the mouse to form a marquee around the objects you want to select.
   c. When all objects you want selected are within the marquee, release the pointer. All the objects within the marquee are selected and have control points or handles.

4. Select the **Subselect** tool, which is the hollow arrow to the right of the Pointer tool. Again experiment with selecting objects on the page.

5. Select the **Lasso** tool from the Tools panel. Experiment by drawing a lasso around an object to select it. Try this several times—the Lasso can take a while to get used to. Remain in this screen for the next Step-by-Step.

Changing the View of a Document

While you are working on a design, you might need to change the magnification of the Document window so you can see an area more clearly or to get a better look at details. You can do this quickly by using the Magnification pop-up menu on the Status toolbar in the lower-left corner of the window. You can select percentages to view. You can also select from fixed items such as Fit Page, which always adjusts the view so that the current page fits in the Document window, or Fit All, which shows all the pages in the current document. These magnification options are also available from the View menu.

Additionally, you can use the Zoom tool to change the magnification of the Document window or to zoom in on an object or page. As you use the Zoom tool, the value on the Magnification button changes to reflect the current magnification. You can keep clicking on the document to zoom in more and more, to a maximum of 256x.

If you want to move to a different area of the page after you have zoomed in, you don't have to zoom out and then zoom back in on a different object. Instead, you can use the panning feature. With the Zoom tool still selected, hold down the spacebar. The magnifying glass turns into a hand. Drag while you continue holding down the spacebar. The Document window moves or "pans" to a different area of the page.

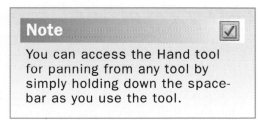

Note ✓

You can access the Hand tool for panning from any tool by simply holding down the spacebar as you use the tool.

STEP-BY-STEP 1.4

Changing the View

1. Click the list arrow on the **Magnification** pop-up menu located on the Status toolbar and choose **Fit All**, as shown in Figure 1-4. The view in the Document window changes to include all the pages in the document.

FIGURE 1-4
The Magnification pop-up menu

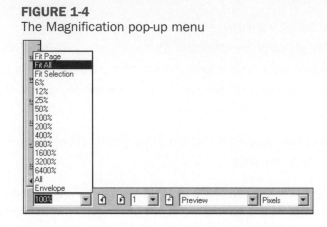

2. Now choose **Fit Page** from the Magnification list. The view in the Document window reverts to show only page 1.

3. Select the **Zoom** tool on the Tools panel. Your pointer now looks like a magnifying glass. Move the pointer until you are over an area you want to see more clearly. Then click once to zoom in on that object.

4. Hold down the spacebar and then drag to experiment with the panning feature.

5. Choose **Fit Page** from the **Magnification** pop-up menu. The view in the Document window once again reverts to include only page 1.

6. Click the **File** menu, and then click **Close**. If a warning appears asking you to save changes to the file, click **No** (Windows) or **Don't Save** (Macintosh). The document closes. Keep FreeHand open for the next Step-by-Step.

Using FreeHand Tools to Create a Logo

Now that you've been introduced to some of the basic features of the FreeHand user interface, you can move on to the next part of this project, creating a logo for Andes Coffee.

When you are creating artwork or pages, you need to keep in mind the size of the medium on which they will be seen. Artwork created for the Web is targeted for display on a monitor, which has a typical resolution of 72 pixels per inch. Not all monitors have this precise 72-pixels-per-inch resolution, however, so you should allow for some variance when sizing your page. If you are designing a page intended for a typical screen size of 640 × 480 pixels, make the actual size smaller (600 × 440) to be sure the page will fill a variety of screens without being cut off.

FreeHand offers a number of predefined sizes such as letter, tabloid, legal, and Web. When designing your Web site, you might want to create a number of pages with a custom size, such as 600 × 440. You can define and save this custom size in the Edit Page Sizes dialog box, which you open from the Page Size pop-up menu in the Document panel, as shown in Figure 1-5.

FIGURE 1-5
The Document panel

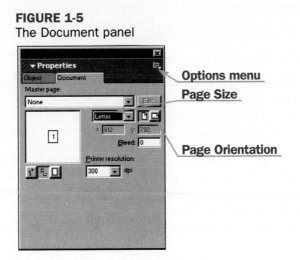

To begin the creation process, you first need to create a new page (in an existing document) where you will draw a logo. To create a new page, you use the Document panel, which you open from the Window menu.

STEP-BY-STEP 1.5

Using the Document Panel to Create a New Page

1. Click the **File** menu, click **Open**, navigate to the data files supplied for this project, select **Andes_L1.fh11**, and click **Open** (Windows) or **Choose** (Macintosh).

2. Make sure **Fit All** is selected on the **Magnification** pop-up menu on the Status toolbar to display all the pages in the document.

3. Make sure the units are set to pixels (on the Status toolbar).

4. If necessary, click the **Window** menu, and then click **Document** to display the Document panel shown in Figure 1-5.

5. On the Document panel, open the page size list and choose **Edit**. The Edit Page Sizes dialog box opens.

6. Click **New** to define a new custom page size. A new page size is created with the name SizeX (where X is the number of the custom size you are defining). For example, if you have two custom sizes already defined, the name would be Size3.

STEP-BY-STEP 1.5 Continued

7. In the Page Size text box, select the existing text if necessary and then key **Flash 600x440**, replacing the Size*X* page size. In the x box, select the current size and then key **600** to define the width of the page; in the y box, select the current size and then key **440** to define the height. Then click **Close**. The Edit Page Sizes dialog box closes.

8. Create a new page using your new custom page size:

   a. Click the Options menu control in the upper-right corner of the Document panel to display the Options menu, and choose **Add pages**. The Add Pages dialog box opens.

   b. Choose **Flash 600x440** from the page size list. Click **OK** to add the new page.

> **Note** ☑️
>
> The new page should be in landscape orientation, with the width greater than the height. If your new page is not, click the Landscape button next to the page size list to rotate the page to landscape.

9. Click the **View** menu, and then click **Fit to Page** to zoom and center your new page in the Document window. The newly created page fills the view.

10. Click the **File** menu, and then click **Save As**. Name the file **Andes_L1** followed by your initials, and then click **Save**. (If you're using Windows, the extension .fh11 will be added automatically.)

Other FreeHand Panels

Panels and panel groups are an essential part of the FreeHand user interface. Panels are organized into panel groups. For example, the Properties panel group contains the Object panel and the Document panel. You can expand or collapse a panel group by clicking its name.

To switch between panels, open a panel group and then click the tabs at the top of the panel group. You can also open the desired panel from the Window menu. As you continue with this project, examine the various panels you use while you edit the selected objects.

The Object panel is one of the most important panels you'll work with. It displays properties for a selected object or objects. You'll use it for most drawing tasks, and you'll use it to set the style of your text. The top half of the panel displays a list of properties, such as stroke, fill, and effect, applied to a selected object. The bottom half of the panel changes to display attributes for the selected property in the list above it.

Now that you have created a blank page with the appropriate dimensions and layout, you will create the logo for Andes Coffee that will be used on the Web site.

S TEP-BY-STEP 1.6

Creating a Logo

1. Create one vertical guide (by dragging from the vertical ruler). Position the vertical guide at about **160 pixels**, using the horizontal ruler to determine the position. *Hint:* You may want to use the Magnification pop-up menu to get a better view of the page and the ruler.

STEP-BY-STEP 1.6 Continued

2. Select the **Rectangle** tool from the Tools panel.

3. Press and hold the **Shift** key and draw a square in the center of the page. Release the pointer and then release the Shift key. (Don't worry about size or color at this point; you will be changing the size in the next step and color a little later.)

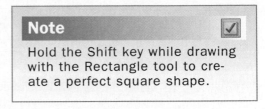

Note ☑

Hold the Shift key while drawing with the Rectangle tool to create a perfect square shape.

4. Click the **Object** tab on the Properties panel group; you will use the Object panel to edit the size of the first element in the logo. The panel switches to show the attributes for the selected object, similar to those shown in Figure 1-6.

FIGURE 1-6
The Object panel

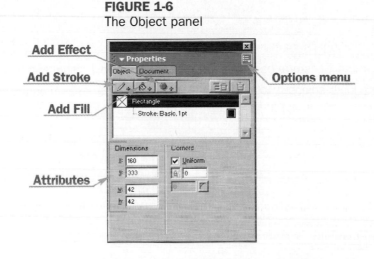

5. On the Object panel, under Dimensions, replace the existing values with **42** for the width (w) and **42** for the height (h). Then press **Enter** (Windows) or **Return** (Macintosh).

6. Make sure Snap to Guides is turned on. (Click the **View** menu, point to **Guides**, and click **Snap to Guides**—there should now be a check mark next to this menu item.)

Note ☑

The specific dimensions in your Object panel will vary from those shown in Figure 1-6 depending on the size of the square you drew and where you placed it.

7. Select the **Pointer** tool from the Tools panel. Click on the square to be sure it is selected and then move the square toward the guide you created earlier. (When a shape has no fill, you must click on one of the edges of the object to move it.) Move the square until the left side touches the vertical guide. Notice that as the square approaches the guide, it snaps into place.

STEP-BY-STEP 1.6 Continued

You now have one square exactly 42 pixels wide by 42 pixels high, snapped to a vertical guide, as shown in Figure 1-7.

FIGURE 1-7
A single square positioned by a vertical guide

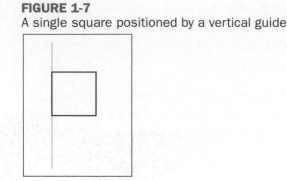

8. Create four additional squares:

   a. Make sure the Transform panel is open. (Click the **Window** menu, and then click **Transform**.)

   b. With the square selected, locate **Move distance** on the Transform panel, as shown in Figure 1-8. Key **42** in the x field and **0** in the y field. In the Copies field, key **4** and then click **Move**.

FIGURE 1-8
With the Move feature, you can precisely move or copy objects along the x (left to right) and y (up and down) axes

Click here to see
Move Distance

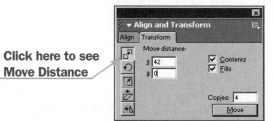

9. Click the **Save** button to save your changes. Remain in this screen for the next Step-by-Step.

The Copies option enables you to duplicate the Transform operation by the specified number; by entering 4, you moved and copied the square four times. You should now have five identical squares in a row, as shown in Figure 1-9.

FIGURE 1-9
Five identical squares adjacent to each other

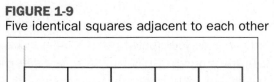
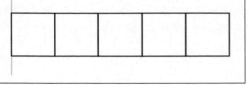

Adding Color

To add color to your squares, you use the Swatches panel shown in Figure 1-10. Color applied to a closed path or text is called a *fill*. Color applied to the outline of a path or text is called a *stroke*. You can change or remove a selected object's stroke and fill colors by using the Swatches panel. The Swatches panel is part of the Assets panel group. It can be opened from the Window menu.

FIGURE 1-10
The Swatches panel stores, tracks, and organizes colors

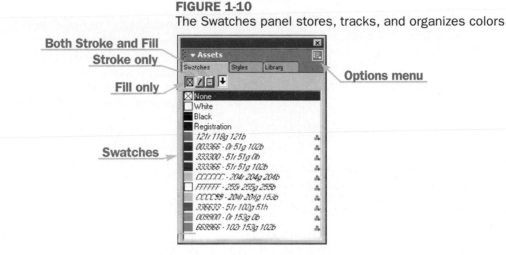

S TEP-BY-STEP 1.7

Adding Color to Your Logo

1. Open the Swatches panel by clicking the **Window** menu and then **Swatches**.

2. Select the first square (by clicking on one of its edges).

3. On the Swatches panel, select the **Fill** selector and then click on the color name **336633 - 51r 102g 51b**. This sets the fill to this color. Don't worry about the stroke; you will change that later.

4. Select the second square and set the fill color to **009900 - 0r 153g 0b**.

5. Select the third square and set the fill color to **669966 - 102r 153g 102b**.

6. Select the fourth square and set the fill color to **CCCC99 - 204r 204g 153b**.

> **Note** ☑
> The colors you need for building the logo are already present on the Swatches panel. These colors are also Web safe. Not all colors are reproducible on the Web. FreeHand offers a *library* or set of colors that are reproducible on the Web.

STEP-BY-STEP 1.7 Continued

7. Select the fifth square and set the fill color to **White**. All five squares should now have color, with the exception of the last square, which you set to White.

Now that you have set the fill color on all the squares, you will set the stroke width and stroke color by using the Object panel.

8. Select all five squares. To do this, select the first square, hold down the **Shift** key, and then select the remaining four squares.

9. Set the stroke width by using the Object panel:

a. In the top half of the Object panel, select the **Stroke** property to display the stroke attributes, as shown in Figure 1-11.

b. In the bottom half of the Object panel, open the width pop-up menu and select the value of **1pt** to apply a stroke width of 1 point to all five squares.

> **Did You Know?**
>
> Use the Shift key while selecting objects to select multiple objects. When multiple elements are selected, applied changes affect each element. You can also select multiple elements by using the Pointer tool and creating a marquee around the objects or by using the Lasso tool.

FIGURE 1-11
The Object panel with the Stroke property selected

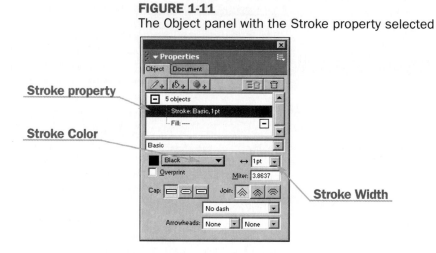

Stroke property

Stroke Color

Stroke Width

10. In the bottom half of the Object panel, open the stroke color pop-up menu and choose the color **333300 - 51r 51g 0b**. All five squares have different fill colors but now have the same stroke color, as shown in Figure 1-12.

FIGURE 1-12
The squares have different fill colors but the same stroke color and stroke width

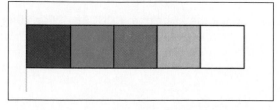

STEP-BY-STEP 1.7 Continued

11. Press the **Tab** key to deselect all the squares. (You can also deselect objects by simply clicking anywhere in the Document window and not on another object.)

12. Click the **File** menu, and then click **Save** to save your changes to the document. Remain in this screen for the next Step-by-Step.

Note ✓

You can also change the stroke and fill colors of a path by using the Stroke, Fill, or Both selectors on the Swatches panel. Simply click on any selector and then click a color. For example, with a path selected, if you click on the Stroke selector and then choose a color, the stroke of the selected path changes to that color.

Adding Text

To add text to the logo, you use the Text tool. When you select the Text tool in the Tools panel, the mouse pointer turns from an arrow or pointer to a vertical bar with short horizontal bars at the top and bottom (an I-beam). Click once on the page to begin a text block. Before you key any text, you should select an appropriate font. You do this from the Object panel or the Text toolbar, which you view by clicking the Window menu, pointing to Toolbars, and clicking Text. Select the font you want from the Font Name pop-up menu on the Text toolbar.

Once you have a block of text, you can select the text and use the Object panel to modify text attributes. There are five type attribute buttons on the left side of the bottom half of the panel. You can use these to open five sets of options to apply precise type specifications to characters, lines of text, paragraphs, and entire text blocks.

STEP-BY-STEP 1.8

Adding Text to the Logo

1. Select the **Text** tool from the Tools panel.

2. In the Properties panel group, select the **Object** tab to access the Object panel.

3. On the page, click to create a text box above the five squares. The pointer automatically reverts to a flashing pointer, and a vertical bar appears where you clicked. This bar indicates where the text will appear when you begin. The Text property should already be selected for you, displaying the text options shown in Figure 1-13. Click the **Character Attributes** button if it is not already selected.

STEP-BY-STEP 1.8 Continued

FIGURE 1-13
The Object panel with the Text property selected

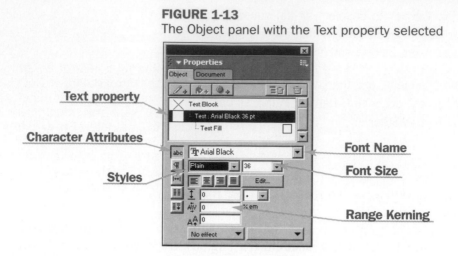

4. In the bottom half of the Object panel, click the **Font Name** list arrow and select the font **Arial Black**. Click the **Style** list arrow and select the style **Plain**. Make sure the **Font Size** is set to **36**. With these attributes, you will be creating Arial Black text with no style (plain) at 36 points in size.

5. Set the color of the text you will key:
   a. On the Object panel, click the **Text Fill** property.
   b. In the bottom half of the Object panel, use the Fill Color pop-up menu to choose the color **333300 - 51r 51g 0b**.

6. Key and position the logo text:
   a. Press the **Caps Lock** key. You want the text to be all uppercase.
   b. Click the **Text** tool again if it is not selected and then key **ANDES**.
   c. Hold down **Ctrl** (Windows) or **Command** (Macintosh) to revert the Text tool to the Pointer. Click once on the text to select the entire text block, and release the key. A selected text block appears in the Document window as an outline with eight control points and a link box (a small square below the lower-right corner).
   d. Click the **Pointer** tool and position it over the text block. Drag toward the guide you created earlier (it may help to change the page magnification). Stop when the left side of the text box snaps to the guide. With the text box snapped to the guide, move the text over the squares until it is centered vertically on the squares, as shown in Figure 1-14.

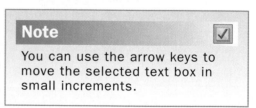

Note ☑

You can use the arrow keys to move the selected text box in small increments.

FIGURE 1-14
The five colored squares and the Andes text aligned to the guide

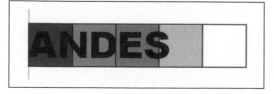

STEP-BY-STEP 1.8 Continued

7. Now you'll format the text so each letter is centered in a square. With the text still selected, locate the **Range Kerning** text box on the Object panel, key **38**, and press **Enter** (Windows) or **Return** (Macintosh). The spaces between the letters increase and the letter "S" should fall on top of the last square.

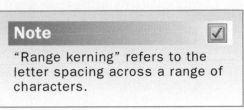

> **Note** ☑
>
> "Range kerning" refers to the letter spacing across a range of characters.

8. With the text still selected, go to the **Transform** panel (the Move subpanel). Key **7** in the x field and **0** in the y field. Make sure Copies is set to **0**. Then click **Move**. The text should move to the right, with each letter centered over a square. Results might vary, however. If the letters do not fall on top of the squares correctly, adjust the Range Kerning to 40. Also try using the left and right arrow keys to move the text.

9. Finally, you need to group all your artwork:

   a. Select the **Pointer** tool and draw a marquee around all the squares and text to select all the artwork.

   b. Click the **Modify** menu, and then click **Group** to group all the objects together as one element. (This allows them to be moved as one and keeps all your spacing and settings accurate.) Your logo is now complete and should look like Figure 1-15.

FIGURE 1-15
The finished logo

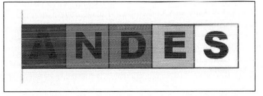

10. Click the **File** menu, and then click **Save**.

11. Close your document and close FreeHand.

> **Extra Challenge** 📐
>
> Explore the other tools on the Tools panel. You will be using some of them later in the curriculum. Try creating more shapes by using the Rectangle tool and the Ellipse tool. Also, set different fill and stroke colors to the objects you draw and set different stroke widths. Review all the panels you used in this project. Choose Using FreeHand on the Help menu for complete, illustrated information about FreeHand and its many features.

SUMMARY

In this lesson, you learned to:

- Create a logo by using tools available in FreeHand.
- Create pages in which to place your graphics.
- Use page rulers and guides.
- Use panels and panel groups.

WORKING IN FREEHAND

OBJECTIVES

Upon completion of this lesson, you should be able to:

- Customize the FreeHand workspace.

- Organize your graphics by using layers.

- Place images.

- Use the Paste Contents (Windows) or Paste Inside (Macintosh) feature.

Customizing the FreeHand Interface

In Lesson 1 you were introduced to the Macromedia FreeHand MX interface and some basic features. You opened a FreeHand document and explored the Tools panel, Main toolbar, and Status toolbar. You also created a new page and constructed a logo for Andes Coffee, using various panels.

In this lesson, you will use some of the more sophisticated tools available in FreeHand. When you've completed this lesson, you will have a better working knowledge of FreeHand that you can then apply in the rest of this course.

Adding Buttons to the Toolbars

The form, location, and contents of all the toolbars are customizable. The Status toolbar is customizable only in Windows.

You can use the Toolbars tab in the Customize dialog box to change what buttons are available on a particular toolbar. The dialog boxes appear slightly different in Windows than on a Macintosh computer, as shown in Figures 2-1 and 2-2, but their functionality is essentially the same. On the left side of the dialog box is the Commands list. This list mirrors the FreeHand menus—with some additional features. To access the commands on a menu, click the plus (+) signs (Windows) or the triangles (Macintosh). On the right side of the dialog box are buttons that represent the commands. Selecting a command from the list highlights the corresponding button. Holding your pointer over any of the buttons causes a tooltip to appear with the name of the tool.

> **Note** ☑
>
> You can also create custom shortcuts by clicking **Edit** on the menu bar and then **Keyboard Shortcuts**. A shortcut is a combination of keys that perform a menu command. Many shortcuts are already established. You can see these when you view menus—the shortcut combinations are listed next to the menu items.

> **Note** ☑
>
> Selecting the menu name displays all the buttons for all the commands in that menu.

FIGURE 2-1
The Toolbars tab in the Customize dialog box (Windows)

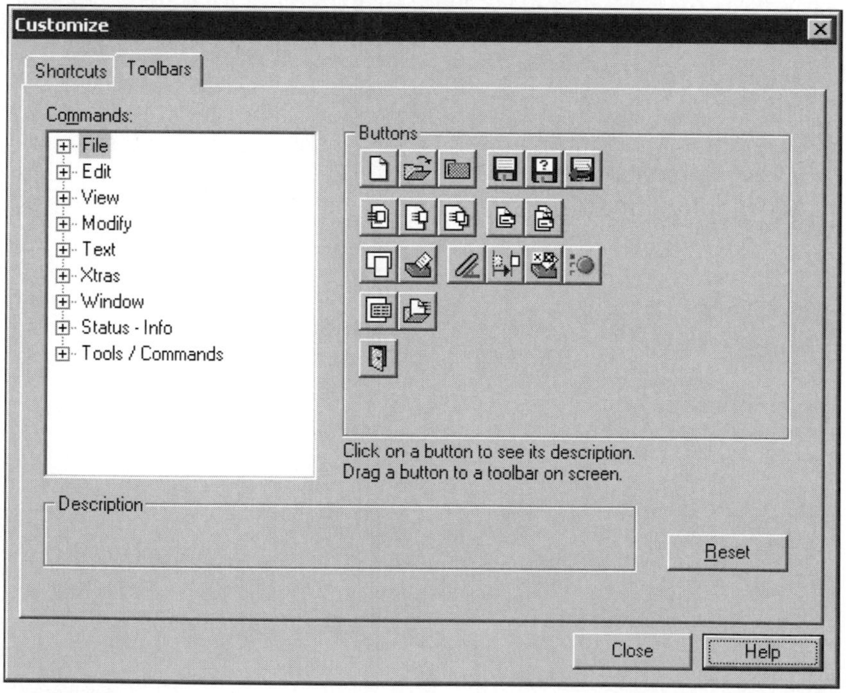

FIGURE 2-2
The Customize Toolbars dialog box (Macintosh)

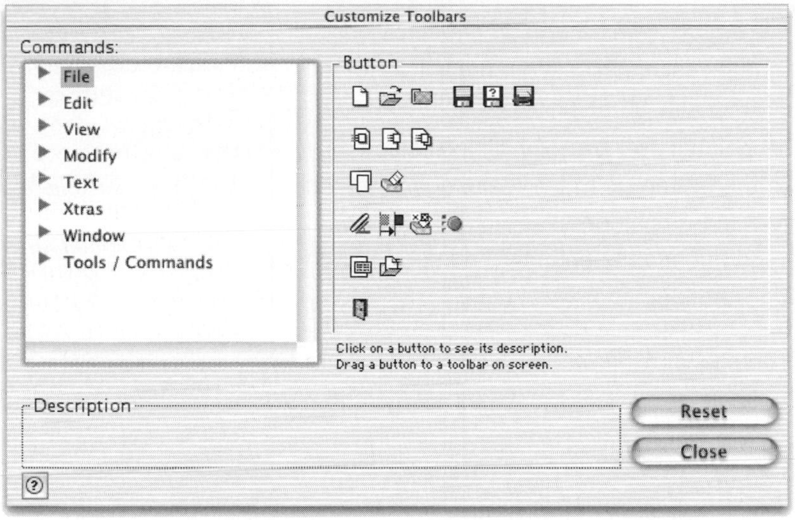

To add a button to a toolbar, you drag the button from the right side of the dialog box to the toolbar where you would like to place it. In Windows, a small gray rectangle appears directly below the pointer as you drag a button. This is your indication that you are moving the button to an acceptable position, such as the Main toolbar. When you release the pointer, the button is added to that position. If you drag the pointer over an area where the button cannot be placed, such as the Document window, a small box with an X appears. If you release the pointer this time, the button is not placed. (Note that if the button was already on the toolbar, it is removed from the toolbar when you release.)

If you're using a Macintosh computer, an outline of the button forms as you drag. If you release the button over an acceptable area, the button is placed. If you release the pointer over an unacceptable area, such as the Document window, the button is not placed (or the button is removed from the toolbar). Unlike in Windows, the pointer gives no indication of whether you are moving a button to a proper position.

STEP-BY-STEP 2.1

Adding Buttons to the Main Toolbar

1. Open the file **Andes_L2.fh11** from the data files supplied for this project. This file has been started for you, so some of the artwork elements are already present. During this project you will add additional artwork elements and pages to prepare the file for the Web.

2. Click the **Window** menu, point to **Toolbars**, and then click **Customize**. The Customize (Windows) or Customize Toolbars (Macintosh) dialog box appears.

3. Later in this lesson you will import an image into your file, so now add a button for the Import command:

  a. In the Commands list, make sure **File** is selected. The buttons in that menu are on the right.

  b. Click the **plus (+)** sign (Windows) or **triangle** (Macintosh) next to the **File** menu in the Commands list. A hierarchical list appears, showing all the commands available under the File menu.

STEP-BY-STEP 2.1 Continued

c. Select the **Import** command (use the scroll bar to move down the list, if necessary). The button for the Import command is now highlighted on the right.

d. Move the pointer over the highlighted Import button. Drag the button up to the Main toolbar on the right side. Find a position near the end of a row of buttons and release the pointer. The Import button is added to the Main toolbar.

4. Close the Customize (Windows) or Customize Toolbars (Macintosh) dialog box. Leave the Andes_L2 file and FreeHand open for the next Step-by-Step.

> **Hot Tip** ⊚
>
> You can also reposition the existing buttons without using the Customize or Customize Toolbars dialog box. Hold down the **Alt** key (Windows) or **Command** key (Macintosh) and drag a button. Disabled or "dimmed" buttons, however, cannot be moved or deleted.

Customizing Toolbars

In addition to customizing the buttons that appear on the toolbars, you can move and reposition the toolbars themselves. They can be turned into resizable floating toolbars or docked to any side of the Document window: left, right, top, or bottom. Toolbars can be moved onto the pasteboard (the area around the document) or even overlaying the document—though this can be bothersome.

To move a toolbar from its docked position, point to the gray area at either end of the toolbar (Windows) or to the toolbar handle at either end of the toolbar (Macintosh) and then drag the toolbar to the area where you would like it to float. As you drag the toolbar, it changes to an outline shape to give you an idea of the size, shape, and location of the floating toolbar. When it is positioned where you want it, release the pointer.

To dock a floating toolbar, you select either the title bar or an empty area of the toolbar and drag. When you start to drag, the toolbar window becomes an outline, and as it approaches the toolbar area, the outline changes shape. This change represents the position of the toolbar when you release it.

STEP-BY-STEP 2.2

Customizing a Toolbar

1. Turn a toolbar into a floating toolbar as follows:

a. Move the pointer over either end of the toolbar.

b. Drag the toolbar out onto the pasteboard or the area beyond the toolbars and release. The toolbar turns into a floating window.

2. Return a toolbar to the toolbar area as follows:

a. Move the pointer over the gray area of a toolbar window, an area without a button, or the title bar.

b. Click and hold as you drag the toolbar back to the top toolbar area. Keep the Andes_L2 file and FreeHand open for the next Step-by-Step.

Using the Layers Panel

Layers help you organize your artwork. You can think of layers as stacked planes or overlays. You can have multiple layers in a document, each containing different artwork elements. The Layers panel shown in Figure 2-3 can be opened from the Window menu.

FIGURE 2-3
The Layers panel

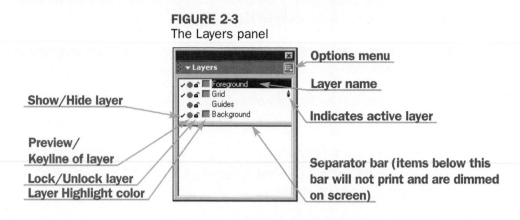

The Layers panel shown in Figure 2-3 is for the Andes_L2.fh11 document with which we are currently working. This file has four layers: Foreground, Grid, Guides, and Background. Each layer has three options you can toggle on or off. The show/hide option is represented by a check mark. To affect the visibility of a layer, move the pointer over the check mark next to the layer. Click the check mark to hide the layer. To unhide the layer, click in the same area and a check mark will reappear.

With the second option (the gray circle), you can view the contents of any layer in either Preview mode or Keyline mode. Preview mode, represented by the gray circle, displays the document as it would print. Keyline mode, represented by a circle outline with a dot (Windows) or an X (Macintosh), displays the artwork as black outlines with no fills, no strokes, and x-boxes for placed images.

You can use the third option to lock the layer to keep changes from occurring on it. The open lock image represents the unlocked state and the closed lock image represents the locked state.

Every FreeHand document has a Guides layer, which you cannot rename or delete. However, the Guides layer can be moved, locked, turned on or off, and set to Keyline mode or Preview mode.

Additionally, you can add layers or change the names of existing layers (except Guides) to help you organize your artwork. You add new layers through the Options menu (the button on the right side of the panel title bar) on the Layers panel. You rename layers by double-clicking to select the current name and then keying the new name.

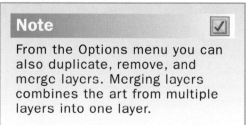

Note ☑

From the Options menu you can also duplicate, remove, and merge layers. Merging layers combines the art from multiple layers into one layer.

It is also important to note that you can change the order of the layers in the Layers panel. The order of the layers affects the visibility of the artwork. Layers at the top of the list will appear on top of layers further down in the list. To change the order of the layers, select the layer you want to move and drag it to a new location in the list. The Layers panel has a separator line. Any layers placed below the separator line will not print and will appear dimmed.

S TEP-BY-STEP 2.3

Using the Layers Panel

1. Continue in the Andes_L2.fh11 file. If the Layers panel is not open, click the **Window** menu, and then click **Layers**. The Layers panel looks like Figure 2-3.

2. To hide the Grid layer, move the pointer over the check mark next to the **Grid** layer and click. On the page, all the artwork that was on the Grid layer disappears.

3. To show the Grid layer, click in the same area. A check mark reappears and all the artwork on the Grid layer reappears.

4. Move the pointer over the small gray circle next to the **Grid** layer and click. The small circle reverts to an outlined circle with a dot in the middle (Windows) or an "x" in the middle (Macintosh), and the artwork on this layer is in Keyline mode.

5. To return the layer to Preview mode, select the circle again.

6. Hide all layers except the Grid layer.

7. Move the pointer over the small open lock icon next to the **Grid** layer and click. The icon changes to a closed lock and the artwork on the layer becomes uneditable. Experiment by trying to select some of the artwork on the page—because the layer is locked, you can't select it.

8. On the Layers panel, open the **Options** menu and click **New** (Windows) or **New Layer** (Macintosh). A new layer is added.

9. Double-click the name of the new layer to highlight the text. Then key **Images** and press **Enter** (Windows) or **Return** (Macintosh). The name of this layer changes to Images.

10. Make all the layers visible.

11. Select the new **Images** layer and drag that layer directly below the Foreground layer.

12. Select the **Grid** layer and drag it to the bottom of the list, but not below the separator line. The artwork on the Grid layer seems to disappear. In reality, the artwork has moved below the artwork on the Background layer. The art on the Background layer is blocking your view.

Hot Tip

You can change the visibility, locking, and view mode of more than one layer at a time by clicking and dragging across a range of layers. You can also change all the layers at one time by holding down **Ctrl** (Windows) or **Option** (Macintosh) and clicking the visibility, lock, or view of one layer.

13. Move the pointer over the check mark next to the **Background** layer and click to hide the layer. The Grid layer artwork is visible again because the Background layer is no longer blocking your view. Drag the Grid layer back to a position just above the Background layer, and make the Background layer visible again. Remain in this screen for the next Step-by-Step.

Working with Images and Lens Fills

In this part of the lesson you create a lens fill, place an image on the page, and paste that image inside an object.

Using Lens Fills

A *lens fill* transforms a selected object into any of six special-effect lenses: Transparency, Magnify, Invert, Lighten, Darken, or Monochrome. Any of these effects will modify the appearance of objects placed under a lens-filled object. For this Step-by-Step, you use a Transparency lens fill to create a see-through effect.

STEP-BY-STEP 2.4

Applying a Lens Fill

1. On the Layers panel, hide all the layers except the Images layer.

2. Now select the **Images** layer, if necessary. This is the layer you will be working on. Notice a small Pen icon next to the layer name. This shows that this layer is the active drawing layer.

3. Select the **Rectangle** tool from the Tools panel and draw a rectangle on the page. Size and position do not matter at this point; you will adjust them next.

4. With the rectangle still selected, go to the Object panel. Key **385** in the x box, **95** in the y box, **232** in the w box, and **212** in the h box. Then press **Enter** (Windows) or **Return** (Macintosh). The rectangle changes size and moves to the correct location on the page.

5. Select the **Stroke** property. In the Stroke options (at the bottom of the Object panel), make sure the stroke type is **Basic**, the stroke color is **Black**, and the stroke width is **1 pt**.

6. Add a Fill property to the rectangle. Click the **Add Fill** button (the button with a paint bucket and a plus sign) at the top of the Object panel.

7. In the Fill options at the bottom of the Object panel:
   a. Choose **Lens** from the **fill type** pop-up menu. If a warning window appears, click **OK**. This warning tells you that any object with a lens fill will automatically print in process colors, or CMYK, which is not really a concern when you're building objects for the Web.
   b. Set the lens type (the menu directly below the fill type pop-up menu) to **Transparency**, if necessary.

STEP-BY-STEP 2.4 Continued

c. Set the Color to **003366 - 0r 51g 102b** (a blue color already present in the color list) and set the Opacity to **65%**. The rectangle fills with a color equivalent to 65% of 003366, a blue-gray color (see Figure 2-4). Remain in this screen for the next Step-by-Step.

FIGURE 2-4
The rectangle filled with a 65% Transparency lens fill of the color 003366

Importing Images into FreeHand

FreeHand can import a variety of images, both vector images (such as other FreeHand files) and raster images (such as Photoshop, GIF, JPEG, and EPS).

S TEP-BY-STEP 2.5

Importing Images

1. With the rectangle still selected, click the **Edit** menu, and then click **Clone**. The Clone command creates an exact copy of a selected element, in the same position, directly on top of the original. Set the fill type to **Basic** and the Stroke Color to **003366 - 0r 51g 102b**.

2. Make sure nothing is currently selected on the page (press **Tab** to deselect everything). Click the **File** menu, and then click **Import**, or click the new **Import** button you created earlier. The Import Document dialog box opens.

3. Navigate to the **L2_Images** folder supplied with the data files for this project. Select the **NA001536b.tif** file and click **Open** (Windows) or **Choose** (Macintosh). When the dialog box closes, the pointer changes to the Import pointer—a backward, upside-down "L." Clicking with this pointer determines where the upper-left corner of the file you are importing will be positioned.

4. Move the pointer to about the center of the page and click to place the image. An image of a mountain appears on the page.

STEP-BY-STEP 2.5 Continued

5. With the newly placed image selected, go to the Object panel and key **235** in the x box, and **–56** in the y box. Then press **Enter** (Windows) or **Return** (Macintosh). The image moves to the position shown in Figure 2-5. Remain in this screen for the next Step-by-Step.

FIGURE 2-5
The mountain image positioned on the page

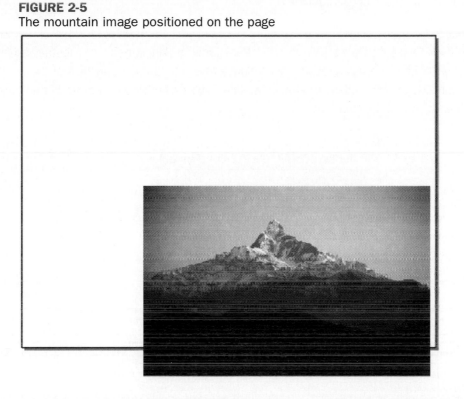

Using Paste Contents

The image you placed in the previous exercise is too large. To fix this, you will mask off the unneeded parts of the image by turning the cloned rectangle into a clipping path. A *clipping path* is a closed path with an object pasted inside. The objects pasted inside a path are called *contents*. Only the portion of the contents that fall within the selected path will be visible on the page; the remainder will be masked (not visible). Images can be pasted inside of, behind, or in front of other images.

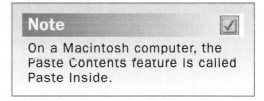

Note ☑

On a Macintosh computer, the Paste Contents feature is called Paste Inside.

S TEP-BY-STEP 2.6

Using Paste Contents

1. With the mountain image still selected, click the **Edit** menu, and then click **Cut**. This removes the image and places it on the Clipboard.

2. Select the blue rectangle (you might need to select your **Pointer** tool first), click the **Edit** menu, and then click **Paste Contents** (Windows) or **Paste Inside** (Macintosh). The rectangle turns into a clipping path with the image placed inside. Notice that you can see only part of the image. Pasting an object inside another object creates a "window," cutting from view all parts of the image outside the window, as shown in Figure 2-6.

FIGURE 2-6
The mountain image pasted inside the rectangle

Remember, there are two shapes here. One is a clipping path with the mountain pasted inside; the other is filled with a Transparency fill. You want the mountain to be placed behind the Transparency fill to achieve the desired effect.

3. With the mountain image selected, click **Edit**, and then click **Cut**. The mountain image again disappears, leaving the Transparency-filled rectangle on the page.

4. Select the Transparency-filled rectangle, click **Edit**, point to **Special**, and then click **Paste Behind**. This pastes the image back onto the page, directly behind the Transparency-filled rectangle. You can also see now how the Transparency fill affects the mountain image, creating a tint of blue over the image, as in Figure 2-7.

STEP-BY-STEP 2.6 Continued

FIGURE 2-7
The mountain image appears to have a blue tint

5. Click the **File** menu, and then click **Close** to close the file. When you are prompted to save your work, choose **No** (Windows) or **Don't Save** (Macintosh).

Extra Challenge

Try to customize the interface more, moving the toolbars around until you find a place for them that works better for you. Add more buttons and shortcuts for some of the commands used frequently in this project. Explore the other tools on the Tools panel. Draw more shapes, using the Pencil and Pen tools. Experiment with gradient fills and lens fills.

SUMMARY

In this lesson, you learned to:

■ Customize the FreeHand workspace.

■ Organize your graphics by using layers.

■ Place images.

■ Use the Paste Contents (Windows) or Paste Inside (Macintosh) feature.

EXPLORING OTHER FREEHAND FEATURES

OBJECTIVES

Upon completion of this lesson, you should be able to:

- Take advantage of additional FreeHand features.
- Use contour gradients.
- Use the Trace tool and the Trace wand.
- Work with symbols.
- Create and use master pages.
- Define and use brush strokes.
- Use envelopes and the perspective grid.

Additional FreeHand Features

From the exercises in Lesson 1 you have gained a good working knowledge of Macromedia FreeHand MX and an understanding of its basic features. Lesson 2 introduced you to some more sophisticated features. Now we will take a look at the Trace tool, the Trace wand, envelopes, and the perspective grid. We'll also examine the techniques behind contour gradients, brush strokes, symbol editing, and master pages.

You will use contour gradients to create unique three-dimensional effects; they're an ideal tool for innovative Web graphics. You will learn how to define and use brush strokes. This new feature puts a vast array of creative possibilities at your fingertips. You can use brush strokes to enhance your paths as well as to create random patterns and simple animations. The Library panel has been updated to provide the same easy access to symbol editing available in Macromedia Flash MX 2004. Finally, master pages will form the foundation for your site or publication's creative development by providing a powerful and simple way to define your overall graphical look.

The Contour Gradient

A *gradient* is a fill attribute that gives a shaded texture to a shape. A contour gradient is one of several gradient options. When you use the contour gradient, the color gradation follows the perimeter of the shape being filled.

In this project, you apply a contour gradient to the Andes Coffee logo.

STEP-BY-STEP 3.1

Applying the Contour Gradient to a Logo and Editing It

1. Open the document **Andes_L3.FH11** from the data files supplied for this project. Verify that you are on page 1. If not, use the **Go to Page** pop-up menu on the Status toolbar.

2. Click the **Zoom** tool and draw a marquee selection around the word *ANDES*. This lets you zoom in so it is easier to view and select the letters.

3. Using the **Subselect** tool, select the letter **A** of the Andes Coffee logo.

4. Hold down the **Shift** key and select the rest of letters in the word *ANDES*, as shown in Figure 3-1.

FIGURE 3-1
The ANDES logo with each letter selected

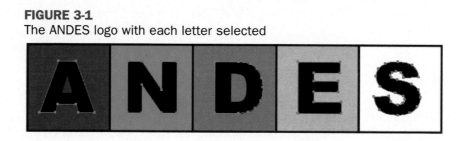

5. On the Object panel, select the Fill property. You can now see the Fill options available for the selected objects.

6. In the options section of the Object panel, choose **Gradient** from the **fill type** pop-up menu. By default the Linear gradient type is selected, graduating from black to white as shown in Figure 3-2.

FIGURE 3-2
The Object panel with the Fill property selected

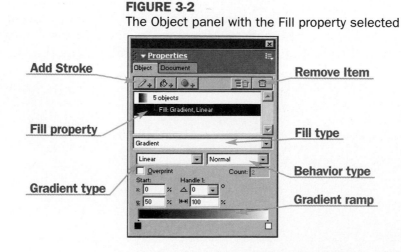

STEP-BY-STEP 3.1 Continued

7. Select the fill property again. Select **Contour** from the **gradient type** pop-up menu. The word ANDES is now filled with a contour gradient from black to white, as shown in Figure 3-3.

FIGURE 3-3
Filling with the contour gradient

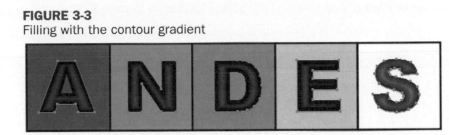

8. Select the fill property again. Drag the swatch for the color **CC9933 - 204r 153g 51b** from the Swatches panel (in the Assets panel group) to the white swatch (bottom right corner) on the Gradient ramp of the Object panel. The gradient is now filled with black and CC9933 - 204r 153g 51b.

9. Select the fill property again. In the field properties, set the x field to **40**, the y field to **60**, and the Taper to **30**.

10. Select the fill property again. Change the **Behavior type** to **Auto Size**. The letters gain a three-dimensional effect, and the width of the contour gradient along the perimeter of the path becomes a bit narrower, as shown in Figure 3-4.

FIGURE 3-4
The final contour gradient

11. Click the **File** menu, and then click **Save As**. Name the file **Andes_L3** followed by your initials, and then click **Save**. Remain in this screen for the next Step by Step.

The Andes Coffee logo now sports a fresher, three-dimensional look. By experimenting with the various Fill attributes, you can create a variety of unique contour gradients.

The Trace Tool

The Trace tool can trace any visible objects on the page: bitmaps, text, vector paths, and fills. The settings in the Trace Tool dialog box affect the results of the operation. In addition, the Trace wand (it's called the Trace wand when it's used to make selections) samples areas of contiguous color based on the settings in the Wand Options dialog box. In the following Step-by-Step, you trace the image of the mountain range.

S TEP-BY-STEP 3.2

Using the Trace Tool to Vectorize an Image

1. Using the **Go to Page** pop-up menu on the Status toolbar, go to page **2**, as shown in Figure 3-5.

FIGURE 3-5
Page 2 of the Andes_L3 document

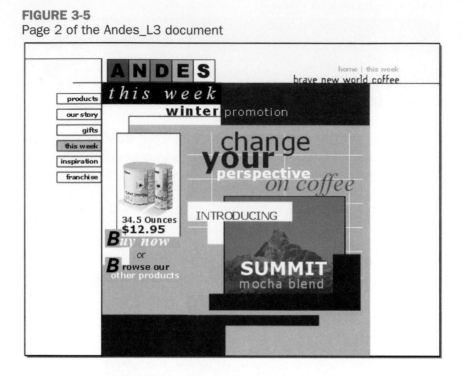

2. Hide all layers except the one named Mountain.

3. Double-click the **Trace** tool on the Tools panel. The Trace Tool dialog box opens.

4. Set the options in the Trace Tool dialog box as indicated in Figure 3-6. These options specify the parameters and color tolerances used in tracing an object.

STEP-BY-STEP 3.2 Continued

FIGURE 3-6
The Trace Tool dialog box with desired settings

Trace Tool

Color mode:
| 8 ▼ | Colors ▼ |
| | RGB ▼ |

Resolution: Normal ▼

Trace layers: All ▼

Path conversion:
Outline ▼

Path overlap: Loose ▼

Trace conformity:
5 ◄ [   ] ►
loose   tight

Noise tolerance:
15 ◄ [   ] ►
min   max

Wand color tolerance:
5 ◄ [ ] ►
narrow   wide

[OK] [Cancel]

5. Click **OK** to close the Trace Tool dialog box.

6. Select the **Mountain** layer on the Layers panel. Using the **Trace** tool, draw a rectangle marquee around the entire image of the mountain. After several seconds, a vector version of the image appears over the original. This new image is made up of dozens of interlocking vector shapes. Each shape is selected, making the image look like a bundle of control points, as shown in Figure 3-7.

FIGURE 3-7
The mountain image converted to vectors with the Trace tool

STEP-BY-STEP 3.2 Continued

7. You need to group this new vector image (the original TIFF is still under it, and grouping lets you keep the two separated). Click the **Modify** menu, and then click **Group** or use **Ctrl-G** (Windows) or **Command-G** (Macintosh).

8. Press **Tab** to deselect the object. Look at the image and notice how FreeHand has re-created the jagged, rocky detail with colors derived from the original image.

9. Save your changes and remain in this screen for the next Step-by-Step.

The Trace Wand

In the next Step-by-Step, you use the Trace wand to trace part of the Andes Coffee product TIFF and part of its surrounding vector background. The Trace wand extends the capabilities of the Trace tool by selecting color areas based on the color tolerance settings within the Trace Tool dialog box. The Trace wand does not differentiate between types of objects; it just targets color. If a raster image and a background share the same color, they become part of the same selection.

STEP-BY-STEP 3.3

Selecting a Color Area with the Trace Wand

1. Continuing with the Andes_L3 file, turn on all the invisible layers by opening the Layers panel **Options** menu and choosing **All On**.

2. Reopen the Trace Tools dialog box (by double-clicking the **Trace** tool) and set the options in the Trace Tool dialog box as follows:
   Resolution: **High**
   Path Overlap: **Tight**
   Trace Conformity: **10** (tight)
   Noise Tolerance: **1** (min)
   Wand Color Tolerance: **5** (narrow)

3. Click **OK** to save your settings and close the Trace Tools dialog box.

4. Select the **Images** layer on the Layers panel. Click once with the Trace wand toward the top of the white background area within the product image (the photo of the two coffee cans). The white background becomes selected (a line of "marching ants"—or a moving marquee—appears around the perimeter of the selection as well as the items within the selection area). The border around the white area stops the selection from spilling out onto the rest of the page.

STEP-BY-STEP 3.3 Continued

5. Click one more time inside the marching ants selection area to open the Wand Options panel shown in Figure 3-8. On this panel, you can specify how to convert the currently active selection.

FIGURE 3-8
Wand Options panel

6. Select **Convert Selection Edge** if necessary and click **OK**. The selection area is now converted to a vector object. This object should appear black, with a white silhouette depicting the shape of the product.

7. Click the **Modify** menu, and then click **Join** or press **Ctrl-J** (Windows) or **Command-J** (Macintosh). The vector is now a compound path. The white silhouette area has become a hole through which you can view the original image.

8. Select the **Rectangle** tool from the Tools panel and draw a rectangle over the top half of the newly traced vector. Make three sides of the rectangle larger than the vector tracing, as shown in Figure 3-9.

> **Note** ☑
> If the object has jumped to a different layer, bring it back to the Images layer by clicking on the layer name on the Layers panel.

STEP-BY-STEP 3.3 Continued

FIGURE 3-9
Overlap the rectangle over the top of the product image

9. Use the **Pointer** tool to select the rectangle. Hold down the **Shift** key, and then select the vector tracing so that both objects are now selected.

10. Click the **Modify** menu, point to **Combine**, and then click **Intersect**. A new vector shape is created from the intersection of the traced vector and the drawn rectangle. This intersection represents the new background for the product shot.

    You need to remove the stroke from the new background. Shapes resulting from path operations (Combine, Intersect, Punch) always contain a stroke. Deleting the stroke blends the vector with the photo.

11. To delete the stroke, either use the Swatches panel by dragging the **None** swatch over the Stroke box or select the Stroke property in the Object panel and click the **Remove Item** button (the button with the trash icon in the upper right of the Object panel).

12. Next, apply a gradient fill to the new background:
    a. Select the Fill property and choose **Gradient** from the fill type pop-up menu. The background vector fills with a gradation of black to white, making the background appear dimensional and photographic.
    b. Make sure that the gradient properties are set as follows: Under Start, set x to **0** and set y to **100**. Under Handle 1, set the angle to **270** and set the length to **100**.
    c. Drag the swatch for the color **999966 - 153r 153g 102b** from the Swatches panel and drop it on top of the black color box in the Object panel. The background fills with a soft tan color that blends into the white background in the middle of the product image, as shown in Figure 3-10.

STEP-BY-STEP 3.3 Continued

FIGURE 3-10
A gradient background

13. Save your edits and remain in this screen for the next Step-by-Step.

Using Symbols

The Library panel in FreeHand provides a way to keep graphics consistent and organized throughout a project, as shown in Figure 3-11. An object defined as a symbol is saved in a *library*, where it can be used over and over within a document (each use is called an *instance*). If the original symbol is edited—that is, recolored, reshaped, tweaked, and so on—all the instances of the symbol are automatically updated throughout the document. Symbols can be made from any type of object drawn or imported into FreeHand: grouped objects, joined objects, blends, text, TIFFs, JPEGs, EPS files, and so on.

FIGURE 3-11
The Library panel in the Assets panel group

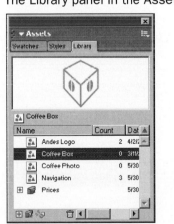

The Library panel is divided into two areas: a top half for displaying the thumbnail of a selected symbol and a bottom half (under the Name label) for displaying a list of available symbols.

S TEP-BY-STEP 3.4

Making the Logo into a Symbol

1. Go to page 1 (use Go to Page on the Status toolbar).

2. Select the **Andes** logo (the same logo you used for the contour gradient earlier in the project).

3. Open the Library panel by clicking the **Window** menu, and then **Library**. At the moment, as Figure 3-12 shows, there are no symbols in this panel.

FIGURE 3-12
An empty Library panel

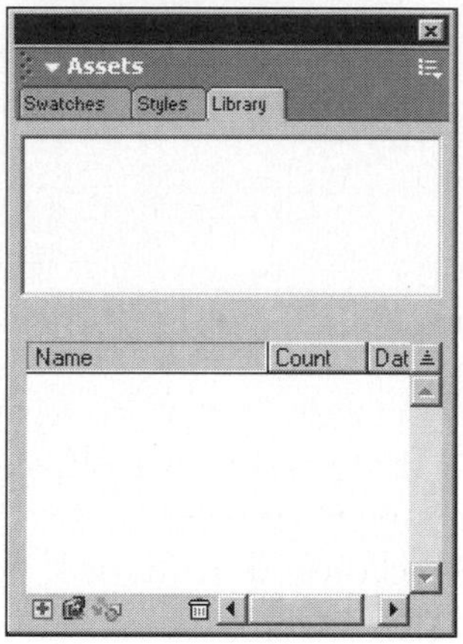

4. Drag the **Andes** logo onto the bottom half of the Library panel and release. A small icon appears on the panel with the name Graphic-01, and the top of the panel displays a full-color thumbnail of the Andes logo, as shown in Figure 3-13.

FIGURE 3-13
The Library panel with the Andes logo symbol

5. Double-click (Windows) or single-click (Macintosh) the name **Graphic-01** (not the small icon next to it). Key **Andes Logo** and press **Enter** (Windows) or **Return** (Macintosh). Remain in this screen for the next Step-by-Step.

Editing a Symbol

The original logo graphic on the page is now an instance of the Andes logo. A symbol's instance can be edited only if released or if the symbol itself is edited (which would affect all instances of the symbol).

S TEP-BY-STEP 3.5

Editing a Symbol

1. Double-click the icon for the symbol **Andes Logo** on the Library panel. A new window displays the logo centered on the page. This is the symbol-editing window, where you can make changes to symbol graphics in their original state.

2. Using the **Subselect** tool, select the letter **A** within the logo. Click the **Edit** menu, point to **Select**, and then click **Superselect** to select the rest of the letter **A**. Use **Superselect** again to select the rest of the word **ANDES**.

> **Note** ✓
>
> Because the letter *A* is made up of two joined shapes (the outer outline and the inner triangular opening), using **Superselect** the first time does not select the word ANDES but only the rest of the letter A. To select the entire word you need to apply the **Superselect** command twice.

3. On the Object panel, you will see a Group object with a Contents attribute under it, as shown in Figure 3-14. Double-click the **Contents** to select the five objects in the group.

FIGURE 3-14
Grouped objects in the Object panel

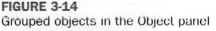

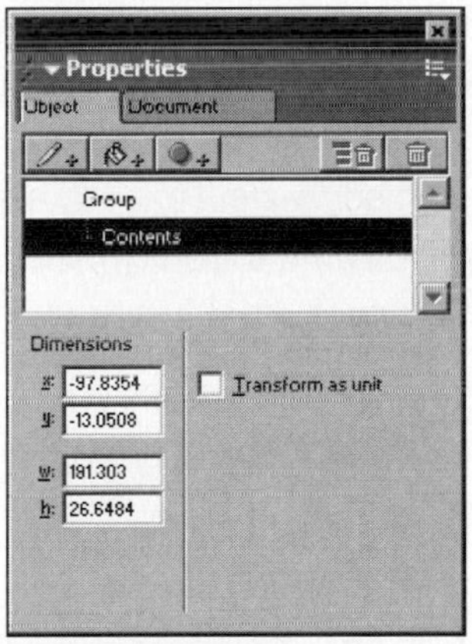

4. Select the Fill property for the five objects. Drag the color swatch **333366 - 51r 51g 102b** from the Swatches panel to the black color swatch on the Contour Gradient ramp. The gradient color in the logo changes to reflect the new colors.

5. Close the Edit Symbol window to return to your document. Notice that the logo symbol on the page has been updated to reflect your recent color change.

STEP-BY-STEP 3.5 Continued

6. With the logo symbol selected, click the **Modify** menu, point to **Symbol**, and then click **Release Instance** to release a specific instance of a symbol, which you can then edit without affecting other instances of the same symbol on the page.

7. Save your changes to the file. Leave the file open for use in a later Step-by-Step.

Master Pages

Master pages are defined in FreeHand as a special type of symbol: they are stored in the library and affect the look of an entire page. Master pages provide an efficient, timesaving method for updating even the largest graphics projects within FreeHand. By placing commonly used backgrounds, borders, and titles on master pages, you can edit and update multiple pages in one step for a faster production time.

STEP-BY-STEP 3.6

Creating and Applying a Master Page

1. Click the **File** menu, click **Open**, navigate to the data files for this course, and open the **AndesMasters_L3.FH11** file. Make sure the Document panel and the Library panel are visible.

2. Click in the upper-right corner of the Document panel to open the **Options** menu. Then choose **Convert to Master Page**.

The label *Master Page-01* appears in the Master Page text box of the Document panel, as shown in Figure 3-15. A new symbol, also named *Master Page-01*, appears on the Library panel. Master pages are defined as symbols and displayed on the Library panel.

FIGURE 3-15
The new master page

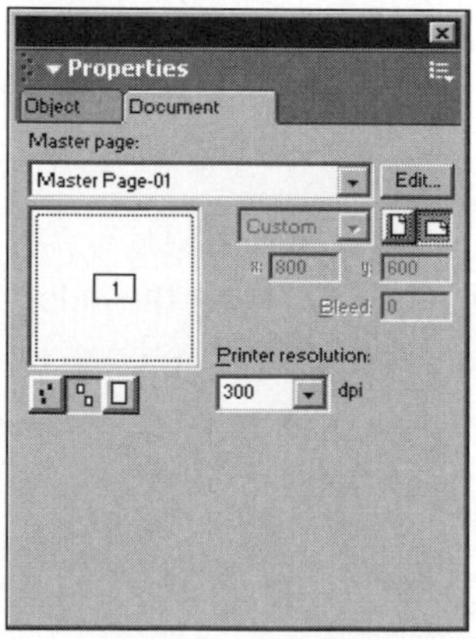

STEP-BY-STEP 3.6 Continued

3. Open the **Options** menu on the Document panel again and click **Add Pages**.

4. In the Number of New Pages text box, key **3**. Click **OK**. Three new pages appear on the pasteboard area.

Note ☑

Graphic elements belonging to a master page cannot be edited within the Document window.

5. Choose **Fit All** from the **Magnification** menu on the Status toolbar to view all the document pages at the same time on the pasteboard, as shown in Figure 3-16. Remain in this screen for the next Step-by-Step.

FIGURE 3-16
All four master pages

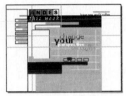

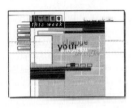

Editing Master Pages

Elements belonging to a master page cannot be edited unless the master page is released or the original symbol is edited.

STEP-BY-STEP 3.7

Releasing and Editing a Master Page

1. Choose **Go to Page 1** from the Status toolbar.

2. Select the **Pointer** tool and click on any of the graphic elements on page 1. Notice that you cannot select any of the elements.

3. Choose **Release Child Page** from the **Options** menu on the Document panel. Page 1 is no longer a master page.

4. Use the **Pointer** tool to click on the Andes logo. The group to which the logo belongs is now selected. The page is no longer a master page, so all graphic elements can be selected and edited.

STEP-BY-STEP 3.7 Continued

5. Move the selected group to a new position on the page. Because you have released the page, the edits on this page will not appear on the remaining three pages, which are still based on the original master page symbol. This page is independent of the master page applied to the rest of the document.

6. Click the **Edit** menu, and then click **Undo Move**.

7. Locate the symbol **Master Page-01** on the Library panel and double-click it. A new window displaying the master page is now visible.

8. With the **Pointer** tool, select the Andes logo.

9. Move the logo to the left of the vertical row of six rectangles that start with the word *products*.

10. Click and hold the mouse pointer over the Scale tool. From the menu that appears, select the **Rotate** tool.

11. Hold down the **Shift** key and use the Rotate tool to rotate the logo by 90 degrees. Holding down the Shift key constrains the rotation angle to 45-degree increments. The logo is now positioned vertically to the left of the page graphics, as shown in Figure 3-17.

FIGURE 3-17
The edited master page

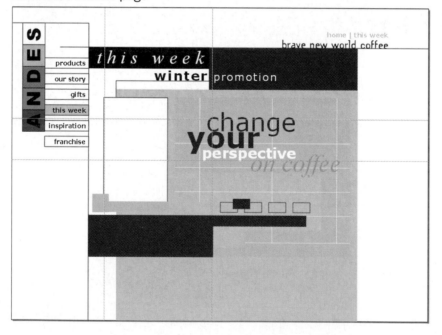

STEP-BY-STEP 3.7 Continued

12. Close the symbol-editing window to return to the main Document window. Choose **Fit All** from the **Magnification** menu to inspect all the master pages. Notice that all pages defined as Master Page-01 have been updated to reflect the change. Page 1 was released in the previous exercise and was not affected by your edit.

Master pages let you define the look of a document or Web site with only a few steps. Defining specific pages for specific functions can facilitate the graphic development of even the most sophisticated project.

13. Click the **File** menu, click **Save** to save the changes to the file, and then close it. Leave FreeHand and Andes_L3 open for the next Step-by-Step.

The Brush Strokes

Brush strokes are yet another type of symbol. They also reside in the library and can be described as graphics that are mapped to a path: they are applied to a path as a stroke. In the next Step-by-Step, you define and apply a brush stroke. Brush strokes offer additional techniques for creating borders and animations. You can accumulate an extensive library of brushes over time—a valuable asset for any graphics professional.

Any brushes you create can be edited through the Edit Brush dialog box (available through Stroke property options on the Object panel). By editing the options in the Edit Brush dialog box, you can create unique looks to use when designing pages for a Web site. Because brush strokes are defined as symbols, you can update every instance of a brush within a document by editing the defining symbol.

S TEP-BY-STEP 3.8

Defining a Brush Stroke

1. With the Andes_L3 file open, use the **Go to Page** menu on the Status toolbar to go to page **3**.

2. Use the Pointer tool to select the cube graphic on page 3. Click the **Modify** menu, point to **Brush**, and then click **Create Brush**.

STEP-BY-STEP 3.8 Continued

3. When you are asked whether you want to copy or convert the graphic to a symbol to use as a brush, select the **Copy** option. The Edit Brush dialog box opens, as shown in Figure 3-18.

FIGURE 3-18
The Edit Brush dialog box

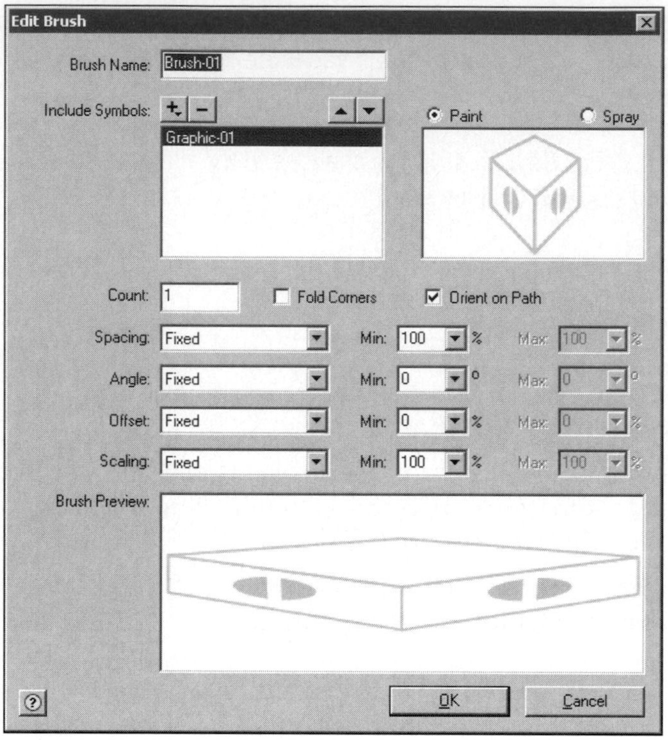

4. Key **Coffee Brush** in the **Brush Name** field. Leave all other options as they are and click **OK**.

5. Use the **Pencil** tool to draw a wavy path across the bottom of page 2. Keep the path selected.

6. In the Object panel, click the **Add Stroke** button (the button with the pencil icon).

7. Select **Brush** from the **stroke type** pop-up menu. Make sure **Coffee Brush** is selected in the list of available brushes. The new brush is now mapped to the shape and direction of your stroke path, as shown in Figure 3-19. (Your image will vary depending on the shape and location of the wavy path you drew.) You have defined and applied a custom brush to a path. This brush, however, lends itself better to the Spray Brush option.

STEP-BY-STEP 3.8 Continued

FIGURE 3-19
The new Coffee Brush

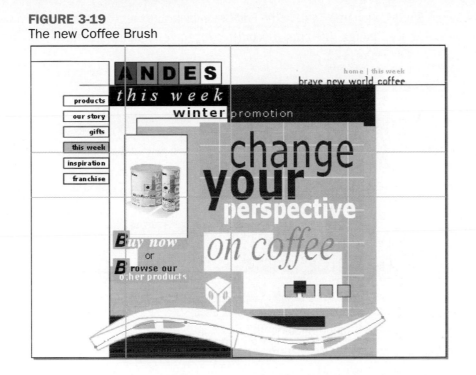

8. With the Stroke property still selected, click the **Options** button in the Stroke options portion of the Object panel, as shown in Figure 3-20. Then choose **Edit**. The Edit Brush window opens again.

FIGURE 3-20
The Brush Options menu in the Object panel

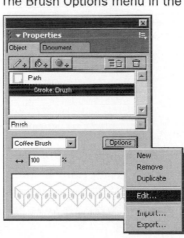

STEP-BY-STEP 3.8 Continued

9. Choose the **Spray** option (top right) in the Edit Brush dialog box and click **OK**. When a warning dialog box opens, choose **Change**. The brush becomes a repeating instance that follows the direction of the path, as shown in Figure 3-21.

FIGURE 3-21
Using the Coffee Brush with the Spray option

10. With the path still selected, open the Edit Brush dialog box again. Choose the following options and then click **OK** to create a random look in the brush instances:

Spacing: **Variable**, Min: **50%**, Max: **200%**

Angle: **Random**, Min: **0**, Max: **60**

Offset: **Random**, Min: **-200%**, Max: **200%**

Scaling: **Random**, Min: **20%**, Max: **200%**

11. When a warning dialog box opens, choose **Change**.

12. Delete the path.

13. Save your changes and remain in this screen for the next Step-by-Step.

The Envelope Toolbar

Envelopes are a powerful way of applying custom transformations such as warps and bends to vector objects and groups. Envelopes treat a group as an individual object, enabling transformations that would be extremely difficult with other editing tools. Using envelopes, you can warp an object to simulate a waving flag, "wrap" text around a cylinder, spherize objects on a beach ball—the applications are endless. For the following Step-by-Steps, you use the SUMMIT text to create two keyframes you will save for an animation in Lesson 5.

To proceed, you need to have access to the Envelope toolbar, as shown in Figure 3-22. You access this toolbar through the Toolbars option on the Window menu.

FIGURE 3-22
The Envelope toolbar

Create   Remove

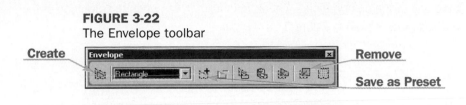

Save as Preset

STEP-BY-STEP 3.9

Using the Envelope Toolbar to Edit a Vector Object

1. Verify that you are on page 2 of the Andes_L3 file, and make sure the Envelope toolbar is open. (Click the **Window** menu, point to **Toolbars**, and then click **Envelope**.)

2. Use your Pointer tool to select the word **SUMMIT** and click the **Create** button on the Envelope toolbar.

   The selection box around the word changes to include not only the corner points of the grouped object but also the center points on each of the selection sides. Each point can be used to change the shape or size of the object.

   > **Note** ✓
   >
   > Envelopes can transform vector graphics and text but not imported images. If you apply an envelope to a text object, you can edit the text later by using the Text tool.

3. Click one of the control points and drag away from the word. The word warps in the direction of the movement, similar to that shown in Figure 3-23.

FIGURE 3-23
Moving one of the envelope's control points

Control point

Handle

STEP-BY-STEP 3.9 Continued

4. Move one of the point handles. The word is further warped in the direction of the handle's movement, similar to that shown in Figure 3-24.

FIGURE 3-24
Moving one of the envelope's control handles

5. With the word **SUMMIT** still selected, click the **Remove** button on the Envelope toolbar. The word returns to its original, unwarped state.

6. The word might have changed its position when you removed the envelope effect from it. On the Object panel, set the x field to **418** and the y field to **156**. Then press **Enter** (Windows) or **Return** (Macintosh).

7. With **SUMMIT** still selected, click the **Edit** menu and then click **Clone**. A copy of the word is placed directly over the original.

8. Create a new layer by choosing **New** (Windows) or **New Layer** (Macintosh) from the **Options** menu on the Layers panel.

9. Name the layer by double-clicking the new layer's name and keying **Summit** over the highlighted text. Press **Enter** (Windows) or **Return** (Macintosh) to apply the name. The clone moves to the new layer.

10. Save your changes and remain in this screen for the next Step-by-Step.

Saving Presets

You will keep one original SUMMIT and one warped SUMMIT so you can create an animated transformation later in Macromedia Flash MX 2004. You now need to warp the SUMMIT on the new layer. Start by saving a preset of SUMMIT text. *Presets* are specific envelope shapes that have been saved to be used over and over.

S TEP-BY-STEP 3.10

Creating a Preset Envelope

1. Turn off the Hide layer by clicking the check mark to the left of the layer name on the Layers panel. This makes it easier to separate the cloned SUMMIT from the original.

2. With **SUMMIT** still selected, click the **Create** button on the Envelope toolbar.

3. Select the center top point of the envelope's bounding box. While holding down the **Shift** key, move the point upward. Holding down the Shift key constrains movement to a horizontal, vertical, or 45-degree diagonal axis.

4. Keep moving the point until the overall height of the object is about two to three times the original height and the word looks like a mountain peak, as shown in Figure 3-25.

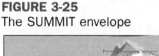

FIGURE 3-25
The SUMMIT envelope

5. With the object still selected, click **Save As Preset** on the Envelope toolbar. A dialog box opens, prompting you to name this new preset.

6. Key **Summit** in the Name field of the dialog box and click **OK**. This name appears in the Preset list on the Envelope toolbar.

7. Close the Envelope toolbar. Save your changes and remain in this screen for the next Step-by-Step.

Extra Challenge

You can use the SUMMIT preset with other words and objects in your document. Experiment with the SUMMIT preset and other presets by applying them to different objects in the document. Remember that envelopes cannot be applied to imported images. Undo any changes you have made or close your document without saving and then reopen your Andes_L3 document for the next Step-by-Step.

Perspective Grids

FreeHand provides a powerful means of moving vector objects in a three-dimensional space that is easy to understand and easy to implement. The perspective grid brings these basic 3-D rendering functions to FreeHand. The grid displays guidelines that converge to a vanishing point. You can define the number of lines and the number of vanishing points (any number of guidelines and up to three vanishing points). The purpose of the grid is not just to provide a static visual aid—graph paper, if you will; the grid enables you to manually create 3-D objects.

You use the Perspective tool (shown in Figure 3-26) on the Tools panel to "snap" an object to a perspective grid to automatically apply a 3-D effect. By dragging an object over the perspective grid with the Perspective tool, you can "move" the object in a three-dimensional space. The object aligns itself to the vanishing points as it is being moved. You can also resize objects while they're selected by the Perspective tool, and this transformation takes into account the vanishing points as well.

FIGURE 3-26
The Perspective tool from the Tools panel

S TEP-BY-STEP 3.11

Applying Perspective to a Group of Objects

1. Go to page 3 and select the group with the text *change your perspective on coffee*.

2. Click the **View** menu, point to **Perspective Grid**, and then click **Show**. A green perspective grid appears on the page, as shown in Figure 3-27.

FIGURE 3-27
The perspective grid provides guidelines and a vanishing point

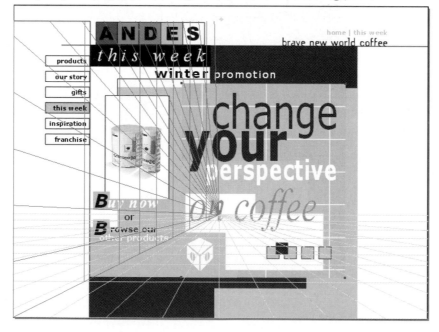

STEP-BY-STEP 3.11 Continued

3. Select the **Perspective** tool from the Tools panel and place it at the intersection of the horizontal and vertical axes of the grid, just at the vanishing point. Then drag to the right until the vertical axis is aligned with the number 928 on the page ruler, as shown in Figure 3-28.

FIGURE 3-28
Aligning the vertical axis to the horizontal page ruler

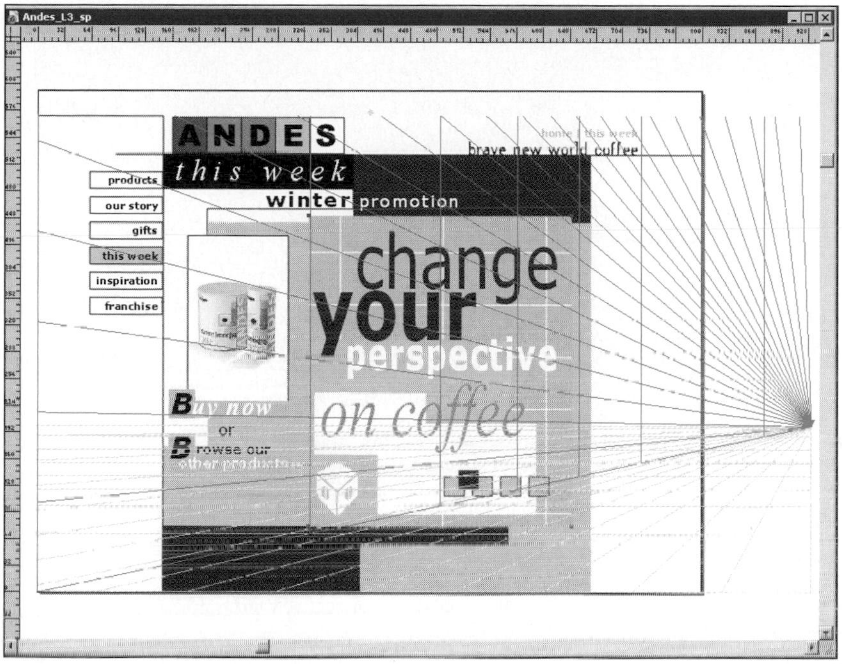

4. Click and hold down the **Perspective** tool over the text selection. While still holding it down, tap the left arrow key on the keyboard. An outline of the object "snaps" to the left, rendered in perspective. The outline is oriented toward the vanishing point.

5. Without releasing the Perspective tool, move the outline about on the page. As the outline moves, notice how it reorients itself to remain in perspective.

6. Without releasing the Perspective tool, move the outline until it is centered in the gray area to the right of the product illustration.

STEP-BY-STEP 3.11 Continued

7. Without releasing the Perspective tool, tap the number **2** on the keyboard several times to enlarge the image while keeping it in perspective. You want to fill the space as much as possible. If, after releasing, you notice that the image is still too small, click and hold the image again and continue tapping the **2** key until most of the space is filled, as shown in Figure 3-29.

FIGURE 3-29
The finished perspective applied to the group

8. Click and hold the image again and tap the numbers **1** through **6** on the keyboard to see their effects on the sizing of the object. Also experiment with tapping each of the arrow keys while holding the Perspective tool down on an object.

Did You Know?

While you are editing an object with the Perspective tool, you cannot recolor or reshape the object with other FreeHand tools.

9. When the text is sized and positioned in the proper place, you need to release the perspective grid from the text object. Click the **View** menu, point to **Perspective Grid**, and then click **Release With Perspective**.

10. Save your changes and remain in this screen for the next Step-by-Step.

Defining Custom Grids

After you release the object, it is a plain vector object again, although it appears to be sitting in a three-dimensional space. You can control this three-dimensional space by defining custom grids.

S TEP-BY-STEP 3.12

Defining a Custom Perspective Grid

1. Click the **View** menu, point to **Perspective Grid**, and then click **Define Grids** to open the Define Grids dialog box shown in Figure 3-30.

FIGURE 3-30
The Define Grids dialog box

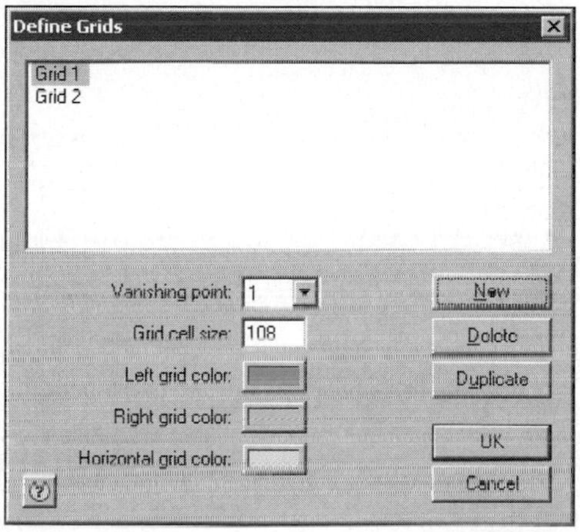

2. Click **New**. An additional name appears in the list window. By default, it is Grid 3. Grid 1 and Grid 2 are already listed in the window.

3. Double-click on the name of the new grid and enter a custom name such as **Grid_YourName**.

4. Set the number of vanishing points to **2** and the grid cell size to **200**.

5. Click **OK** to close the Define Grids dialog box and return to the page. The perspective grid has changed to a two-point perspective.

6. Click the **File** menu, click **Save**, and then close the file and FreeHand.

Did You Know?

By default, the grid cell size is 108 points. This measurement reflects the measurement unit selected on the Status toolbar. (Changing the measurement unit to inches would convert this value to 1.5 inches.)

Extra Challenge

Create a variety of objects, and experiment with contour gradients. Experiment with the Brush Strokes options in the Edit Brush window. Create several master pages within the same document. Try updating them, applying them to different pages, and changing their sizes.

SUMMARY

In this lesson, you learned how to:

- Take advantage of additional FreeHand features.
- Use contour gradients.
- Use the Trace tool and the Trace wand.
- Work with symbols.
- Create and use master pages.
- Define and use brush strokes.
- Use envelopes and the perspective grid.

DESIGNING SCENES FOR MACROMEDIA FLASH MX 2004

OBJECTIVES

Upon completion of this lesson, you should be able to:

- Define the storyboard workflow within FreeHand in preparation for creating Flash animations.

- Use the Page tool to storyboard an animation.

- Use the Blend command to morph between two objects.

- Use the Release to Layers command to create an animation.

- Use brush strokes as an animation technique.

- Use the Controller to test sophisticated animation techniques.

- Export a SWF (Flash) file.

The Storyboard

This lesson introduces more sophisticated drawing techniques available within Macromedia FreeHand MX. It also shows you how FreeHand can help you produce animations in Macromedia Flash MX 2004. You will continue to work on the Andes Coffee file and start to develop keyframes for a more concise storyboard. A *keyframe* defines an important event within an animation—the introduction of a new graphic, a blending effect, a new title, or a change in motion, direction, or speed. To create the necessary objects for these key events and to keep track of the animation's progression, you can develop a *storyboard*—a collection of keyframes encompassing the entire movie (an animation in Flash is called a movie).

Think of each page within your document as a keyframe. Within each page, think of each layer as an individual frame for a specific scene. In this lesson, you learn to manage pages with the Page tool, create animations with brush strokes, and convert the layers into individual frames with the Release to Layers option. You also learn to export elements of your document into a Flash movie to complete the animation.

The Navigation Panel

The Navigation panel is where you define hyperlinks and object animation behavior within FreeHand. The Script Actions contained within the panel are simplified versions of Flash actions. Defining links and actions in FreeHand means you can test them before exporting to Flash. In the following Step-by-Step exercises, you create two types of links: page links for navigating through a multipage document and URL links for connecting to a Web site. An *URL (uniform resource locator)* is a link containing information about where a file is located on the Web.

S TEP-BY-STEP 4.1

Creating a Page Link

1. Launch FreeHand and open **Andes_L4.FH11** from the data files supplied for this lesson.

2. Use the **Go to Page** pop-up menu on the Status toolbar to go to page 1 if you're not there already.

3. Click the **Window** menu, and then click **Navigation** to open the Navigation panel.

4. Select the arrow symbol on the bottom right of page 1. On the Navigation panel, choose the following options from the list menus in the Action section:

Action: **Go To and Stop**

Event: **on (press)**

Parameters: **Page 2, Background**

These options define the arrow as a navigation button with a link to page 2. The *on (press)* event specifies that the action is to take place when the user clicks the arrow symbol.

5. Notice that the Navigation panel has a Name text box in which you can name your links so you can keep your document organized. Click in the Name text box and key FWD Arrow. Figure 4-1 shows what your finished Navigation panel should look like.

STEP-BY-STEP 4.1 Continued

FIGURE 4-1
The navigation arrow on page 1 and the Navigation panel

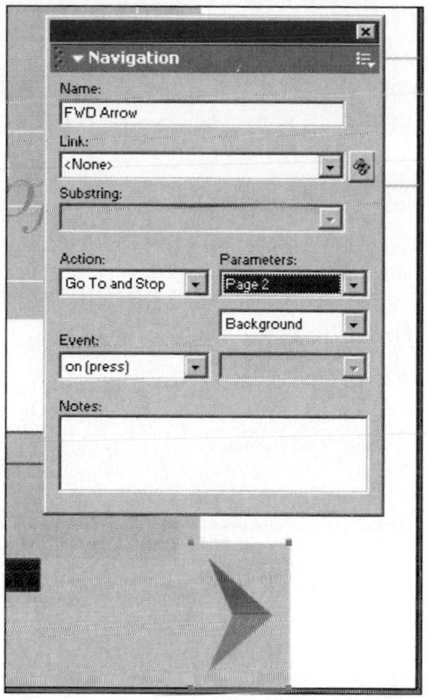

6. Go to page 2 and select the arrow at the bottom right of the page. On the Navigation panel, choose the same Action and Event options outlined in step 4, except in the **Parameters** list, choose **Page 1, Foreground**. You have now created a Back button that navigates from page 2 to page 1 of the document.

7. Name this arrow **BACK Arrow**.

8. Click the **Window** menu, point to **Movie**, and then click **Settings** to define the preview of the Movie.

9. In the Export Options section of the Movie Settings dialog box, make the following changes:
   a. For Movie, choose **Single**.
   b. For Layers, choose **Flatten**.
   c. For Page Range, choose **From: 1, To: 2** to limit the navigation to pages 1 and 2 (the other pages do not have navigation arrows).

10. In the Movie Properties section, make sure the **Autoplay** check box is not selected.

11. Click **OK** to exit the Movie Settings dialog box.

12. Click the **Window** menu, point to **Movie**, and then click **Test**. A new window opens, with the title Andes_L4: Macromedia Flash (SWF). When you place the Pointer tool over the arrow, notice that the pointer icon changes to a link icon.

STEP-BY-STEP 4.1 Continued

13. Now test the button. Click the arrow to jump to page 2. Click the arrow on page 2 to return to page 1.

14. Close the Flash Playback window.

15. Click the **File** menu, click **Save As**, name the file **L4_Animation** followed by your initials, and click **Save**. Remain in this screen for the next Step-by-Step.

Creating an URL Link

You have created and tested navigation buttons within FreeHand without the need to export your document to Flash. Now define an URL (Uniform Resource Locator) link to access Web pages over the Internet from your FreeHand document.

STEP-BY-STEP 4.2

Creating an URL Link

1. Go to page 1. Select the **Andes** logo at the top of the page.

2. In the Link text box of the Navigation panel, select **<None>**, and key **http://www.macromedia.com**.

3. Close the Navigation panel or move it off to the side.

4. Click the **Window** menu, point to **Movie**, and then click **Test** to display page 1 in the movie window. Place the Pointer tool over the Andes logo. When the pointer changes to the link icon, click the logo.

Hot Tip

To test a movie, you can press **Ctrl + Enter** (Windows) or **Command + Return** (Macintosh).

Your default Web browser opens and logon procedures to the Internet are initiated. You can cancel the logon routine by quitting your browser application, or you can allow it to proceed with the connection.

5. When you finish viewing the Macromedia Web site, close your browser.

6. Close the Flash Playback window.

7. Save your changes and remain in this screen for the next Step-by-Step.

The Page Tool

The Page tool provides a variety of page- and document-editing options that do not require menus or windows. It is an important tool for organizing your pages for the storyboard. In the following Step-by-Steps, you isolate the "perspective" text and graphics to create a simple animation storyboard in the file you have been working with.

STEP-BY-STEP 4.3

Setting Page Options

1. Select the **Page** tool from the **Tools** panel and then go to page 3 on the pasteboard (by using the horizontal scroll bar) and select it. Control points appear around the perimeter of the page.

2. Using the Page tool, click the lower-left corner control point of the page (the Page Tool pointer becomes a double-headed arrow) and drag toward the center of the page and release. The page is resized. The Document panel displays the new size.

3. Key the following dimensions in the x and y fields of the Document panel to define an accurate page size: x = **448**, y = **337**. Press **Enter** (Windows) or **Return** (Macintosh).

4. The page orientation is not correct. You need to use the Page tool to change it. Choose the **Page** tool to select the page again. Place the Page tool close to one of the corner points until the pointer changes to a rotation symbol (a bent double-headed arrow).

5. Drag diagonally until the page orientation changes from a horizontal (landscape) orientation to a vertical (portrait) orientation.

6. Align graphics to page coordinates:
   a. Unlock the **Grid** layer.
   b. Hide all other layers (except the Grid layer) by clicking the check mark to the left of their names.
   c. Click with the Pointer tool to select the perspective graphic.
   d. On the Object panel, key the following coordinates: x = **0**, y = **40**. Press **Enter** (Windows) or **Return** (Macintosh). The perspective graphic becomes aligned to the top left of the page.

> ### Did You Know?
> When you align graphics by adjusting X and Y coordinates instead of manually, you can be more precise and consistent. Using the same coordinates for similar graphics on other pages will produce identical results.

7. Click the **File** menu, click **Revert**, and then click **Revert** in the dialog box to return the page to its original state. Remain in this screen for the next Step-by-Step.

Duplicating Pages

You now need to create additional pages to continue with the storyboard.

STEP-BY-STEP 4.4

Duplicating Pages

1. Select the **Page** tool and click on page 3. Press and hold **Alt** (Windows) or **Option** (Macintosh) and drag the page toward the right.

STEP-BY-STEP 4.4 Continued

2. When the outline of the page is no longer overlapping page 3, release the mouse and the key. A second, identical page appears, as shown in Figure 4-2. You now have two keyframes for the Flash animation.

> **Note** ☑
>
> By holding down the **Alt** (Windows) or **Option** (Macintosh) key, you can select components that are part of a group without ungrouping them. The Shift key enables you to select multiple objects. Therefore, you can use **Shift + Alt/Option** to select multiple objects that are part of separate groups.

FIGURE 4-2
Another keyframe page added to the document

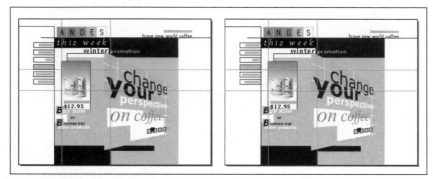

3. Go to page 1 and unlock the Grid layer.

4. Press **Shift + Alt** (Windows) or **Shift + Option** (Macintosh) and use the Pointer tool to select the words **change**, **your perspective**, and **on coffee** (they're in three text boxes). Then click the **Edit** menu and click **Copy**.

5. Go to page 4 and select the **change your perspective on coffee** graphic.

6. Hold down **Alt** (Windows) or **Option** (Macintosh) and click on one of the letters of the phrase *on coffee*. Click the **Edit** menu, point to **Select**, and then click **Superselect** to select the entire phrase (you might have to repeat this command several times to select the words *on coffee*). Then press **Delete**.

7. Click the **Edit** menu, and then click **Paste** to place the text from page 1 onto page 4. Then click the **Modify** menu and click **Group**. Click the **Foreground** layer on the Layers panel to move the new group to this layer.

8. With the new text still selected, key the following values in the Object panel: x = **325**, y = **200**. Press **Enter** (Windows) or **Return** (Macintosh). This keyframe defines a change in the placement of the text within the animation.

9. Hold down **Alt** (Windows) or **Option** (Macintosh) and use the Page tool to drag page 4 to add yet another page (page 5).

STEP-BY-STEP 4.4 Continued

10. Lock all layers except the Hide and Mountain layers.

11. Go to page 2. Use the Pointer tool to select the mountain elements by drawing a marquee selection area like the one in Figure 4-3. Include the *Introducing* text and the two dark blue rectangles at the lower right. Notice that two layers are highlighted when you make the selection: the Hide and Mountain layers.

FIGURE 4-3
The selection marquee around the mountain graphics

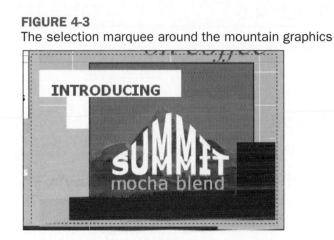

12. Click the **Edit** menu, and then click **Copy**.

13. Unlock all the layers.

14. Go to page 5, and then click **Paste** on the **Edit** menu. The elements appear centered on page 5, still active. The Hide and Mountain layers are still highlighted; FreeHand has pasted the graphics on them.

15. Click the **Mountain** layer to bring all the elements to the same layer.

16. Align the new graphic flush with the lower-right edge of the page by dragging with the Pointer tool, as shown in Figure 4-4.

FIGURE 4-4
Aligning the mountain graphic on the page

17. Save your changes and remain in this screen for the next Step-by-Step.

The Blend Command

The Blend command creates a number of intermediate steps between two or more anchor objects. For example, if you create a square on the left of the page and a circle on the right and then blend them, FreeHand creates a number of in-between objects that morph from one shape to the other.

S TEP-BY-STEP 4.5

Blending Multiple Objects

1. From the data files supplied for this lesson, open the **Cup.FH11** file. This file contains a vector graphic of a cup.

2. Select the **Text** tool and click above the cup.

3. On the Object panel, set the style for the text block. Select **Arial** as the font and **Bold** as the style.

4. Key **ANDES** (all caps).

5. Hold down the **Ctrl** key (Windows) or **Command** key (Macintosh) to revert the Text tool to the Pointer. Click once on the text to select the entire text block, and then release.

6. Click the **Text** menu, and then click **Convert to Paths**. The text is now a grouped vector object.

7. Click the **Modify** menu, and then click **Join** to change the object into a compound path. Complex objects need to be defined as compound paths to blend properly.

8. Move the word, if necessary, to center it over the cup. Hold down **Shift** and use the Pointer tool to drag one of the text group's corner points to resize the text as needed to make it almost as wide as the cup. Your page should look similar to Figure 4-5.

FIGURE 4-5
Centering the word over the cup

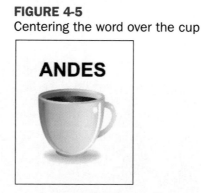

9. Click the **Options** menu control on the Swatches panel (if the panel is not open, click the **Window** menu, and then click **Swatches**).

STEP-BY-STEP 4.5 Continued

10. From the **Options** menu, select **Web Safe Color Library**, and then select the color **CCFFFF** (you will have to scroll to locate this color, or you can key the value in the text box to locate it more quickly). Click **OK** to close the Library panel and add this color to your Swatches list.

11. With this color added to your Swatches list, select it as a fill for the word *Andes*. (Drag it onto the word.)

12. Make sure the word Andes is selected. Then click the **Modify** menu, point to **Transform**, and then click **Move** to open the Transform panel. Make sure the Move button is selected.

13. Set the **Move distance** to x = **0**, y = **120**. Set Copies to **3** and then click **Move**. Close the Transform panel.

14. Select all four copies of the word *ANDES* (use the **Shift** key to select multiple objects) and then click the **Modify** menu, point to **Combine**, and then click **Blend**. All the words are now blended together.

15. Click the **File** menu, click **Save As**, and name the file **L4_Cup** followed by your initials. Remain in this screen for the next Step-by-Step.

Editing a Blend

A FreeHand blend is an editable group. The color, number of steps, direction, and shape of the original objects can all be interactively edited. For this document, the default number of steps is 25.

STEP-BY-STEP 4.6

Editing a Blend

1. If the blend object is not selected, click on it with the Pointer tool. Then key **10** for the number of steps in the Object panel. Press **Enter** (Windows) or **Return** (Macintosh). The number of objects created between the originals is now 10. Next you can recolor the blend.

2. Drag the **White** color from the Swatches panel on top of the word at the very top of the blend. The blend steps change color to simulate a fade to white on the page.

3. Drag the **White** color again on top of the part of the blend closest to the cup. The steam now appears to fade in and out of the page above the coffee cup.

4. To create a more realistic, undulating steam effect, you can reposition the original *Andes* words:
   a. Hold down **Alt** (Windows) or **Option** (Macintosh) and click with the Pointer tool on the bottom of the blend to select a part of the original *ANDES* word (which is now all white).
   b. Click the **Edit** menu, point to **Select**, and then click **Superselect** to select the entire word.

STEP-BY-STEP 4.6 Continued

c. Move the selected word to the right (keep it over the cup). The blend reshapes itself.

d. **Alt-click** (Windows) or **Option-click** (Macintosh) the second (original) **ANDES** word from the bottom of the blend. (Because you can't tell where the original words are exactly, just click in the general area and the selection will snap to the appropriate spot.)

e. Be sure the entire word is selected (click **Edit**, **Select**, and **Superselect**).

f. Move the word to the left.

g. Continue with the two other (original) words to create an S-shaped blend.

5. Save your changes and remain in this screen for the next Step-by-Step.

> **Hot Tip**
>
> You might find it easier to move the words more precisely where you want them by using the arrow keys on the keyboard.

> **Note**
>
> You can also resize an element after selecting it within a blend.

Using Release to Layers

You now have the components for creating a simple Flash animation. The Release to Layers command automatically places each group in the illustration on its own layer. In doing so, it creates a number of sequentially numbered layers. This step helps when you're importing animations into Flash, because each layer becomes one of the animation frames. A file with 10 sequentially numbered layers becomes a 10-frame animation in Flash.

STEP-BY-STEP 4.7

Releasing to Layers

1. Make sure no objects are selected. Switch to the Layers panel and create a new layer by clicking the **Options** menu control and then choosing **New** (Windows) or **New Layer** (Macintosh). Rename this layer **Steam Sequence**. Press **Enter** (Windows) or **Return** (Macintosh).

2. Select the blend and click the **Steam Sequence** layer to move the object to this layer.

3. Click the **Xtras** menu, point to **Animate**, and then click **Release to Layers**. The Release to Layers panel opens, as shown in Figure 4-6.

FIGURE 4-6
The Release to Layers panel

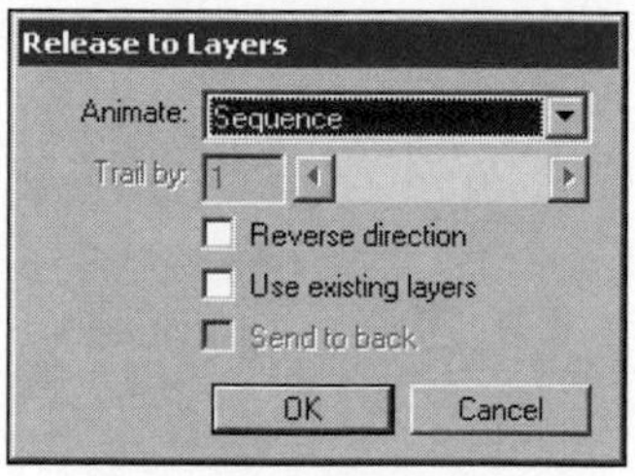

STEP-BY-STEP 4.7 Continued

4. Make sure Animate is set to **Sequence** and then click **OK**. Many new layers (33, to be exact) are created.

5. Save your changes and remain in this screen for the next Step-by-Step.

Each step of the blend is on its own layer, and each layer will become an animation frame.

Creating Animations with Brush Strokes

You can also create animations by using brush strokes. The advantage of using this method is that you can control the size, spacing, rotation, and offset of the individual frames of the animation. The defined brush stroke can also be more complex than a graphic created though a Blend and Release to Layers technique. In the following Step-by-Step, you create a simple animation based on brush strokes.

STEP-BY-STEP 4.8

Creating an Animation with Brush Strokes

1. Switch to the **L4_Animation.FH11** document. Choose **Add Pages** from the **Options** menu on the Document panel to add a new page (page 6). Choose **Custom** page with the landscape orientation and set the size to **800** × **600**. Click **OK**.

2. Go to page 6. Open the **Library** panel from the **Window** menu and locate the **Coffee Box** symbol. Drag the symbol onto page 6.

STEP-BY-STEP 4.8 Continued

3. With the symbol selected, click the **Modify** menu, point to **Brush**, and click **Create Brush** to open the Edit Brush dialog box. Enter the new name and the settings shown in Figure 4-7. (Make sure you select the spray option.)

FIGURE 4-7
Settings for the Box Brush stroke

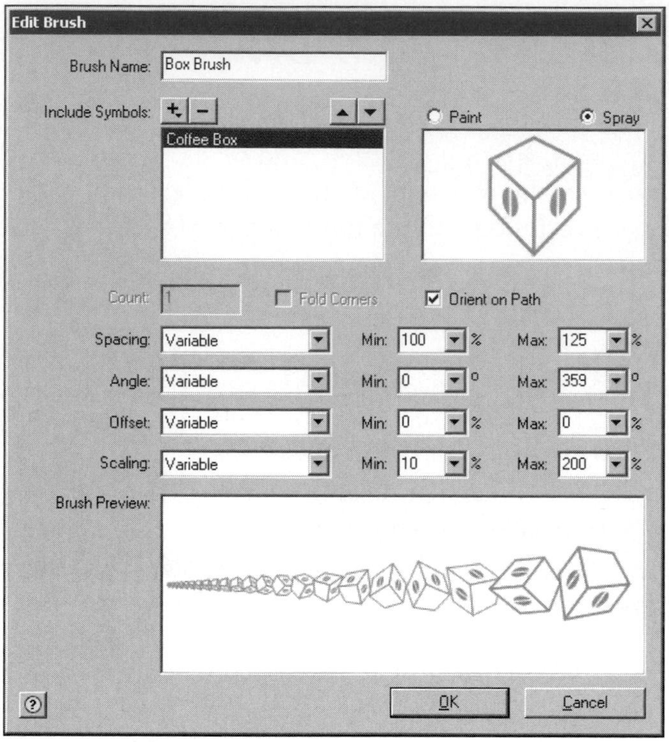

4. Click **OK** to return to the page.

5. Delete the box symbol you placed on this page.

6. Click and hold the Line tool to reveal the Spiral tool. Use the **Spiral** tool to draw a spiral in the middle of page 6. (Start in the middle of the page and drag toward an edge without going outside the page borders.)

7. On the Object panel, click the **Add Stroke** button. Make sure **Brush** is selected (use the stroke type pop-up menu if necessary), and then select **Box Brush** from the brush pop-up menu. Your graphic should look similar to Figure 4-8.

STEP-BY-STEP 4.8 Continued

FIGURE 4-8
The Box Brush applied to a spiral

8. With the spiral still selected, click the **Modify** menu, point to **Brush**, and click **Release Brush**. Deselect the spiral by clicking elsewhere on the page with the Pointer tool.

9. If the entire spiral object is not within the page borders, use the Pointer tool to double-click on the spiraling boxes and then drag the object until it is within the page borders. Then press **Tab** to deselect the object.

10. On the Layers panel, locate the current layer (the one highlighted, with the image of the pen next to it) and switch to Keyline mode (by clicking on the gray circle).

11. Shift-click with the Pointer tool to select the boxes; then click the **Modify** menu and click **Ungroup**.

12. Select **Modify** and **Ungroup** a second time. Repeat until you see each box individually selected.

13. Use the Pointer tool to select the spiraling boxes again. Click the **Modify** menu, and then click **Group**.

14. Click the **Xtras** menu, point to **Animate**, and then click **Release to Layers**. Accept the default sequence animation setting and click **OK**.

15. Save your changes and remain in this screen for the next Step-by-Step.

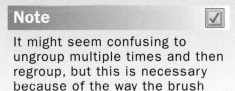

Note ☑

It might seem confusing to ungroup multiple times and then regroup, but this is necessary because of the way the brush strokes are released and grouped by FreeHand.

Extra Challenge

A variety of other effects are possible; try experimenting with brush strokes and Release to Layers.

You have created a sophisticated animation showing a coffee box spiraling toward the viewer and getting closer. In the next section you will preview the animation by using the Controller.

The Controller

You can use the Controller to control the playback of navigation and animation sequences within FreeHand. It works as a shortcut for the Window menu, Movie, Test command. By editing the movie settings and then using the Controller, you can preview your work before exporting it to Flash.

With the Controller, you can stop, rewind, and navigate through your animation frames with total freedom.

STEP-BY-STEP 4.9

Previewing a Movie with the Controller

1. Click the **Window** menu, point to **Movie**, and click **Settings**, and make sure the options match those shown in Figure 4-9. Then click **OK**.

FIGURE 4-9
The Movie Settings dialog box

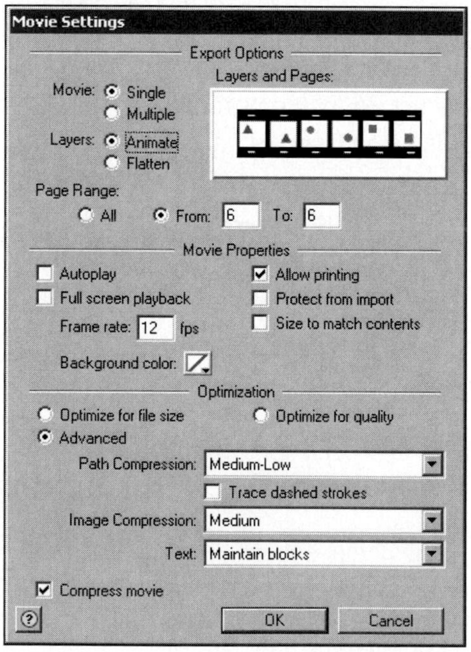

STEP-BY-STEP 4.9 Continued

2. Click the **Window** menu, point to **Toolbars**, and then click **Controller** to open the Controller.

3. Click the **Test** button within the Controller, as shown in Figure 4-10. The preview window appears, displaying the first frame of your animation.

FIGURE 4-10
The Controller for Flash movie files

Play   Test   Settings

4. Click **Play** on the Controller to view the animation sequence.

5. When you are satisfied with your animation, close the Flash Playback window. You can also close the Controller. You are now ready to export to Flash.

6. Save your changes and remain in this screen for the next Step-by-Step.

Exporting to Flash

It is now time to export your file to Flash. You want to be able to bring the vector elements you created in FreeHand into Flash, but you want to do so in an organized manner. The L4_Cup file you have created has only one element, so the export procedure is simple. The L4_Animation file is more intricate, with five pages involved (you will not export page 6). The first two pages were used as a template to further develop the animation keyframes. Pages 3 through 5 show the specific keyframes. Pages 3 and 4 contain the beginning and ending keyframes of a blend of the word *perspective*. Page 5 contains the image of the mountain, with the *Summit* text. Let's first review the export options for L4_Cup and then address the L4_Animation file. Exported SWF files are ready to add to an HTML page through a program such as Macromedia Dreamweaver MX 2004 (introduced in Lesson 6).

STEP-BY-STEP 4.10

Exporting to Flash

1. Switch to the **L4_Cup** file, click the **File** menu, and then click **Export** to open the Export Document (Windows) or Export (Macintosh) dialog box shown in Figure 4-11.

FIGURE 4-11
The Export Document dialog box

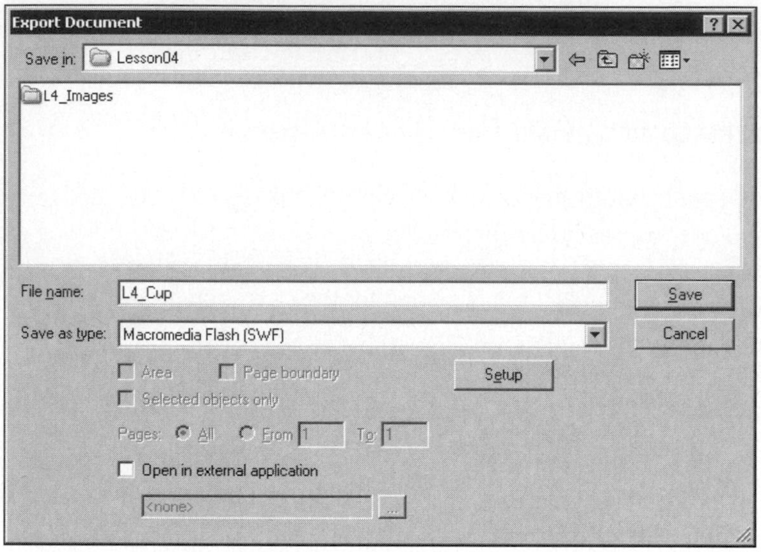

Export Document

Save in: ☐ Lesson04

☐ L4_Images

File name: L4_Cup   Save

Save as type: Macromedia Flash (SWF)   Cancel

☐ Area   ☐ Page boundary   Setup
☐ Selected objects only

Pages: ● All   ○ From 1   To 1

☐ Open in external application
<none>   ...

2. For format type, make sure **Macromedia Flash (SWF)** is selected.

3. Click **Setup** (not Save). A new window appears in which you can customize the way you export files into Flash.

4. The Optimization section (at the bottom) controls how artwork is compressed for transfer to the Web. Verify that all the default settings match those shown in Figure 4-12. This lets the export module use the numbered layers to create sequential animation frames.

STEP-BY-STEP 4.10 Continued

FIGURE 4-12
The Setup window for export options

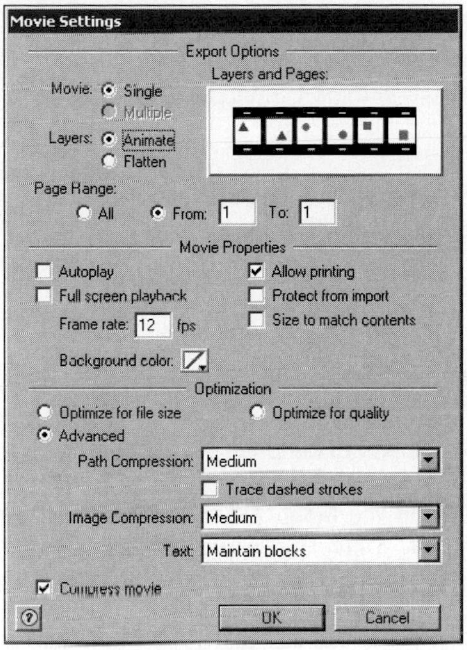

5. Click **OK** to return to the Export Document (Windows) or Export (Macintosh) dialog box.

6. Name the export file **Steam_Sequence** and save it in the **L4_Images** folder. Click **Save** (Windows) or **Export** (Macintosh).

7. Save the changes and close the L4_Cup file, but leave L4_Animation open for the next Step-by-Step.

Your first Flash export has been completed, and the layers will play back as a sequential animation within the Flash Player. This SWF file can also be added to an HTML document as is, provided you are satisfied with the animation results. Now it's time to export the keyframes from the L4_Animation file.

S TEP-BY-STEP 4.11

Exporting Pages as Animation Keyframes

1. With **L4_Animation.FH11** open, go to page 3. Click the **File** menu, click **Export**, and make sure **Macromedia Flash (SWF)** is selected under Save as Type (Windows) or Format (Macintosh).

2. Click **Setup**.

3. In the Export Options section of the Movie Settings dialog box, select the **Flatten** option, specify pages **From 3 to 3** (so you can export only the page you're viewing), and verify that **Autoplay** is unchecked.

STEP-BY-STEP 4.11 Continued

4. Click **OK** to return to the Export Document (Windows) or Export (Macintosh) dialog box. Name the file **Andes_Anim**, with the Macromedia Flash (SWF) file format, and make sure you're in the **L4_Images** folder. Then click **Save** (Windows) or **Export** (Macintosh). Your file has been exported.

5. Go to page 4. Turn off all layers except the **Grid** layer. (*Tip*: Use the **Options** menu to select **All Off** and then just turn on the one required.)

6. Click the **File** menu, and then click **Export**. Name the file **Andes_PerspAn**. Click **Setup** and define pages **From 4 to 4**. Click **OK**. Then click **Save** (Windows) or **Export** (Macintosh). (Settings from the last export are still loaded, so you do not need to redefine them.)

7. Go to page 5 and turn on only the **Mountain** layer. Click off the **Keyline** view. Click the **File** menu, click **Export**, and name the file **Andes_Summit**. Click **Setup** and define pages **From 5 to 5**. Click **OK**. Click **Save** (Windows) or **Export** (Macintosh).

8. Save and close the file and then close FreeHand.

Extra Challenge

Explore blends for creating additional animation effects. Blend between a variety of colors or between varieties of shapes. Explore the options within the Navigation panel. Test some of the ActionScripts available. Explore the Page tool for creating a variety of page sizes and orientations within the same document.

SUMMARY

In this lesson, you learned to:

■ Define the storyboard workflow within FreeHand in preparation for creating Flash animations.

■ Use the Page tool to storyboard an animation.

■ Use the Blend command to morph between two objects.

■ Use the Release to Layers command to create an animation.

■ Use brush strokes as an animation technique.

■ Use the Controller to test sophisticated animation techniques.

■ Export a SWF (Flash) file.

CREATING A FLASH ANIMATION

OBJECTIVES

Upon completion of this lesson, you should be able to:

- Identify the differences in interface and function between FreeHand and Flash.
- Understand how Flash creates animations.
- Import FreeHand files into a Flash document.
- Use Flash for basic animations.
- Create basic interactive elements.

Using Flash

In this lesson, you will integrate Macromedia FreeHand MX with Macromedia Flash MX 2004. You will import into Flash the SWF files you exported from FreeHand. You will review basic tools and functions and understand the reasons for the steps you took in creating and exporting the FreeHand files. You will view your progress by playing back the animation as it is being developed and also add some interactivity in the process.

The Flash Interface

Flash documents have three main areas: the *Timeline*, which controls the scenes, frames, and layers; the *Stage*, where the artwork you build is visible in the browser or movie; and the *workspace* outside the Stage that is not visible in the browser or movie, as shown in Figure 5-1. In addition, several panels surround the work area: the Actions panel and the Property inspector on the bottom and various design and development panels on the right.

FIGURE 5-1
The Flash Document window

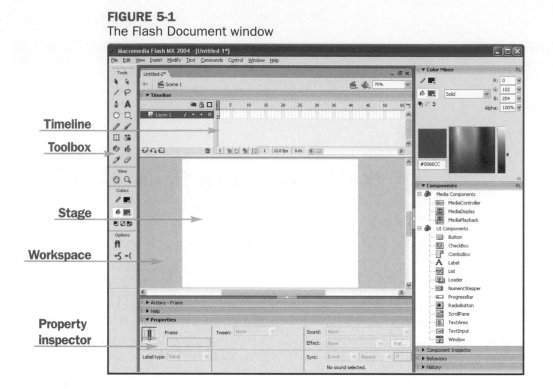

The Timeline, shown in Figure 5-2, is the heart of a Flash document. Using the Timeline, you create the Flash animations, or *movies*. A movie can be divided into scenes, with each scene having its own Timeline, layers, and frames. By using these elements correctly, you can create simple animations—such as a bouncing ball—or author an entire Web site.

FIGURE 5-2
The Flash Timeline

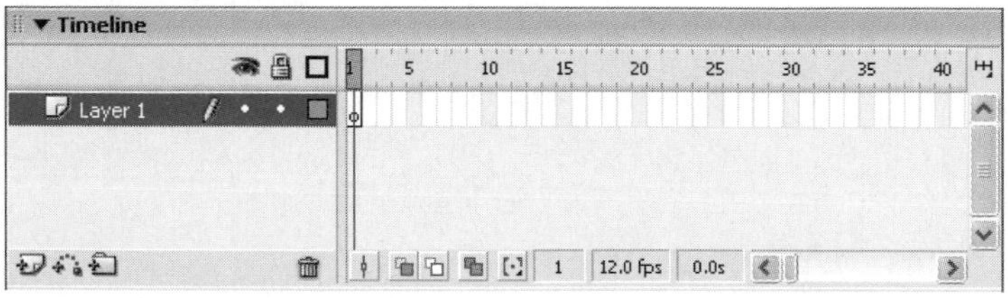

You can break up your Flash movie into manageable segments, or *scenes*. If your animation contains hundreds of frames, you might want to create an introduction scene, a main scene, and then a closing scene. For simple animations, however, you might want to use only one scene, as you will be doing in this project.

Frames are segments within a scene. A Flash movie is a visual progression from one frame to another until it reaches the end, very much like the frames in a movie reel. Each image you create for a Flash movie resides in a frame. You create animations by changing the content of successive frames.

Layers in Flash are similar to those in FreeHand. Each layer can contain individual elements to help you keep your file organized. You can also lock, hide, and reorder layers, just as in FreeHand.

Before you begin building your files, you need to set some parameters. Just as in FreeHand, you need to determine the dimensions of the "page" where you will be placing your images. The page is actually the Stage, the visible area in the browser or Flash movie that displays your images and animation. When you start Flash, you automatically open a new, empty file. In the following Step-by-Step, you work within this new file.

STEP-BY-STEP 5.1

Setting the Document Properties

1. Start Flash.

2. Click the **Modify** menu, and then click **Document** to open the Document Properties dialog box shown in Figure 5-3.

<table>
<tr><td>**Hot Tip**   ⊙</td></tr>
<tr><td>You can also access the Document Properties dialog box by selecting the **Size** button in the Property inspector at the bottom of the display. Or you can press **Ctrl + J** (Windows) or **Command + J** (Macintosh).</td></tr>
</table>

FIGURE 5-3
The Document Properties dialog box

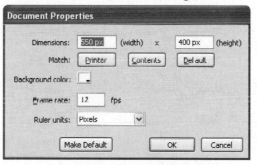

3. For the Dimensions, key **360** for width and **472** for height.

4. At the bottom of the Document Properties dialog box, select **Pixels** from the **Ruler units** (units of measure) menu if necessary, and then click **OK**. Notice that the size of the Stage area on your screen adjusts to reflect the new dimensions.

5. Save this document as **Steam_Sequence_in_Flash** and remain in this screen for the next Step-by-Step.

You used pixels while working in FreeHand, so it makes sense to continue using pixels because your target medium is still the Web.

The Flash Toolbox

You use the Flash toolbox (shown in Figure 5-4) to create and edit artwork. The basic tools are comparable to those you have used in FreeHand and include the Selection tool (similar to the Pointer in FreeHand), the Subselection tool, the Lasso tool (which allows for free-form selection areas), and the Line, Text, Oval, and Rectangle tools. You mostly use the Selection tool in this project.

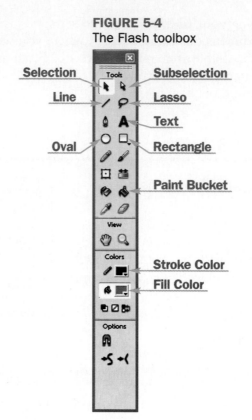

FIGURE 5-4
The Flash toolbox

After preparing and exporting your files in Lesson 4, you are ready to import these files into Flash.

STEP-BY-STEP 5.2

Importing Layered Files

1. Click the **File** menu, point to **Import**, and click **Import to Stage**. Locate the file **Steam_Sequence.swf** in your **L4_Images** folder. (This is a file you created in Lesson 4.) Select it and click **Open** (Windows) or **Import** (Macintosh). A series of individual frames appears on the Timeline. Each frame is one step within the animation. When played back, this sequence of frames creates motion. By default, Flash displays Frame 1.

STEP-BY-STEP 5.2 Continued

2. Open the Controller (shown in Figure 5-5) by clicking the **Window** menu, pointing to **Toolbars**, and then clicking **Controller**.

FIGURE 5-5
The Controller

Play

3. Click the **Play** button to preview the steam animation. Notice that because the cup is present only in the first frame, it disappears as soon as the animation starts playing. Throughout most of the animation, you will see only the steam rising toward the top of the document. In the next three steps, you will remedy this.

4. Click on Frame **1** on the Timeline. When you click on a frame, all objects on the Stage belonging to the frame are selected. The cup is now selected.

5. Click the **Edit** menu, and then click **Copy**.

6. Click the **Insert** menu, point to **Timeline**, and then click **Layer**. A new layer appears on the Timeline above the original layer.

7. Click on Frame **1** of the new layer. Then click the **Edit** menu and click **Paste in Place**. The cup has now been pasted within the new layer, in the same location as the original and within the same number of frames (Frames 1 through 33). When you play the animation, the cup will not disappear.

8. Save your changes and then close the document. Leave Flash open for the next Step-by-Step.

Motion Tweening

In this section, you will continue to import files while exploring how Flash creates animations. *Tweening* is a method by which Flash automatically creates in-between frames to complete an animation. By specifying beginning and ending keyframes and then changing the size, position, color, and rotation of an element between these two keyframes, you can use motion tweening to fill the frames and create a variety of movements.

STEP-BY-STEP 5.3

Animating Motion and Changing Colors

1. Click the **File** menu, and then click **New** to create a new document file. On the General tab of the New Document dialog box, select **Flash Document** and click **OK**.

2. Click the **File** menu, point to **Import**, and click **Import to Stage**. Import the file **Andes_Anim.swf**, which you exported from Lesson 4. The graphic takes up only one frame on the Timeline.

STEP-BY-STEP 5.3 Continued

3. Click on Frame **15** on the Timeline. Then, click the **Insert** menu, point to **Timeline**, and click **Keyframe**.

4. Drag from Frame 1 to Frame 15 to select all the frames.

5. Right-click (Windows) or Control-click (Macintosh) on the selected frames and select **Create Motion Tween;** a solid arrow appears, pointing to Frame 15. The motion tween is complete; however, you need to apply some size and color changes to create an interesting animation.

6. Click on Frame **15**. Open the Transform panel by clicking the **Window** menu, pointing to **Design Panels**, and then clicking **Transform**. Enter a scale of **65%** in both the horizontal and vertical fields. (If the Constrain box is checked, you can enter a value in either the horizontal or vertical fields and it will be automatically applied to the other field.) Press **Enter** (Windows) or **Return** (Macintosh) to apply the scale change.

7. Close the Transform panel.

8. If the Property inspector at the bottom of the Stage is not open, click the **Window** menu, and then click **Properties**. Use the Selection tool to select the graphics in Frame 15. In the Property inspector, set the X and Y coordinates to **0**. This will align the top left corner of the graphics to the top left corner of the Stage.

9. Locate the Controller and click **Play** to view the animation.

10. Save the new file as **Flash_L5** followed by your initials. (In Windows, the .fla extension is added automatically.)

11. Click on Frame **1** on the Timeline, and then click the graphic on the Stage.

12. Select **Alpha** from the **Color** pop-up menu in the Property inspector at the bottom of the Stage. Then key **10** in the numeric field to the right. When the animation is played, the graphic will now fade in from 10% opacity to 100% opacity.

13. Play the movie again with the Controller to see the alpha effect.

14. Save your work and remain in this screen for the next Step-by-Step.

It's time to add some interactivity to the animation. When this animation is downloaded on the Internet, it will start playing automatically and continuously (looping back to the beginning and playing over and over). To control when the animation should play, you will add a button so viewers can start the movie manually.

Interactive Elements

You have probably noticed rollover buttons on many Web pages. The effect is created by a mini-movie of one to four frames. To control the playback of animations, you can use Flash to create interactive navigation buttons (which you will create in the following Step-by-Step) and other much more complex scripts that control the behavior of objects.

When you are creating a navigation button, you see four large frame icons with the labels Up, Over, Down, and Hit across the top of the Stage, in place of the Timeline. These frames specify what the button looks like when the pointer is not over it (Up), when the pointer is over it (Over), and when it is being clicked (Down). The Hit frame determines the shape and size of the area that can be clicked to trigger the button.

S TEP-BY-STEP 5.4

Making a Button

1. The Flash_L5 file should still be open. Click the **Insert** menu, and then click **New Symbol** to display the Create New Symbol dialog box. Select the **Button** option, key the name **Play Button** in the text box, as shown in Figure 5-6, and click **OK**. A new, empty Stage appears.

   FIGURE 5-6
   The Create New Symbol dialog box

   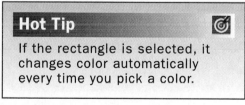

2. In the Colors section of the toolbox (below the Hand tool), are color swatches that specify the stroke and fill colors. Click on the **Fill Color** swatch—it's the one with the paint bucket next to it. A color palette opens.

3. Select a mid-tone gray (for example, #999999) from the left column of colors. This color is now a default fill color for any shapes you draw.

4. Using the **Rectangle** tool from the toolbox, drag to draw a rectangle. (Don't worry about location or size— these will be set precisely in the next step.) Notice the mid-tone gray fill color.

   > **Hot Tip**
   > If the rectangle is selected, it changes color automatically every time you pick a color.

5. Double-click the rectangle with the Selection tool. The fill and stroke of the rectangle become selected (selected objects display a uniform pattern of small white dots).

6. Within the Property inspector at the bottom of the screen, enter **120** for W, **15** for H, **–60** for X, and **–7** for Y. The rectangle is now properly sized and positioned in the center of the Stage.

7. Click the **Over** frame at the top of the Stage area. Click the **Insert** menu, point to **Timeline**, and click **Keyframe**. The frame is highlighted and red shading appears over the frame to verify that it is now a keyframe. The rectangle you drew in the Up frame also appears on the Stage.

STEP-BY-STEP 5.4 Continued

8. Click the **Paint Bucket** tool. Click on the **Fill Color** swatch below the toolbox, and this time select a medium blue color. Click in the center of the rectangle to apply the color if it isn't applied automatically. Now when the pointer passes over this button on a Web page, the rectangle will change color from gray to blue.

9. Click the **Up** keyframe, select the **Text** tool, and key **PLAY ANIMATION** (all caps) over the rectangle. Notice that the Property inspector now includes text-editing options.

10. Select the text and choose **Helvetica Bold** and **12**-point size (or **Arial Black**, **10**-point) and choose **White** for the text color.

11. Use the Selection tool to select the text and center it inside the rectangle. (You might also find it easier to use the arrow keys on the keyboard to get the exact placement you want for the text.)

12. Select the text and copy it. Click the **Over** keyframe, click the **Edit** menu, and then click **Paste in Place**. The text appears over the blue button.

13. Click the **Scene 1** icon at the top left of the Stage window to return the preview to the main animation. Then click the **Insert** menu, point to **Timeline**, and click **Layer**. A new layer appears on the Timeline above the original layer.

14. To name the new layer, double-click its name to highlight it and then key **Button Layer**.

15. Make sure Frame **1** is selected in the new Button Layer. Then locate and drag the **Play Button** icon from the Library panel to the Stage. (If the Library panel is not visible, click on the **Window** menu and then on **Library**.) When the button appears on-screen, place it in the lower-right corner of the animation. The button image is automatically placed in Frames 1–15.

16. Save your changes and remain in this screen for the next Step-by-Step.

Creating ActionScript

Now that you've established the rollover state for the button, you need to "tell" the button what to do when it is clicked. An instruction to perform a specific task is called a script. In Flash, you write scripts in *ActionScript*, a built-in programming language similar to JavaScript. Flash contains a series of preset instructions that can be edited for specific purposes. You can apply these presets to individual frames on the Timeline for quick scripting.

S TEP-BY-STEP 5.5

Adding an ActionScript and Viewing Your Movie

1. Click in the **Actions** panel below the Stage to view ActionScript options available within Flash. If you don't see the Actions panel, click the **Window** menu, point to **Development Panels**, and then click **Actions**.

STEP-BY-STEP 5.5 Continued

2. Make sure your Play Animation button is selected. Notice that the title of the Actions panel is Actions - Button, as shown in Figure 5-7; the title reflects the object currently selected.

FIGURE 5-7
The Actions panel

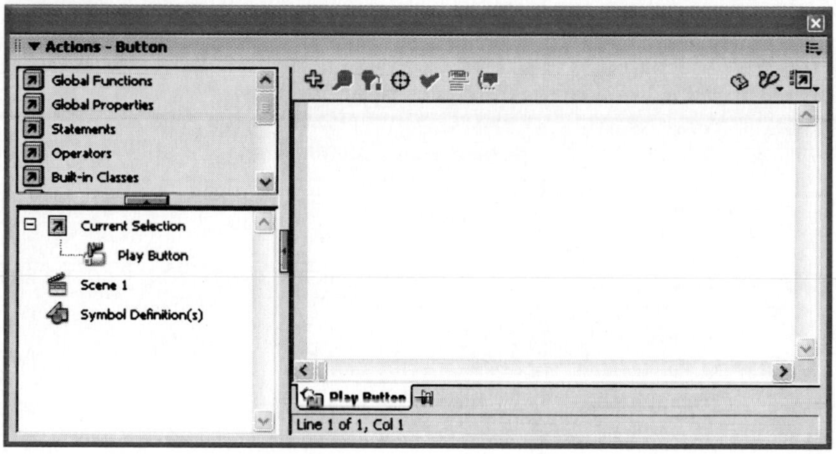

3. In the upper-left corner of the Actions panel, click on the **Global Functions** icon. A list of action types is now visible below the Global Functions icon. Click on the **Movie Clip Control** icon to access an additional list of actions specific to movie clips.

4. Double-click the **on** icon in the list of Movie Clip Control actions. Notice that the word *on* is displayed in the Script pane to the right of the list. A drop-down list of movie events appears. Double-click the mouse event **press**. You can also key the word *press* in the parentheses that follow the word *on*.

At the end of the first line of ActionScript is an open bracket. There is a closing bracket on the second line. Any ActionScript commands you place between the brackets will be executed whenever the button is pressed.

STEP-BY-STEP 5.5 Continued

5. Place the text insertion point at the end of the first line. Press **Enter** (Windows) or **Return** (Macintosh) to start a new line. Then, in the Actions list on the left, click the **Timeline Control** icon. Double-click the **play** icon in the list of Timeline Control actions. In the Actions panel you should now see the script shown in Figure 5-8.

FIGURE 5-8
The Actions panel showing a script for the Play Animation button

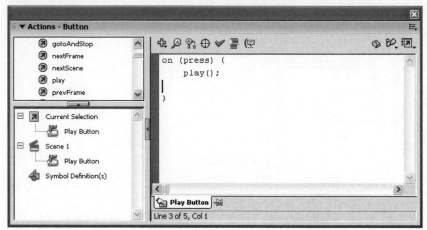

6. Click the **Insert** menu, point to **Timeline**, and click **Layer** to create another new layer. Name it **Action Layer**. You will use this layer to add actions to a frame.

7. Click Frame **1** of the Action Layer. The title of the Actions panel is now Actions - Frame.

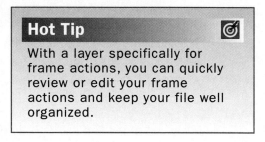

Hot Tip

With a layer specifically for frame actions, you can quickly review or edit your frame actions and keep your file well organized.

8. Double-click on the **Stop** action from the list of Timeline Control actions. The Stop action is applied to the frame instead of to an object. It keeps the animation from playing unless the viewer clicks the **Play** button. Let's see how it works.

9. Click the **Control** menu, and then click **Test Movie**. A new animation window opens, but the animation will not play until you click on the button you just created. Notice the rollover effect when your pointer passes over the button.

10. Click the **Play Animation** button to make the animation play. You have just created an interactive element from within Flash. You can also use existing FreeHand graphics to create interactive buttons.

11. Close the animation preview to return to the main Stage.

12. Save your changes and then close the document and close Flash.

Extra Challenge

Experiment with additional motion tweens. Create original graphics within Flash and animate them by changing their color and size properties. Create an interactive button and experiment with the Actions options.

In Lesson 6, you will use Macromedia Dreamweaver MX 2004 to finish the site.

SUMMARY

In this lesson, you learned to:

- Identify the differences in interface and function between FreeHand and Flash.
- Understand how Flash creates animations.
- Import FreeHand files into a Flash document.
- Use Flash for basic animations.
- Create basic interactive elements.

INTEGRATING FREEHAND WITH OTHER MACROMEDIA WEB APPLICATIONS

OBJECTIVES

Upon completion of this lesson, you should be able to:

■ Work with the basic functions of Fireworks and Dreamweaver.

■ Edit your FreeHand layouts in Fireworks and Dreamweaver to develop a Web page.

■ Slice an image and create a hotspot in Fireworks.

■ Optimize files in Fireworks.

■ Export GIFs and JPEGs directly from FreeHand.

■ Export a file from FreeHand directly to HTML.

Exploring Integration Features

In this lesson, you will use Macromedia Fireworks MX 2004 (a Web graphics editor) and Macromedia Dreamweaver MX 2004 (a Web-page development tool) to prepare images for use in building a basic Web page. As you learned in Lesson 1, one of the great advantages to creating concept Web pages in Macromedia FreeHand MX is that you can use the same artwork to build the actual Web pages. You can open FreeHand files in Fireworks, which means no rebuilding is required. You simply open the vector file in Fireworks, perform any necessary editing, and export to HTML, which you can then import into Dreamweaver for further manipulation.

Slicing Your FreeHand File

In the following Step-by-Step, you open a page for the Andes Coffee Web site in FreeHand and create *slices* (divided graphics for minimizing file size). In a later Step-by-Step, you will import this file into Fireworks.

S TEP-BY-STEP 6.1

Slicing Your FreeHand File

1. Start FreeHand and open **This_Week.fh11** from the data files supplied for this lesson. To save time, we have constructed this page for you. Notice that the page looks similar to the pages you have worked on in previous lessons.

2. Click the **Window** menu and then click **Layers** to open the Layers panel. Make the **FHMXSlices** layer visible by clicking in the empty space to the far left of the layer name.

Note ☑

If necessary, select the **L6_Images** folder in the Locate File dialog box and select the appropriate image. Select the **Search the Current Folder for Missing Links** check box and then click **OK** to close the dialog box and resume opening the FreeHand file.

The FHMXSlices layer represents the sections of this page that you will later "slice" in Fireworks. As shown in Figure 6-1, rectangles were created and filled with transparent lens fills so you can see the artwork underneath. As you will see when you bring this file into Fireworks, the FHMXSlices layer will aid you in creating the slices.

FIGURE 6-1
Areas that will be sliced in Fireworks

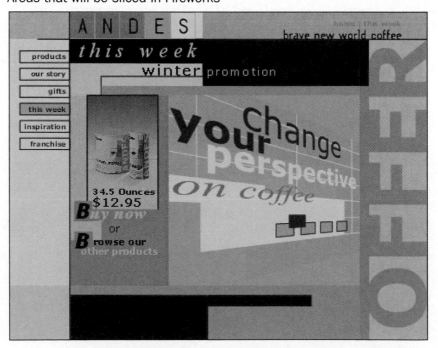

STEP-BY-STEP 6.1 continued

    3. Click the **File** menu, then click **Save As**, and save this file as **This_Week** followed by your initials. Close FreeHand. Remain in this screen for the next Step-by-Step.

Introduction to Fireworks

Fireworks is a complete tool for creating graphics for the Web. Fireworks can create all the necessary elements for a Web page, including images, text, buttons, animation, and HTML.

STEP-BY-STEP 6.2

Exploring the Fireworks Interface

    1. Start Fireworks. Click the **File** menu, and then click **New** to create a new document. The New Document dialog box opens.

    2. Enter a Width of **600** pixels, a Height of **440** pixels, and a Resolution of **72**. Then click **OK**.

Let's use the blank page to take a brief tour of the Fireworks interface. Take a look at the Document window shown in Figure 6-2, which displays the document artwork. Along the top of the Document window are the preview buttons. The Original view shows the document as it was first opened; the Preview button lets you view the document per the settings shown on the Optimize panel in Figure 6-3. Click the 2-Up button to view a split screen of the Original view and the Preview view; click the 4-Up button to split the screen into four views that include the Original view and three additional views set by the Optimize panel.

FIGURE 6-2
The Fireworks Document window and Preview buttons

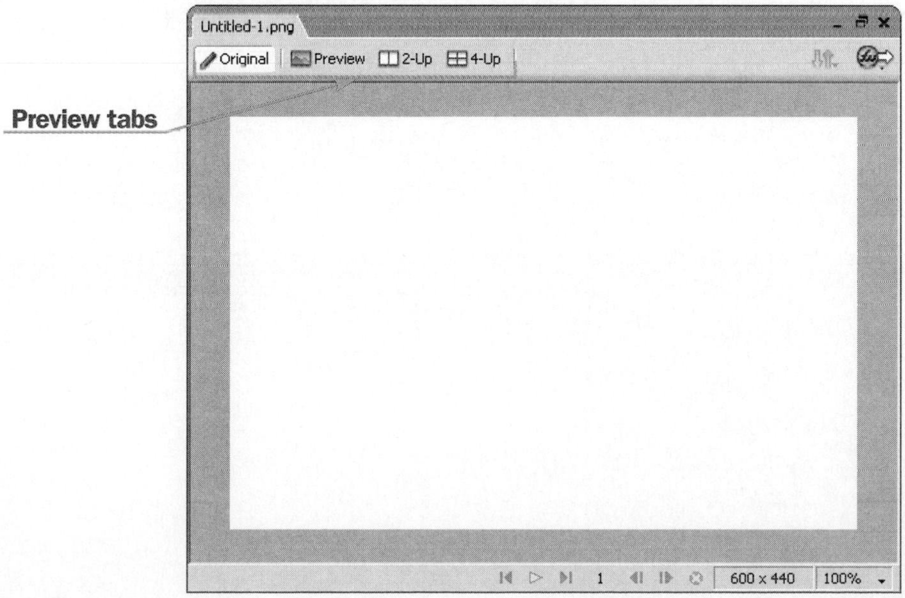

FIGURE 6-3
The Fireworks Optimize panel

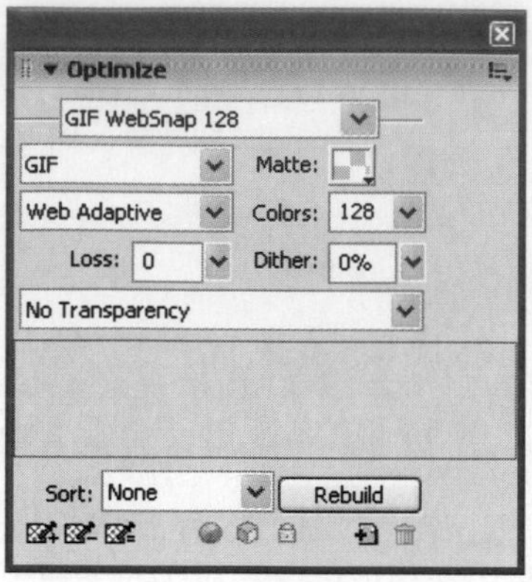

When you choose the Preview, 2-Up, or 4-Up view in the Document window, you can set the optimization for each view in the Optimize panel to see how optimization affects your images. You will learn more about optimization a little later in this lesson.

Like FreeHand and Macromedia Flash MX 2004, Fireworks has a Tools panel that contains the tools you need to manipulate and edit objects and the environment, as shown in Figure 6-4. Many of these are comparable to those you are already familiar with from FreeHand and Flash. Hold your pointer over the buttons, tabs, and fields in Fireworks to activate the tooltips, which give a brief description of each item.

FIGURE 6-4
The Fireworks Tools panel

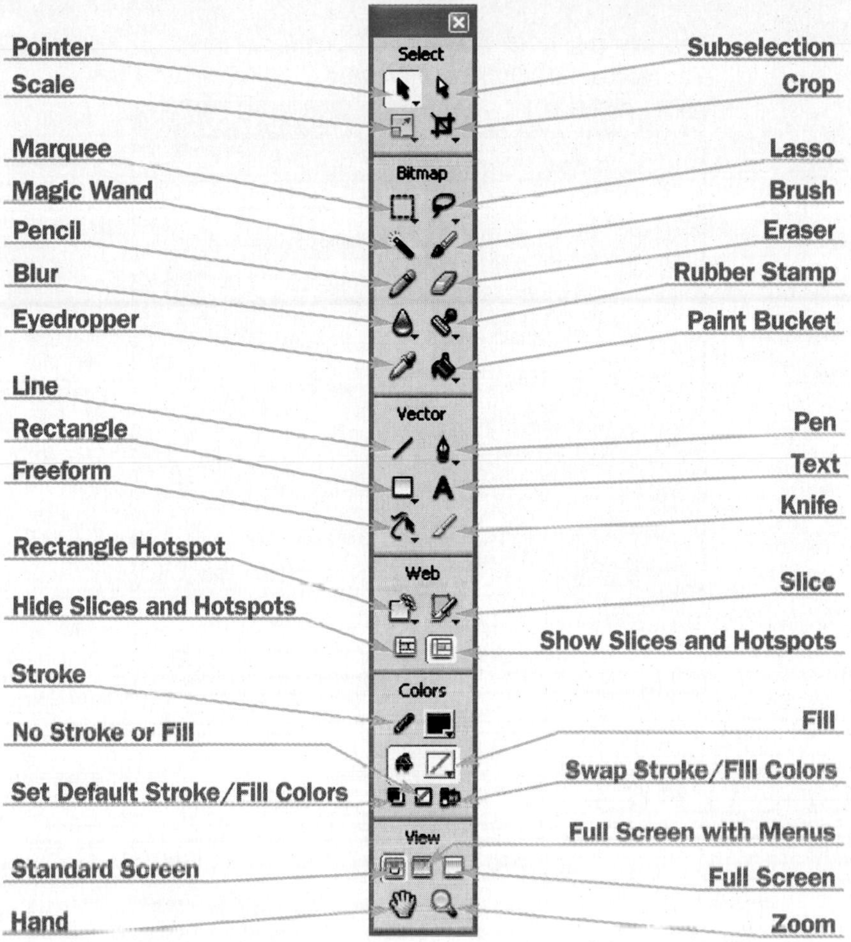

Pointer	Subselection
Scale	Crop
Marquee	Lasso
Magic Wand	Brush
Pencil	Eraser
Blur	Rubber Stamp
Eyedropper	Paint Bucket
Line	
Rectangle	Pen
Freeform	Text
	Knife
Rectangle Hotspot	
Hide Slices and Hotspots	Slice
	Show Slices and Hotspots
Stroke	
No Stroke or Fill	Fill
Set Default Stroke/Fill Colors	Swap Stroke/Fill Colors
	Full Screen with Menus
Standard Screen	Full Screen
Hand	Zoom

As in FreeHand, the Layers panel, shown in Figure 6-5, helps you keep your file organized. You can show and hide layers, lock them, and reorder them to change the visibility of your images. The Web layer holds the objects used to define slices and hotspots, as you will see a little later in the lesson.

FIGURE 6-5
The Fireworks Layers panel

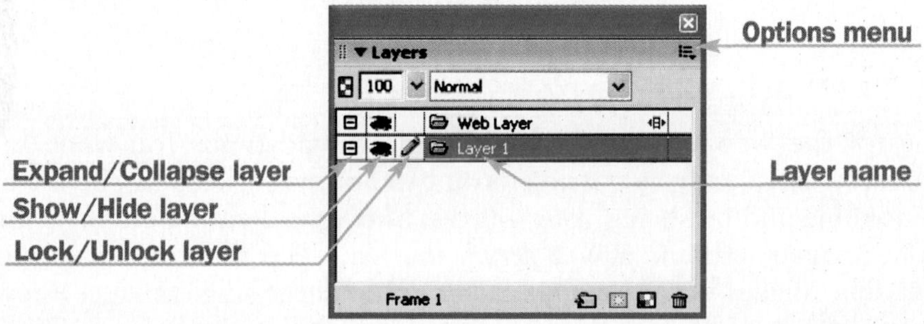

Options menu

Expand/Collapse layer
Show/Hide layer
Lock/Unlock layer

Layer name

Importing an Image into Fireworks

Fireworks can open vector files, such as those created in FreeHand. This enables you to use the more sophisticated drawing tools of a vector program and then import the files into Fireworks.

When you open a vector file, the Vector File Options dialog box opens automatically, as shown in Figure 6-6.

FIGURE 6-6
The Vector File Options dialog box

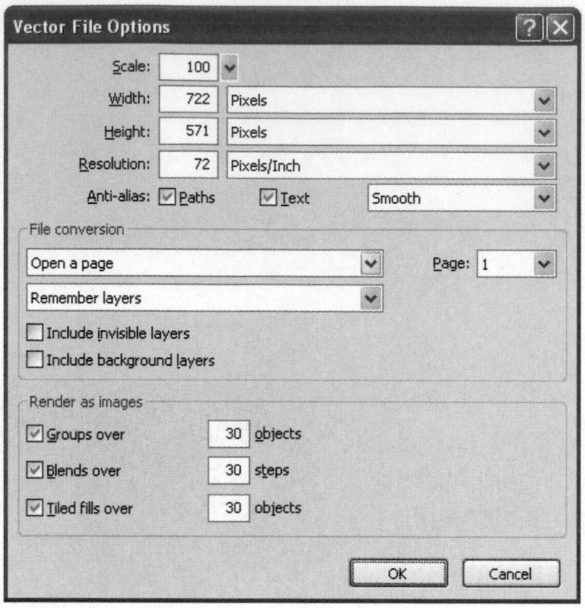

S TEP-BY-STEP 6.3

Importing a Vector File into Fireworks

1. Click the **File** menu, click **Open**, navigate to the **This_Week.fh11** file you saved earlier (the one with your initials), and click **Open**. The Vector File Options dialog box opens.

> **Note** ☑
>
> Use the **Remember Layers** option under File Conversion in the Vector File Options dialog box to retain the layer names from a FreeHand file.

2. In the Vector File Options dialog box, make sure the options match those shown in Figure 6-6. Then click **OK** to close the Vector File Options dialog box and open the FreeHand file in Fireworks. Remain in this screen for the next Step-by-Step.

Slicing a File in Fireworks

When designing for the Web, always think about download time: You want your page to load in the user's browser as quickly as possible. You can do this by keeping the file size of your images as small as possible and by slicing your images. *Slicing* is dividing graphics into separate sections. If your split image resides on a Web server that can send multiple images to the user's browser, the smaller split images will download faster than a large single image. Fireworks gives you a number of ways to slice an object or a page: by using the Slice and Polygon Slice tools from the Tools panel to manually define slices; by using guides in the Document window and choosing the Slice Along Guides option as you export; or by creating slices from objects. In the following Step-by-Step, you create slices from the objects on the FHMXSlices layer created in FreeHand.

S TEP-BY-STEP 6.4

Slicing a File in Fireworks

1. With This_Week.fh11 open, make sure the Layers panel is open (click **Layers** on the **Window** menu).

2. On the Layers panel, click the Options menu control in the upper-right corner to open the **Options** menu. Choose **Hide All** to hide all the layers.

> **Note** ☑
>
> The Web layer is always present on the Layers panel and cannot be removed or renamed.

3. Click the **FHMXSlices** layer to make it visible again. (You might have to scroll to locate it.)

4. Click in the Document window. Click the **Select** menu, and then click **Select All** to select the colored rectangles on the FHMXSlices layer.

5. Click the **Edit** menu, point to **Insert**, and then click **Slice**.

6. Because you have more than one object selected, a dialog box appears asking if you would like to create one slice or multiple slices. Choose **Multiple**. For each rectangle, a separate slice (green rectangle) is created on the Web Layer.

7. Select the **FHMXSlices** layer on the Layers panel and choose **Delete Layer** from the Layers panel Options menu (you no longer need it). Remain in this screen for the next Step-by-Step.

Creating Hotspots in Fireworks

Hotspots are areas associated with an URL. When you click a hotspot in your browser, an action is performed, such as switching to another page. You can create a hotspot by using the Hotspot tools in the Tools panel or by selecting an object and defining a hotspot from the shape, the way you defined slices in the previous Step-by-Step. In the following Step-by-Step, you create a hotspot by using the Rectangle Hotspot tool.

S TEP-BY-STEP 6.5

Creating a Hotspot

1. On the Layers panel, open the Layers panel **Options** menu and choose **Show All** to make all layers visible.

2. Select the **Zoom** tool from the Tools panel. Draw a selection marquee around the text *Browse our other products* and then release to fit the view around this text.

3. Make sure the **Web Layer** is visible on the Layers panel. Select the **Rectangle Hotspot** tool and draw a rectangle around the text. Make sure the rectangle you draw completely surrounds the text and stays within the slice containing the text. Slices are indicated by the red lines and green boxes on the Web layer. The rectangle turns blue and is added to the Web layer on the Layers panel.

STEP-BY-STEP 6.5 Continued

4. Click the **View** menu, and then click **Fit All** to fit the view to the page. You now have a hotspot (blue rectangle) on the Web layer, as shown in Figure 6-7. Remain in this screen for the next Step-by-Step.

FIGURE 6-7
The Web layer with a single hotspot

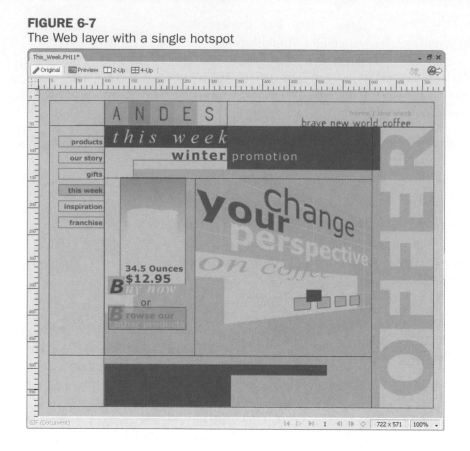

Exporting from Fireworks

Fireworks has very powerful optimization capabilities. *Optimizing* is the process of finding the best balance of visual quality and file size. You want the images to look good, but you also want them to download quickly. The Export Preview feature visually aids you in optimizing your pages.

S TEP-BY-STEP 6.6

Exporting a File by Using the Export Preview Feature

1. Click the **File** menu, and then click **Export Preview**. If a dialog box appears telling you how to stop the redraw of an image, click **OK**. The Export Preview dialog box opens, in which you can choose an optimization setting and view its effects on your images, as shown in Figure 6-8.

FIGURE 6-8
The Export Preview dialog box

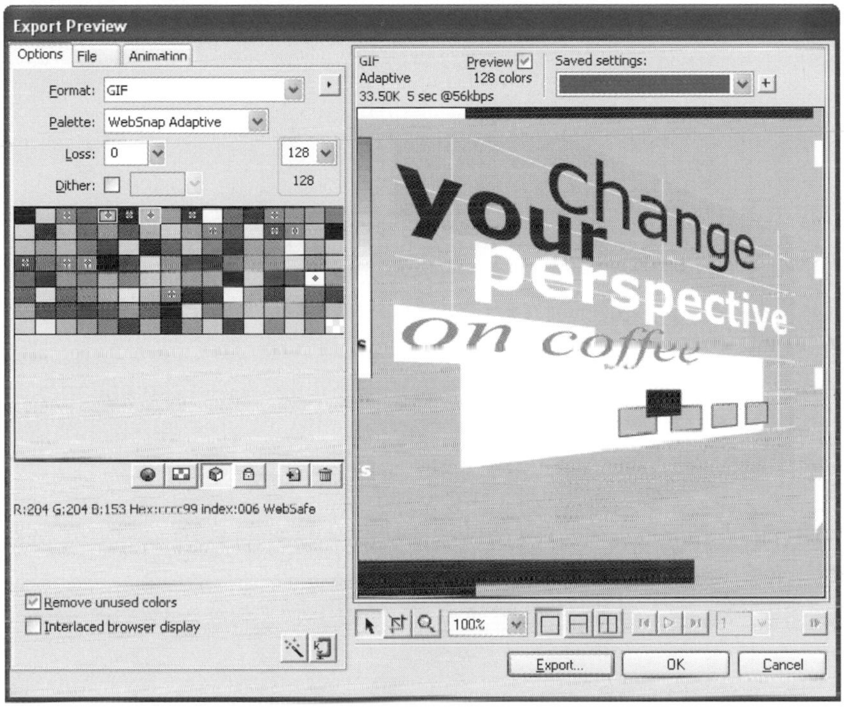

Take a moment to choose different export settings to see how the file size is affected.

2. On the left side of the Export Preview dialog box, select the **Format** pop-up menu and choose **JPEG**. The information in the dialog box changes to show the attributes for the JPEG file format.

3. Make sure the **Quality** is set to **80%** and make sure **Remove Unused Colors** is selected.

4. Click the **Export** button to open the Export dialog box, where you can choose a destination folder and choose to slice the page.

5. Navigate to the **Andes_Site** folder (in the data files for this lesson). Create a new folder and name it **This_Week_Page**.

6. Open the **This_Week_Page** folder. Make sure the following are set:
   a. From the Save as Type (Windows) or Save As (Macintosh) list, choose **HTML and Images**.
   b. From the HTML list, choose **Export HTML File**.
   c. From the Slices list, choose **Export Slices**.

STEP-BY-STEP 6.6 Continued

7. Click the **Options** button. In the HTML Setup dialog box, select **Dreamweaver HTML** from the **HTML Style** menu. Choose **.htm** from the **Extension** list. On the Macintosh, choose **Dreamweaver** from the **File Creator** list.

8. Click **OK** to exit the HTML Setup dialog box and then click **Save** in the Export dialog box. Fireworks generates and saves the appropriate HTML code and creates a separate file for each of the sliced areas on the page.

9. Click the **File** menu (Windows) or click the **Fireworks** menu and click **Quit Fireworks** (Macintosh) to close Fireworks. When you are prompted to save your work, choose **No** (Windows) or **Don't Save** (Macintosh).

Exporting GIF and JPEG Files from FreeHand

GIF and JPEG are two of the most popular file formats for Web images and are widely used across the Web. FreeHand can convert your document to a GIF or JPEG when you use Export. As you saw in Fireworks, choosing either GIF or JPEG in the Export Preview dialog box can affect the look, quality, and size of your images. You should give some thought to how your files are built before you choose either format.

You can export a FreeHand file by using the Export command on the File menu. By selecting the options for either format, you can adjust the size and quality of your images. Refer to Table 6-1 to determine which export format is best for your files.

TABLE 6-1
Comparing GIF and JPEG file formats

FORMAT	GIF	JPEG
Color depth	8-bit maximum	Up to 24-bit
Compression	Lossless; compresses solid areas of color	Lossy; compresses subtle color transitions
Transparency support	Yes	No
Advantages	Lossless compression Transparency	Ability to control quality loss in compression Excellent compression of photographic images
Disadvantages	Maximum of 256 colors Does not compress gradient colors well	No transparency Loss of quality when compressed
Typical uses	Cartoon images Logos Animated banners	Scanned photographs Images with complex textures Images with complex radiant colors

Working in Dreamweaver

Dreamweaver is a professional WYSIWYG (what-you-see-is-what-you-get) Web-page authoring program. Using Dreamweaver, you can create and position elements to build a Web page. Dreamweaver can also open HTML files created by other applications, such as Fireworks and FreeHand. You can edit these files and re-save them as HTML for publishing on the Web.

The main area where the pages are built in Dreamweaver is the Document window. A number of panels along the top, bottom, and sides of the Document window contain the various tools available for building your pages. At the top of the screen is the main menu bar, from which you can access various commands as shown in Figure 6-9.

FIGURE 6-9
The Dreamweaver Document window

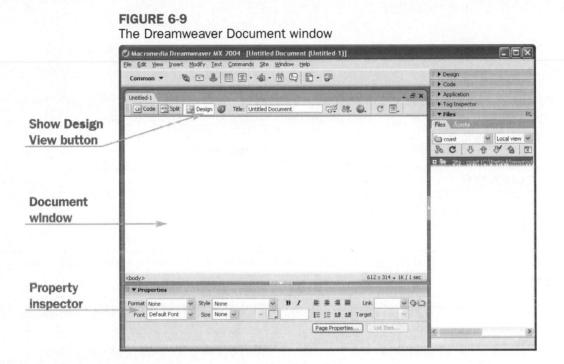

S TEP-BY-STEP 6.7

Opening an HTML File in Dreamweaver

1. Start Dreamweaver. If you are asked to choose which workspace you want to use, choose **Designer** and then click **OK**.

2. Click the **File** menu, click **Open**, and navigate to the **Andes_Site/This_Week_Page** folder you created earlier. Select the **This_Week.htm** file and click **Open** (Windows) or **Choose** (Macintosh).

3. On the Document toolbar, make sure the **Show Design View** button is selected. Remain in this screen for the next Step-by-Step.

You created the This_Week.htm file in the previous Step-by-Step, using Fireworks. As you can see, this page looks very similar to the way it looked in Fireworks.

Adding URLs in Dreamweaver

Now you will add an URL to the hotspot. When you click a hotspot in a browser, you are brought to the page or Web site attached to that hotspot.

S TEP-BY-STEP 6.8

Adding an URL to a Hotspot

1. Move the pointer over the **Browse our other products** hotspot and select it.

2. Go to the Property inspector, as shown in Figure 6-10. If the Property inspector is not open, click **Properties** on the **Window** menu.

> **Note** ☑
>
> The hotspot you created should be visible on the page. If not, click the **View** menu, point to **Visual Aids**, and click **Image Maps**.

FIGURE 6-10
Property inspector for the selected hotspot

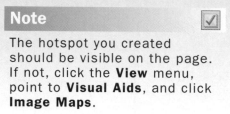

3. In the Property inspector, click the folder icon to the right of the **Link** text box. In the Select File dialog box that opens, navigate to the **Andes_Site/Product** folder. Select the file **Andes_Product.htm** and click **OK** (Windows) or **Choose** (Macintosh). (If you see a message box saying that the location of these files is outside your root directory, click **No** to avoid copying files to your root directory.)

This hotspot now has a link to the Product page of the Andes site. Later when you open this site in a browser, you will see this link in action.

4. From the list box next to the **Target** text box (in the Property inspector), choose **_self**.

5. Click the **File** menu, and then click **Save**. Dreamweaver saves the HTML file for this page under the default name This_Week.htm.

6. Click the **File** menu, and then click **Exit** (Windows) or **Quit** (Macintosh) to close Dreamweaver.

Creating HTML from FreeHand and Opening It in Dreamweaver

You can use the Publish as HTML feature to instantly convert your FreeHand document to a Web page. You can also assign URLs to images in your FreeHand files. When you create the HTML file, these links are written into the code.

> **Note** ☑
>
> When you use the Publish as HTML feature, each group of objects in your FreeHand file becomes a single object when your file is converted to HTML.

STEP-BY-STEP 6.9

Adding an URL and Creating HTML from FreeHand

1. Start FreeHand and open **AndesHome.fh11** from the data files. The Andes home page opens. This page was created for this Step-by-Step.

2. With the **Pointer** tool, click the **This Week** button from the vertical navigation bar on the left side of the page.

3. Click the **Window** menu, and then click **Navigation** to open the Navigation panel shown in Figure 6-11.

FIGURE 6-11
The Navigation panel in FreeHand

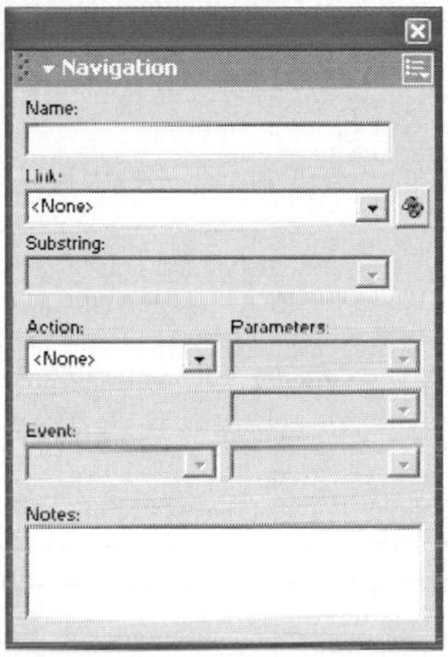

You need to assign an URL to the This Week button. Later you will edit this URL in Dreamweaver, but for now just create a dummy link or placeholder. You will easily see the dummy link when you open this page in Dreamweaver.

4. With the This Week button still selected, key **This Week Button** in the Name text box and **DummyLink** in the Link text box, and then press **Enter** (Windows) or **Return** (Macintosh). Close the Navigation panel.

5. Click the **File** menu, and then click **Publish as HTML** to open the HTML Output dialog box. Make sure the **Show Output Warnings** and the **View in Browser or HTML Editor** options are not selected.

6. Click the **Setup** button to open the HTML Setup dialog box.

7. Click the **Browse** button under the Document root section and navigate to the **Andes_Site** folder. Create a new folder and name it **Home**. Open the new folder and then click **Select** (Windows) or **Choose** (Macintosh) at the bottom of the dialog box.

8. In the **Layout** pop-up menu, make sure that **Positioning with Layers** is selected.

> **Note** ✓
>
> When the **Show Output Warnings** option is selected, FreeHand warns you of any potential problems with the HTML being generated. Because we created this file for you, you don't need this option now; however, remember the option when you convert your own FreeHand files to HTML.

STEP-BY-STEP 6.9 Continued

9. Under Export Defaults, make sure that **Vector Art** is set to **GIF**, and that **Images** is set to **JPEG**. Click **OK** to return to the HTML Output dialog box.

10. Click **Save as HTML**. FreeHand creates the necessary HTML code and saves all the images of the page as either GIF or JPEG files.

11. Close FreeHand. When you see a warning message about unsaved files, choose **Exit** (Windows) or **Quit Anyway** (Macintosh).

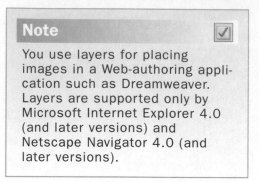

If you're using a Macintosh, open up the **Andes_Site** window in the Finder. FreeHand may have placed the new **AndesHomeFH11001.html** it created and a new **images** folder inside the Andes_Site folder, instead of the Home folder. If so, move the HTML file and the images folder to the **Home** folder before you go on to the next Step-by-Step.

Opening a FreeHand-Generated HTML File in Dreamweaver

Now it's time to open the HTML file you created in FreeHand and finish the URL or link for the This Week navigation button.

STEP-BY-STEP 6.10

Opening an HTML File Generated by FreeHand and Adding an URL

1. Start Dreamweaver. Click the **File** menu, click **Open**, and navigate to the **Andes_Site/Home** folder. Select **AndesHomeFH11001.html** and click **Open** (Windows) or **Choose** (Macintosh). This is the HTML file that was generated by FreeHand. (The images that were on the page were saved in the images folder.)

2. When the file opens, it looks almost the same as it did in FreeHand. Select the **This Week** button in the navigation bar on the left side of the page.

3. Make sure the Property inspector is open (click **Properties** on the **Window** menu if it is not). In the Link field, you will see the DummyLink text (the link you set in FreeHand). Click the folder icon next to the **Link** field to find the page to link to.

4. Navigate to the **Andes_Site/This_Week_Page** folder. Select the **This_Week.htm** file and click **OK** (Windows) or **Choose** (Macintosh). You created the This_Week.htm page earlier in Fireworks and Dreamweaver, and now you are adding a link to it by replacing the dummy link you originally created in FreeHand. (If you see a message box saying that the location of these files is outside of your root directory, click **No** to avoid copying files to your root directory.)

STEP-BY-STEP 6.10 continued

5. Click the **File** menu, and then click **Save As**. Name the file **AndesHome.html**, and save it to the **Andes_Site/Home** folder.

6. Close Dreamweaver.

Opening Your Completed Web Pages in a Web Browser

Your Web pages are complete. You can now open them in a browser and test them.

S TEP-BY-STEP 6.11

Opening and Testing Your Finished Pages in a Browser

1. Start your browser. From the browser's **File** menu, click **Open**, and then navigate to the **Andes_Site/Home** folder. Select the **AndesHome.html** file and open it. The Andes home page opens in the browser.

2. Move the pointer over the **This Week** button and click to open the This_Week page.

3. Move the pointer over the **Browse our other products** text and click to open the **Andes_Product** page.

4. When you finish reviewing your pages, close your browser.

> **Extra Challenge**
>
> Learn more about Fireworks and Dreamweaver by working through the projects and examining the online Help files **Using Fireworks** and **Using Dreamweaver** found on the Help menu of each application. In Fireworks, try various optimization options to see how they affect your images. Try to bring other FreeHand files into Fireworks and create manual slices by using the Rectangle Slice and Polygon Slice tools.

You have now been introduced to the basic tools for creating your own Web pages. You used FreeHand to create the artwork, Flash to animate, Fireworks to optimize, and Dreamweaver to bring it all together. If you explore these applications further, the only limitation to making Web pages will be your imagination.

SUMMARY

In this lesson, you learned to:

- Work with the basic functions of Fireworks and Dreamweaver.

- Edit your FreeHand layouts in Fireworks and Dreamweaver to develop a Web page.

- Slice an image and create a hotspot in Fireworks.

- Optimize files in Fireworks.

- Export GIFs and JPEGs directly from FreeHand.

- Export a file from FreeHand directly to HTML.

GLOSSARY

A

Absolute path Path that provides the complete URL of a linked document, including the protocol. You must use an absolute path to link to a document on another server. You should not use absolute paths for local links.

ActionScript In Macromedia Flash, an instruction to perform a specific task.

Animation plan Helps a Web designer visualize and lay out complex animation, often involving several graphic elements, size changes, and fading. The plan contains sketches or rough images of what the transformations will look like. It is similar to a storyboard for a cartoon or a film, but it also contains information on the numerical transformation and position changes of the graphic.

B

Behaviors Prewritten JavaScript codes used to add interactivity to Web pages, enabling users to change or control the information they see. A behavior combines a user event (for example, moving the pointer over a graphic button) with an action or series of actions that take place as result of that event.

Button An object that performs some action when you click it.

C

Clipping path In FreeHand, a closed path with an object pasted inside.

Cloning In Fireworks, the process of painting a copy of some area of a bitmap object onto another area of the bitmap object.

Components In Macromedia Flash, ready-made movie clips for commonly used controls such as check boxes, drop-down menus, and buttons.

D

Document-relative path Define the path to take to find the linked file, starting from the current file. This is the best choice for most local links.

Document-relative referencing Refers to how Dreamweaver references an image; with document-relative referencing, it displays every other pixel on every other line and then goes back and repeats the process, filling in areas not already displayed.

F

Fill Color applied to a closed path or text.

Frames Segments within a scene of a Macromedia Flash movie.

G

Gamma setting Setting on a computer that affects the apparent brightness and contrast of the monitor display.

H

Hotspots Areas associated with an URL that when clicked, trigger an action.

I

Instance The use of an object defined as a symbol and saved in a library.

Interlacing A method of defining the way an image is displayed in a Web browser; it displays every other pixel on every other line and then goes back and repeats the process, filling in areas not already displayed.

K

Kerning Refers to the amount of space between letters.

Keyframe In FreeHand, it defines an important event within an animation—the introduction of a new graphic, a blending effect, a new title, or a change in motion, direction, or speed. In Macromedia Flash, you use keyframes to mark a change in what appears on the Timeline.

L

Layers In a Macromedia Flash document, you use layers to help organize the artwork, animation, and other elements in your document.

Leading Refers to the amount of space between lines of text.

Lens fill A FreeHand special effect that can be applied to an object; the six special-effect lenses are Transparency, Magnify, Invert, Lighten, Darken, and Monochrome.

Library In FreeHand, a set of colors, which are reproducible on the Web. In Macromedia Flash and Freehand, the library stores symbols created in these programs, and also imported files such as video clips, sound clips, bitmaps, and imported vector artwork.

Live Effects In Fireworks, Live Effects are filters that apply to vector, bitmap, and text objects.

M

Marquee In FreeHand, a dotted line square you create to select multiple objects or groups.

Mask In Fireworks, it is a window to something underneath. You can think of the mask as a mat within a picture frame: only the area inside the mat is visible.

Mini-movie A movie or animation with four or fewer frames.

Movie An animation in Macromedia Flash.

N

Named anchor A link, normally created in a document that is long or has many sections, that jumps the user to a specific place in the document.

Nested grouping Combination of groups of objects that have already been grouped. Groups and nested groups can be manipulated as a single unit.

O

Optimizing The process of converting images to the proper format and making sure they are as small as possible, resulting in faster downloads.

P

Paths In Fireworks, the lines you draw to form basic shapes.

Pixels Colored picture elements that are grouped to form a bitmap graphic.

Presets In FreeHand, specific envelope shapes that have been saved to be reused over and over.

Projector A standalone executable version of a Macromedia Flash movie.

R

Raster images Also called bitmaps, these graphics are created with pixels. When you create a raster image, you map out the placement and color of each pixel, and the resulting bitmap is what you see on the screen.

Rollover An image that changes when the user moves the pointer over the image.

S

Scenes Smaller, more manageable segments in a Macromedia Flash movie.

Site map Visual representation of a Web site and all its linked pages.

Site-root-relative path The path from the site's root folder to a linked document. Useful for large Web sites that use several servers.

Site-root-relative referencing Refers to how Dreamweaver references an image; with site-root-relative referencing, it constructs the path to the image based on the relative location of that image from your site root.

Slicing Dividing graphics into separate sections in order to keep the file size of images as small as possible.

Spacer image Used to control the spacing in a Web page layout but is not visible in the browser window.

Stage In Macromedia Flash, the area where the artwork you build is visible in the browser or movie.

Storyboard A collection of frames or panels encompassing an entire animation or movie.

Stroke Refers to the width, color, and style of lines, as well as the lines that border the shapes you create.

Symbol In Macromedia Flash, a graphic, button, or movie clip that you create once and can reuse throughout a document.

T

Timeline In Macromedia Flash, the area that controls the scenes, frames, and layers.

Tools panel The main working set of tools in FreeHand. You can use the tools to create, select, and modify graphics; create and edit text; zoom in and out; select and trace placed bitmap graphics; complete perspective renderings; and more.

Tweening A method by which Macromedia Flash automatically creates "in-between" frames to complete an animation.

U

URL (uniform resource locator) A link containing information about where a file is located on the Web.

V

Vector graphics Graphics created with lines and curves and descriptions of their properties. Commands within the vector graphic tell your computer how to display the lines and shapes, what colors to use, how wide to make the lines, and so on.

W

Workspace In Macromedia Flash, the space outside the Stage that is not visible in the browser or movie.

INDEX